Additional Praise for
Financial Statement Analysis, Fourth Edition

"This is an illuminating and insightful tour of financial statements, how they can be used to inform, how they can be used to mislead, and how they can be used to analyze the financial health of a company."
—Jay O. Light, Dean Emeritus, Harvard Business School

"*Financial Statement Analysis* should be required reading for anyone who puts a dime to work in the securities markets or recommends that others do the same."
—Jack L. Rivkin, Director, Neuberger Berman Mutual Funds and Idealab

"Fridson and Alvarez provide a valuable practical guide for understanding, interpreting, and critically assessing financial reports put out by firms. Their discussion of profits—'quality of earnings'—is particularly insightful given the recent spate of reporting problems encountered by firms. I highly recommend their book to anyone interested in getting behind the numbers as a means of predicting future profits and stock prices."
—Paul Brown, Associate Dean, Executive MBA Programs,
Leonard N. Stern School of Business, New York University

"Let this book assist in financial awareness and transparency and higher standards of reporting, and accountability to all stakeholders."
—Patricia A. Small, Treasurer Emeritus, University of California;
Partner, KCM Investment Advisors

"This book is a polished gem covering the analysis of financial statements. It is thorough, skeptical, and extremely practical in its review."
—Daniel J. Fuss, Vice Chairman, Loomis, Sayles & Company, LP

Financial
Statement
Analysis

Founded in 1807, John Wiley & Sons is the oldest independent publishing company in the United States. With offices in North America, Europe, Australia and Asia, Wiley is globally committed to developing and marketing print and electronic products and services for our customers' professional and personal knowledge and understanding.

The Wiley Finance series contains books written specifically for finance and investment professionals as well as sophisticated individual investors and their financial advisors. Book topics range from portfolio management to e-commerce, risk management, financial engineering, valuation and financial instrument analysis, as well as much more.

For a list of available titles, visit our Web site at www.WileyFinance.com.

Financial Statement Analysis

A Practitioner's Guide

Fourth Edition

MARTIN FRIDSON
FERNANDO ALVAREZ

WILEY

John Wiley & Sons, Inc.

Published by John Wiley & Sons, Inc., Hoboken, New Jersey.
Published simultaneously in Canada.

For general information on our other products and services or for technical support, please contact our Customer Care Department within the United States at (800) 762-2974, outside the United States at (317) 572-3993 or fax (317) 572-4002.

Wiley also publishes its books in a variety of electronic formats. Some content that appears in print may not be available in electronic books. For more information about Wiley products, visit our web site at www.wiley.com.

Library of Congress Cataloging-in-Publication Data

Fridson, Martin S.
  Financial statement analysis : a practitioner's guide / Martin S. Fridson and Fernando Alvarez. – 4th ed.
      p. cm. – (Wiley finance ; 597)
  Includes bibliographical references and index.
  ISBN 978-0-470-63560-5 (hardback); ISBN 978-1-118-06418-4 (ebk);
  ISBN 978-1-118-06419-1 (ebk); ISBN 978-1-118-06420-7 (ebk)
  1. Financial statements.   2. Ratio analysis.   I. Alvarez, Fernando, 1964–   II. Title.
  HF5681.B2F772 2011
  657′.3–dc22

                                                                        2010054229

Printed in the United States of America

10 9 8 7 6 5 4 3 2

In memory of my father, Harry Yale Fridson, who introduced me to accounting, economics, and logic, as well as the fourth discipline essential to the creation of this book—hard work!
M. F.

For Shari, Virginia, and Armando.
F. A.

Contents

Preface to Fourth Edition

This fourth edition of *Financial Statement Analysis,* like its predecessors, seeks to equip its readers for the practical challenges of contemporary business. Once again, the intention is to acquaint readers who have already acquired basic accounting skills with the complications that arise in applying textbook-derived knowledge to the real world of extending credit and investing in securities. Just as a swiftly changing environment necessitated extensive revisions and additions in the second and third editions, new concerns and challenges for users of financial statements have emerged during the first decade of the twenty-first century.

A fundamental change reflected in the third edition was the shift of corporations' executive compensation plans from a focus on reported earnings toward enhancing shareholder value. In theory, this new approach aligned the interests of management and shareholders, but the concept had a dark side. Chief executive officers who were under growing pressure to boost their corporations' share prices could no longer increase their bonuses by goosing reported earnings through financial reporting tricks that were transparent to the stock market. Instead, they had to devise more opaque methods that gulled investors into believing that the reported earnings gains were real.

To adapt to the new environment, corporate managers became far more aggressive in misrepresenting their performance. They moved beyond exaggeration to outright fabrication of earnings through the use of derivatives and special purpose vehicles that never showed up in financial statements and had little to do with the production and sale of goods and services. This insidious trend culminated in colossal accounting scandals involving companies such as Enron and WorldCom, which shook confidence not only in financial reporting but also in the securities markets.

Government responded to the outrage over financial frauds by enacting the Sarbanes-Oxley Act of 2002. Under its provisions, a company's chief executive officer and chief financial officer were required to attest to the integrity of the financial statements. They were thereby exposed to greater risk than formerly of prosecution and conviction for misrepresentation. Sarbanes-Oxley did create a deterrent to untruthful reporting, but as case studies in this new edition demonstrate, users of financial statements still cannot breathe easy.

To help readers avoid being misled by deceptive financial statements, we continue to urge them to combine an understanding of accounting principles with a corporate finance perspective. We facilitate such integration of disciplines throughout *Financial Statement Analysis,* making excursions into economics and business management as well. In addition, we encourage analysts to consider the institutional context in which financial reporting occurs. Organizational pressures result in divergences from elegant theories, both in the conduct of financial statement analysis and in auditors' interpretations of accounting principles. The issuers of financial statements also exert a strong influence over the creation of the accounting principles, with powerful politicians sometimes carrying their water.

As in the third edition, we highlight success stories in the critical examination of financial statements. Wherever we can find the necessary documentation, we show not only how a corporate debacle could have been foreseen through application of basis analytical techniques but also how practicing analysts actually did detect the problem before it became widely recognized. Readers will be encouraged by these examples, we hope, to undertake genuine, goal-oriented analysis, instead of simply going through the motions of calculating standard financial ratios. Moreover, the case studies should persuade them to stick to their guns when they spot trouble, despite management's predictable litany. ("Our financial statements are consistent with generally accepted accounting principles. They have been certified by one of the world's premier auditing firms. We will not allow a band of greedy short sellers to destroy the value created by our outstanding employees.") Typically, as the vehemence of management's protests increases, conditions deteriorate, and accusations of aggressive accounting give way to revelations of fraudulent financial reporting.

A new chapter (Chapter 11) titled "Is Fraud Detectable?" serves as a cautionary note. Some companies continue to succeed in burying misrepresentations in ways that cannot be detected by standard techniques such as ratio analysis. They manage to keep their auditors in the dark or succeed in corrupting them, removing a key line of defense for users of financial statements. By reading the case studies presented in this chapter, readers can observe corporate behavior that puts companies under suspicion by seasoned financial detectives such as short sellers. We also highlight recent research linking financial misreporting to words and phrases used by corporate managers in conference calls with investors and analysts.

As for the plan of *Financial Statement Analysis,* readers should not feel compelled to tackle its chapters in the order we have assigned to them. To aid those who want to jump in somewhere in the middle of the book, we provide cross-referencing and a glossary. Words that are defined in the glossary are shown in bold-faced type in the text. Although skipping around will be the most efficient approach for many readers, a logical flow does underlie the sequencing of the material.

In Part One, "Reading between the Lines," we show that financial statements do not simply represent unbiased portraits of corporations' financial performance and explain why. The section explores the complex motivations of issuing firms and their managers. We also study the distortions produced by the organizational context in which the analyst operates.

Part Two, "The Basic Financial Statements," takes a hard look at the information disclosed in the balance sheet, income statement, and statement of cash flows. Under close scrutiny, terms such as *value* and *income* begin to look muddier than they appear when considered in the abstract. Even cash flow, a concept commonly thought to convey redemptive clarification, is vulnerable to stratagems designed to manipulate the perceptions of investors and creditors.

In Part Three, "A Closer Look at Profits," we zero in on the lifeblood of the capitalist system. Our scrutiny of profits highlights the manifold ways in which earnings are exaggerated or even fabricated. By this point in the book, the reader should be amply imbued with the healthy skepticism necessary for a sound, structured approach to financial statement analysis.

Application is the theme of Part Four, "Forecasts and Security Analysis." For both credit and equity evaluation, forward-looking analysis is emphasized over seductive but ultimately unsatisfying retrospection. Tips for maximizing the accuracy of forecasts are included, and real-life projections are dissected. We cast a critical eye on standard financial ratios and valuation models, however widely accepted they may be.

Financial markets continue to evolve, but certain phenomena appear again and again in new guises. In this vein, companies never lose their resourcefulness in finding new ways to skew perceptions of their performance. By studying their methods closely, analysts can potentially anticipate the variations on old themes that will materialize in years to come.

MARTIN FRIDSON
FERNANDO ALVAREZ

Acknowledgments

Mukesh Agarwal
John Bace
Mimi Barker
Mitchell Bartlett
Richard Bernstein
Richard Byrne
Richard Cagney
George Chalhoub
Tiffany Charbonier
Sanford Cohen
Margarita Declet
Mark Dunham
Kenneth Emery
Bill Falloon
Sylvan Feldstein
David Fitton
Thomas Flynn III
Daniel Fridson
Igor Fuksman
Ryan Gelrod
Kenneth Goldberg
Susannah Gray
Evelyn Harris
David Hawkins
Emilie Herman
Avi Katz
Rebecca Keim
James Kenney
Andrew Kroll
Les Levi
Ross Levy
Michael Lisk
David Lugg
Jennie Ma

Stan Manoukian
Michael Marocco
Tom Marshella
Eric Matejevich
John Mattis
Pat McConnell
Oleg Melentyev
Krishna Memani
Ann Marie Mullan
Kingman Penniman
Stacey Rivera
Richard Rolnick
Clare Schiedermayer
Gary Schieneman
Bruce Schwartz
Devin Scott
David Shapiro
Elaine Sisman
Charles Snow
Vladimir Stadnyk
John Thieroff
Scott Thomas
John Tinker
Kivin Varghese
Diane Vazza
Pamela Van Giessen
Sharyl Van Winkle
David Waill
Steven Waite
Douglas Watson
Burton Weinstein
Stephen Weiss
David Whitcomb
Mark Zand

Financial Statement Analysis

PART One

Reading between the Lines

The Adversarial Nature of Financial Reporting

Financial statement analysis is an essential skill in a variety of occupations, including investment management, corporate finance, commercial lending, and the extension of credit. For individuals engaged in such activities, or who analyze financial data in connection with their personal investment decisions, there are two distinct approaches to the task.

The first is to follow a prescribed routine, filling in boxes with standard financial ratios, calculated according to precise and inflexible definitions. It may take little more effort or mental exertion than this to satisfy the formal requirements of many positions in the field of financial analysis. Operating in a purely mechanical manner, though, will not provide much of a professional challenge. Neither will a rote completion of all of the proper standard analytical steps ensure a useful, or even a nonharmful, result. Some individuals, however, will view such problems as only minor drawbacks.

This book is aimed at the analyst who will adopt the second and more rewarding alternative, the relentless pursuit of accurate financial profiles of the entities being analyzed. Tenacity is essential because financial statements often conceal more than they reveal. To the analyst who embraces this proactive approach, producing a standard spreadsheet on a company is a means rather than an end. Investors derive but little satisfaction from the knowledge that an untimely stock purchase recommendation was supported by the longest row of figures available in the software package. Genuinely valuable analysis begins *after* all the usual questions have been answered. Indeed, a superior analyst adds value by raising questions that are not even on the checklist.

Some readers may not immediately concede the necessity of going beyond an analytical structure that puts all companies on a uniform, objective scale. They may recoil at the notion of discarding the structure altogether when a sound assessment depends on factors other than comparisons of standard financial ratios. **Comparability**, after all, is a cornerstone of **generally accepted accounting principles (GAAP)**. It might therefore seem to follow that financial statements prepared in accordance with GAAP necessarily produce fair and useful indications of relative value.

The corporations that issue financial statements, moreover, would appear to have a natural interest in facilitating convenient, cookie-cutter analysis. These companies spend heavily to disseminate information about their financial performance. They employ investor-relations managers, they communicate with existing and potential shareholders via interim financial reports and press releases, and they dispatch senior management to periodic meetings with securities analysts. Given that companies are so eager to make their financial results known to investors, they should also want it to be easy for analysts to monitor their progress. It follows that they can be expected to report their results in a transparent and straightforward fashion . . . or so it would seem.

THE PURPOSE OF FINANCIAL REPORTING

Analysts who believe in the inherent reliability of GAAP numbers and the good faith of corporate managers misunderstand the essential nature of financial reporting. Their conceptual error connotes no lack of intelligence, however. Rather, it mirrors the standard accounting textbook's idealistic but irrelevant notion of the purpose of financial reporting. Even Howard Schilit (see the MicroStrategy discussion, later in this chapter), an acerbic critic of financial reporting as it is actually practiced, presents a high-minded view of the matter:

> *The primary goal in financial reporting is the dissemination of financial statements that accurately measure the profitability and financial condition of a company.*[1]

Missing from this formulation is an indication of *whose* primary goal is accurate measurement. Schilit's words are music to the ears of the financial statements users listed in this chapter's first paragraph, but they are not the ones doing the financial reporting. Rather, the issuers are for-profit companies, generally organized as corporations.[2]

A corporation exists for the benefit of its shareholders. Its objective is not to educate the public about its financial condition, but to maximize its shareholders' wealth. If it so happens that management can advance that objective through "dissemination of financial statements that accurately measure the profitability and financial condition of the company," then in principle, management should do so. At most, however, reporting financial results in a transparent and straightforward fashion is a means unto an end.

Management may determine that a more direct method of maximizing shareholder wealth is to reduce the corporation's *cost of capital.* Simply stated, the lower the interest rate at which a corporation can borrow or the higher the price at which it can sell stock to new investors, the greater the wealth of its shareholders. From this standpoint, the best kind of financial statement is not one that represents the corporation's condition most fully and most fairly, but rather one that produces the highest possible credit rating (see Chapter 13) and price-earnings **multiple** (see Chapter 14). If the highest ratings and multiples result from statements that measure profitability and financial condition *inaccurately,* the logic of fiduciary duty to shareholders obliges management to publish that sort, rather than the type held up as a model in accounting textbooks. The best possible outcome is a cost of capital lower than the corporation deserves on its merits. This admittedly perverse argument can be summarized in the following maxim, presented from the perspective of issuers of financial statements:

The purpose of financial reporting is to obtain cheap capital.

Attentive readers will raise two immediate objections. First, they will say, it is fraudulent to obtain capital at less than a fair rate by presenting an unrealistically bright financial picture. Second, some readers will argue that misleading the users of financial statements is not a sustainable strategy over the long run. Stock market investors who rely on overstated historical profits to project a corporation's future earnings will find that results fail to meet their expectations. Thereafter, they will adjust for the upward bias in the financial statements by projecting lower earnings than the historical results would otherwise justify. The outcome will be a stock valuation no higher than accurate reporting would have produced. Recognizing that the practice would be self-defeating, corporations will logically refrain from overstating their financial performance. By this reasoning, the users of financial statements can take the numbers at face value, because corporations that act in their self-interest will report their results honestly.

The inconvenient fact that confounds these arguments is that financial statements do *not* invariably reflect their issuers' performance faithfully. In lieu of easily understandable and accurate data, users of financial statements often find numbers that conform to GAAP yet convey a misleading impression of profits. Worse yet, outright violations of the accounting rules come to light with distressing frequency. Not even the analyst's second line of defense, an affirmation by independent auditors that the statements have been prepared in accordance with GAAP, assures that the numbers are reliable.

A few examples from recent years indicate how severely an overly trusting user of financial statements can be misled.

Interpublic Tries Again . . . and Again

Interpublic Group of Companies announced on August 13, 2002, that it had improperly accounted for $68.5 million of expenses and would restate its financial results all the way back to 1997. The operator of advertising agencies said the restatement was related to transactions between European offices of the McCann-Erickson Worldwide Advertising unit. Sources indicated that when different offices collaborated on international projects, they effectively booked the same revenue more than once. In the week before the restatement announcement, when the company delayed the filing of its quarterly results to give its audit committee time to review the accounting, its stock sank by nearly 25 percent.

Perhaps not coincidentally, Interpublic's massive revision coincided with the effective date of new **Securities and Exchange Commission** (**SEC**) certification requirements. Under the new rules, a company's chief executive officer and chief financial officer could be subject to fines or prison sentences if they certified false financial statements. It was an opportune time for any company that had been playing games with its financial reporting to get straight.

The August 2002 restatement did not clear things up once and for all at Interpublic. In October, the company nearly doubled the amount of the planned restatement to $120 million, and in November, it emerged that the number might go even higher. By that time, Interpublic's stock was down 55 percent from the start of the year, Standard & Poor's had downgraded its credit rating from BBB+ to BBB, and several top executives had been dismissed.

Like many other companies that have issued financial statements that subsequently needed revision, Interpublic was under earnings pressure. Advertising spending had fallen drastically, producing the worst industry results in decades. Additionally, the company was having difficulty assimilating a huge number of acquisitions. Chairman John J. Dooner was understandably eager to shift the focus from all that. "The finger-pointing is about the past," he said. "I'm focusing on the present and future."[3]

Unfortunately, the future brought more accounting problems. A few days after Dooner's statement, the company upped its estimated restatement to $181.3 million, nearly triple the original figure. Another blow arrived a week later as the SEC requested information related to the errors that gave rise to the restatement. It also turned out that the misreporting was not limited to double-counting of revenue by McCann-Erickson's European offices. Other items included an estimate of not-yet-realized insurance proceeds, write-offs of accounts receivable and work in progress, and understated liabilities at other Interpublic subsidiaries dating back as far as 1996. Dooner commented, "The restatement that we have been living through is finally filed."[4] He also stated that he was resolved that the turmoil created by the accounting problems would never happen again.

Fast-forward to September 2005. Dooner's successor and the third CEO since the accounting problems first surfaced, Michael I. Roth, declared that his top priority was to put Interpublic's financial reporting problems behind it. For the first time, the company acknowledged that honest mistakes might not have accounted for all of the erroneous accounting. Furthermore, said Interpublic, investors should not rely on previous estimates of the restatements, which also involved procedures for tracking the company's hundreds of agency acquisitions. That proved to be something of an understatement. Interpublic ultimately announced a restatement of $550 million, three times the previous estimate, for the period 2000 through September 30, 2004. In May 2008, the company paid $12 million to settle the SEC's accusation that it fraudulently misstated its results by booking intercompany charges as receivables instead of expenses.

MicroStrategy Changes Its Mind

On March 20, 2000, MicroStrategy announced that it would restate its 1999 revenue, originally reported as $205.3 million, to around $150 million. The company's shares promptly plummeted by $140 to $86.75 a share, slashing Chief Executive Officer Michael Saylor's paper wealth by over $6 billion. The company explained that the revision had to do with recognizing revenue on the software company's large, complex projects.[5] MicroStrategy and its auditors initially suggested that the company had been obliged to restate its results in response to a recent (December 1999) SEC advisory on rules for booking software revenues. After the SEC objected to that explanation, the company conceded that its original accounting was inconsistent with accounting principles published way back in 1997 by the American Institute of Certified Public Accountants.

Until MicroStrategy dropped its bombshell, the company's auditors had put their seal of approval on the company's revenue recognition policies. That was despite questions raised about MicroStrategy's financials by accounting expert Howard Schilit six months earlier and by reporter David Raymond in an issue of *Forbes ASAP* distributed on February 21.[6] It was reportedly only after reading Raymond's article that an accountant in the auditor's national office contacted the local office that had handled the audit, ultimately causing the firm to retract its previous certification of the 1998 and 1999 financials.[7]

No Straight Talk from Lernout & Hauspie

On November 16, 2000, the auditor for Lernout & Hauspie Speech Products (L&H) withdrew its clean opinion of the company's 1998 and 1999 financials. The action followed a November 9 announcement by the Belgian producer of speech-recognition and translation software that an internal investigation had uncovered accounting errors and irregularities that would require restatement of results for those two years and the first half of 2000. Two weeks later, the company filed for bankruptcy.

Prior to November 16, 2000, while investors were relying on the auditor's opinion that Lernout & Hauspie's financial statements were consistent with generally accepted accounting principles, several events cast doubt on that opinion. In July 1999, short seller David Rocker criticized transactions such as L&H's arrangement with Brussels Translation Group (BTG). Over a two-year period, BTG paid L&H $35 million to develop translation software. Then L&H bought BTG and the translation product along with it. The net effect was that instead of booking a $35 million research and development expense, L&H recognized $35 million of revenue.[8] In August 2000, certain Korean companies that L&H claimed as customers said that they in fact did no business with the corporation. In September, the Securities and Exchange Commission and Europe's EASDAQ stock market began to investigate L&H's accounting practices.[9] Along the way, Lernout & Hauspie's stock fell from a high of $72.50 in March 2000 to $7 before being suspended from trading in November. In retrospect, uncritical reliance on the company's financials, based on the auditor's opinion and a presumption that management wanted to help analysts get the true picture, was a bad policy.

THE FLAWS IN THE REASONING

As the preceding deviations from GAAP demonstrate, neither fear of antifraud statutes nor enlightened self-interest invariably deters corporations from cooking the books. The reasoning by which these two forces ensure honest accounting rests on hidden assumptions. None of the assumptions can stand up to an examination of the organizational context in which financial reporting occurs.

To begin with, corporations can push the numbers fairly far out of joint before they run afoul of GAAP, much less open themselves to prosecution for fraud. When major financial reporting violations come to light, as in most other kinds of white-collar crime, the real scandal involves what is *not* forbidden. In practice, generally accepted accounting principles countenance a lot of measurement that is decidedly inaccurate, at least over the short run.

For example, corporations routinely and unabashedly smooth their earnings. That is, they create the illusion that their profits rise at a consistent rate from year to year. Corporations engage in this behavior, with the blessing of their auditors, because the appearance of smooth growth receives a higher price-earnings multiple from stock market investors than the jagged reality underlying the numbers.

Suppose that, in the last few weeks of a quarter, earnings threaten to fall short of the programmed year-over-year increase. The corporation simply borrows sales (and associated profits) from the next quarter by offering customers special discounts to place orders earlier than they had planned. *Higher*-than-trendline growth, too, is a problem for the earnings-smoother. A sudden jump in profits, followed by a return to a more ordinary rate of growth, produces volatility, which is regarded as an evil to be avoided at all costs. Management's solution is to run up expenses in the current period by scheduling training programs and plant maintenance that, while necessary, would ordinarily be undertaken in a later quarter.

These are not tactics employed exclusively by fly-by-night companies. Blue chip corporations openly acknowledge that they have little choice but to smooth their earnings, given Wall Street's allergy to surprises. Officials of General Electric have indicated that when a division is in danger of failing to meet its annual earnings goal, it is accepted procedure to make an acquisition in the waning days of the reporting period. According to an executive in the company's financial services business, he and his colleagues hunt for acquisitions at such times, saying, "Gee, does somebody else have some income? Is there some other deal we can make?"[10] The freshly acquired unit's profits for the full quarter can be incorporated into GE's, helping to ensure the steady growth so prized by investors.

Why do auditors not forbid such gimmicks? They hardly seem consistent with the ostensible purpose of financial reporting, namely, the accurate portrayal of a corporation's earnings. The explanation is that sound principles of accounting theory represent only one ingredient in the stew from which financial reporting standards emerge.

Along with accounting professionals, the issuers and users of financial statements also have representation on the **Financial Accounting Standards Board (FASB)**, the rule-making body that operates under authority delegated by the Securities and Exchange Commission. When FASB identifies an area in need of a new standard, its professional staff typically defines the theoretical issues in a matter of a few months. Issuance of the new standard may take several years, however, as the corporate issuers of financial statements pursue their objectives on a decidedly less abstract plane.

From time to time, highly charged issues, such as executive stock options and mergers, lead to fairly testy confrontations between FASB and the corporate world. The compromises that emerge from these dustups fail to satisfy theoretical purists. On the other hand, rule making by negotiation heads off all-out assaults by the corporations' allies in Congress. If the lawmakers were ever to get sufficiently riled up, they might drastically curtail FASB's authority. Under extreme circumstances, they might even replace FASB with a new rule-making body that the corporations could more easily bend to their will.

There is another reason that enlightened self-interest does not invariably drive corporations toward candid financial reporting. The corporate executives who lead the battles against FASB have their own agenda. Just like the investors who buy their corporations' stock, managers seek to maximize their wealth. If producing bona fide economic profits advances that objective, it is rational for a chief executive officer (CEO) to try to do so. In some cases, though, the CEO can achieve greater personal gain by taking advantage of the compensation system through financial reporting gimmicks.

Suppose, for example, the CEO's year-end bonus is based on growth in earnings per share. Assume also that for financial reporting purposes, the corporation's **depreciation** schedules assume an average life of eight years for fixed assets. By arbitrarily amending that assumption to nine years (and obtaining the auditors' consent to the change), the corporation can lower its annual depreciation expense. This is strictly an accounting change; the actual cost of replacing equipment worn down through use does not decline. Neither does the corporation's tax deduction for depreciation expense rise nor, as a consequence, does cash flow[11] (see Chapter 4). Investors recognize that bona fide profits (see Chapter 5) have not increased, so the corporation's stock price does not change in response to the new accounting policy. What *does* increase is the CEO's bonus, as a function of the artificially contrived boost in earnings per share.

This example explains why a corporation may alter its accounting practices, making it harder for investors to track its performance, even though the shareholders' enlightened self-interest favors straightforward, transparent financial reporting. The underlying problem is that corporate executives sometimes put their own interests ahead of their shareholders' welfare. They beef up their bonuses by overstating profits, while shareholders bear the cost of reductions in price–earnings ratios to reflect deterioration in the quality of **reported earnings**.[12]

The logical solution for corporations, it would seem, is to align the interests of management and shareholders. Instead of calculating executive bonuses on the basis of earnings per share, the board should reward senior management for increasing shareholders' wealth by causing the stock price to rise. Such an arrangement gives the CEO no incentive to inflate reported earnings through gimmicks that transparently produce no increase in bona fide profits and therefore no rise in the share price.

Following the logic through, financial reporting ought to have moved closer to the ideal of accurate representation of corporate performance as companies have increasingly linked executive compensation to stock price appreciation. In reality, though, no such trend is discernible. If anything, the preceding examples of Interpublic, MicroStrategy, and Lernout & Hauspie suggest that corporations have become more creative and more aggressive over time in their financial reporting.

Aligning management and shareholder interests, it turns out, has a dark side. Corporate executives can no longer increase their bonuses through financial reporting tricks that are readily detectable by investors. Instead, they must devise better-hidden gambits that fool the market and artificially elevate the stock price. Financial statement analysts must work harder than ever to spot corporations' subterfuges.

SMALL PROFITS AND BIG BATHS

Certainly, financial statement analysts do not have to fight the battle single-handedly. The Securities and Exchange Commission and the Financial Accounting Standards Board prohibit corporations from going too far in prettifying their profits to pump up their share prices. These regulators refrain from indicating exactly how far is too far, however. Inevitably, corporations hold diverse opinions on matters such as the extent to which they must divulge bad news that might harm their stock market valuations. For some, the standard of disclosure appears to be that if nobody happens to ask about a specific event, then declining to volunteer the information does not constitute a lie.

The picture is not quite that bleak in every case, but the bleakness extends pretty far. A research team led by Harvard economist Richard Zeckhauser has compiled evidence that lack of perfect candor is widespread.[13] The researchers focus on instances in which a corporation reports quarterly earnings that are only slightly higher or slightly lower than its earnings in the corresponding quarter of the preceding year.

Suppose that corporate financial reporting followed the accountants' idealized objective of depicting performance accurately. By the laws of probability, corporations' quarterly reports would include about as many cases of earnings that barely exceed year-earlier results as cases of earnings that fall just shy of year-earlier profits. Instead, Zeckhauser and colleagues find that corporations post small increases far more frequently than they post small declines. The strong implication is that when companies are in danger of showing slightly negative earnings comparisons, they locate enough discretionary items to squeeze out marginally improved results.

On the other hand, suppose a corporation suffers a quarterly profit decline too large to erase through discretionary items. Such circumstances create an incentive to take a big bath by maximizing the reported setback. The reasoning is that investors will not be much more disturbed by a 30 percent drop in earnings than by a 20 percent drop. Therefore, management may find it expedient to **accelerate** certain future expenses into the current quarter, thereby ensuring positive reported earnings in the following period. It may also be a convenient time to recognize long-run losses in the value of assets such as outmoded production facilities and **goodwill** created in unsuccessful acquisitions of the past. In fact, the corporation may take a larger write-off on those assets than the principle of accurate representation would dictate. Reversals of the excess write-offs offer an artificial means of stabilizing reported earnings in subsequent periods.

Zeckhauser and his associates corroborate the big bath hypothesis by showing that large earnings declines are more common than large increases. By implication, managers do not passively record the combined results of their own skill and business factors beyond their control, but intervene in the calculation of earnings by exploiting the latitude in accounting rules. The researchers' overall impression is that corporations regard financial reporting as a technique for propping up stock prices, rather than a means of disseminating objective information.[14]

If corporations' gambits escape detection by investors and lenders, the rewards can be vast. For example, an interest-cost savings of half a percentage point on $1 billion of borrowings equates to $5 million (pretax) per year. If the corporation is in a 34 percent tax bracket and its stock trades at 15 times earnings, the payoff for risk-concealing financial statements is $49.5 million in the cumulative value of its shares.

Among the popular methods for pursuing such opportunities for wealth enhancement, aside from the big bath technique studied by Zeckhauser, are:

- Maximizing growth expectations.
- Downplaying contingencies.

MAXIMIZING GROWTH EXPECTATIONS

Imagine a corporation that is currently reporting annual net earnings of $20 million. Assume that five years from now, when its growth has leveled off somewhat, the corporation will be valued at 15 times earnings. Further assume that the company will pay no dividends over the next five years and that investors in growth stocks currently seek returns of 25 percent (before considering capital gains taxes).

Based on these assumptions, plus one additional number, the analyst can place an aggregate value on the corporation's outstanding shares. The final required input is the expected growth rate of earnings. Suppose the corporation's earnings have been growing at a 30 percent annual rate and appear likely to continue increasing at the same rate over the next five years. At the end of that period, earnings (rounded) will be $74 million annually. Applying a multiple of 15 times to that figure produces a valuation at the end of the fifth year of $1.114 billion. Investors seeking a 25 percent rate of return will pay $365 million today for that future value.

These figures are likely to be pleasing to a founder or chief executive officer who owns, for the sake of illustration, 20 percent of the outstanding shares. The successful entrepreneur is worth $73 million on paper, quite possibly up from zero just a few years ago. At the same time, the newly minted multimillionaire is a captive of the market's expectations.

Suppose investors conclude for some reason that the corporation's potential for increasing its earnings has declined from 30 to 25 percent per annum. That is still well above average for corporate America. Nevertheless, the value of the corporation's shares will decline from $365 million to $300 million, keeping previous assumptions intact.

Overnight, the long-struggling founder will see the value of his personal stake plummet by $13 million. Financial analysts may shed few tears for him. After all, he is still worth $60 million on paper. If they were in his shoes, however, how many would accept a $13 million loss with perfect equanimity? Most would be sorely tempted, at the least, to avoid incurring a financial reverse of comparable magnitude via every means available to them under GAAP.

That all-too-human response is the one typically exhibited by owner-managers confronted with falling growth expectations. Many, perhaps most, have no intention to deceive. It is simply that the entrepreneur is by nature a self-assured optimist. A successful entrepreneur, moreover, has had this optimism vindicated. Having taken his company from nothing to $20 million of earnings against overwhelming odds, he believes he can lick whatever short-term problems have arisen. He is confident that he can get the business back onto a 30 percent growth curve, and perhaps he is right. One thing is certain: If he were not the sort who believed he could beat the odds one more time, he would never have built a company worth $300 million.

Financial analysts need to assess the facts more objectively. They must recognize that the corporation's predicament is not unique, but on the contrary, quite common. Almost invariably, senior managers try to dispel the impression of decelerating growth, since that perception can be so costly

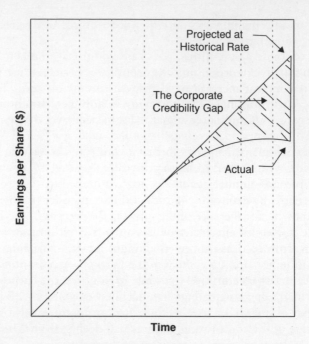

EXHIBIT 1.1   The Inevitability of Deceleration

Note: Shifting investors' perceptions upward through the Corporate Credibility Gap between actual and management-projected growth is a potentially valuable but inherently difficult undertaking for a company. Liberal financial reporting practices can make the task somewhat easier. In this light, analysts should read financial statements with a skeptical eye.

to them. Simple mathematics, however, tends to make false prophets of corporations that extrapolate high growth rates indefinitely into the future. Moreover, once growth begins to level off (see Exhibit 1.1), restoring it to the historical rate requires overcoming several powerful limitations.

Limits to Continued Growth

Saturation   Sales of a hot new consumer product can grow at astronomical rates for a time. Eventually, however, everybody who cares to will own one (or two, or some other finite number that the consumer believes is enough). At that point, potential sales will be limited to replacement sales plus growth in population, that is, the increase in the number of potential purchasers.

Entry of Competition   Rare is the company with a product or service that cannot either be copied or encroached on by a knockoff sufficiently similar to tap the same demand, yet different enough to fall outside the bounds of patent and trademark protection.

Increasing Base A corporation that sells 10 million units in Year 1 can register a 40 percent increase by selling just 4 million additional units in Year 2. If growth continues at the same rate, however, the corporation will have to generate 59 million new unit sales to achieve a 40 percent gain in Year 10.

In absolute terms, it is arithmetically possible for volume to increase indefinitely. On the other hand, a growth rate far in excess of the **gross domestic product**'s annual increase is nearly impossible to sustain over any extended period. By definition, a product that experiences higher-than-**GDP** growth captures a larger percentage of GDP each year. As the numbers get larger, it becomes increasingly difficult to switch consumers' spending patterns to accommodate continued high growth of a particular product.

Market Share Constraints For a time, a corporation may overcome the limits of growth in its market and the economy as a whole by expanding its sales at the expense of competitors. Even when growth is achieved by market share gains rather than by expanding the overall demand for a product, however, the firm must eventually bump up against a ceiling on further growth at a constant rate. For example, suppose a producer with a 10 percent share of market is currently growing at 25 percent a year while total demand for the product is expanding at only 5 percent annually. By Year 14, this supergrowth company will require a 115 percent market share to maintain its rate of increase. (Long before confronting this mathematical impossibility, the corporation's growth will probably be curtailed by the antitrust authorities.)

Basic economics and compound-interest tables, then, assure the analyst that all growth stories come to an end, a cruel fate that must eventually be reflected in stock prices. Financial reports, however, frequently tell a different tale. It defies common sense yet almost has to be told, given the stakes. Users of financial statements should acquaint themselves with the most frequently heard corporate versions of "Jack and the Beanstalk," in which earnings—in contradiction to a popular saw—do grow to the sky.

Commonly Heard Rationalizations for Declining Growth

"Our Year-over-Year Comparisons Were Distorted" Recognizing the sensitivity of investors to any slowdown in growth, companies faced with earnings deceleration commonly resort to certain standard arguments to persuade investors that the true, underlying profit trend is still rising at its

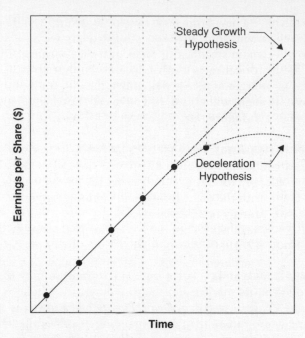

EXHIBIT 1.2 "Our Year-over-Year Comparisons Were Distorted"
Note: Is the latest earnings figure an outlier or does it signal the start of a slowdown in growth? Nobody will know for certain until more time has elapsed, but the company will probably propound the former hypothesis as forcefully as it can.

historical rate (see Exhibit 1.2). Freak weather conditions may be blamed for supposedly anomalous, below-trendline earnings. Alternatively, the company may allege that shipments were delayed (never canceled, merely delayed) because of temporary production problems caused, ironically, by the company's explosive growth. (What appeared to be a negative for the stock price, in other words, was actually a positive. Orders were coming in faster than the company could fill them—a high-class problem indeed.) Widely publicized macroeconomic events such as the Y2K problem[15] receive more than their fair share of blame for earnings shortfalls. However plausible these explanations may sound, analysts should remember that in many past instances, short-term supposed aberrations have turned out to be advance signals of earnings slowdowns.

"New Products Will Get Growth Back on Track"   Sometimes, a corporation's claim that its obviously **mature** product lines will resume their former growth path becomes untenable. In such instances, it is a good idea for management to have a new product or two to show off. Even if the products are still in development, some investors who strongly wish to believe in the corporation will remain steadfast in their faith that earnings will continue growing at the historical rate. (Such hopes probably rise as a function of owning stock on margin at a cost well above the current market.) A hard-headed analyst, though, will wait to be convinced, bearing in mind that new products have a high failure rate.

"We're Diversifying Away from Mature Markets" If a growth-minded company's entire industry has reached a point of slowdown, it may have little choice but to redeploy its earnings into faster-growing businesses. Hunger for growth, along with the quest for cyclical balance, is a prime motivation for the corporate strategy of **diversification**.

Diversification reached its zenith of popularity during the conglomerate movement of the 1960s. Up until that time, relatively little evidence had accumulated regarding the actual feasibility of achieving high earnings growth through acquisitions of companies in a wide variety of growth industries. Many corporations subsequently found that their diversification strategies worked better on paper than in practice. One problem was that they had to pay extremely high price-earnings multiples for growth companies that other conglomerates also coveted. Unless earnings growth accelerated dramatically under the new corporate ownership, the acquirer's return on investment was fated to be mediocre. This constraint was particularly problematic for managers who had no particular expertise in the businesses they were acquiring. Still worse was the predicament of a corporation that paid a big premium for an also-ran in a hot industry. Regrettably, the number of industry leaders available for acquisition was by definition limited.

By the 1980s, the stock market had rendered its verdict. The price-earnings multiples of widely diversified corporations carried a conglomerate discount. One practical problem was the difficulty security analysts encountered in trying to keep tabs on companies straddling many different industries. Instead of making 2 plus 2 equal 5, as they had promised, the conglomerates' managers presided over corporate empires that traded at cheaper prices than their constituent companies would have sold for in aggregate had they been listed separately.

Despite this experience, there are periodic attempts to revive the notion of diversification as a means of maintaining high earnings growth indefinitely into the future. In one variant, management makes lofty claims about the potential for cross-selling one division's services to the customers of another. It is not clear, though, why paying premium acquisition prices to assemble the two businesses under the same corporate roof should prove more profitable than having one independent company pay a fee to use the other's mailing list. Battle-hardened analysts wonder whether such corporate strategies rely as much on the vagaries of mergers-and-acquisitions accounting (see Chapter 10) as they do on bona fide **synergy**.

All in all, users of financial statements should adopt a show-me attitude toward a story of renewed growth through diversification. It is often nothing more than a variant of the myth of above-average growth forever. Multi-industry corporations bump up against the same arithmetic that limits earnings growth for focused companies.

DOWNPLAYING CONTINGENCIES

A second way to mold disclosure to suit the issuer's interests is by downplaying extremely significant contingent liabilities. Thanks to the advent of **class action** suits, the entire net worth of even a multibillion-dollar corporation may be at risk in litigation involving environmental hazards or product liability. Understandably, an issuer of financial statements would prefer that securities analysts focus their attention elsewhere.

At one time, analysts tended to shunt aside claims that ostensibly threatened major corporations with bankruptcy. They observed that massive lawsuits were often settled for small fractions of the original claims. Furthermore, the outcome of a lawsuit often hinged on facts that emerged only when the case finally came to trial (which by definition never happened if the suit was settled out of court). Considering also the susceptibility of juries to emotional appeals, securities analysts of bygone days found it extremely difficult to incorporate legal risks into earnings forecasts that relied primarily on **microeconomic** and **macroeconomic** variables. At most, a contingency that had the potential of wiping out a corporation's equity became a qualitative factor in determining the multiple assigned to a company's earnings.

Manville Corporation's 1982 bankruptcy marked a watershed in the way analysts have viewed legal contingencies. To their credit, specialists in the building products sector had been asking detailed questions about Manville's exposure to asbestos-related personal injury suits for a long time before the company filed. Many investors nevertheless seemed to regard the corporation's August 26, 1982, filing under **Chapter 11** of the Bankruptcy Code as a sudden calamity. Manville's stock plunged by 35 percent on the day following its filing.

In part, the surprise element was a function of disclosure. The corporation's last quarterly report to the Securities and Exchange Commission prior to its bankruptcy had implied a total cost of settling asbestos-related claims of about $350 million. That was less than half of Manville's $830 million of shareholders' equity. On August 26, by contrast, Manville estimated the potential damages at no less than $2 billion.

For analysts of financial statements, the Manville episode demonstrated the plausibility of a scenario previously thought inconceivable. A bankruptcy at an otherwise financially sound company, brought on solely by legal claims, had become a nightmarish reality. Intensifying the shock was that the problem had lain dormant for many years. Manville's bankruptcy resulted from claims for diseases contracted decades earlier through contact with the company's products. The long-tailed nature of asbestos liabilities was underscored by a series of bankruptcy filings over succeeding years. Prominent examples, each involving a billion dollars or more of assets, included Walter Industries (1989), National Gypsum (1990), USG Corporation (1993 and again in 2001), Owens Corning (2000), and Armstrong World Industries (2000).

Bankruptcies connected with asbestos exposure, silicone gel breast implants, and assorted environmental hazards (see Chapter 13) have heightened analysts' awareness of legal risks. Even so, analysts still miss the forest for the trees in some instances, concentrating on the minutiae of financial ratios of corporations facing similarly large contingent liabilities. They can still be lulled by companies' matter-of-fact responses to questions about the gigantic claims asserted against them.

Thinking about it from the issuer's standpoint, one can imagine several reasons that the investor-relations officer's account of a major legal contingency is likely to be considerably less dire than the economic reality. To begin with, the corporation's managers have a clear interest in downplaying risks that threaten the value of their stock and options. Furthermore, as parties to a highly contentious lawsuit, the executives find themselves in a conflict. It would be difficult for them to testify persuasively in their company's defense while simultaneously acknowledging to investors that the plaintiffs' claims have merit and might, in fact, prevail. (Indeed, any such public admission could compromise the corporation's case. Candid disclosure may therefore not be a viable option.) Finally, it would hardly represent aberrant behavior if, on a subconscious level, management were to deny the real possibility of a company-wrecking judgment. It must be psychologically very difficult for managers to acknowledge that their company may go bust for reasons seemingly outside their control. Filing for bankruptcy may prove to be the only course available to the corporation, notwithstanding an excellent record of earnings growth and a conservative balance sheet.

For all these reasons, analysts must take particular care to rely on their independent judgment when a potentially devastating contingent liability looms larger than their conscientiously calculated financial ratios. It is not a matter of sitting in judgment on management's honor and forthrightness.

If corporate executives remain in denial about the magnitude of the problem, they are not deliberately misleading analysts by presenting an overly optimistic picture. Moreover, the managers may not provide a reliable assessment even if they soberly face the facts. In all likelihood, they have never worked for a company with a comparable problem. They consequently have little basis for estimating the likelihood that the worst-case scenario will be fulfilled. Analysts who have seen other corporations in similar predicaments have more perspective on the matter, as well as greater objectivity. Instead of relying entirely on the company's periodic updates on a huge class action suit, analysts should also speak to representatives of the plaintiffs' side. Their views, while by no means unbiased, will expose logical weaknesses in management's assertions that the liability claims will never stand up in court.

THE IMPORTANCE OF BEING SKEPTICAL

By now, the reader presumably understands why this chapter is titled "The Adversarial Nature of Financial Reporting." The issuer of financial statements has been portrayed in an unflattering light, invariably choosing the accounting option that will tend to prop up its stock price, rather than generously assisting the analyst in deriving an accurate picture of its financial condition. Analysts have been warned not to partake of the optimism that drives all great business enterprises, but instead to maintain an attitude of skepticism bordering on distrust. Some readers may feel they are not cut out to be financial analysts if the job consists of constant nay-saying, of posing embarrassing questions, and of being a perennial thorn in the side of companies that want to win friends among investors, customers, and suppliers.

Although pursuing relentless antagonism can indeed be an unpleasant way to go through life, the stance that this book recommends toward issuers of financial statements implies no such acrimony. Rather, analysts should view the issuers as adversaries in the same manner that they temporarily demonize their opponents in a friendly pickup basketball game. On the court, the competition can be intense, which only adds to the fun. Afterward, everyone can have a fine time going out together for pizza and beer. In short, financial analysts and investor-relations officers can view their work with the detachment of litigators who engage in every legal form of shin-kicking out of sheer desire to win the case, not because the litigants' claims necessarily have intrinsic merit.

Too often, financial writers describe the give-and-take of financial reporting and analysis in a highly moralistic tone. Typically, the author exposes a tricky presentation of the numbers and reproaches the company for greed and chicanery. Viewing the production of financial statements as an epic struggle between good and evil may suit a crusading journalist, but financial analysts need not join the ethics police to do their job well.

An alternative is to learn to understand the gamesmanship of financial reporting, perhaps even to appreciate on some level the cleverness of issuers who constantly devise new stratagems for leading investors off the track. Outright fraud cannot be countenanced, but disclosure that shades economic realities without violating the law requires truly impressive ingenuity. By regarding the interaction between issuers and users of financial statements as a game, rather than a morality play, analysts will find it easier to view the action from the opposite side. Just as a chess master anticipates an opponent's future moves, analysts should consider which gambits they themselves would use if they were in the issuer's seat.

"Oh no!" some readers must be thinking at this point. "First the authors tell me that I must not simply plug numbers into a standardized spreadsheet. Now I have to engage in role-playing exercises to guess what tricks will be embedded in the statements before they even come out. I thought this book was supposed to make my job easier, not more complicated."

In reality, this book's goal is to make the reader a better analyst. If that goal could be achieved by providing shortcuts, the authors would not hesitate to do so. Financial reporting occurs in an institutional context that obliges conscientious analysts to go many steps beyond conventional calculation of financial ratios. Without the extra vigilance advocated in these pages, the user of financial statements will become mired in a system that provides excessively simple answers to complex questions, squelches individuals who insolently refuse to accept reported financial data at face value, and inadvisably gives issuers the benefit of the doubt.

These systematic biases are inherent in selling stocks. Within the universe of investors are many large, sophisticated financial institutions that utilize the best available techniques of analysis to select securities for their **portfolios**. Also among the buyers of stocks are individuals who, not being trained in financial statement analysis, are poorly equipped to evaluate annual and quarterly earnings reports. Both types of investors are important sources of financing for industry, and both benefit over the long term from the returns that accrue to capital in a market economy. The two groups cannot be sold stocks in the same way, however.

What generally sells best to individual investors is a story. Sometimes the story involves a new product with seemingly unlimited sales potential. Another kind of story portrays the recommended stock as a play on some current economic trend, such as declining interest rates or a step-up in defense spending. Some stories lie in the realm of rumor, particularly those that relate to possible corporate takeovers. The chief characteristics of most stories are the promise of spectacular gains, superficially sound logic, and a paucity of quantitative verification.

No great harm is done when an analyst's stock purchase recommendation, backed up by a thorough study of the issuer's financial statements, is translated into soft, qualitative terms for laypersons' benefit. Not infrequently, though, a story originates among stockbrokers or even in the executive offices of the issuer itself. In such an instance, the zeal with which the story is disseminated may depend more on its narrative appeal than on the solidity of the supporting analysis.

Individual investors' fondness for stories undercuts the impetus for serious financial analysis, but the environment created by institutional investors is not ideal, either. Although the best investment organizations conduct rigorous and imaginative research, many others operate in the mechanical fashion derided earlier in this chapter. They reduce financial statement analysis to the bare bones of forecasting earnings per share, from which they derive a price-earnings multiple. In effect, the less conscientious investment managers assume that as long as a stock stacks up well by this single measure, it represents an attractive investment. Much Wall Street research, regrettably, caters to these institutions' tunnel vision, sacrificing analytical comprehensiveness to the operational objective of maintaining up-to-the-minute earnings estimates on vast numbers of companies.

Investment firms, moreover, are not the only workplaces in which serious analysts of financial statements may find their style crimped. The credit departments of manufacturers and wholesalers have their own set of institutional hazards.

Consider, to begin with, the very term *credit approval process.* As the name implies, the vendor's bias is toward extending rather than refusing credit. Up to a point, this is as it should be. In Exhibit 1.3, neutral Cutoff Point A, where half of all applicants are approved and half are refused,

EXHIBIT 1.3   The Bias toward Favorable Credit Evaluations

represents an unnecessarily high credit standard. Any company employing it would turn away many potential customers who posed almost no threat of delinquency. Even Cutoff Point B, which allows more business to be written but produces no credit losses, is less than optimal. Credit managers who seek to maximize profits aim for Cutoff Point C. It represents a level of credit extension at which losses on receivables occur but are slightly more than offset by the profits derived from incremental customers.

To achieve this optimal result, a credit analyst must approve a certain number of accounts that will eventually fail to pay. In effect, the analyst is required to make mistakes that could be avoided by rigorously obeying the conclusions derived from the study of applicants' financial statements. The company makes up the cost of such mistakes by avoiding mistakes of the opposite type (rejecting potential customers who will not fail to pay).

Trading off one type of error for another is thoroughly rational and consistent with sound analysis, so long as the objective is truly to maximize profits. There is always a danger, however, that the company will instead maximize sales at the expense of profits. That is, the credit manager may bias the system even further, to Cutoff Point D in Exhibit 1.3. Such a problem is bound to arise if the company's salespeople are paid on commission and their compensation is not tightly linked to the collection experience of their customers. The rational response to that sort of incentive system is to pressure credit analysts to approve applicants whose financial statements cry out for rejection.

A similar tension between the desire to book revenues and the need to make sound credit decisions exists in commercial lending. At a bank or a finance company, an analyst of financial statements may be confronted by special pleading on behalf of a loyal, long-established client that is under allegedly temporary strain. Alternatively, the lending officer may argue that a loan request ought to be approved, despite substandard financial ratios, on the grounds that the applicant is a young, struggling company with potential to grow into a major client. Requests for exceptions to established credit policies are likely to increase in both number and fervor during periods of slack demand for loans.

When considering pleas of mitigating circumstances, the credit analyst should certainly take into account pertinent qualitative factors that the financial statements fail to capture. At the same time, the analyst must bear in mind that qualitative credit considerations come in two flavors, favorable and unfavorable. It is also imperative to remember that the cold, hard statistics show that companies in the temporarily impaired and start-up categories have a higher-than-average propensity to **default** on their debt.

Every high-risk company seeking a loan can make a plausible soft case for overriding the financial ratios. In aggregate, though, a large percentage of such borrowers will fail, proving that many of their seemingly valid qualitative arguments were specious. This unsentimental truth was driven home by a massive 1989–1991 wave of defaults on high-yield bonds that had been marketed on the strength of supposedly valuable assets not reflected on the issuers' balance sheets. Bond investors had been told that the bold dreams and ambitions of management would suffice to keep the companies solvent. Another large default wave in 2001 involved early-stage telecommunications ventures for which there was scarcely any financial data from which to calculate ratios. The rationale advanced for lending to these nascent companies was the supposedly limitless demand for services made possible by miraculous new technology.

To be sure, defaults also occur among companies that satisfy established quantitative standards. The difference is that analysts can test financial ratios against a historical record to determine their reliability as predictors of bankruptcy (see Chapter 13). No comparable testing is feasible for the highly idiosyncratic, qualitative factors that weakly capitalized companies cite when applying for loans. Analysts are therefore on more solid ground when they rely primarily on the numbers than when they try to discriminate among companies' soft arguments.

CONCLUSION

A primary objective of this chapter has been to supply an essential ingredient that is missing from many discussions of financial statement analysis. Aside from accounting rules, cash flows, and definitions of standard ratios, analysts must consider the motivations of corporate managers, as well as the dynamics of the organizations in which they work. Neglecting these factors will lead to false assumptions about the underlying intent of issuers' communications with users of financial statements.

Moreover, analysts may make incorrect inferences about the quality of their own work if they fail to understand the workings of their own organizations. If a conclusion derived from thorough financial analysis is deemed wrong, it is important to know whether that judgment reflects a flawed analysis or a higher-level decision to override analysts' recommendations. Senior managers sometimes subordinate financial statement analysis to a determination that idle funds must be put to work or that loan volume must be increased. At such times, organizations rationalize their behavior by persuading themselves that the principles of interpreting financial statements have fundamentally changed. Analysts need not go to the extreme of resigning in protest, but they will benefit if they can avoid getting caught up in the prevailing delusion.

To be sure, organizational behavior has not been entirely overlooked up until now in the literature of financial statement analysis. Typically, academic studies depict issuers as profit-maximizing firms, inclined to overstate their earnings if they can do so legally and if they believe it will boost their equity market valuation. This model lags behind the portrait of the firm now prevalent in other branches of finance.[16] Instead of a monolithic organization that consistently pursues the clear-cut objective of share price maximization, the corporation is now viewed more realistically as an aggregation of individuals with diverse motivations.

Using this more sophisticated model, an analyst can unravel an otherwise vexing riddle concerning corporate reporting. Overstating earnings would appear to be a self-defeating strategy in the long term, since it has a tendency to catch up with the perpetrator. Suppose, for example, a corporation depreciates assets over a longer period than can be justified by physical wear and tear and the rate of technological change in manufacturing methods. When the time comes to replace the existing equipment, the corporation will face two unattractive options. The first is to penalize reported earnings by writing off the remaining undepreciated balance on equipment that is obsolete and hence of little value in the resale market. Alternatively, the company can delay the necessary purchase of more up-to-date equipment, thereby losing ground competitively and reducing future earnings. Would the corporation not have been better off if it had refrained from overstating its earnings in the first place, an act that probably cost it some measure of credibility among investors?

If the analyst considers the matter from the standpoint of management, a possible solution to the riddle emerges. The day of reckoning, when the firm must pay back the reported earnings borrowed via underdepreciation, may be beyond the planning horizon of senior management. A chief executive officer who intends to retire in five years, and who will be compensated in the interim according to a formula based on reported earnings growth, may have no qualms about exaggerating current results at the expense of future years' operations. The long-term interests of the firm's owners, in other words, may not be consistent with the short-term interests of their agents, the salaried managers.

Plainly, analysts cannot be expected to read minds or to divine the true motives of management in every case. There is a benefit, however, in simply being cognizant of objectives other than the ones presupposed by introductory accounting texts. If nothing else, the awareness that management may have something up its sleeve will encourage readers to trust their instincts when some aspect of a company's disclosure simply does not ring true. In a given instance, management may judge that its best chance of minimizing analysts' criticism of an obviously disastrous corporate decision lies in stubbornly defending the decision and refusing to change course. Even though the chief executive officer may be able to pull it off with a straight face, however, the blunder remains a blunder. Analysts who remember that managers may be pursuing their own agendas will be ahead of the game. They will be properly skeptical that management is genuinely making tough choices designed to yield long-run benefits to shareholders, but which individuals outside the corporation cannot envision.

Armed with the attitude that the burden of proof lies with those making the disclosures, the analyst is now prepared to tackle the basic financial statements. Methods for uncovering the information they conceal, as well as that which they reveal, constitute the heart of the next three chapters. From that elementary level right on up to making investment decisions with the techniques presented in the final two chapters, it will pay to maintain an adversarial stance at all times.

PART TWO

The Basic
Financial Statements

The Balance Sheet

The balance sheet is a remarkable invention, yet it has two fundamental shortcomings. First, while it is in theory quite useful to have a summary of the values of all the assets owned by an enterprise, these values frequently prove elusive in practice. Second, many kinds of things have value and could be construed, at least by the layperson, as assets. Not all of them can be assigned a specific value and recorded on a balance sheet, however. For example, proprietors of service businesses are fond of saying, "Our assets go down the elevator every night." Everybody acknowledges the value of a company's human capital—the skills and creativity of its employees—but no one has devised a means of valuing it precisely enough to reflect it on the balance sheet. Accountants do not go to the opposite extreme of banishing all intangible assets from the balance sheet, but the dividing line between the permitted and the prohibited is inevitably an arbitrary one.[1]

During the late 1990s, doctrinal disputes over accounting for assets intensified as intellectual capital came to represent growing proportions of many major corporations' perceived value. A study conducted on behalf of Big Five accounting firm Arthur Andersen showed that between 1978 and 1999, **book value** fell from 95 percent to 71 percent of the stock market value of public companies in the United States.[2] Increasingly, investors were willing to pay for things other than the traditional assets that generally accepted accounting principles (GAAP) had grown up around, including buildings, machinery, inventories, receivables, and a limited range of capitalized expenditures.

At the extreme, start-up Internet companies with negligible physical assets attained gigantic **market capitalizations.** Their valuations derived from business models purporting to promise vast profits far in the future. Building up subscriber bases through heavy consumer advertising was an expensive proposition, but one day, investors believed, a large, loyal following would translate into rich revenue streams.

Much of the dot-coms' stock market value disappeared during the tech wreck of 2000, but the perceived mismatch between the information-intensive New Economy and traditional notions of assets persisted. Prominent accounting theorists argued that financial reporting practices rooted in an era more dominated by heavy manufacturing grossly understated the value created by research and development outlays, which GAAP was resistant to capitalizing. They observed further that traditional accounting generally permitted assets to rise in value only if they were sold. "Transactions are no longer the basis for much of the value created and destroyed in today's economy, and therefore traditional accounting systems are at a loss to capture much of what goes on," argued Baruch Lev of New York University. As examples, he cited the rise in value resulting from a drug passing a key clinical test and from a computer software program being successfully beta-tested. "There's no accounting event because no money changes hands," Lev noted.[3]

THE VALUE PROBLEM

The problems of value that accountants wrestle with have also historically plagued philosophers, economists, tax assessors, and the judiciary. Moral philosophers over the centuries grappled with the notion of a fair price for merchants to charge. Early economists attempted to derive a product's intrinsic value by calculating the units of labor embodied in it. Several distinct approaches have evolved for assessing real property. These include **capitalization** of rentals, inferring a value based on sales of comparable properties, and estimating the value a property would have if put to its highest and best use. Similar theories are involved when the courts seek to value the assets of bankrupt companies, although vigorous negotiations among the different classes of creditors play an essential role in the final determination.

With commendable clarity of vision, the accounting profession long ago cut through the thicket of competing theories by establishing **historical cost** as the basis for valuing nonfinancial assets. The cost of acquiring or constructing an asset has the great advantage of being an objective and verifiable figure. As a benchmark for value, it is, therefore, compatible with accountants' traditional principle of conservatism.

Whatever its strengths, however, the historical cost system also has disadvantages that are apparent even to the beginning student of accounting. As already noted, basing valuation on transactions means that no asset can be reflected on the balance sheet unless it has been involved in a transaction. The most familiar difficulty that results from this convention involves goodwill. Company A has value above and beyond its tangible assets, in the form of well-regarded brand names and close relationships with merchants built up over many years. None of this intangible value appears on Company A's balance sheet, however, for it has never figured in a transaction. When Company B acquires Company A at a premium to book value, though, the intangibles are suddenly recognized. To the benefit of users of financial statements, Company A's assets are now more fully reflected. On the negative side, Company A's balance sheet now says it is more valuable than Company C, which has equivalent tangible and intangible assets but has never been acquired.

The difficulties a person may encounter in the quest for true value are numerous. Consider, for example, a piece of specialized machinery, acquired for $50,000. On the day the equipment is put into service, even before any controversies surrounding depreciation rates arise, value is already a matter of opinion. The company that made the purchase would presumably not have paid $50,000 if it perceived the machine to be worth a lesser amount. A secured lender, however, is likely to take a more conservative view. For one thing, the lender will find it difficult in the future to monitor the value of the collateral through comparables, since only a few similar machines (perhaps none, if the piece is customized) are produced each year. Furthermore, if the lender is ultimately forced to foreclose, there may be no ready purchaser of the machinery for $50,000, since its specialized nature makes it useful to only a small number of manufacturers. All of the potential purchasers, moreover, may be located hundreds of miles away, so that the machinery's value in a liquidation would be further reduced by the costs of transporting and reinstalling it.

The problems encountered in evaluating one-of-a-kind industrial equipment might appear to be eliminated when dealing with actively traded commodities such as crude oil reserves. Even this type of asset, however, resists precise, easily agreed-on valuation. Since oil companies frequently buy and sell reserves in the ground, current transaction prices are readily available. These transactions, however, are based on estimates of eventual production from unique geologic formations, for there are no means of directly measuring oil reserves. Even when petroleum engineers employ the most advanced technology, their estimates rely heavily on judgment and inference. It is not unheard of, moreover, for a well to begin to produce at the rate predicted by the best scientific methods, only to peter out a short time later, ultimately yielding just a fraction of its estimated reserves. With this degree of uncertainty, recording the true value of oil reserves is not a realistic objective for accountants. Users of financial statements can, at best, hope for informed guesses, and there is considerable room for honest people (not to mention rogues with vested interests) to disagree.

COMPARABILITY PROBLEMS IN THE VALUATION OF FINANCIAL ASSETS

The numerous difficulties of evaluating physical assets make historical cost an appealing, if imperfect, solution by virtue of its objectivity. Some financial assets are unaffected by those difficulties, however. They trade daily and actively in well-organized markets such as the New York Stock Exchange. It is feasible to value such assets on the basis of market quotations at the end of the financial reporting period, rather than according to historical cost, and achieve both objectivity and accuracy.

Analysts must keep in mind, however, that the values assigned to huge amounts of financial assets on many companies' balance sheets are *not* verifiable on the basis of continuously quoted prices determined in deep, liquid markets. Under **Fair Value Accounting**, an asset of this sort is valued at the amount at which it currently could be bought or sold in a transaction between willing parties, not including a liquidation sale. If no active market for the asset exists, a company can determine its balance sheet value on the basis of quoted prices for similar assets that do trade actively. In this case, the company must make assumptions about how the market would adjust for the fact that the actively traded and non-actively-traded assets are not identical. If no comparables exist, a company can use its own assumptions about the assumptions market participants would use to offer or bid for the asset it is valuing. Users of financial statements can reasonably expect that some companies' assumptions about assumptions will be on the liberal side, potentially inflating the value of non-actively-traded assets. Abuse of this discretion was one element of the Enron fraud (see Chapter 11.)

Thanks to market innovations of recent decades, a large category of subjectively valued financial assets consists of non-exchange-traded **derivatives**. (The collective term for these assets reflects that their valuations derive from the values of other assets, such as commodities or indexes of securities.) In a financial market crisis, the price at which such instruments can be bought or sold is subject to violent swings. Companies understandably would prefer that the investors who determine their stock prices not see or consider such losses in value, which the companies invariably (but not always correctly) characterize as temporary. For a financial institution, an even bigger worry is that its regulator will declare the institution insolvent, based on a market-induced and genuinely temporary decline in the balance sheet value of its derivatives.

Seeing these disadvantages to themselves, issuers of financial statements have resisted the imposition of full-blown fair value accounting. Under the compromise embodied in Statement of Financial Accounting Standards (**SFAS**) 115, financial instruments are valued according to their intended use by the company issuing the financial statements. If the company intends to hold a debt security to maturity, it records the value at amortized cost less impairment, if any. (The amortization is the write-down of a premium over face value or write-up of discount from face value, over the remaining period to maturity. Impairment is a loss of value arising from a clear indication that the obligor will be unable to satisfy the terms of the obligation.) If the company intends to sell a debt or equity security in the near term, hoping to make a trading profit, it records the instrument at fair value and includes unrealized gains and losses in earnings. A third option is for the company to classify a debt or equity security as neither held-to-maturity or a trading security, but instead in the noncommittal category of available for sale. In that case, the instrument is recorded at fair value, but unrealized gains and losses are excluded from earnings and instead reported in other comprehensive income, a separate component of shareholders' equity.

The essential point is that an asset may be valued on one company's balance sheet at a substantially different value than an identical asset is valued on another company's balance sheet, all based on the different companies' representations of their intentions.

It is even possible for an asset to be carried at two different values on a single balance sheet. For instance, when equity values plummeted in 2008, managers of leveraged buyout partnerships varied in the severity with which they wrote down their holdings. Many deals were shared by multiple private equity firms. A university endowment fund or pension plan sponsor might be a limited partner in a privately owned company held by two or more private equity funds that placed different values on the company. Underlying the value for those funds on the institution's balance sheet would be nonequivalent valuations of identical shares.

Inconsistent valuations can also undermine the integrity of an enterprise's balance sheet without involvement of outside parties such as private equity firms. An inquest into the September 2008 bankruptcy of Lehman Brothers found that each trading desk within the investment bank had its own methodology for pricing assets. Methodologies differed even within a single asset class, and the Product Control Group, which was supposed to enforce standardization in valuation, was understaffed for the task. Incidentally, some of the methodologies employed at Lehman Brothers were dubious, to say the least. For example, the investment bank based its second-quarter 2008 prices for one group of assets on a Morgan Stanley research note published in the first quarter of that year.[4]

INSTANTANEOUS WIPEOUT OF VALUE

Because the value of many assets is so subjective, balance sheets are prone to sudden, arbitrary revisions. To cite one dramatic example, on July 27, 2001, JDS Uniphase, a manufacturer of components for telecommunications networks, reduced the value of its goodwill by $44.8 billion. It was the largest write-off in corporate history up to that time.

This drastic decline in economic value did not occur in one day. Several months earlier, JDS Uniphase had warned investors to expect a big write-off arising from declining prospects at businesses that the company had acquired during the telecommunications euphoria of the late 1990s.[5] If investors had relied entirely on JDS's balance sheet, however, they would have perceived the loss of value as a sudden event.

Shortly before JDS Uniphase's action, Nortel Networks took a $12.3 billion goodwill write-off, and several major companies in such areas as Internet software and optical fiber quickly followed suit. High-tech companies had no monopoly on instantaneous evaporation of book value, however. In the fourth quarter of 2000, Sherwin-Williams recognized an impairment charge of $352 million ($293.6 million after taxes). Most of the write-off represented a reduction of goodwill that the manufacturer of paint and related products had created through a string of acquisitions. Even after the huge hit, goodwill represented 18.8 percent of Sherwin-Williams's assets and accounted for 47.9 percent of shareholders' equity.

Both Old Economy and New Economy companies, in short, are vulnerable to a sudden loss of stated asset value. Therefore, users of financial statements should not assume that balance sheet figures invariably correspond to the current economic worth of the assets they represent. A more reasonable expectation is that the numbers have been calculated in accordance with GAAP. The trick is to understand the relationship between these accounting conventions and reality.

If this seems a daunting task, the reader may take encouragement from the success of the bond-rating agencies (see Chapter 13) in sifting through the financial reporting folderol to get to the economic substance. The multibillion-dollar goodwill write-offs in 2001 did not, as one might have expected, set off a massive wave of rating downgrades. As in many previous instances of companies writing down assets, Moody's and Standard & Poor's did not equate changes in accounting values with reduced protection for lenders. To be sure, if a company wrote off a billion dollars' worth of goodwill, its ratio of assets to liabilities declined. Its ratio of *tangible* assets to liabilities did not change, however. The rating agencies monitored both ratios but had customarily attached greater significance to the version that ignored intangible assets such as goodwill.

HOW GOOD IS GOODWILL?

By maintaining a skeptical attitude to the value of intangible assets throughout the New Economy excitement of the late nineties, Moody's and Standard & Poor's were bucking the trend. The more stylish view was that balance sheets constructed according to GAAP seriously understated the value of corporations in dynamic industries such as computer software and e-commerce. Their earning power, so the story went, derived from inspired ideas and improved methods of doing business, not from the bricks and mortar for which conventional accounting was designed. To adapt to the economy's changing profile, proclaimed the heralds of the new paradigm, the accounting rule makers had to allow all sorts of items traditionally expensed to be capitalized onto the asset side of the balance sheet. Against that backdrop, analysts who questioned the value represented by goodwill, an item long deemed legitimate under GAAP, look conservative indeed.

In reality, the stock market euphoria that preceded Uniphase's mind-boggling write-off illustrated in classic fashion the reasons for rating agency skepticism toward goodwill. Through stock-for-stock acquisitions, the sharp rise in equity prices during the late 1990s was transformed into increased balance sheet values, despite the usual assumption that fluctuations in a company's stock price do not alter its stated net worth. It was a form of financial alchemy as remarkable as the transmutation of proceeds from stock sales into revenues described in Chapter 3.

The link between rising stock prices and escalating goodwill is illustrated by the fictitious example in Exhibit 2.1. In Scenario I, the shares of Associated Amalgamator Corporation ("Amalgamator") and United Consolidator Inc. ("Consolidator") are both trading at multiples of 1.0 times book value per share. Shareholders' equity is $200 million at Amalgamators and $60 million at Consolidator, equivalent to the companies' respective market capitalizations. Amalgamator uses stock held in its treasury to acquire Consolidator for $80 million. The purchase price represents a premium of $33^1/_3$ percent above the prevailing market price.

Let us now examine a key indicator of credit quality. Prior to the acquisition, Amalgamator's ratio of total assets to total liabilities (see Chapter 13) is 1.25 times, while the comparable figure for Consolidator is 1.18 times. The stock-for-stock acquisition introduces no new hard assets (e.g., cash, inventories, or factories). Neither does the transaction eliminate any existing liabilities. Logically, then, Consolidator's 1.18 times ratio should drag down Amalgamator's 1.25 times ratio, resulting in a figure somewhere in between for the combined companies.

In fact, though, the total-assets-to-total-liabilities ratio after the deal is 1.25 times. By paying a premium to Consolidator's tangible asset value,

EXHIBIT 2.1 Pro Forma Balance Sheets, December 31, 20XX ($000 omitted)

	Associated Amalgamator Corporation	United Consolidator Inc.	Purchase Price	Combined Companies Pro Forma
Scenario I				
Tangible assets	$1,000	$400		$1,400
Intangible assets	0	0		20
Total assets	1,000	400		1,420
Liabilities	800	340		1,140
Shareholders' equity (SE)	200	60	80	280
Total liabilities and SE	$1,000	$400		$1,420
Tangible assets/total liabilities	1.25	1.18		1.23
Total assets/total liabilities	1.25	1.18		1.25
Market capitalization	200	60		280
Scenario II				
Tangible assets	$1,000	$400		$1,400
Intangible assets	0	0		60
Total assets	1,000	400		1,460
Liabilities	800	340		1,140
Shareholders' equity (SE)	200	60	120	320
Total liabilities and SE	$1,000	$400		$1,460
Total assets/total liabilities	1.25	1.18		1.28
Tangible assets/total liabilities	1.25	1.18		1.23
Market capitalization	300	90		480*

*Ignores possible impact of earnings per share dilution.

Amalgamator creates $20 million of goodwill. This intangible asset represents just 1.4 percent of the combined companies' total assets, but that suffices to enable Amalgamator to acquire a company with a weaker debt-quality ratio without showing any deterioration on that measure.

If this outcome seems perverse, consider Scenario II. As the scene opens, an explosive stock market rally has driven up both companies' shares to 150 percent of book value. The ratio of total assets to total liabilities, however, remains at 1.25 times for Amalgamator and 1.18 times for Consolidator. Conservative bond buyers take comfort from the fact that the assets remain on the books at historical cost less depreciation, unaffected by euphoria on the stock exchange that may dissipate at any time without notice.

As in Scenario I, Amalgamator pays a premium of $33\frac{1}{3}$ percent above the prevailing market price to acquire Consolidator. The premium is calculated on a higher market capitalization, however. Consequently, the purchase price rises from $80 million to $120 million. Instead of creating $20 million of goodwill, the acquisition gives rise to a $60 million intangible asset.

When the conservative bond investors calculate the combined companies' ratio of total assets to total liabilities, they make a startling discovery. Somehow, putting together a company boasting a 1.25 times ratio with another sporting a 1.18 times ratio has produced an entity with a ratio of 1.28 times. Moreover, a minute of experimentation with the numbers will show that the ratio would be higher still if Amalgamator had bought Consolidator at a higher price. Seemingly, the simplest way for a company to improve its credit quality is to make stock-for-stock acquisitions at grossly excessive prices.

Naturally, this absurd conclusion embodies a fallacy. In reality, the receivables, inventories, and machinery available to be sold to satisfy creditors' claims are no greater in Scenario II than in Scenario I. Given that the total-assets-to-total-liabilities ratio is lower at Consolidator than at Amalgamator, the combined companies' ratio logically must be lower than at Amalgamator. Common sense further states that Amalgamator cannot truly have better credit quality if it overpays for Consolidator than if it acquires the company at a fair price.

As it happens, there is a simple way out of the logical conundrum. Let us exclude goodwill in calculating the ratio of assets to liabilities. As shown in the exhibit, Amalgamator's ratio of *tangible* assets to total liabilities following its acquisition of Consolidator is 1.23 times in both Scenario I and Scenario II. This is the outcome that best reflects economic reality. To ensure that they reach this commonsense conclusion, credit analysts must follow the rating agencies' practice of calculating balance sheet ratios both with and without goodwill and other intangible assets, giving greater emphasis to the latter version.

Calculating ratios on a tangibles-only basis is not equivalent to saying that the intangibles have no value. Amalgamator is likely to recoup all or most of the $60 million accounted for as goodwill if it turns around and sells Consolidator tomorrow. Such a transaction is hardly likely, however. A sale several years hence, after stock prices have fallen from today's lofty levels, is a more plausible scenario. Under such conditions, the full $60 million probably will not be recoverable.

Even leaving aside the possibility of a plunge in stock prices, it makes eminent sense to eliminate or sharply downplay the value of goodwill in a balance-sheet-based analysis of credit quality. Unlike inventories or accounts receivable, goodwill is not an asset that can be readily sold or **factored** to raise cash. Neither can a company enter into a **sale-leaseback** of its goodwill, as it can with its plant and equipment. In short, goodwill is not a separable asset that management can either convert into cash or use to raise cash to extricate itself from a financial tight spot. Therefore, the relevance of goodwill to an analysis of asset protection is questionable.

On the whole, the rating agencies appear to have shown sound judgment during the 1990s by resisting the New Economy's siren song. While enthusiasm mounted for all sorts of intangible assets, they continued to gear their analysis to tangible-assets-only versions of key balance sheet ratios. By and large, therefore, companies did not alter the way they were perceived by Moody's and Standard & Poor's when they suddenly took an ax to their intangible assets.

More generally, asset write-offs do not cause ratings to fall. Occasionally, to be sure, the announcement of a write-off coincides with the disclosure of a previously unrevealed impairment of value, ordinarily arising from operating problems. That sort of development may trigger a downgrade. In addition, a write-off sometimes coincides with a decision to close down certain operations. The associated severance costs (payments to terminated employees) may represent a substantial cash outlay that does weaken the company's financial position. Finally, a write-off can put a company in violation of a debt covenant (see Chapter 12). Nervous lenders may exploit the **technical default** by canceling the company's credit lines, precipitating a **liquidity** crisis. In and of itself, however, adjusting the balance sheet to economic reality does not represent a reduction in credit protection measures.

LOSING VALUE THE OLD-FASHIONED WAY

Goodwill write-offs by technology companies such as JDS Uniphase make splashy headlines in the financial news, but they by no means represent the only way in which balance sheet assets suddenly and sharply decline in value. In the Old Economy, where countless manufacturers earn slender margins on low-tech industrial goods, companies are vulnerable to long-run erosion in profitability. Common pitfalls include fierce price competition and a failure, because of near-term pressures to conserve cash, to invest adequately in modernization of plants and equipment. As the rate of return on their fixed assets declines, producers of industrial commodities such as paper, chemicals, and steel must eventually face up to the permanent impairment of their reported asset values.

It is not feasible, in the case of a chronically low rate-of-return company, to predict precisely the magnitude of a future reduction in accounting values.

Indeed, there is no guarantee that a company will fully come to grips with its overstated net worth, especially on the first round. To estimate the expected order of magnitude of future write-offs, however, an analyst can adjust the shareholders' value shown on the balance sheet to the rate of return typically being earned by comparable corporations.

To illustrate, suppose Company Z's average net income over the past five years has been $24 million. With most of the company's modest earnings being paid out in dividends, shareholders' equity has been stagnant at around $300 million. Assume further that during the same period, the average return of companies in the Standard & Poor's 400 index of industrial corporations has been 14 percent.

Does the figure $300 million accurately represent Company Z's equity value? If so, the implication is that investors are willing to own the company's shares and accept a return of only 8 percent ($24 million divided by $300 million), even though a 14 percent return is available on other stocks. There is no obvious reason that investors would voluntarily make such a sacrifice, however. Therefore, Company Z's book value is almost certainly overstated.

A reasonable estimate of the low-profit company's true equity value would be the amount that produces a return on equity equivalent to the going rate:

$$\frac{\text{Company Z average earnings stream}}{X} = \frac{\text{Average return on equity}}{\text{for U.S. corporations}}$$

$$\frac{\$24 \text{ million}}{X} = 14\%$$

$$X = \$171 \text{ million}$$

Although useful as a general guideline, this method of adjusting the shareholders' equity of underperforming companies neglects a number of important subtleties. For one thing, Company Z may be considered riskier than the average company. In that case, shareholders would demand a return higher than 14 percent to hold its shares. Furthermore, cash flow may be a better indicator of the company's economic performance than net income. This would imply that the adjustment ought to be made to the ratio of cash flow to market capitalization, rather than return on equity. Furthermore, investors' rate-of-return requirements reflect expected future earnings, rather than past results. Depending on the outlook for its business, it might be reasonable to assume that Company Z will either realize higher profits in the next five years than in the past five or see its profits plunge further. By the same token, securities analysts may expect the peer group of stocks that represent alternative investments to produce a return higher or lower than 14 percent in coming years. The further the analyst travels in search of true value, it seems, the murkier the notion becomes.

TRUE EQUITY IS ELUSIVE

What financial analysts are actually seeking, but are unable to find in the financial statements, is equity as economists conceive of it. In scholarly studies, the term *equity* generally refers not to accounting book value, but to the present value of future cash flows accruing to the firm's owners. Consider a firm that is deriving huge earnings from a trademark that has no accounting value because it was developed **internally** rather than acquired. The present value of the profits derived from the trademark would be included in the economist's definition of equity but not in the accountant's, potentially creating a gap of billions of dollars between the two.

The contrast between the economist's and the accountant's notions of equity is dramatized by the phenomenon of negative equity. In the economist's terms, equity of less than zero is synonymous with bankruptcy. The reasoning is that when a company's liabilities exceed the **present value** of all future income, it is not rational for the owners to continue paying off the liabilities. They will stop making payments currently due to lenders and trade creditors, which will in turn prompt the holders of the liabilities to try to recover their claims by forcing the company into bankruptcy. Suppose, on the other hand, that the present value of a highly successful company's future income exceeds the value of its liabilities by a substantial margin. If the company runs into a patch of bad luck, recording net losses for several years running and writing off selected operations, the book value of its assets may fall below the value of its liabilities. In accounting terms, the result is negative shareholders' equity. The economic value of the assets, however, may still exceed the stated value of the liabilities. Under such circumstances, the company has no reason to consider either suspending payments to creditors or filing for bankruptcy.

The Western Union Company's September 2006 spin-off from First Data Corporation demonstrated that negative equity in an accounting sense is not synonymous with insolvency. In connection with the spin-off, the provider of money transfer services distributed approximately $3.5 billion to First Data in the form of cash and debt securities. Net of other events during the period, shareholders' equity fell to –$314.8 million on December 31, 2006, from $2.8 billion one year earlier. By producing solid earnings over the next three years, Western Union boosted shareholders' equity to $353.5 million by December 31, 2009. Anyone who mistook the year-end

2006 negative figure as an indication of Western Union's economic value would have deemed its stock grossly overvalued at $18.85 a share. Through the end of 2009, however, Western Union shares performed far better than the stock market as a whole. The Standard & Poor's 500 Index fell by 21.4 percent versus a decline of only 15.9 percent for Western Union.

PROS AND CONS OF A MARKET-BASED EQUITY FIGURE

Relying on market capitalization is the practical means by which financial analysts commonly estimate the economists' more theoretically rigorous definition of equity as the present value of expected future cash flows. Monumental difficulties confront anyone who instead attempts to arrive at the figure through conventional financial reporting systems. The problem is that traditional accounting favors items that can be objectively measured. Unfortunately, future earnings and cash flows are unobservable. Moreover, calculating present value requires selecting a **discount rate** representing the company's **cost of capital.** Determining the cost of capital is a notoriously controversial subject in the financial field, complicated by thorny tax considerations and risk adjustments. The figures needed to calculate economists' equity are not, in short, the kind of numbers accountants like to deal with. Their ideal value is a price on an invoice that can be independently verified by a canceled check.

Market capitalization has additional advantages beyond its comparative ease of calculation. For one thing, it represents the consensus of large numbers of analysts and investors who constantly monitor companies' future earnings prospects as the basis for their evaluations. In addition, an up-to-the-minute market capitalization can be calculated on any day that the stock exchange is open. This represents a considerable advantage over the shareholders' equity shown on the balance sheet, which is updated only once every three months. Market capitalization adjusts instantaneously to news such as a surprise product launch by a competitor, an explosion that halts production at a key plant, or a sudden hike in interest rates by the Federal Reserve. In contrast, these events may never be reflected in book value in a discrete, identifiable manner. Ardent advocates of market capitalization cannot conceive of any more accurate estimate of true equity value.

Against these advantages, however, the analyst must weigh several drawbacks to relying on market capitalization to estimate a company's actual equity value. For one thing, while the objectivity of a price quotation established in a competitive market is indeed a benefit, it is obtainable only for corporations with publicly traded stocks. For privately owned companies, the proponents of market capitalization typically generate a proxy for true equity through reference to industry-peer public companies. For example, to calculate the equity of a privately owned paper producer, an analyst might multiply the publicly traded peer group's average price-earnings ratio (see Chapter 14) by the private company's earnings. Often, the peer-group multiple is based on **EBITDA** (see Chapter 8) rather than net income. This method can expand the peer group to include companies no longer publicly traded but recently acquired in leveraged buyouts. A limitation of the peer-group approach is that it fails to capture company-specific factors and therefore does not reap one major benefit of using market capitalization as a gauge of actual equity value.

Even if analysts restrict their reliance on market capitalization to publicly traded companies, they will still encounter pitfalls. Consider, for example, that on October 22, 2008, the **Dow Jones Industrial Average** plunged by 190 points, or 5.7 percent. The price of Dow component Walt Disney plummeted by 8.9 percent, representing a $4 billion loss in market value, without any major negative news reported about the entertainment company that day. Less than a week later, the stock market gauge had fully recovered its loss, and Disney's shares took just nine days to rebound to their October 21 level.

Notwithstanding the theoretical arguments for regarding market capitalization as a company's true equity value, short-run changes of the magnitude experienced by Disney on October 22, 2008, raise a caution. In a literal interpretation, even a huge, sudden swing in market capitalization indicates a change in a company's earnings prospects. In extreme cases, though, a temporary shift in the aggregate value of a company's shares can appear to reveal more about the dynamics of the stock market. An inference along those lines is supported by extensive academic research conducted under the rubric of behavioral finance. In contrast to more traditional financial economists, the behavioralists doubt that investors invariably process information accurately and act on it according to rules of rationality, as defined by economists. Empirical studies by adherents of behavioral finance show that instead of faithfully tracking companies' intrinsic values, market prices frequently overreact to news events. Even though investors supposedly evaluate stocks on the basis of expected future dividends (see Chapter 14), the behavioralists find that the stock market is far more volatile than the variability of dividends can explain.[6]

To be sure, these conclusions remain controversial. Traditionalists have challenged the empirical studies that underlie them, producing a vigorous debate. Nevertheless, the findings of behavioral finance lend moral support to analysts who find it hard to believe that the one-day erasure of billions of market capitalization must automatically be a truer representation of the company's change in equity value than a figure derived from financial statement data.

Market capitalization, then, is a useful tool but not one to be heeded blindly. In the end, true equity remains an elusive number. Instead of striving for theoretical purity on the matter, analysts should adopt a flexible attitude, using the measure of equity value most useful to a particular application.

For example, stated balance sheet figures, derived mainly from historical cost, are the ones that matter in estimating the risk that a company will violate a loan covenant requiring maintenance of a minimum ratio of debt to net worth (see Chapter 12). The historical cost figures are less relevant to a liquidation analysis aimed at gauging creditors' asset protection. That is, if a company were sold to pay off its debts, the price it would fetch would probably reflect the market's current valuation of its assets more nearly than the carrying cost of those assets.

Neither measure, however, could be expected to equate precisely to the proceeds that would actually be realized in a sale of the company. Between the time that a sale was decided on and executed, its market capitalization might change significantly, purely as a function of the stock market's dynamics. By the same token, the current balance sheet values of certain assets could be overstated, through tardy recognition of impairments in value, or understated, reflecting the prohibition on writing up an asset that has not changed hands.

THE COMMON FORM BALANCE SHEET

As the technology companies' huge 2001 write-offs demonstrate, deterioration in a company's financial position may catch investors by surprise because it occurs gradually and is reported suddenly. It is also possible for an increase in financial risk to sneak up on analysts even though it is reported as it occurs. Many companies alter the mix of their assets, or their methods of financing them, in a gradual fashion. To spot these subtle yet frequently significant changes, it is helpful to prepare a common form balance sheet.

Also known as the percentage balance sheet, the common form balance sheet converts each asset into a percentage of total assets and each liability or component of equity into a percentage of total liabilities and shareholders' equity. Exhibit 2.2 applies this technique to the 2009 balance sheet of Starbucks, a processor and marketer of coffee.

The analyst can view a company's common form balance sheets over several quarters to check, for example, whether inventory is increasing significantly as a percentage of total assets. An increase of that sort might signal **involuntary inventory buildup** resulting from an unanticipated slowdown in

EXHIBIT 2.2   Starbucks Corp. Balance Sheet in Thousands

	Sep 27, 2009	Percent Total
ASSETS		
Current assets:		
Cash and cash equivalents	$ 599.8	10.76%
Short-term investments—available-for-sale securities	21.5	0.39%
Short-term investments—trading securities	44.8	0.80%
Accounts receivable, net	271.0	4.86%
Inventories	664.9	11.92%
Prepaid expenses and other current assets	147.2	2.64%
Deferred income taxes, net	286.6	5.14%
Total current assets	2,035.8	36.50%
Long-term investments—available-for-sale securities	71.2	1.28%
Equity and cost investments	352.3	6.32%
Property, plant, and equipment, net	2,536.4	45.48%
Other assets	253.8	4.55%
Other intangible assets	68.2	1.22%
Goodwill	259.1	4.65%
TOTAL ASSETS	$5,576.8	100.00%
LIABILITIES AND SHAREHOLDERS' EQUITY		
Current liabilities:		
Commercial paper and short-term borrowings	—	—
Accounts payable	$ 267.1	4.79%
Accrued compensation and related costs	307.5	5.51%
Accrued occupancy costs	188.1	3.37%
Accrued taxes	127.8	2.29%
Insurance reserves	154.3	2.77%
Other accrued expenses	147.3	2.64%
Deferred revenue	388.7	6.97%
Current portion of long-term debt	0.2	0.00%
Total current liabilities	1,581.0	28.35%
Long-term debt	549.3	9.85%
Other long-term liabilities	400.8	7.19%
Total liabilities	$2,531.1	45.39%
Shareholders' equity:		
Common stock ($0.001 par value)—authorized, 1,200.0 shares; issued and outstanding, 742.9 and 735.5 shares, respectively (includes 3.4 common stock units in both periods)	0.7	0.01%

EXHIBIT 2.2   *(Continued)*

	Sep 27, 2009	Percent Total
Additional paid-in capital	147.0	2.64%
Other additional paid-in-capital	39.4	0.71%
Retained earnings	2,793.2	50.09%
Accumulated other comprehensive income	65.4	1.17%
Total shareholders' equity	3,045.7	54.61%
TOTAL LIABILITIES AND SHAREHOLDERS' EQUITY	$5,576.8	100.00%

Source: Company 10-K, Capital IQ, and author calculations.

sales. Similarly, a rise in accounts receivable as a percentage of assets may point to increasing reliance on the extension of credit to generate sales or a problem in collecting on credit previously extended. Over a longer period, a rise in the percentage of assets represented by a manufacturing company's property, plant, and equipment can signal that a company's business is becoming more capital-intensive. By implication, fixed costs are probably rising as a percentage of revenues, making the company's earnings more volatile.

CONCLUSION

By closely examining the underlying values reflected in the balance sheet, this chapter emphasizes the need for a critical, rather than a passive, approach to financial statement analysis. The discussions of return on equity, goodwill, and **leveraged recapitalizations** underscore the chapter's dominant theme, the elusiveness of true value. Mere tinkering with the conventions of historical cost cannot bring accounting values into line with equity as economists define it and, more to the point, as financial analysts would ideally like it to be. Market capitalization probably represents a superior approach in many instances. Under certain circumstances, however, serious questions can be raised about the validity of a company's stock price as a standard of value. In the final analysis, users of financial statements cannot retreat behind the numbers derived by any one method. They must instead exercise judgment to draw sound conclusions.

The Income Statement

T he goal of analyzing an income statement is essentially to determine whether the story it tells is good, bad, or indifferent. To accomplish this objective, the analyst draws a few initial conclusions, then puts the income statement into context by comparing it with income statements of earlier periods, as well as statements of other companies. These steps are described in the section of this chapter titled "Making the Numbers Talk."

Simple techniques of analysis can extract a great deal of information from an income statement, but the quality of the information is no less a concern than the quantity. A conscientious analyst must determine how accurately the statement reflects the issuer's revenues, expenses, and earnings. This deeper level of scrutiny requires an awareness of imperfections in the accounting system that can distort economic reality.

The section titled "How Real Are the Numbers?" documents the indefatigability of issuers in devising novel gambits for exploiting these vulnerabilities. Analysts must be equally resourceful. In particular, students of financial statements must keep up with innovations in transforming rising stock values into revenues of dubious quality.

MAKING THE NUMBERS TALK

By observing an income statement in its raw form, the reader can make several useful, albeit limited, observations. Peet's Coffee & Tea's income statement for 2009 (Exhibit 3.1) shows, for example, that the company was profitable rather than unprofitable. The statement also provides some sense of the firm's cost structure. Cost of goods sold (COGS) was the largest component of total costs, at about 10 times selling, general, and administrative expenses (SG&A). Depreciation and amortization, essentially a fixed expense in the short run, was a minor factor.

Based on these observations, we can infer that Peet's profitability is highly sensitive to changes in the prices of materials and labor that are

EXHIBIT 3.1   Peet's Coffee & Tea Inc. Income Statement in $ Millions

For the Fiscal Period Ending Dec 2009 12 months	(NasdaqGS:PEET)
Total Revenue	311.3
Cost of Goods Sold	248.5
Gross Profit	62.7
Selling, General, & Admin Exp.	24.5
Pre-Opening Costs	
Depreciation & Amort.	15.2
Other Operating Expense/(Income)	—
Other Operating Exp., Total	39.7
Operating Income	23.1
Interest Expense	—
Interest and Invest. Income	0.1
Net Interest Exp.	0.1
Income/(Loss) from Affiliates	
Currency Exchange Gains (Loss)	
Other Nonoperating Inc. (Exp.)	—
EBT Excl. Unusual Items	23.2
Restructuring Charges	4.2
Gain (Loss) on Sale of Invest.	7.3
Asset Writedown	(0.9)
Other Unusual Items	(3.0)
EBT Incl. Unusual Items	30.8
Income Tax Expense	11.6
Minority Int. in Earnings	—
Earnings from Cont. Ops.	19.3
Earnings of Discontinued Ops.	—
Extraord. Item & Account. Change	—
Net Income	19.3

Source: Capital IQ and author calculations.

included in COGS. Companies generally have limited control over those costs. Management has more discretion with SG&A, but changes in that category have a proportionally smaller impact on profits.

The relative importance of the various cost components is largely a function of Peet's business, which consists of selling tea, coffee, specialty foods, and related merchandise through its own retail stores, as well as a network of grocery stores, home delivery operations, offices, and restaurant and food service accounts. Depreciation is a larger component of the income statements of heavy manufacturing companies that require huge production facilities (e.g., steel mills, automobile plants).

Peet's income statement is void in two categories that are significant cost items for many other companies—research and development (R&D) and interest expense. For pharmaceutical producers and companies that create and market electronics and computer software, R&D is generally a significant cost element. Similarly, interest expense is an important cost for banks and finance companies, as well as for electric utilities. Unlike Peet's, which has no debt outstanding, those companies borrow heavily, so their profits are more sensitive than Peet's to fluctuations in interest rates.

Even within an industry, the breakdown of expenses can vary from company to company as a function of differing business models and financial policies. This is illustrated by Exhibit 3.2, which compares the income statements of Peet's Coffee & Tea and two other food and beverage companies that sell through retail stores, coffee shop operator Starbucks and Panera Bread, which specializes in baked goods. To facilitate the comparison, the exhibit converts the components of the companies' income statements to percentages of revenues. Note that percentage breakdowns are also helpful for comparing a single company's performance with its results in previous years and for comparing two different companies on the basis of their effectiveness in controlling costs.

Like Peet's, Starbucks roasts and sells whole-bean coffee, beverage-related accessories, and other food items through retail stores and other marketing channels. Despite being in the same line of business, however, it has a much different cost structure. Its COGS represents only 43.25 percent of revenue versus 79.83 percent for Peet's. On the other hand, Starbucks spends 39.04 percent of its revenue dollar on SGA versus only 7.87 percent for Peet's. One other difference is that Starbucks employs debt and therefore incurs a modest amount of interest expense.

The dramatic difference in cost structures reflects differences in the two companies' business models. Starbucks more heavily emphasizes retailing of coffee through its ubiquitous stores, while Peet's sales are proportionately more concentrated in its other marketing channels. In essence, Peet's is more of a coffee roaster, and Starbucks is more involved in brewing coffee to serve to consumers on premise.

Another factor that may give rise to differences in cost structures within an industry is the availability of **economies of scale**, as discussed later. Greater size does not invariably confer an advantage in operating margin, however. Starbucks had more than 30 times the revenue of Peet's in 2009 and did in fact achieve a higher percentage of operating income to revenues, 9.74 percent versus 7.42 percent. On the other hand, Panera Bread had only about one-seventh the revenues of Starbucks in 2009, yet achieved a 10.62 percent operating margin versus Starbucks's 9.74 percent. Panera's

EXHIBIT 3.2 Starbucks Corp., Panera Bread Co, and Peet's Coffee & Tea Inc. Income Statements in $ Millions

Income Statement in $ Millions For the Fiscal Period Ending Dec. 2009 12 months	Starbucks Corp. (NasdaqGS:SBUX)		Panera Bread Co. (NasdaqGS:PNRA)		Peet's Coffee & Tea Inc. (NasdaqGS:PEET)	
Total Revenue	9,882.1	100.00%	1,353.5	100.00%	311.3	100.00%
Cost of Goods Sold	4,273.8	43.25%	904.4	66.82%	248.5	79.85%
Gross Profit	5,608.3	56.75%	449.1	33.18%	62.7	20.15%
Selling, General, & Admin Exp.	3,858.2	39.04%	83.2	6.14%	24.5	7.87%
Pre-Opening Costs			2.5	0.18%		
Depreciation & Amort.	531.0	5.37%	67.2	4.96%	15.2	4.87%
Other Operating Expense/(Income)	256.2	2.59%	152.5	11.27%	—	
Other Operating Exp., Total	4,645.4	47.01%	305.3	22.55%	39.7	12.75%
Operating Income	962.9	9.74%	143.8	10.62%	23.1	7.41%
Interest Expense	(34.3)	−0.35%	(0.7)	−0.05%	—	
Interest and Invest. Income	48.3	0.49%	0.9	0.07%	0.1	
Net Interest Exp.	14.0	0.14%	0.2	0.01%	0.1	
Income/(Loss) from Affiliates	127.8	1.29%				
Currency Exchange Gains (Loss)	(19.8)	−0.20%				
Other Nonoperating Inc. (Exp.)	43.8	0.44%	(2.5)	−0.18%	—	
EBT Excl. Unusual Items	1,128.7	11.42%	141.5	10.45%	23.2	7.44%

Restructuring Charges	(275.2)	−2.78%	—		4.2	1.34%
Gain (Loss) on Sale of Invest.	(12.4)	−0.13%	1.3	0.10%	7.3	2.35%
Asset Writedown	(11.1)	−0.11%	(2.9)	−0.21%	(0.9)	−0.29%
Other Unusual Items	—		—		(3.0)	−0.96%
EBT Incl. Unusual Items	830.0	8.40%	139.9	10.34%	30.8	9.90%
Income Tax Expense	260.4	2.64%	53.1	3.92%	11.6	3.71%
Minority Int. in Earnings	(1.6)	−0.02%	(0.8)	−0.06%		
Earnings from Cont. Ops.	568.0	5.75%	86.1	6.36%	19.3	6.18%
Earnings of Discontinued Ops.	—		—		—	
Extraord. Item & Account. Change	—		—		—	
Net Income	568.0	5.75%	86.1	6.36%	19.3	6.18%

Source: Capital IQ and author calculations.

COGS as a percentage of sales was half again as great as Starbucks's, at 66.82 percent versus 43.25 percent. Its advantage was in a far lower SG&A expense ratio, 6.14 percent versus 39.04 percent.

The contrasting cost structures reflected a major difference in the two companies' business models. At the end of 2009, 42 percent of Panera's stores were company owned, and 58 percent were franchised operations. The Starbucks chain, in contrast, was entirely company owned and operated.

Costs as percentages of sales also vary among companies within an industry for reasons other than differences in business models. Some companies operate more efficiently than others, generating more revenue from each dollar of expenditures. Where a company stands in its life cycle can also make a difference. For example, in 2009 Starbucks had a total of 8,800 retail stores and was encountering constraints on its ability to expand further. Beginning in 2008, the company closed a number of stores, suggesting that it had saturated some of its markets. Panera, on the other hand, had a total of 1,380 cafés and did not yet appear to be bumping up against limits on growth. Its profitability was helped by not having to choose more marginal locations in order to maintain the pace of new store openings.

The variation in cost structures and profit margins that Peet's, Starbucks, and Panera Bread exhibit within food and beverages is paralleled in other industries. For example, some pharmaceutical manufacturers also produce and market medical devices, nonprescription health products, toiletries, and beauty aids. A more widely diversified manufacturer can be expected to have a higher percentage of product costs, as well as a lower percentage of research and development expenses, than industry peers that focus exclusively on prescription drugs. Analysts must take care not to mistake a difference that is actually a function of business strategy as evidence of inferior or superior management skills.

Segment reporting data in the notes to financial statements can provide a measure of insight into the underlying differentiators of profit margins among companies that tend to be grouped together. Unfortunately, companies have considerable discretion in defining their segments, resulting in a lack of standardization that often makes comparisons difficult. In such cases, an analyst must dig deeper for an understanding of the competitors' cost structures by obtaining as much information as their **investor relations officers** will divulge and drawing on industry sources.

HOW REAL ARE THE NUMBERS?

Many individuals are attracted to business careers not only by monetary rewards but also by the opportunity, lacking in many other professions, to be measured against an objective standard. The personal desire to improve the bottom line, that is, a company's net profit, challenges a businessperson in much the same way that an athlete is motivated by the quantifiable goal of breaking a world record. The income statement is the stopwatch against which a company runs; net profit is the corporation's record of wins and losses for the season.

The analogy between business and athletics extends to the fact, which is apparent to any close observer, that superior skills and teamwork alone do not win championships. A baseball manager can intimidate the umpire by heatedly protesting a call on the base paths, hoping thereby to have the next close ruling go in his team's favor. A corporation has the power to fire its auditor and may use that power to influence accounting decisions that are matters of judgment rather than clear-cut reporting standards. A baseball team's front office can shorten the right-field fence in its home stadium to favor a lineup stocked with left-handed power hitters; a corporation's management can select the accounting method that shows its results in the most favorable light. Collectively, the team owners can urge the rules committee to lower the pitching mound if they believe that a predictable increase in base hits and runs will boost attendance. Similarly, a group of corporations can try to block the introduction of new accounting standards that might reduce their reported earnings.

Attempts to transform the yardstick become most vigorous when the measure of achievement becomes more important to participants than the accuracy of the measure itself. Regrettably, this is often the case when corporations seek to motivate managers by linking their compensation to the attainment of specific financial goals. Executives whose bonuses rise in tandem with earnings per share have a strong incentive not only to generate bona fide earnings but also to use every lawful means of inflating the figures through accounting sleight of hand.

It would take many more pages than are allotted to this chapter to detail all the ways that companies can manipulate the accounting rules to inflate their earnings. Instead, the following examples should convey to the reader the thought process involved in this rule bending. Equipped with an understanding of how the rule benders think, users of financial statements will be able to detect other ruses they are sure to encounter.

Not All Sales Are Final

"Take care of the top line and the bottom line will take care of itself." So goes a business bromide, which underscores the importance of revenues (the top line) to net income (the bottom line). The point is that if a company wants to cure an earnings problem, it should concentrate on bringing in more sales.

Generally, this is sound advice, as long as the needed sales are brought in by the sales force. A company can compound its problems, however, if the financial staff makes up the shortfall in revenues through accounting gimmicks. Some revenue-inflating tricks are achievable within generally accepted accounting principles (GAAP) boundaries, whereas others clearly fall outside the law. They all produce similar ill effects, however. Enhancements to reported sales boost reported earnings without increasing cash flow commensurately.

Often, a company's earnings and cash flow diverge to an extent that becomes unsustainable. The eventual result is an abrupt adjustment to the financial statements of previous periods. In the process, earnings and cash flow come back into alignment, but management's credibility plummets. Even when no such shock occurs, the practice of pumping up revenues through discretionary accounting decisions represents a hazard for analysts. At a minimum, it reduces the comparability of a company's financial statements from one period to the next.

Additional Reasons to Be Skeptical about Revenues

Unfortunately for analysts, companies do not always spell out in the notes to financial statements the means by which they have artificially inflated their revenues. A company might lower the credit standards it applies to prospective customers without simultaneously raising the percentage of reserves it establishes for losses on receivables. The result would be a rise in both revenues and earnings in the current period, with the corresponding increase in credit losses not becoming apparent until a later period. Alternatively, a manufacturer may institute short-term discounts that encourage its dealers or wholesalers to place orders earlier than they otherwise would. In this case, sales and earnings will be higher in the current quarter than they would be in the absence of the incentives, but the difference will represent merely a shifting of revenues from a later to an earlier period. Analysts will face disappointment if they regard such inflated quarterly sales as indicative of the future.

Although the current-period income statement may offer no clues that these gambits have been used, several techniques can help the analyst detect artificial expansion of revenues. On a retrospective basis, a surge in credit losses or an unexpected shortfall in revenues may indicate that revenues were inflated in an earlier period with the techniques described in the preceding paragraph. (Hindsight of this kind is not without value; an analyst who finds a historical pattern of hyperbolized sales will be appropriately skeptical about future income statements that look surprisingly strong.) On a current basis, analysts should take notice if a company posts a substantially greater sales increase than its competitors. If discussions with the company and other industry sources fail to elicit a satisfactory explanation (such as the introduction of a successful new product), artificial methods may be the root of the matter. Industry sources can also provide direct testimony about tactics being used to shift revenues from future periods to the present.

Extraordinary and Nonrecurring Items

To most individuals who examine a company's income statement, the document is less important for what it tells about the past than for what it implies about future years.[1] Last year's earnings, for example, have no direct impact on a company's stock price, which represents a discounting of a future stream of earnings (see Chapter 14). An equity investor is therefore interested in a company's income statement from the preceding year primarily as a basis for forecasting future earnings. Similarly, a company's creditors already know whether they were paid the interest that came due in the previous year before the income statement arrives. Their motivation for studying the document is to form an opinion about the likelihood of payment in the current year and in years to come.

In addition to recognizing that readers of its income statement will view the document primarily as an indicator of the future, a company knows that creating more favorable expectations about the future can raise its stock price and lower its borrowing cost. It is therefore in the company's interest to persuade readers that a major development that hurt earnings last year will not adversely affect earnings in future years. One way of achieving this is to suggest that any large loss suffered by the company was somehow outside the normal course of business, anomalous, and, by implication, unlikely to recur.

To create the desired impression that a loss was alien to the company's normal pattern of behavior, the loss can be shown on a separate line on the income statement and labeled an "extraordinary item." Note that an extraordinary item is reported on an after-tax basis, below the line of income (or loss) from continuing operations. This presentation creates the strongest possible impression that the loss was outside the ordinary course of business. It maximizes the probability that analysts of the income statement will give it little weight in forecasting future performance.

Because the effect created by a below-the-line treatment is so strong, the accounting rules carefully limit its use. To qualify as extraordinary under the relevant **Accounting Principles Board** (**APB**) opinion, events must be "distinguished by their unusual nature and by the infrequency of their occurrence."[2] These criteria are not easily satisfied. According to the opinion, *unusual nature* means that "the underlying event or transaction should possess a high degree of abnormality and be of a type clearly unrelated to, or only incidentally related to, the ordinary and typical activities of the entity, taking into account the environment in which the entity operates." Lest the *extraordinary* label be employed indiscriminately, the opinion prohibits its use for several types of events considered unusual in nature under the strict standard being applied. Among these are:

- Write-offs of receivables and inventories.
- Gains or losses on foreign currency translation (even when they result from major devaluations or revaluations).
- Gains or losses on disposal of a segment of a business or the sale or abandonment of property, plant, or equipment.

Not even the September 11, 2001, terrorist attacks on the Pentagon and World Trade Center qualified as an extraordinary event under the stringent criteria of the Financial Accounting Standards Board (FASB). After tentatively deciding that companies could break out costs arising from the disaster as below-the-line items, the task force on the subject voted not to allow the practice. The chairman of the task force, FASB Research Director Timothy S. Lucas, noted that even the airlines, which were plainly hurt by the events, would have difficulty separating the impact of the attacks from other revenue and earnings pressures during the period.[3]

Considering the exacting tests that an item must meet to be considered extraordinary, analysts may consider themselves on solid ground if they largely disregard any such item in forecasting future earnings. The APB opinion, after all, adds that "infrequency of occurrence" means that the event or transaction in question must be "of a type not reasonably expected to recur in the foreseeable future." Occasionally, one would suppose, an event meeting this strict standard might be followed just a few years later by an event at the same company, radically different in nature but also qualifying for classification as extraordinary and below-the-line reporting. On even rarer occasions, an extraordinary event might be followed the very next year by a qualifying event of a similar nature, even though such a recurrence was "not reasonably expected," to quote the accounting standard. Judging by the highly restrictive language of the APB opinion, however, it would be extremely surprising if any company ever booked an extraordinary item more than twice in a matter of several years.

Improbable though it might seem, however, a search of the Capital IQ database identified 30 companies that recorded extraordinary gains or losses in at least three of the eight years ending in 2009. Among the companies that repeatedly experienced events of an allegedly infrequent and unusual nature were such stalwarts as Allstate, Conagra Foods, Kimberly-Clark, Monsanto,

Occidental Petroleum, and Time Warner. American Electric Power recorded six extraordinary items during the period. In light of actual experience, analysts cannot simply project a company's future earnings as though an extraordinary event had never occurred, however fervently management might wish them to do precisely that.

Actually, companies lean on analysts to be even more accommodating when they evaluate past results to forecast future performance. Corporate officials not only encourage users of their financial statements to disregard losses that qualify for the label extraordinary but also ask them to ignore certain hits to earnings simply because management pronounces them aberrant. To steer analysts toward the true (that is, higher trajectory) trend of earnings deemed official by management fiat, companies break out the supposed aberrations from their other operating earnings. The accounting rules require such carve-outs to be reported above the line (that is, on a pretax basis) and prohibit use of the label *extraordinary*. Accordingly, companies employ designations such as *nonrecurring* or *unusual*. These terms have no official standing under GAAP, but they foster the impression that the highlighted items are exceptional in nature. Sometimes, losses that fail to meet the criteria of extraordinary items appear under the more neutral heading, "special charges." Even this terminology, however, leaves the impression that the company has put the problem behind itself. The semantics are so appealing to corporate managers that a search of the Capital IQ database revealed that 487 of the companies represented in Standard & Poor's 500 Index reported unusual items in at least half of the years from 2002 to 2009. Nearly half (230) recorded unusual items in all eight years of that span, including such blue chips as Exxon Mobil, JPMorgan Chase, McDonald's, Microsoft, and Sprint Nextel. Many of the eight-timers reported both positive and negative unusual items, strongly hinting at a desire to persuade users of financial statements that their true earnings progression was much smoother than the GAAP figures showed.

Over time, restructuring has become a catchall for charges that companies wish analysts to consider outside the normal course of business but that do not qualify for below-the-line treatment. The term has a positive connotation, implying that the corporation has cast off its money-losing operations and positioned itself for significantly improved profitability. If abused, the segregation of restructuring charges can create too rosy a picture of past performance. It can entrap the unwary analyst by downplaying the significance of failed business initiatives, which have a bearing on management's judgment. Additionally, the losses associated with a restructuring may be blamed on the company's previous chief executive officer, provided they are booked early in the successor CEO's tenure. Within a year's time, the new kingpin may be able to take credit for a turnaround, based on an improvement in earnings relative to a large loss that can be conveniently attributed to the predecessor regime.

Even more insidiously, companies sometimes write off larger sums than warranted by their actual economic losses on a failed business. Corporate managers commonly perceive that the damage to their stock price will be no greater if they take (for sake of argument) a $1.5 billion write-off than if they write off $1.0 billion. The benefit of exaggerating the damage is that in subsequent years, the overcharges can be reversed in small amounts that do not generate any requirement for specific disclosure. Management can use these gains to supplement and smooth the corporation's bona fide operating earnings.

The most dangerous trap that users of financial statements must avoid, however, is inferring that the term *restructuring* connotes finality. Some corporations have a bad habit of remaking themselves year after year. For such companies, the analyst's baseline for forecasting future profitability should be earnings after, rather than before, restructuring charges.

Procter & Gamble (P&G) is a case in point. As of April 2001, the consumer goods company had booked restructuring charges in seven consecutive quarters, aggregating to $1.3 billion. Moreover, management indicated that it planned to continue taking these ostensibly nonrecurring charges until mid-2004, ultimately charging off approximately $4 billion.

Defending its reporting, P&G said that Securities and Exchange Commission (SEC) accounting rules precluded it from taking one huge charge at the outset of the restructuring program launched in June 1999. Instead, the company was required to record the charges in the periods in which it actually incurred them. Granting the point, the SEC did not compel Procter & Gamble to segregate the costs of closing factories and laying off workers from its other operating expenses. Indeed, the arguments were stronger for treating the charge-offs as normal costs of operating in P&G's highly competitive consumer goods business, where countless products fail or become obsolete over time.

Abstract issues of accounting theory, however, had little impact on brokerage house securities analysts' treatment of P&G's earnings record. All 14 analysts who followed the company and submitted earnings per share forecasts to Thomson Financial/First Call excluded the restructuring charges from their calculations, and P&G management was bound to like Wall Street's interpretation of the numbers. Including all of the ostensibly unusual gains and losses, operating income declined in all four quarters of 2000. Leaving out all the items deemed aberrant by management, net income rose in all quarters but the first. The latter interpretation surely gave investors a more optimistic view of P&G's prospects than the sourpuss GAAP numbers.[4]

Naturally, companies encourage analysts to *include* special items in their earnings calculations when they happen to be gains, rather than losses. They evidently reason that turnabout is fair play, and judging by the results, many securities analysts apparently agree. The 14 Wall Street analysts mentioned earlier unanimously chose to include in their "core net earnings" figures the gains that Procter & Gamble classified as nonrecurring or extraordinary, even as they excluded the extraordinary and nonrecurring losses.

Transforming Stock Market Proceeds into Revenues

At the same time that corporate managers have been supplementing their traditional tactics with new adjustments to earnings, they have also concentrated in recent years on applying their ingenuity to revenues. This focus makes eminent sense for corporations that want to present the best possible, if not necessarily most accurate, profile to investors. If a company achieves its revenue objectives, its battle for profitability is more than half won. To be sure, success also depends on controlling expenses. Without a robust top line, however, the company cannot economize its way to a respectable bottom line.

Garnering sales is not only a vital task, but a tough job as well. Competitors are forever striving to snatch away revenues by introducing superior products or devising means of lowering prices to customers. From the standpoint of maximizing value to consumers and promoting economic efficiency, management's optimal response to this challenge is to upgrade its own products and generate cost savings that it can pass along to customers. Stepping up expenditures on advertising or expanding the sales force can also lead to increased revenues. Along with effective execution of product design or marketing plans, however, another option exists. Management can boost sales through techniques that more properly fall into the category of corporate finance.

Raising the rate of revenue increases through mergers and acquisitions is the most common example. A corporation can easily accelerate its sales growth by buying other companies and adding their sales to its own. Creating genuine value for shareholders through acquisitions is more difficult, although unwary investors sometimes fail to recognize the distinction.

In the fictitious example in Exhibit 3.3, Big Time Corporation's sales increase by 5 percent between Year 1 and Year 2. Small Change, a smaller, privately owned company in the same industry, also achieves 5 percent year-over-year sales growth. Suppose that at the end of Year 1, Big Time acquires Small Change with shares of its own stock. The Big Time income statements under this assumption ("Acquisition Scenario") show a 10 percent sales

EXHIBIT 3.3 Small Sales Growth Acceleration without Profitability Improvement: Big Time Corporation and Small Change, Inc. ($000 omitted)

| | Nonacquisition Scenario | | | | Acquisition Scenario | |
| | Big Time Corporation | | Small Change Inc. | | Big Time Corporation | |
	Year 1	Year 2	Year 1	Year 2	Year 1	Year 2
Sales	$5,000.0	$5,250.0	$238.1	$250.0	$5,000.0	$5,500.1
Costs and expenses						
Cost of goods sold	3,422.7	3,591.4	160.6	171.1	3,422.7	3,762.5
Selling, general, and administrative expenses	1,250.0	1,315.0	61.9	62.5	1,250.0	1,377.5
Interest expense	100.0	105.0	4.8	5.0	100.0	110.0
Total costs and expenses	4,772.7	5,011.4	227.3	238.6	4,772.7	5,250.0
Income before income taxes	227.3	238.6	10.8	11.4	227.3	250.0
Income taxes	77.3	81.1	3.7	3.9	77.3	85.0
Net income	$ 150.0	$ 157.5	$ 7.1	$ 7.5	$ 150.0	$ 165.0
Year-over-year sales increase	—	5%	—	5%	—	10%
Net income as a percentage of sales	3%	3%	3%	3%	3%	3%
Shares outstanding (million)	75	75			75	75
Earnings per share	$ 2.00	$ 2.10			$ 2.00	$ 2.10
Price-earnings multiple (times)	14	14			14	14
Price per share	$ 28.00	$ 29.40			$ 28.00	$ 29.40

increase between Year 1 and Year 2. (Note that Year 1 is shown as originally reported, with Small Change still an independent company, while in Year 2, the results of the acquired company, Small Change, are consolidated into the parent's financial reporting. Analysts might also examine a pro forma income statement showing the levels of sales, expenses, and earnings that Big Time would have achieved in Year 1, if the acquisition had occurred at the beginning of that year.)

On the face of it, a company growing at 10 percent a year is sexier than one growing at only 5 percent a year. Observe, however, that Big Time's profitability, measured by net income as a percentage of sales, does not improve as a result of the acquisition. Combining two companies with equivalent profit margins of 3 percent produces a larger company that also earns 3 percent on sales. Shareholders do not gain anything in the process, as the supplementary figures in Exhibit 3.3 demonstrate.

If Big Time decides not to acquire Small Change, its number of shares outstanding remains at 75.0 million. The earnings increase from $150.0 million in Year 1 to $157.5 million in Year 2 raises earnings per share from $2.00 to $2.10. With the price-earnings multiple constant at 14 times, equivalent to the average of the company's industry peers, Big Time's stock price rises from $28.00 to $29.40 a share.

In the Acquisition Scenario, on the other hand, Big Time pays its industry-average earnings multiple of 14 times for Small Change, for a total acquisition price of $7.1 million × 14 = $99.4 million. At Big Time's Year 1 share price of $28.00, the purchase therefore requires the issuance of $99.4 million ÷ $28.00 = 3.6 million shares. With the addition of Small Change's net income, Big Time earns $165.0 million in Year 2. Dividing that figure by the increased number of shares outstanding (78.6 million) produces earnings per share of $2.10. At a price-earnings multiple of 14 times, Big Time is worth $29.40 a share, precisely the price calculated in the Nonacquisition Scenario. The mere increase in annual sales growth from 5 percent to 10 percent has not benefited shareholders, whose shares increase in value by 5 percent whether Big Time acquires Small Change or not.

Analysts should note that this analysis is sensitive to the assumptions underlying the scenarios. Suppose, for instance, that instead of issuing stock, Big Time finances the acquisition of Small Change with borrowed money. Let us suppose that Big Time must pay interest at a rate of 8 percent on the $99.4 million of new borrowings. Interest expense in Year 2 of the Acquisition Scenario is now $118.0 million, rather than $100.0 million. Pretax income therefore falls from $250.0 million to $242.0 million, reducing net income from $165.0 million to $159.7 million at the company's effective tax rate of 34 percent. Only 75.0 million shares are outstanding at the conclusion of the transaction, however, rather than the 78.6 million observed in the acquisition-for-stock case. As a result, Big Time's earnings per share rise to $159.7 million ÷ 75.0 million = $2.13.

Assuming the market continues to assign a multiple of 14 times to Big Time's earnings, the stock is now worth $29.82, a bit more than in the Nonacquisition Scenario. In practice, the investors may reduce Big Time's price-earnings multiple slightly to reflect the heightened risk represented by its decreased interest coverage. (Following the formulas laid out in Chapter 13, income before interest and taxes declines from $360.0 million ÷ $110.0 million = 3.3 times in the stock-acquisition case to $360.0 million ÷ $118.0 million = 3.1 times in the debt financed-acquisition case.) If the price-earnings multiple falls only from 14 to 13.8 times as a result of this decline in debt protection, Big Time's stock price in this variant again comes to $29.40, equivalent to the Year 2 price in the Nonacquisition Scenario. As in the case of Big Time paying with stock for the acquisition of Small Change, shareholders do not benefit if Big Time instead borrows the requisite funds, assuming investors are sensitive to the impact of the company's increased debt load on its credit quality.

Internal versus External Growth

More important than the fine-tuning of the calculations is the principle that a company cannot truly increase shareholders' wealth by accelerating its revenue growth without also improving profitability. This does not dissuade companies from attempting to mesmerize analysts with high rates of sales growth generated by grafting other companies' sales onto their own through acquisitions. Analysts may fall for the trick by failing to distinguish between **internal growth** and **external growth.**

Internal growth consists of sales increases generated from a company's existing operations, while the latter represents incremental sales brought in through acquisitions. An internal (or organic) growth rate greater than the average recorded for the industry implies that the company is gaining market share from its competitors. As a precaution, the analyst must probe further to determine whether management has merely increased unit sales by accepting lower gross margins. If that is not the case, however, the company may in fact be improving its competitive position and, ultimately, increasing its value. On the other hand, if Company A generates external growth by acquiring Company B and neither Company A nor its new subsidiary increases its profitability, then the intrinsic value of the merged companies is no greater than the sum of the two companies' values.

External growth can increase shareholders' wealth, however, if the mergers and acquisitions lead to improvements in profitability. This effect is commonly referred to as *synergy*. It is a term much abused by companies that promise to achieve operating efficiencies, without offering many specific examples, through acquisitions that appear to offer few such opportunities. Nevertheless, even analysts who have grown cynical after years of seeing purported synergies remain unrealized will acknowledge the existence of several bona fide means of raising a company's profit margins through external growth.

For one thing, a company may be able to reduce its cost per unit by increasing the size of its purchases. Suppliers commonly offer volume discounts to their large customers, which they can service more efficiently than customers who order in small quantities. If the cost of materials, fuel, and transportation required to produce each widget goes down while the selling price of widgets remains unchanged in a stable competitive environment, the company's gross margin increases.

Another way to increase profitability through external growth involves **economies of scope**. In a simple illustration, a manufacturer of potato chips has a sales force calling on retail stores. Much of the associated expense represents the time and transportation costs incurred as the salespeople travel from store to store, as well as the salespeople's health insurance and other benefits. Now suppose that the potato chip manufacturer acquires a pretzel manufacturer. For the sake of explication, assume that the pretzel company formerly relied on food brokers rather than an in-house sales force. The acquiring company terminates the contracts with the brokers and adds pretzels to its potato chip sales force's product line. Revenues and gross profits per sales call rise with the addition of the pretzel line. The number of sales calls per salesperson remains essentially constant, because taking orders for the additional product consumes little time. Accordingly, time and transportation costs per sales call do not rise materially, while the cost of health insurance and other benefits does not rise at all. Adding it all up, the profitability of selling both potato chips and pretzels through the same distribution channel is greater than the profitability of selling one snack food only.

Analysts should be forewarned that claims of potential economies of scope often prove, in retrospect, to be exaggerated. Over a period of several decades, for example, banks, brokerage houses, and insurance companies have frequently proclaimed the advent of the financial supermarket, in which a single distribution channel will efficiently deliver all classes of financial services to consumers. A fair amount of integration between these businesses has certainly occurred, but cultural barriers between the businesses have turned out to be more formidable than corporate planners have foreseen. Considerable training is required to teach salespeople how to shift gears between the fast-paced business of dealing in stocks and the more painstaking process of selling insurance policies. In general, the less closely related the combining businesses are, the less certain it is that the hoped-for economies of scope will be realized. When disparate companies combine in pursuit of novel synergies, analysts should treat with extreme caution the margin increases shown in pro forma income statements produced by management.

Capturing Economies of Scale

Finally, and perhaps most famously, mergers can genuinely increase profitability and shareholder wealth through economies of scale. As illustrated in Exhibit 3.4, Central Widget is currently utilizing only 83.3 percent of its

EXHIBIT 3.4 Economies of Scale

Selected Production and Financial Statement Data			
	Central Widget	Excelsior Widget	Central Widget (Pro Forma)
Units of capacity (million)	300	36	300
Unit sales	250	30	280
Capacity utilization	83.3%	83.3%	93.3%
Unit sales (million)	250	30	280
Price per unit	$ 10.00	$ 10.00	$ 10.00
Variable costs per unit			
Labor	$ 4.75	$ 4.75	$ 4.75
Materials	3.00	3.00	3.00
Variable sales costs	0.75	0.75	0.75
Total	$ 8.50	$ 8.50	$ 8.50
Total fixed costs ($million)			
Depreciation	$ 200.00	$ 24.00	$ 200.00
Interest expense	25.00	3.00	28.00
General and administrative	75.00	20.00	85.00
Total	$ 300.00	$ 47.00	$ 313.00
($000,000 omitted)			
Sales	$2,500.00	$300.00	$2,800.00
Variable costs	2,125.00	255.00	2,380.00
Fixed costs	300.00	47.00	313.00
Income before income taxes	75.00	2.00	107.00
Income tax	25.00	0.70	35.30
Net income	$ 50.00	$ 1.30	$ 71.70
Net income as a percentage of sales	2.0%	0.4%	2.6%
Shares outstanding (million)	20	3	22.2
Earnings per share	$ 2.50	$ 0.43	$ 3.33
Price-earnings multiple (times)	13	N.M.	13
Price per share	$ 32.50	$ 18.00	$ 43.29

productive capacity. At the present production level, the company's **fixed costs** amount to \$300 million ÷ 250 million = \$1.20 per unit, or 12 percent of each sales dollar. These irreducible costs represent a major constraint on the company's net profit margin, just 2.0 percent, and in turn its return on equity (see Chapter 13), which is an unexciting 11.1 percent.

Central Widget spies an opportunity in the form of its smaller competitor, Excelsior Widget. Because the two companies operate in the same geographic region, it would be feasible to consolidate production in Central Widget's underutilized factories. Management proposes a merger premised on achieving economies of scale.

Excelsior's cost structure is similar to Central's, except that its general and administrative expense is higher as percentage of sales (6.7 percent versus 3.0 percent). The problem is that certain costs (such as the upkeep on a headquarters building and salaries of senior executives) are nearly as great for Excelsior as for Central, but Excelsior has a smaller base of sales over which to spread them. As a result, Excelsior is running at a loss at current operating levels. Its board of directors therefore accepts the acquisition offer. Central pays \$23.40 worth of its own stock (0.72 shares) for each share of Excelsior, a 30 percent premium to Excelsior's prevailing market price.

Unlike the acquisition of Small Change by Big Time depicted in Exhibit 3.3, this transaction not only increases the acquiring company's sales but also improves its profitability. Following the acquisition, on a pro forma basis, Central Widget's fixed cost per unit is \$313.0 million ÷ 280 million = \$1.12, down from \$1.20. The net margin is up from 2.0 percent to 2.6 percent, while earnings per share have jumped from \$2.50 to \$3.33, pro forma. If the market continues to assign a multiple of 13 times to Central's earnings, the stock should theoretically trade at \$43.29, up from \$32.50 before the transaction. Realistically, that increase probably overstates the actual rise that Central Widget shareholders can expect. Aside from severance costs not shown in the pro forma income statement, investors may reduce the price-earnings multiple to reflect the myriad uncertainties faced in any merger, such as potential loss of key personnel and the predictable traumas of melding distinct corporate cultures. After all the dust has settled, however, Central Widget's shareholders will assuredly benefit from the economies of scale achieved through the acquisition of Excelsior Widget.

Scale economies become available for a variety of reasons. Technological advances can make a sizable portion of existing capacity redundant. For example, computerization has increased the productivity of financial services workers engaged in clearing transactions. **Consolidation** in the banking and brokerage industries has been hastened by cost savings achievable through handling two companies' combined volume of transactions with fewer back office workers than the companies previously employed in aggregate.

Economies of scale also arise through consolidation of a mom-and-pop business, that is, an industry characterized by many small companies operating within small market areas. For example, waste hauling has evolved from a highly localized business to an industry with companies operating on a national scale. Among the associated efficiencies is the ability to reduce garbage trucks' idle time by employing them in several adjacent municipalities.

Behind the Numbers: Fixed versus Variable Costs

As synergies go, projections of economies of scale in combinations of companies within the same business tend to be more plausible than economies of scope purportedly available to companies in tangentially connected businesses. The existence of chronically underutilized capacity is apparent to operations analysts within corporations and to outside management consultants. Word inevitably spreads from there until the possibility of achieving sizable efficiencies through consolidation becomes common knowledge among investors. Companies' published financial statements typically provide too little detail to quantify directly the potential for realizing economies of scale.

Companies do not generally break out their fixed and **variable costs** in the manner shown in Exhibit 3.4. Instead, they include a combination of variable and fixed costs in cost of goods sold. Somewhat helpfully, the essentially fixed costs of depreciation and interest appear as separate lines. On the whole, however, a company's published income statement provides only limited insight into its **operating leverage,** or the rate at which net income escalates once sales volume rises above the **breakeven rate.** This is unfortunate, because a breakout of fixed and variable costs would be immensely helpful in quantifying the economies of scale potentially achievable through a merger. More generally, such information would greatly facilitate the task of forecasting a company's earnings as a function of projected sales volume.

Exhibit 3.5 uses data from the Central Widget example to plot the relationship between sales volume and pretax income (income before income taxes). The company breaks even at a sales volume of 200 million units, the level at which the $1.50 per unit **contribution** (margin of revenue over variable cost) exactly offsets the $300 million of fixed costs. Once fixed costs are covered, the contribution on each incremental unit sold flows directly to the pretax income line. At full capacity, 300 million units, Central Widget earns $150 million before taxes. (Note that analysts can alternatively remove interest expense from the calculation and base a breakeven analysis on operating income.)

In theory, an analyst can back out the fixed and variable components of a company's costs from reported sales and income data. The object is to

EXHIBIT 3.5 Operating Leverage—Central Widget

produce a graph along the lines of the one shown in Exhibit 3.5, while also estimating the contribution per unit. At that point, the analyst can create a table like that shown in the exhibit and establish the sensitivity of profits to the portion of capacity being utilized.

Exhibit 3.6 presents the fictitious case of West Coast Whatsit. The top graph plots the company's reported unit sales volume versus pretax income for each of the past 10 years. (West Coast is debt-free and has no other non-operating income or expenses, so the company's operating income is equivalent to its pretax income.) Observe that the plotted points are concentrated

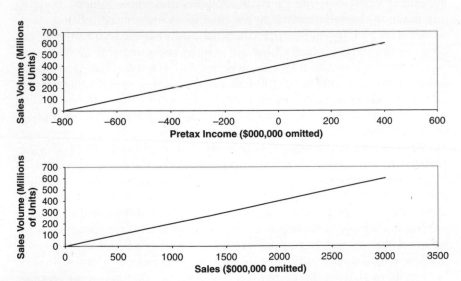

EXHIBIT 3.6 Backing Out Fixed and Variable Costs—West Coast Whatsit

in the upper right-hand corner of the graph, reflecting that annual sales volume never declined to less than 380 million units (63 percent of capacity) during the period. At that low ebb, pretax income fell below zero.

The next step is to fit a diagonal line through the points, as shown in the upper graph. (For a precise technique of fitting a line, see the discussion of the least-squares method in Chapter 14.) According to the line derived from the empirical observations, the company's breakeven sales volume is 400 million units, that is, the point on the diagonal line that corresponds to zero on the horizontal scale (pretax income). Although West Coast Whatsit has not utilized 100 percent of its capacity in any of the past 10 years, the graph indicates that at that level (600 million on the vertical scale), pretax income would amount to $400 million.

To complete the analysis, the analyst must also plot the reported unit sales volume versus dollar sales for the past 10 years, as shown in the lower graph. The remaining task is to back into the data required to fill in the table at the bottom of Exhibit 3.6. At the outset, the analyst knows only the figures shown in boldface, which can be derived directly from the two graphs. For example, the fitted line shows that at full capacity (600 million units), sales would total $3.0 billion.

According to the known data, the increase in pretax income between the breakeven volume (400 million units) and a volume of 500 million units is $200 million. That dollar figure must represent the contribution on 100 million units. Dividing $200 million by 100 million yields the contribution per unit of $2.00, enabling the analyst to fill in that whole column. Dividing any figure in the sales column by its corresponding number of units (e.g., $2.5 billion and 500 million) provides the unit price of $5.00, which goes on every line in that column. Cost per unit, by subtraction, is $3.00.

At the breakeven level (pretax income = $0), the contribution totals 400 million units times $2.00 = $800 million. The analyst can put that number on every line in the entire "Fixed Costs" column. All that remains is to fill in the "Contribution" column by multiplying each remaining line's number of units by the $2.00 contribution per unit figure.

Regrettably, the elegant procedure just described tends to be highly hypothetical, even though it is useful to go through the thought process. To begin with, companies engaged in a wide range of products do not disclose the explicit unit volume figures that the analysis requires. Relating their sales volumes to prices and costs is more complicated than in the case of a producer of a basic metal or a single type of paper. The management discussion and analysis section of a multiproduct company's financial report may disclose period-to-period *changes* in unit volume, but not absolute figures, by way of explaining fluctuations in revenues. A rise or drop in revenue, however, may also reflect changes in the sales price per unit, which may in turn be sensitive to industrywide variance in capacity utilization. In addition, revenue may vary with product mix. When a recession causes consumers to turn cautious about spending on major appliances, for example, they may trade down to lower-priced models that provide smaller contributions to the manufacturers. Finally, multiproduct companies' product lines typically change significantly over periods as long as the 10 years assumed in Exhibit 3.6.

For all these reasons, analysts generally cannot back out fixed and variable costs in practice. When projecting a company's income statement for the coming year, they instead work their way down to the operating income line by making assumptions about cost of goods sold (COGS) and selling, general, and administrative expenses (SG&A) as percentages of sales (see Chapter 12). They try in some sense to take into account the impact of fixed and variable costs, but they cannot be certain that their forecasts are internally consistent.

In Exhibit 3.6, total pretax costs are equivalent to the sum of COGS and SG&A. (Remember that West Coast Whatsit has no interest expense or other nonoperating items.) An analyst who projects that the two together will represent 92 percent of sales is making a forecast consistent with sales volume of 500 million units, or 83 percent of capacity. At that unit volume, variable costs total 500 million × $3.00 = $1.5 billion, which when added to fixed costs of $800 million, produces total costs of $2.3 billion, or 92 percent of sales measuring $2.5 billion. The assumption of a total pretax cost 92 percent ratio would be too pessimistic if the analyst actually expected West Coast to operate in line with the whatsit industry as a whole at 90 percent of capacity. That would imply unit sales of 540 million, resulting in variable costs of $1.62 billion and total costs of $2.42 billion. The ratio of operating expenses to sales of $2.7 billion (540 million units @ $5.00) would be only 90 percent. Observe that not only operating income but also the operating margin rises as sales volume increases.

Estimating COGS and SG&A as percentages of sales is an imperfect, albeit necessary, substitute for an analysis of fixed and variable costs. Conscientious analysts must strive to mitigate the distortions introduced by the shortcut method. They should avoid the trap of uncritically adopting the projected COGS and SG&A percentages kindly provided by companies' investor relations departments. Analysts who do so risk sacrificing their independent judgment. After all, the preceding paragraph demonstrates that a forecast of the operating margin must reflect an implicit assumption about sales volume. Accordingly, a company's guidance regarding COGS and SG&A percentages necessarily incorporates management's assumption about the coming year's sales volume. At the risk of stating the obvious, management's embedded sales projection will often be more optimistic than the analyst's independently generated forecast.

Readers should not infer from the absence of disclosure about fixed and variable costs that the information is unimportant to understanding companies' financial performance. On the contrary, a company's fixed-variable mix can be a dominant factor in analyzing both its credit quality and its equity value (see Chapters 13 and 14, respectively). A company with relatively large fixed costs has a high breakeven level. Even a modest economic downturn will reduce its capacity utilization below the rate required to keep the company profitable. A cost structure of this sort poses a substantial risk of earnings falling below the level needed to cover the company's interest expense. On the other hand, if the same company has low variable costs, its earnings will rise dramatically following a recession. Each incremental unit of sales will contribute prodigiously to operating income. Two real-life examples demonstrate the analytical value of understanding the fixed-versus-variable nature of a company's cost structure, even though it may not be feasible to document the mix precisely from the financial statements.

As an amusement park operator, Cedar Fair exemplifies the high-fixed-cost company. Attendance (and therefore revenue) shows wide seasonal variations, but the company's costs are concentrated in categories that do not vary with attendance. Examples include occupancy, depreciation on rides, insurance, and wages of employees who must be on site whether the parks are full or nearly empty.

A time series of the company's cost of sales as a percentage of sales (see Exhibit 3.7) shows wide quarterly fluctuations, largely reflecting extreme

EXHIBIT 3.7   Cedar Fair LP Cost of Goods Sold as Percentage of Sales
Source: Capital IQ and author calculations.

seasonality in the company's business. In 2009, for example, the warm-weather second and third calendar quarters accounted for 86 percent of the year's sales. During those quarters, cost of sales typically runs about 50 percent of sales. The profit margin is slimmer in the fourth quarter, and in the first quarter, Cedar Fair operates at a loss, with cost of sales typically running 150 percent or higher.

Fluor Corporation (see Exhibit 3.8) represents the opposite extreme of cost structures. The engineering and construction concern incurs variable labor and material costs with each contract it obtains. Once Fluor completes the project, the associated costs cease. If the volume of available work declines from one year to the next, the company's total costs decline nearly in proportion, as fixed costs are too low to have a large impact.

Throughout the five-year period depicted, cost of sales remained in a range of 98.91 percent to 93.98 percent. In the quarters ending December 2006 through December 2009, the range was even narrower, 95.57 percent to 93.98 percent. The biggest swings in Fluor's normal profit margins did not reflect seasonality but unusual business developments. For example, in the quarter ending September 30, 2006, Fluor took $133 million in provisions for estimated cost overruns on embassy projects for the U.S. Department of State. A substantial portion of the loss was related to a project in Haiti, where work was delayed by civil unrest.

Fluor's margin squeeze in 2006 shows that even with a predominantly variable cost structure, a company can experience unexpected variability in profits. Indeed, the engineering and construction firm Washington Group International (formerly Morrison Knudsen), which maintained a pattern like the one shown in Exhibit 3.8 over a long period, filed for bankruptcy

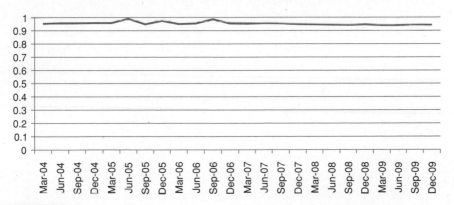

EXHIBIT 3.8 Fluor Corporation Cost of Goods Sold as Percentage of Sales
Source: Capital IQ and author calculations.

in May 2001. The company suffered severe liquidity problems as a result of taking over unprofitable contracts in conjunction with its April 2000 acquisition of Raytheon Engineers & Constructors. Still, credit analysts generally perceive greater risk in the high-fixed-cost pattern exemplified by Cedar Fair. For highly seasonal companies, classically represented by toy manufacturers and general merchandisers, a lackluster winter holiday sales season can drive operating income below the level required to cover interest expense.

Playing with Price-Earnings Multiples

Vigilance, as exemplified by the need to watch for earnings discontinuities, has been a recurring theme throughout this exploration of the ins and outs of income statements. Other pitfalls to watch out for include unrealizable synergies and company-furnished projections of cost ratios that incorporate management's assumptions regarding sales volume. Before moving on, vigilant analysts should familiarize themselves with a device that companies have developed to get around the general proposition that mergers do not increase value unless they increase profitability.

Turning back to the fictitious acquisition case presented in Exhibit 3.3, let us change one assumption (see Exhibit 3.9). As a comparatively small company within its industry, Small Change probably will not command as high a price-earnings multiple as its larger industry peers. Therefore, we shall assume that Big Time is able to acquire the company for only 12 times earnings, rather than 14 times, as indicated in Exhibit 3.3.

Our revised assumption does not alter the income statements in either year under either the Acquisition Scenario or the Nonacquisition Scenario. The acquisition price, however, falls from $99.4 million to $7.1 million × 12 = $85.2 million. Big Time issues only $85.2 million ÷ $28.00 = 3.0 million shares to pay for the acquisition, rather than 3.6 million under the previous assumption. Consequently, Big Time has 78.0 million shares outstanding at the end of Year 2 under the Acquisition Scenario, instead of 78.6 million. Earnings per share come to $165.0 million ÷ 78.0 million = $2.12. At a price-earnings multiple of 14 times, Big Time's stock is valued at $29.68 a share following the Small Change acquisition, slightly higher than the $29.40 figure shown in the Nonacquisition Scenario. Big Time could vault its share price to a considerably loftier level by making a series of acquisitions on a similar basis.

In contrast to the outcome depicted in Exhibit 3.3, Big Time increases the value of its stock through the acquisition of Small Change. The company achieves this effect without realizing operating efficiencies through the

EXHIBIT 3.9 Exploiting a Difference in Price-Earnings Multiples: Big Time Corporation and Small Change, Inc. ($000 omitted)

	Nonacquisition Scenario				Acquisition Scenario	
	Big Time Corporation		Small Change, Inc.		Big Time Corporation	
	Year 1	Year 2	Year 1	Year 2	Year 1	Year 2
Sales	$5,000.0	$5,250.0	$238.1	$250.0	$5,000.0	$5,500.0
Cost and Expenses Cost of goods sold	3,422.7	3,591.4	160.6	171.1	3,422.7	3,762.5
Selling, general, and administrative expenses	1,250.0	1,315.0	61.9	62.5	1,250.0	1,377.5
Interest expense	100.0	105.0	4.8	5.0	100.0	110.0
Total costs and expenses	4,772.7	5,011.4	227.3	238.6	4,772.7	5,250.0
Income before income expenses	227.3	238.6	10.8	11.4	227.3	250.0
Income taxes	77.3	81.1	3.7	3.9	77.3	85.0
Net income	$ 150.0	$ 157.5	$ 7.1	$ 7.5	$ 150.0	$ 165.0
Year-over-year sales increase	—	5%	—	5%	—	10%
Net income as a percentage of sales	3%	3%	3%	3%	3%	3%
Shares outstanding (million)	75.0	75.0			75.0	78.0
Earnings per share	$ 2.00	$ 2.10			$ 2.00	$ 2.12
Price-earnings multiple (times)	14	14			14	14
Price per share	$ 28.00	$ 29.40			$ 28.00	$ 29.68

combination. Following the transaction, Big Time's ratio of net income to sales is 3 percent, unchanged from its preacquisition level.

The rational explanation of this apparent alchemy lies in Big Time's ability to exchange its stock for shares of privately owned Small Change on highly favorable terms. By acquiring the smaller company at a price of 12 times earnings with stock valued at a multiple of 14 times, Big Time spreads Small Change's earnings across fewer shares than would be the case if the market valued the two companies at the same multiple. The effect, achieved purely through financial engineering, is a parody of the economies of scale realized in mergers premised instead of improvements in operations.

In fairness to the many real-world companies that have exploited disparities in price-earnings multiples over the years, Big Time's share-price-enhancing acquisition rests squarely within the bounds of fair play. Companies legitimately take advantage of favorable currency exchange rates when deciding whether to purchase materials and equipment domestically or overseas. If the dollar is high relative to the euro, companies based in the United States can source goods more economically in Europe than at home. In principle, it is no less appropriate or beneficial to shareholders to buy earnings with a highly valued acquisition currency, that is, its own stock.

Furthermore, as shareholders of a private company, Small Change's owners do not have to be coerced to sell out to Big Time. The disparity in price-earnings multiples is justified by the private company's owners' opportunity to exchange an illiquid investment for public stock, for which a deep and active trading market exists. If anything, the difference between Big Time's multiple of 14 times and Small Change's 12 times understates the valuation gap between the public and private shares. Lacking a secondary market that would reward higher reported income with a higher share price, private owner-managers commonly extract compensation through perquisites that their companies can lawfully account for as business expenses. The result is lower net income than comparably successful public companies would report, but with the value of the perks delivered on a pretax basis. Instead of buying cars with dividends distributed from after-tax income, the owner-managers can drive fancier, more expensive company-provided cars purchased with pretax dollars. After adjusting Small Change's reported income for expenses that would not be incurred at a public company such as Big Time, the $85.2 million acquisition price might represent a multiple of only 10 or 11 times, rather than 12 times.

In short, there is nothing inherently unsavory about paying for low-multiple companies with high-multiple stock. Why, then, does the technique warrant special focus in a chapter covering the broad subject of income statements? The answer is that like many other legitimate financial practices, exploiting disparities in price-earnings multiples is prone to abuse. Capitalizing on disparities in price-earnings multiples can lead to trouble in several ways.

To begin with, suppose a high-multiple company acquires a low-multiple company during a period of exceptionally wide dispersion in valuations. In a shift from normal conditions to a two-tiered market, the respective multiples might go, for the sake of example, from 15 and 12 to 25 and 10. Selling stockholders of the low-multiple company would probably consider it a fair exchange to accept payment in shares of the high-multiple company at the prevailing market price. Their feelings would probably change dramatically, however, if the two-tiered market abruptly ended with the purchaser's stock receding from 25 times earnings to a more ordinary 15 times. Sellers who retained the acquiring company's shares would discover that their value received had suddenly fallen by 40 percent. (It is reasonable to assume that many shareholders would have held on to the shares, because doing so would ordinarily delay the incurrence of capital gains taxes on the sale. Unlike cash-for-stock transactions, stock-for-stock acquisitions generally qualify as tax-free exchanges.)

Readers might accuse the selling shareholders of being crybabies. After all, they knew when they accepted the acquiring company's shares as payment that they would be exposed to stock market fluctuations, much as they were prior to the deal. The difference, however, is that if they had held on to their low-multiple stock, their loss would not have been 40 percent, but only 17 percent, that is, from 12 times to 10 times earnings. (A complete comparison must also take into account any premium over the previously prevailing stock price received by the selling shareholders.)

Financial statement analysis would not have warned the selling shareholders of the impending marketwide drop in price-earnings (P/E) multiples. Careful scrutiny of the acquiring company's income statement might very well have determined, however, that its shares were susceptible to a sharp decline. Over the years, many voracious acquirers have temporarily achieved stratospheric multiples on their acquisition currency through financial reporting gimmicks that hard-nosed analysts were able to detect before the share prices fell back to earth.

In some instances, the basis for an exaggerated P/E multiple is rapid earnings per share (EPS) growth achieved through financial engineering rather than bona fide synergies. Starting with a modest multiple on its stock, a company can make a few small acquisitions of low-multiple companies to get the earnings acceleration started. Each transaction may be too small to be deemed material in itself. That would eliminate any obligation on the company's part to divulge details that would make it easy for analysts to quantify the impact of the company's exploitation of disparities in P/E multiples. As quarter-to-quarter percentage increases in EPS escalate, the company's equity begins to be perceived as a high-growth glamour stock. Obliging investors award the stock a higher multiple, which increases the company's ability to buy earnings on favorable terms. Management may succeed in pumping up the P/E multiple even further by asserting that it can achieve economies of scope through acquiring enterprises outside yet, in some previously unrecognized way, complementary to the company's core business.

The conglomerate craze of the 1960s relied heavily on these techniques, and with variations, they have been reused in more recent times. Massive declines in the share prices of the insatiable acquirers' stock prices have frequently resulted. Contributing to the downslides have been the practical problems of integrating the operations of diverse companies. Deals that work on paper have often foundered on incompatible information systems, disparate distribution channels, clashes of personality among senior executives, and contrasting corporate cultures. In addition, the process of boosting earnings per share through acquisition of lower-multiple companies may prove unsustainable. For example, if competition heats up among corporations seeking to grow through acquisition, the P/E gap between acquirers and target companies may narrow. That could get in the way of the continuous stream of acquisitions needed to maintain EPS growth in the absence of profit improvements. Inevitably, too, the voracious acquirer will suffer a normal cyclical decline in the earnings of its existing operations. The company's price-earnings multiple may then decline relative to the multiples of its potential targets, interrupting the necessary flow of acquisitions.

It is no small task to dissect the income statement of a corporation that makes frequent acquisitions and discloses as few details as possible. Nevertheless, an energetic analyst can go a long way toward segregating ongoing operations from purchased earnings growth. Acquisitions of public companies leave an information trail in the form of regulatory filings. Conscientious searching of the media, including the industry-specialized periodicals and local newspapers, may yield useful tidbits on acquisitions of private companies. Such investigations will frequently turn up the phrase "terms of the acquisition were not disclosed," but reliable sources may provide informed speculation about the prices paid. Finally, the acquirers may furnish general information regarding the range of earnings multiples paid in recent deals. If an analysis of the available data indicates that management is expanding its empire without creating additional value through genuine economies of scale or scope, the prudent action is to sell before the bottom falls out.

CONCLUSION

At several points in this chapter, analysis of the income statement has posed questions that could be answered only by looking outside the statement. Mere study of reported financial figures never leads to a fully informed judgment about the issuer. Financial statements cannot capture certain non-quantitative factors that may be essential to an evaluation. These include industry conditions, corporate culture, and management's ability to anticipate change and respond effectively.

The Statement of Cash Flows

The present version of the statement that traces the flow of funds in and out of the firm, the statement of cash flows, became mandatory, under Statement of Financial Accounting Standards (SFAS) 95, for issuers with fiscal years ending after July 15, 1988. Exhibit 4.1, the 2009 cash flow statement of Cisco Systems, illustrates the statement's division into cash flows from operating activities, investing activities, and financing activities. The predecessor of the statement of cash flows, the statement of changes in financial position, was first required under Accounting Principles Board (APB) opinion 19, in 1971.

Prior to that time, going as far back as the introduction of **double-entry bookkeeping** in Italy during the fifteenth century, financial analysts had muddled through with only the balance sheet and the income statement. Anyone with a sense of history will surely conclude that the introduction of the cash flow statement must have been premised by expectations of great new analytical insights. Such an inference is in fact well founded. The advantages of a cash flow statement correspond to the shortcomings of the income statement and, more specifically, the concept of profit. Over time, profit has proven so malleable a quantity, so easily enlarged or reduced to suit management's needs, as to make it useless, in many instances, as the basis of a fair comparison among companies.

An example of the erroneous comparisons that can arise involves the contrasting objectives that public and private companies have in preparing their income statements.

For financial-reporting (as opposed to tax-accounting) purposes, a publicly owned company generally seeks to maximize its reported net income, which investors use as a basis for valuing its shares. Therefore, its incentive in any situation where the accounting rules permit discretion is to minimize expenses. The firm will capitalize whatever expenditures it can and depreciate its fixed assets over as long a period as possible. All that restrains the public company in this respect (other than conscience) is the wish to avoid

EXHIBIT 4.1   Cisco Systems, Inc. Cash Flow Statement

Company Name: Cisco Systems, Inc.
Form Type: 10-K
Filed On: 9/11/2009

Years Ended	July 25, 2009
Cash flows from operating activities:	
Net income	$ 6,134
Adjustments to reconcile net income to net cash provided by operating activities:	
Depreciation, amortization, and other noncash items	1,768
Employee share-based compensation expense	1,140
Share-based compensation expense related to acquisitions and investments	91
Provision for doubtful accounts	54
Deferred income taxes	(574)
Excess tax benefits from share-based compensation	(22)
In-process research and development	63
Net losses (gains) on investments	80
Change in operating assets and liabilities, net of effects of acquisitions:	
Accounts receivable	610
Inventories	187
Lease receivables, net	(222)
Accounts payable	(208)
Income taxes payable and receivable	768
Accrued compensation	175
Deferred revenue	572
Other assets	(780)
Other liabilities	61
Net cash provided by operating activities	9,897
Cash flows from investing activities:	
Purchases of investments	(41,225)
Proceeds from sales of investments	20,473
Proceeds from maturities of investments	12,352
Acquisition of property and equipment	(1,005)
Acquisition of businesses, net of cash and cash equivalents acquired	(426)
Change in investments in privately held companies	(89)
Other	(39)
Net cash used in investing activities	$ (9,959)

EXHIBIT 4.1 (*Continued*)

Cash flows from financing activities:	
Issuance of common stock	863
Repurchase of common stock	(3,611)
Issuance of long-term debt	3,991
Repayment of long-term debt	(500)
Settlement of interest rate derivatives related to long-term debt	(42)
Excess tax benefits from share-based compensation	22
Other	(134)
Net cash provided by (used in) financing activities	589
Net increase in cash and cash equivalents	527
Cash and cash equivalents, beginning of fiscal year	5,191
Cash and cash equivalents, end of fiscal year	5,718

Source: Company 10-K, Capital IQ, and author calculations.

being perceived as employing liberal accounting practices, which may lead to a lower market valuation of its reported earnings. Using depreciation schedules much longer than those of other companies in the same industry could give rise to such a perception.

In contrast, a privately held company has no public shareholders to impress. Unlike a public company, which shows one set of statements to the public and another to the Internal Revenue Service, a private company typically prepares one set of statements, with the tax authorities foremost in its thinking. Its incentive is not to maximize, but to minimize the income it reports, thereby minimizing its tax bill as well. If an analyst examines its income statement and tries to compare it with those of public companies in the same industry, the result will be an undeservedly poor showing by the private company.

THE CASH FLOW STATEMENT AND THE LEVERAGED BUYOUT

Net income becomes even less relevant when one analyzes the statements of a company that has been acquired in a **leveraged buyout** (**LBO**) (Exhibit 4.2). In a classic LBO, a group of investors acquires a business by putting up a comparatively small amount of equity and borrowing the balance (70 percent in this example) of the purchase price. As a result of this highly leveraged capital structure, interest expense is so large that the formerly quite profitable

EXHIBIT 4.2 Leveraged Buyout Forecast—Base Case ($000,000 omitted)

Capitalization

December 31, 2010

Senior debt	900	45%
Subordinated debt	500	25%
Total debt	1,400	70%
Common equity	600	30%
Total capital	$2,000	100%

Projected Income Statement	2010 (Act.)	2011	2012	2013	2014	2015
Sales	$1,429	$1,543	$1,667	$1,800	$1,944	$2,100
Cost of sales	800	864	933	1,008	1,089	1,176
Depreciation	100	108	117	126	136	147
Selling, general, and administrative expense	286	309	333	360	389	420
Operating income	243	262	283	306	331	357
Interest expense	45	108	100	91	80	68
Income before income taxes	198	154	183	215	250	289
Provision (credit) for income Taxes	65	51	60	71	83	95
Net Income	$ 133	$ 103	$ 123	$ 144	$ 168	$ 194

Projected Cash Flow	2011	2012	2013	2014	2015
Net income	$ 103	$ 123	$ 144	$ 168	$ 194
Depreciation	108	117	126	136	147
Cash from operations	$ 211	$ 239	$ 270	$ 304	$ 341
Less: Property and equipment additions	100	108	117	126	136
Cash available for debt reduction	$ 111	$ 131	$ 153	$ 178	$ 205

Projected Capitalization	2010 (Act.)	2011	2012	2013	2014	2015
Senior debt	$ 900	$ 789	$ 657	$ 504	$ 326	$ 121
Subordinated debt	500	500	500	500	500	500
Total debt	1,400	1,289	1,157	1,004	826	621
Common equity	600	$ 703	$ 826	$ 970	$1,138	$1,332
Total capital	$2,000	$1,992	$1,983	$1,974	$1,964	$1,953

company reports a reduced net income in its first two years as an LBO (2011–2012). Hardly an attractive investment, on the face of it, and one might also question the wisdom of lenders who provide funds to an enterprise that is assured of becoming less profitable.

A closer study, however, shows that the equity investors are no fools. In 2013, the company's sales are expected to bring in $1,800 million in cash. Cash outlays include cost of sales ($1,008 million); selling, general, and administrative expense ($360 million); and interest expense ($91 million), for a total of $1,459 million. Adding in depreciation of $126 million produces total expenses of $1,585 million, which when subtracted from sales results in a $183 million pretax profit. The amount attributable to depreciation, however, does not represent an outlay of cash in the current year. Rather, it is a bookkeeping entry intended to represent the gradual reduction in value, through use, of physical assets. Therefore, the funds generated by the leveraged buyout firm equal sales less the cash expenses only. (Note that the assumed tax rate in this projection is 33 percent.)

	Sales	$1,800 million
Less:	Cash expenses	
	Cost of sales	1,008
	Selling, general, and administrative expense	360
	Interest expense	91
	Provision for income taxes	71
Equals:	Cash generated	$ 270 million

The same figure can be derived by simply adding back depreciation to income.[1]

	Net income	$144 million
Plus:	Depreciation	126
Equals:	Cash generated	$270 million

Viewed in terms of cash inflows and outflows, rather than earnings, the leveraged buyout begins to look like a sound venture. In 2013, net income has increased by only 8 percent since 2010, despite a 26 percent advance in sales, but the company is generating cash and has reduced its borrowings. (Note that the equity investors take no dividends but instead dedicate any surplus cash generated to reduction of debt.)

The story improves even more during subsequent years. As sales grow at an 8 percent annual rate, the projected income statement shows a steady increase in operating income. In addition, the paydown of debt causes interest expense to decline, so net income increases over time. With depreciation rising as well, funds from operations in this example keep ahead of the growing capital expenditure requirements.

If the projections prove accurate, the equity investors will, by the end of 2015, own a company with $2.1 billion in sales and $357 million of operating income, up from $1.4 billion and $243 million, respectively, in 2010. They will have captured that growth without having injected any additional cash beyond their original $600 million investment.

Suppose the investors then decide to monetize the increase in firm value represented by the growth in earnings. Assuming they can sell the company for the same multiple of EBITDA (earnings before interest, taxes, depreciation, and amortization)[2] that they paid for it, they will realize net proceeds of $1,740 million, derived as follows ($000,000 omitted):

1. Calculate the multiple of EBITDA paid in 2010.

$$= \frac{\text{Purchase price (Equity} + \text{Borrowed funds)}}{\text{Net income} + \text{Income taxes} + \text{Interest expense} + \text{Depreciation and Amortization}}$$

$$= \frac{\$2,000}{\$133 + \$65 + \$45 + \$100}$$

$$= 5.8$$

2. Multiply this factor by 2015 EBITDA to determine sale price in that year.

$$(5.8) \times (\$194 + \$95 + \$68 + \$147) = \$2,923$$

3. From this figure, subtract remaining debt to determine pretax proceeds.

$$\$2,923 - \$621 = \$2,301$$

4. Subtract taxes on the gain over original equity investment to determine net proceeds.

$2,301	Pretax proceeds
−600	Original equity investment
$816,400	Capital gain
× 0.33	Capital gains tax rate
$561	Tax on capital gain
$2,301	Pretax proceeds
−561	Tax on capital gain
$1,740	Net proceeds

The increase in the equity holders' investment from $600 million to $1,740 million over five years represents a compounded annual return of 24 percent after tax. Interestingly, the highly leveraged annual return on equity (based on reported net income and the beginning-of-year book value of equity) is significantly lower, at 17 percent during the period of the projection. Analysts evaluating the investment merits of the LBO proposal would miss the point if they focused on earnings rather than cash flow.

The same emphasis on cash flow, rather than reported earnings, is equally important in analyzing the downside in a leveraged buyout.

As one might expect, the equity investors do not reap such spectacular gains without incurring significant risk. There is a danger that everything will not go according to plan and that they will lose their entire investment. Specifically, there is a risk that sales and operating earnings will fall short of expectations, perhaps as a result of a recession or because the investors' expectations were unrealistically high at the outset. With a less debt-heavy capital structure, a shortfall in operating earnings might not be worrisome. In a leveraged buyout, however, the high interest expense can quickly turn disappointing operating income into a sizable net loss (Exhibit 4.3). The loss may be so large that even after depreciation is added back, the company's funds generated from operations may decline to zero or to a negative figure. (Note that the shortfall shown here resulted from a 10 percent drop in sales from 2010 and deviations of just 10 percent each in the projections for cost of sales, and selling, general, and administrative expense, shown in Exhibit 4.2.)

Now the future does not look so rosy for the equity investors. If they cannot reduce operating expenses sufficiently to halt the cash drain, they will

EXHIBIT 4.3 Leveraged Buyout Forecast—Pessimistic Case ($000 omitted)

Projected Income Statement			2011
Sales			$1,286
Cost of sales			950
Depreciation			108
Selling, general, and administrative expense			340
Operating income			(112)
Interest expense			(108)
Income before income taxes			(220)
Provision (credit) for income taxes			(73)
Net income			$ (147)
	Net income	$(147)	million
	Plus: Depreciation	106	
	Equals: Cash generated	$ (39)	million

lack the cash required for the heavy interest expenses they have incurred, much less the scheduled principal payments. Most of the choices available if they cannot cut costs sufficiently are unappealing. One option is for the investors to inject more equity into the company. This will cause any profits they ultimately realize to represent a smaller percentage return on the equity invested, besides possibly straining the investors' finances. Alternatively, the existing equity holders can sell equity to a new group of investors. The disadvantage of this strategy is that anyone putting in new capital at a time when the venture is perceived to be in trouble is likely to exact terms that will severely dilute the original investors' interest and, possibly, control. Comparably harsh terms may be expected from lenders who are willing (if any are) to let the company try to borrow its way out of its problems. A distressed exchange offer, in which bondholders accept reduced interest or a postponement of principal repayment, may be more attractive for the equity holders but is likely to meet stiff resistance.

If all these options prove unpalatable or infeasible, the leveraged company will default on its debt. At that point, the lenders may force the firm into bankruptcy, which could result in a total loss for the equity investors. Alternatively, the lenders may agree to reduce the interest rates on their loans and postpone mandatory principal repayments, but they will ordinarily agree to such concessions only in exchange for a larger influence on the company's management. In short, once cash flow turns negative, the potential outcomes generally look bleak to the equity investors.

The key point here is that the cash flow statement, rather than the income statement, provides the best information about a highly leveraged firm's financial health. Given the overriding importance of generating (and retaining) cash to retire debt, and because the equity investors have no desire for dividends, there is no advantage in showing an accounting profit, the main consequence of which is incurrence of taxes, resulting in turn in reduced cash flow. Neither are there public shareholders clamoring for increases in earnings per share. The cash flow statement is the most useful tool for analyzing highly leveraged companies because it reflects the true motivation of the firm's owners—to generate cash, rather than to maximize reported income.

ANALYTICAL APPLICATIONS

Although privately held and highly leveraged companies illustrate most vividly the advantages of the cash flow statement, the statement also has considerable utility in analyzing publicly owned and more conventionally capitalized firms. One important application lies in determining where a company is in its life cycle, that is, whether it is taking off, growing rapidly, maturing, or declining. Different types of risk characterize these various stages of the life cycle. Therefore, knowing which stage a company is in can focus the analyst's efforts on the key analytical factors. A second use of the cash flow statement is to assess a company's **financial flexibility**. This term refers to a company's capacity, in the event of a business downturn, to continue making expenditures that, over the long term, minimize its cost of capital and enhance its competitive position. Finally, the cash flow statement is the key statement to examine when analyzing a troubled company. When a company is verging on bankruptcy, its balance sheet may overstate its asset value, as a result of write-offs having lagged the deterioration in profitability of the company's operations. On the other hand, the balance sheet may fail to reflect the full value of certain assets recorded at historical cost, which the company might sell to raise cash. The income statement is not especially relevant in the context of pending bankruptcy. For the moment, the company's key objective is not to maintain an impeccable earnings record, but to survive. The cash flow statement provides the most useful information for answering the critical question: Will the company succeed in keeping its creditors at bay?

CASH FLOW AND THE COMPANY LIFE CYCLE

Business enterprises typically go through phases of development that are in many respects analogous to a human being's stages of life. Just as children are susceptible to illnesses different from those that afflict the elderly, the risks of investing in young companies are different from the risks inherent in mature companies. Accordingly, it is helpful to understand which portion of the life cycle a company is in and which financial pitfalls it is therefore most likely to face.

Revenues build gradually in the introductory phase, when the company is just organizing itself and launching its products. From a small base, revenues accelerate rapidly during the growth phase, as the company's products penetrate the market and production reaches a profitable scale. In the maturity phase, sales opportunities are limited to the replacement of products previously sold, plus new sales derived from growth in the population. Price competition often intensifies at this stage, as companies seek sales growth through increased market share (a larger piece of a pie that is growing at a lesser rate). The decline stage does not automatically follow maturity, but over long periods, some industries do get swept away by technological

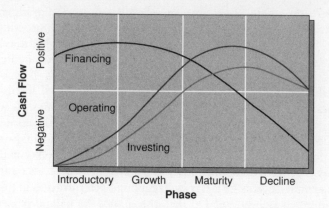

EXHIBIT 4.4   Cash Flows and the Life Cycle
Source: © 2007 *Intermediate Accounting*, 12th ed. (Hoboken, NJ: John Wiley & Sons).

change. Sharply falling sales and earnings, ultimately resulting in corporate bankruptcies, characterize industries in severe decline.

Exhibit 4.4 depicts the business life cycle in terms of operating activities and financing activities, which are usually sources of cash flow, and investing activities, which is ordinarily a use of cash flow. Observe that the financing curve peaks in the earlier (introductory-growth) portion of the life cycle, while the operating and investing curves peak in the later (maturity-decline) portion. A crossover occurs in the maturity phase as cash flows from operating and investing begin to exceed cash flows from financing.

Introductory stage companies subsist primarily on financing as they build their operations toward the point at which they will begin to generate cash. Growth companies can be highly profitable, but they require extensive external capital to keep **funding** their expansion. Mature companies may achieve less impressive profit margins, but as their need to invest levels off, they become self-funding and, ultimately, net generators of cash. This is indicated in the graph by the financing curve falling into negative territory. Companies that throw off cash can be good leveraged buyout candidates. Alternatively, they may seek to bolster profits through industry consolidation (i.e., mergers and acquisitions that reduce the number of competitors) to achieve economies of scale. Declining companies reach a point at which deteriorating cash flows from operating and investing activities cause them to become net cash users. They cannot fill the gap with external financing (as shown by the financing curve moving into the negative zone), because they represent poor credit risks and offer unattractive returns to equity investors.

Tesla Motors illustrates the cash flow pattern of a company in the introductory phase of its life cycle (Exhibit 4.5). Tesla manufactures electric vehicles, a product that was just beginning to gain a foothold with consumers during the period depicted in its statement of cash flows. The company was privately owned during the period shown in the exhibit and did not go public until June 2010.

The net losses recorded by Tesla are not unusual for a company at the introductory stage. It may take several years for a company's sales to reach a level sufficient to cover the sizable fixed costs that are essential to its operations. Young companies may also suffer growing pains. During the 2006–2009 period, Tesla cut its workforce to bring down costs and had four different chief executive officers, including one interim CEO. The company reported a profit in July 2009.

Cash from operations became increasingly negative during the period as losses escalated up until 2009. Investing activities, primarily capital expenditures, did not put a lot of additional strain on cash flow, but Tesla had to issue substantial amounts of debt and preferred stock to continue in business. Funds were provided by Chairman Elon Musk, who took an active role in the company; other entrepreneurs such as Google co-founders Sergey Brin and Larry Page; venture capitalist firms; and German automaker Daimler AG.

Green Mountain Coffee Roasters (Exhibit 4.6) is a rapidly growing company that is well beyond the introductory phase. It was founded in 1981, went public in 1993, and generated revenues of $1.2 billion in fiscal 2010. Green Mountain's revenues expanded at a 50 percent annual rate between 2005 and 2006. Clearly, this is a business in which year-to-year sales increases derive from rising popularity of its products, rather than mere population growth, as in the case of a mature company.

Green Mountain's statement of cash flows shows a steady rise in depreciation and amortization, which accounts for 79 percent of cumulative cash flow from operating activities during the five-year period depicted. Unlike a mature company, Green Mountain is not self-financing. It issues substantial amounts of debt and equity each year to fund its growing needs for **working capital** and acquisitions.

Founded in 1872, paper goods manufacturer Kimberly-Clark (Exhibit 4.7) has gone though a long stretch as a mature company without going into decline. Its major products are essential consumer items such as facial tissue, feminine hygiene products, toilet paper, and disposable diapers. People are not likely to intensify their usage of these products, except as a function of their own life cycles, so demand for Kimberly-Clark's products is largely a function of population growth. By the same token, the company should be able to count on steady demand for its products as long as

EXHIBIT 4.5 Tesla Motors, Inc. Form S-1

Company Name: Tesla Motors, Inc.
Form Type: S-1
Filed On: 1/29/2010

	Years Ended December 31			Nine Months Ended
	2006	2007	2008	Sept. 30, 2009 (Unaudited)
Cash flows from operating activities:				
Net loss	($29,957)	($78,157)	($82,782)	($31,498)
Adjustments to reconcile net loss to net cash used in operating activities:				
Depreciation and amortization	615	2,895	4,157	5,005
Change in fair value of convertible preferred stock warrant liability	($ 196)	($ 36)	2,800	404
Gain on extinguishment of convertible notes and warrants	—	—	($ 1,245)	($ 1,468)
Stock-based compensation	23	198	437	449
Loss on abandonment of fixed assets	—	2,421	—	—
Interest on convertible notes	411	—	3,692	2,686
Changes in operating assets and liabilities:				
Accounts receivable	—	($ 59)	($ 3,261)	1,934
Inventory	—	($ 2,108)	($14,542)	($ 3,003)
Prepaid expenses and other current assets	($ 819)	($ 1,884)	750	($ 2,184)
Other assets	($ 27)	($ 64)	12	($ 654)
Accounts payable	2,242	523	8,815	3,173
Accrued liabilities	2,175	7,572	2,633	($ 79)
Other long-term liabilities	—	—	1,192	2,321

Deferred development compensation	—	—	10,173	($ 6,023)
Deferred revenue	—	—	4,073	326
Refundable reservation payments	22,105	15,230	10,684	($23,207)
Net cash used in operating activities	**($ 3,428)**	**($53,469)**	**($52,412)**	**($51,818)**
Cash flows from investing activities:				
Purchases of property and equipment excluding capital leases	($ 6,505)	($ 9,802)	($ 9,630)	($ 5,685)
Decrease (increase) in restricted cash	($ 300)	40	($ 960)	($ 2,360)
Net cash used in investing activities	**($ 6,805)**	**($ 9,762)**	**($10,590)**	**($ 8,045)**
Cash flows from financing activities				
Proceeds from issuance of Series F convertible preferred stock, net of issuance costs of $122	—	—	—	82,378
Proceeds from issuance of Series E convertible preferred stock, net of issuance costs of $556	—	—	—	49,444
Proceeds from issuance of Series D convertible preferred stock, net of issuance costs of $59	—	44,941	—	—
Proceeds from issuance of Series C convertible preferred stock, net of issuance costs of $211	36,801	—	—	—
Principal payments on capital leases and other debt	—	—	($ 191)	($ 275)
Proceeds from issuance of convertible notes and warrants	3,000	—	54,782	25,468
Proceeds from issuance of common stock to consultant	—	—	21	—
Proceeds from exercise of stock options	6	100	456	118
Net cash provided by financing activities	**39,807**	**45,041**	**55,068**	**157,133**
Net increase (decrease) in cash and cash equivalents	**29,574**	**($18,190)**	**($ 7,934)**	**97,270**

Source: Company S-1.

EXHIBIT 4.6 Green Mountain Coffee Roasters, Inc. Consolidated Statements of Cash Flows (in millions)

Cash Flow

For the Fiscal Period Ending	Restated 12 months Sep-25-2004	Restated 12 months Sep-24-2005	Restated 12 months Sep-30-2006	12 months Sep-29-2007	12 months Sep-27-2008	12 months Sep-26-2009
Net Income	7.8	9.0	8.4	12.8	22.3	55.9
Depreciation & Amort.	4.7	6.0	7.9	10.3	13.5	18.0
Amort. of Goodwill and Intangibles	—	—	1.4	4.8	4.8	5.3
Depreciation & Amort., Total	4.7	6.0	9.3	15.1	18.3	23.3
(Gain) Loss from Sale Of Assets	(0.1)	0	0	0.1	0.2	0.7
(Income) Loss on Equity Invest.	1.8	0.8	1.6	—	—	—
Stock-Based Compensation	0.2	0.2	0.2	0.2	0.2	1.0
Tax Benefit from Stock Options	0.3	2.2	0.3	(3.3)	(6.6)	(11.2)
Provision & Write-off of Bad Debts	0.3	0.3	0.4	0.6	1.2	0.2
Other Operating Activities	0.8	0.2	2.2	4.8	7.0	8.8
Change in Acc. Receivable	(1.3)	(3.1)	(7.9)	(9.9)	(16.6)	(37.0)
Change in Inventories	(2.1)	(4.5)	(8.6)	(7.0)	(46.4)	(49.8)
Change in Acc. Payable	1.3	2.6	5.5	9.0	8.7	25.8
Change in Inc. Taxes	0.3	0.7	(1.3)	5.4	6.8	11.7
Change in Other Net Operating Assets	2.0	0.2	2.8	2.0	6.9	9.1
Cash from Ops.	16.0	14.7	12.8	29.8	1.9	38.5
Capital Expenditure	(18.5)	(9.4)	(13.6)	(21.8)	(48.7)	(48.3)
Sale of Property, Plant, and Equipment	0.5	0.7	0.5	0.2	0.4	0.2
Cash Acquisitions	—	—	(101.1)	—	—	(41.4)
Divestitures	—	—	—	—	—	—
Invest. in Marketable & Equity Securt.	—	—	—	—	—	(50.0)
Net (Inc.) Dec. in Loans Originated/Sold	—	—	—	—	—	—
Other Investing Activities	—	—	—	—	—	—
Cash from Investing	(18.0)	(8.7)	(114.2)	(21.7)	(48.3)	(139.5)

	Dec-14-2006	Dec-13-2007	Dec-11-2008	Nov-25-2009	Nov-25-2009	Nov-25-2009
Short Term Debt Issued	—	—	—	—	—	—
Long-Term Debt Issued	9.0	0.1	102.8	0.0	33.5	50.0
Total Debt Issued	9.0	0.1	102.8	0.0	33.5	50.0
Short Term Debt Repaid	(0.4)	—	—	—	—	—
Long-Term Debt Repaid	(3.4)	(8.7)	(8.6)	(12.9)	(0.1)	(95.7)
Total Debt Repaid	(3.7)	(8.7)	(8.6)	(12.9)	(0.1)	(95.7)
Issuance of Common Stock	0.9	4.3	2.2	3.1	5.7	394.9
Total Dividends Paid	—	—	—	—	—	—
Special Dividend Paid	—	—	—	—	—	—
Other Financing Activities	(0.1)	—	(0.2)	3.3	5.3	(7.2)
Cash from Financing	6.1	(4.2)	96.2	(6.4)	44.4	342.0
Net Change in Cash	4.0	1.7	(5.2)	1.8	(2.0)	241.0
Supplemental Items						
Cash Interest Paid	0.5	0.8	2.2	6.7	6.1	5.1
Cash Taxes Paid	3.5	2.7	5.5	3.2	6.7	20.4
Levered Free Cash Flow	(3.4)	2.2	(8.1)	7.2	(56.5)	(29.6)
Unlevered Free Cash Flow	(3.3)	2.6	(6.7)	11.1	(52.9)	(26.7)
Change in Net Working Capital	(1.3)	4.0	13.7	(0.2)	51.1	51.2
Net Debt Issued	5.3	(8.6)	94.2	(12.9)	33.4	(45.7)
Filing Date	Dec-14-2006	Dec-13-2007	Dec-11-2008	Nov-25-2009	Nov-25-2009	Nov-25-2009
Restatement Type	RS	RS	RS	NC	NC	O
Calculation Type	REP	REP	REP	REP	REP	REP

Source: Company 10-K, Capital IQ, and author calculations.

EXHIBIT 4.7 Kimberly-Clark Corporation Consolidated Statements of Cash Flows (in millions, except per-share items)

For the Fiscal Period Ending	Restated 12 months Dec-31-2005	Restated 12 months Dec-31-2006	Restated 12 months Dec-31-2007	12 months Dec-31-2008	12 months Dec-31-2009
Net Income	1,580.6	1,500.0	1,823.0	1,690.0	1,884.0
Depreciation & Amort.	818.5	894.0	793.0	763.0	765.0
Amort. of Goodwill and Intangibles	26.0	39.0	14.0	12.0	18.0
Depreciation & Amort., Total	844.5	933.0	807.0	775.0	783.0
(Gain) Loss from Sale of Assets	45.8	116.0	30.0	51.0	36.0
Asset Writedown & Restructuring Costs	80.1	—	—	—	—
(Income) Loss on Equity Invest.	(23.8)	27.0	(40.0)	(34.0)	(53.0)
Stock-Based Compensation	32.4	67.0	63.0	47.0	86.0
Minority Int. in Earnings	86.5	95.0	—	—	—
Net Cash from Discontinued Ops.	—	—	—	—	—
Other Operating Activities	(154.2)	(163.0)	76.0	322.0	(360.0)
Change in Acc. Receivable	(41.9)	(231.0)	(192.0)	148.0	(20.0)
Change in Inventories	(81.1)	(252.0)	(439.0)	(45.0)	523.0
Change in Acc. Payable	51.1	150.0	152.0	(43.0)	278.0
Change in Inc. Taxes	13.6	(65.0)	(57.0)	(96.0)	(27.0)
Change in Other Net Operating Assets	(121.8)	403.0	206.0	(299.0)	351.0
Cash from Ops.	2,311.8	2,580.0	2,429.0	2,516.0	3,481.0

Capital Expenditure	(709.6)	(972.0)	(989.0)	(906.0)	(848.0)
Sale of Property, Plant, and Equipment	46.8	44.0	97.0	28.0	25.0
Cash Acquisitions	(17.4)	(100.0)	(16.0)	(98.0)	(458.0)
Divestitures	—	—	—	—	—
Invest. in Marketable & Equity Securt.	100.8	(10.0)	36.0	115.0	(7.0)
Net (Inc.) Dec. in Loans Originated/Sold	—	—	—	—	—
Other Investing Activities	(16.8)	2.0	(26.0)	14.0	—
Cash from Investing	(596.2)	(1,036.0)	(898.0)	(847.0)	(1,288.0)
Total Debt Issued	922.0	262.0	2,171.0	551.0	2.0
Total Debt Repaid	(599.7)	(495.0)	(339.0)	(710.0)	(590.0)
Issuance of Common Stock	142.7	331.0	349.0	113.0	165.0
Repurchase of Common Stock	(1,519.5)	(762.0)	(2,813.0)	(653.0)	(7.0)
Total Dividends Paid	(838.4)	(884.0)	(933.0)	(950.0)	(986.0)
Cash from Financing	(1,929.7)	(1,551.0)	(1,427.0)	(1,747.0)	(1,788.0)
Net Change in Cash	(230.0)	(3.0)	112.0	(109.0)	434.0

Source: Company 10-K, Capital IQ, and author calculations.

it continues investing in its well-known and highly regarded brand names, including Kleenex, Kotex, Cottonelle, and Huggies.

Reflecting the mature state of its business, Kimberly-Clark generates a high and steady level of cash from operations. In the five-year period depicted, the figure ranged between \$2.3 billion and \$2.6 billion, except for a spike to \$3.5 billion in 2009. Sales fell by 1.5 percent in that recession year. To avert a decline in profits, the company instituted cost-saving measures that actually resulted in a year-over-year gain in net income. In that context, Kimberly-Clark reduced inventories by \$523 million and relied more heavily on vendor financing, allowing accounts payable to increase by \$278 million.

By virtue of being long past the high-growth phase of its **business cycle**, Kimberly-Clark did not have to spend heavily on adding to its productive capacity. Capital expenditures, the main component of investing activities, therefore absorbed only about one-third of cash from operating activities during 2005 through 2009. That left the company with cash generation of \$1.5 billion to \$1.7 billion a year (and \$2.2 billion in 2009) before financing activities. After paying annual dividends that rose from \$838.4 million to \$986.0 million during the period, Kimberly-Clark applied the cash generated from its business largely to buying back shares.

Common stock repurchases greatly exceeded net debt issuance (debt issued minus debt repaid) in the period. Far from depending on external capital, this mature company returned capital to investors, giving them the opportunity to reinvest it in higher-growth, cash-hungry businesses. In addition, Kimberly-Clark helped its shareholders by reducing the number of shares outstanding and thereby increasing its earnings per share (see Chapter 14). Some mature companies choose instead to reinvest their positive cash flow internally. They either launch or acquire businesses with higher growth potential than their original core operations. The older businesses become cash cows to be milked for funding the newer activities.

The New York Times Company (Exhibit 4.8) displays cash flow characteristics of a company in the decline phase of its life cycle. This is consistent with the impact of technological change on the newspaper publishing industry. Migration of advertising to new media such as the Internet has undercut the economic basis of advertiser-supported print media. It remains to be seen whether companies tied to older communications technology can reinvent themselves for the new age.

A caveat in analyzing the New York Times Company's statements of cash flows involves the impact of the 2008–2009 recession on advertising sales in all media. It is difficult to separate precisely the respective influences of cyclical and secular forces on net income. This is an analytical problem that applies generally to companies that enter—or appear to enter—the decline phase of their life cycles.

EXHIBIT 4.8 The New York Times Company Consolidated Statements of Cash Flows (in millions, except per-share items)

For the Fiscal Period Ending	Restated 12 months Dec-25-2005	12 months Dec-31-2006	Reclassified 12 months Dec-30-2007	Restated 12 months Dec-28-2008	12 months Dec-27-2009
Net Income	253.5	(543.4)	208.7	(57.8)	19.9
Depreciation & Amort., Total	143.8	169.9	147.0	139.4	133.8
+ Impairment of Assets	—	814,433.0	11,000.0	197,879.0	4,179.0
Net Cash from Discontinued Ops.	—	—	(229.6)	—	(34.9)
= Gain on Sale of Broadcast Media Group	—	—	(190,007.0)	—	—
+ Gain on Sale of Radio Operations	—	—	(39,578.0)	—	(34,914.0)
+ Deferred Income Taxes	(34,772.0)	(139,904.0)	(11,550.0)	(18,958.0)	44,431.0
+ Net Pension Curtailment Gains	—	—	—	—	(53,965)
+ Loss on Leases and Other	—	—	—	—	34,633
+ Pension Withdrawal Expense	—	—	—	—	78,931
Cash from Ops.	294.3	422.3	110.7	246.4	256.8
Capital Expenditure	(221.3)	(332.3)	(380.3)	(167.0)	(51.1)
Sale of Property, Plant, and Equipment	183.2	—	—	—	26.5
Cash Acquisitions	(437.5)	(35.8)	(174.1)	(5.7)	—
+ Acquisitions and Investments	—	—	—	—	—
+ Payment for Purchase of Edison, N.J., Facility	—	—	(139,979.0)	—	—

EXHIBIT 4.8 (Continued)

For the Fiscal Period Ending	Restated 12 months Dec-25-2005	12 months Dec-31-2006	Reclassified 12 months Dec-30-2007	Restated 12 months Dec-28-2008	12 months Dec-27-2009
Divestitures					
= Net Proceeds from Dispositions	—	—	90.8	—	—
+ Proceeds from the Sale of Edison, N.J., Assets	—	—	90,819.0	—	—
Other Investing Activities	(0.6)	(20.6)	611.8	12.2	44.1
+ Proceeds from the Sale of the Broadcast Media Group	—	—	575,427.0	—	—
+ Proceeds from the Sale of Radio Operations	—	—	40,000.0	—	45,424.0
Cash from Investing	(495.5)	(288.7)	148.3	(160.5)	8.1
Total Debt Issued	161.1	61.1	195.0	185.0	431.8
Total Debt Repaid	—	(76.1)	(412.7)	(161.3)	(738.5)
Issuance of Common Stock	14.3	16.0	0.5	—	0.4
Repurchase of Common Stock	(57.4)	(52.3)	(4.5)	(0.2)	(0.5)
Total Dividends Paid	(94.5)	(100.1)	(125.1)	(108.5)	—
Cash from Financing	204.4	(106.2)	(280.5)	(81.2)	(286.2)
Net Change in Cash	2.5	27.4	(20.8)	5.3	(20.3)

Source: Company 10-K, Capital IQ, and author calculations.

At first blush, the New York Times Company's cash flow situation does not look all that bad. During 2005 through 2009, investing activities soaked up only $0.8 billion. Operating activities, meanwhile, generated $1.3 billion. This apparent excess of cash sources over cash uses accounts for the paradox of a declining company being a net payer down of debt and repurchaser of common stock.

Closer examination, however, reveals that the company met its cash needs internally only with the help of approximately $750 million of divestment proceeds and sales of property, plant, and equipment. In effect, the New York Times Company was liquidating itself, the financial equivalent of keeping a train running by ripping down the wooden sides of the coaches and throwing them into the firebox. The biggest divestment, the broadcasting group, was not essential to maintaining the core newspaper publishing business. No company, however, can continue shedding assets indefinitely as a substitute for generating cash from operations, net of capital expenditures and other financing activities.

As noted previously, there is a possibility that companies currently steeped in old media can solve the riddle of how to reinvent themselves to thrive in the new media age. In general, large investments in old technology pose a formidable obstacle to such a thoroughgoing transformation. There are, however, precedents for a mature company heading off decline, taking the higher of the two diverging paths depicted in Exhibit 4.4.

In the mid-2000s, Apple Inc. (Exhibit 4.9) reversed a decline brought on by a series of failed products that reduced its competitiveness. The company's primary focus shifted from computer hardware to mobile electronic devices, as symbolized by the abandonment of its original name, Apple Computer. Highly successful new products such as the iPod, the iPhone, Apple TV, and the iTunes Store made Apple part of the world of entertainment, as well as the technology, world. Cash flow from operating activities turned sharply upward.

THE CONCEPT OF FINANCIAL FLEXIBILITY

Besides reflecting a company's stage of development, and therefore the categories of risk it is most likely to face, the cash flow statement provides essential information about a firm's financial flexibility. By studying the statement, an analyst can make informed judgments on such questions as:

- How safe (likely to continue being paid) is the company's dividend?
- Could the company fund its needs internally if external sources of capital suddenly become scarce or prohibitively expensive?

EXHIBIT 4.9 Apple, Inc. Consolidated Statements of Cash Flows (in millions, except per-share items)

For the Fiscal Period Ending	12 months Sep-25-2003	Restated 12 months Sep-25-2004	Restated 12 months Sep-24-2005	12 months Sep-30-2006	Restated 12 months Sep-29-2007	Restated 12 months Sep-27-2008	Restated 12 months Sep-26-2009	LTM 12 months Dec-26-2009
Net Income	69.0	266.0	1,328.0	1,989.0	3,495.0	6,119.0	8,235.0	9,358.0
Depreciation & Amort.	108.0	132.3	154.0	195.0	279.0	423.0	656.0	697.0
Amort. of Goodwill and Intangibles	5.0	7.0	9.0	12.0	35.0	46.0	53.0	53.0
Depreciation & Amort., Total	113.0	139.3	163.0	207.0	314.0	469.0	709.0	750.0
Other Amortization	–	10.7	16.0	18.0	13.0	27.0	25.0	25.0
(Gain) Loss from Sale of Assets	2.0	7.0	9.0	15.0	12.0	22.0	26.0	25.0
(Gain) Loss on Sale of Invest.	(31.0)	(5.0)	–	–	–	–	–	–
Asset Writedown & Restructuring Costs	12.0	–	–	–	–	–	–	–
Stock-Based Compensation	16.0	46.0	49.0	163.0	242.0	516.0	710.0	745.0
Tax Benefit from Stock Options	7.0	83.0	428.0	–	–	–	–	–
Other Operating Activities	(18.0)	19.0	50.0	53.0	73.0	398.0	1,040.0	1,189.0
Change in Acc. Receivable	(201.0)	(8.0)	(121.0)	(357.0)	(385.0)	(785.0)	(939.0)	(894.0)
Change in Inventories	(11.0)	(45.0)	(64.0)	(105.0)	(76.0)	(163.0)	54.0	(180.0)
Change in Acc. Payable	243.0	297.0	328.0	1,611.0	1,494.0	596.0	92.0	1,815.0
Change in Unearned Rev.	–	–	–	319.0	566.0	718.0	521.0	927.0
Change in Inc. Taxes	–	–	–	–	–	–	–	–
Change in Other Net Operating Assets	88.0	124.0	349.0	(1,693.0)	(278.0)	1,679.0	(314.0)	(1,758.0)
Cash from Ops.	289.0	934.0	2,535.0	2,220.0	5,470.0	9,556.0	10,159.0	12,002.0
Capital Expenditure	(164.0)	(176.0)	(260.0)	(657.0)	(735.0)	(1,091.0)	(1,144.0)	(1,181.0)
Sale of Property, Plant, and Equipment	–	–	–	–	–	–	–	–
Cash Acquisitions	–	–	–	–	–	(220.0)	–	–
Divestitures	–	–	–	–	–	–	–	–
Sale (Purchase) of Intangible Assets	–	–	–	(28.0)	(251.0)	(108.0)	(69.0)	(60.0)
Invest. in Marketable & Equity Securt.	959.0	(1,323.0)	(2,275.0)	1,032.0	(2,312.0)	(6,760.0)	(16,147.0)	(11,434.0)
Net (Inc.) Dec. in Loans Originated/Sold	–	–	–	–	–	–	–	–
Other Investing Activities	33.0	11.0	(21.0)	10.0	49.0	(10.0)	(74.0)	(78.0)
Cash from Investing	828.0	(1,488.0)	(2,556.0)	357.0	(3,249.0)	(8,189.0)	(17,434.0)	(12,753.0)

Short Term Debt Issued	—	—	—	—	—	—	—	—
Long-Term Debt Issued	—	—	—	—	—	—	—	—
Total Debt Issued	—	—	—	—	—	—	—	—
Short Term Debt Repaid	(300.0)	—	—	—	—	—	—	—
Long-Term Debt Repaid	—	—	—	—	—	—	—	—
Total Debt Repaid	(300.0)	—	—	—	—	—	—	—
Issuance of Common Stock	53.0	427.0	543.0	318.0	365.0	483.0	475.0	772.0
Repurchase of Common Stock	(26.0)	—	—	—	—	—	—	—
Issuance of Pref. Stock	—	—	—	—	—	—	—	—
Common Dividends Paid	—	—	—	—	—	—	—	—
Total Dividends Paid	—	—	—	—	—	—	—	—
Special Dividend Paid	—	—	—	—	—	—	—	—
Other Financing Activities	27.0	—	—	6.0	374.0	633.0	188.0	352.0
Cash from Financing	127.0	127.0	543.0	324.0	739.0	1,116.0	663.0	1,124.0
Net Change in Cash	1,144.0	(427.0)	522.0	2,901.0	2,960.0	2,523.0	(6,612.0)	373.0
Supplemental Items								
Cash Interest Paid	20.0	10.0	NA	NA	NA	NA	NA	NA
Cash Taxes Paid	45.0	(7.0)	17.0	194.0	863.0	1,267.0	2,997.0	3,427.0
Levered Free Cash Flow	84.6	510.1	1,333.9	1,669.1	2,761.4	5,257.4	6,807.5	7,206.5
Unlevered Free Cash Flow	89.6	512.0	1,333.9	1,669.1	2,761.4	5,257.4	6,807.5	7,206.5
Change in Net Working Capital	(125.0)	(328.0)	(388.0)	(596.0)	(666.0)	(756.0)	51.0	680.0
Net Debt Issued	NA	NA	NA	NA	NA	NA	NA	NA
Filing Date	Dec-01-2005	Dec-29-2006	Nov-15-2007	Nov-05-2008	Jan-25-2010	Jan-25-2010	Jan-25-2010	Jan-25-2010
Restatement Type	NC	RS	RS	NC	RSA	RSA	RSA	O
Calculation Type	REP	REP	REP	REP	REP	REP	REP	LTM

Source: Company 10-K, Capital IQ, and author calculations.

- Would the company be able to continue meeting its obligations if its business turned down sharply?

Exhibit 4.10 provides a condensed format that can help answer these questions. At the top is basic cash flow, defined as net income (excluding noncash components), depreciation, and deferred income taxes. The various uses of cash are deducted in order, from least to most **discretionary**.

In difficult times, when a company must cut back on various expenditures to conserve cash, management faces many difficult choices. A key objective is to avoid damage to the company's long-term health. Financial flexibility, as captured by the presentation in Exhibit 4.10, is critical to meeting this objective.

Wal-Mart Stores, the world's largest retailer, exhibited exceptional financial flexibility in the fiscal year ended January 31, 2010. Cash generated by operations, at a robust $26.2 billion, precluded any need to borrow or issue stock to pay for the company's ambitious $12.2 billion capital

EXHIBIT 4.10 Wal-Mart Stores, Inc.

Analysis of Financial Flexibility Fiscal Period ending Jan-31-2010 ($000 omitted)	
Basic Cash Flow (1)	*$ 21,881.0*
Change in Adjusted Working Capital (2)	*4,368.0*
Operating Cash flow	*26,249.0*
Capital Expenditures	*(12,184.0)*
Discretionary Cash Flow	*14,065.0*
Total Dividends Paid	(4,217.0)
Other Investing Activities	564.0
Cash flow before financing	*10,412.0*
Net change in long-term debt (3)	(833.0)
Net change in short-term debt	(1,033.0)
Net issuance of common stock	(7,276.0)
Other	*638.0*
Net Change in Cash	*$ 632.0*

(1) Includes net income, depreciation, and amortization, deferred income taxes, and other
(2) Excludes cash and notes payable
(3) Includes capital lease obligations
Source: Company 10-K, Capital IQ, and author calculations.

spending program. Internally generated funds also covered the company's $4.2 billion of dividends. Instead of going to the capital markets to raise money, Wal-Mart achieved net reductions in its long-term and short-term debt, along with a net retirement of $7.3 billion of common stock.

Wal-Mart's ability to self-finance its expansion is a great advantage. At times, new financing becomes painfully expensive, as a function of high interest rates or depressed stock prices. During the credit crunches that occasionally befall the business world, external financing is unavailable at any price.

Underlying Wal-Mart's lack of dependence on external funds is a highly profitable discount store business. If this engine were to slow down for a time, as a result of an economic contraction or increased competitive pressures, the company would have two choices. It could reduce its rate of store additions and profit-enhancing investments in technology, or it could become more dependent on external financing. The former approach could further impair profitability, while the latter option would earmark a greater portion of Wal-Mart's EBITDA for interest and dividends. Loss of financial flexibility, in short, leads to further loss of financial flexibility.

If a corporation's financial strain becomes acute, the board of directors may take the comparatively extreme step of cutting or eliminating the dividend. (About the only measures more extreme than elimination of the dividend are severe retrenchment, entailing a sell-off of core assets to generate cash, and cessation of interest payments, or default.) Reducing the dividend is a step that corporations try very hard to avoid, for fear of losing favor with investors and consequently suffering an increase in cost of capital. Boards sometimes go so far as to borrow to maintain a dividend at its existing rate. This tactic cannot continue over an extended period, lest interest costs rise while internal cash generation stagnates, ultimately leading to insolvency.

Notwithstanding the lengths to which corporations sometimes go to preserve dividends, reducing the dividend must be viewed as a potential means of maintaining financial flexibility in a period of depressed earnings. After all, the term *discretionary,* applied to the cash flow that remains available after operating expenses and capital expenditures, emphasizes that dividends are not contractual payments, but disbursed at the board's discretion. When preservation of the dividend jeopardizes a company's financial well-being, shareholders may actually urge the board to cut the **payout** as a means of enhancing the stock value over the longer term.

To gauge the safety of the dividend, analysts can calculate the margin by which discretionary cash flow covers it. In Wal-Mart's case, the ratio is an extremely comfortable $14.065 billion ÷ $4.217 billion = 3.34X. In fact, if Wal-Mart had earned a zero profit for the year, it still would have covered its dividend. Depreciation alone, at $7.157 billion (not shown in Exhibit 4.10), exceeded dividends.

Wal-Mart's degree of financial flexibility is exceptional. A modest drop in the net income of many other companies would reduce their discretionary cash flow below the level of planned dividend payments. These companies typically have an additional cushion, however, in the form of potential cut-backs in their capital budgets. A retailer could not only reduce the pace of store additions but also defer planned refurbishment of existing stores. The latter measure, though, could cut into future competitiveness. Retailers find that their sales drop off if their stores start to look tired. Similarly, an indus-trial company can lose its competitive edge if it drops back to maintenance-level capital spending for any extended period. This is the amount required just to keep existing plant and equipment in good working order, with no expenditures for adding to capacity or modernizing facilities to enhance productivity. Analysts, by the way, should seek independent confirmation of the figure that management cites as the maintenance level, possibly from an engineer familiar with the business. Companies may exaggerate the ex-tent to which they can reduce capital spending to conserve cash in the event of a downturn.

A final factor in assessing financial flexibility is the change in adjusted working capital. Unlike conventional working capital (current assets minus current liabilities), this figure excludes notes payable, as well as cash and short-term investments. In Exhibit 4.10, the former is part of the net change in short-term debt, while the period's increase or decrease in cash is treated as a residual in the analysis of financial flexibility.

For Wal-Mart, the fiscal year's adjusted working capital requirement represented a much smaller ($4.368 billion) use of funds than capital ex-penditures. In general, a company's inventories and receivables expand as sales grow over time. A company with a strong balance sheet can fund much of that cash need by increasing its trade payables (credit extended by vendors). External financing may be required, however, if accumulation of unsold goods causes inventories to rise disproportionately to sales. Similarly, if customers begin paying more slowly than formerly, receivables can widen the gap between working capital requirements and trade credit availability. The resulting deterioration in credit quality measures (see Chapter 13), in turn, may cause vendors to reduce the amount of credit they are willing to provide. Once again, loss of financial flexibility can feed on itself.

IN DEFENSE OF SLACK

Conditions are tough enough when credit is scarce, either because of gen-eral conditions in the financial markets or as a result of deterioration in a company's debt quality measures. Sometimes the situation is much worse, as a company finds itself actually prohibited from borrowing. Bank credit agreements typically impose restrictive covenants, which may include limitations on total indebtedness (see "Projecting Financial Flexibility" in Chapter 12). Beyond a certain point, a firm bound by such covenants cannot continue borrowing to meet its obligations.

A typical consequence of violating debt covenants or striving to head off bankruptcy is that management reduces discretionary expenditures to avoid losing control. Many items that a company can cut without disrupting operations in the short run are essential to its long-term health. Advertising and research are obvious targets for cutbacks. Their benefits are visible only in future periods, while their costs are apparent in the current period. Over many years, a company that habitually scrimps on such expenditures can impair its competitiveness, thereby transforming a short-term problem into a long-term one.

Avoiding this pattern of decline is the primary benefit of financial flexibility. If during good times a company can generate positive cash flow before financing, it will not have to chop capital expenditures and other outlays that represent investments in its future. Nor, in all likelihood, will a company that maintains some **slack** be forced to eliminate its dividend under duress. The company will consequently avoid tarnishing its image in the capital markets and raising the cost of future financings.

Despite the blessings that financial flexibility confers, however, maintaining a funds cushion is not universally regarded as a wise corporate policy. The opposing view is based on a definition of *free cash flow* as "cash flow in excess of that required to fund all of a firm's projects that have positive **net present values** when **discounted** at the relevant cost of capital."[3] According to this argument, management should dividend all excess cash flow to shareholders. The only alternative is to invest it in low-return projects (or possibly even lower-return marketable securities), thereby preventing shareholders from earning fair returns on a portion of their capital. Left to their own devices, argue the proponents of this view, managers will trap cash in low-return investments because their compensation tends to be positively related to the growth of assets under their control. Therefore, management should be encouraged to remit all excess cash to shareholders. If encouragement fails to do the trick, the threat of **hostile takeover** should be employed, say those who minimize the value of financial flexibility.

The argument against retaining excess cash flow certainly sounds logical. It is supported, moreover, by numerous studies[4] indicating the tendency of companies to continue investing even after they have exhausted their good opportunities. Growing as it does out of economic theory, though, the argument must be applied judiciously in practice. Overinvestment has unquestionably led, in many industries, to prolonged periods of excess capacity, producing in turn chronically poor profitability. In retrospect, the firms involved would have served their shareholders better if they had increased their dividend payouts or repurchased stock, instead of constructing new plants. That judgment, however, benefits from hindsight. Managers may have over-invested because they believed forecasts of economic growth that ultimately proved too optimistic. Had demand grown at the expected rate, a firm that had declined to expand capacity might have been unable to maintain its market share. In the long run, failing to keep up with the scale economies achieved by more expansion-minded competitors could have harmed shareholders more than a few years of excess capacity. The financial analyst's job includes making judgments about a firm's reinvestment policies—without the benefit of hindsight—and does not consist of passively accepting the prevailing wisdom that low returns in the near term prove that an industry has no future opportunities worth exploiting.

A subtler point not easily captured by theorists is that financial flexibility can translate directly into operating flexibility. Keeping cash trapped in marketable securities can enable a firm to gain an edge over lean-and-mean competitors when tight credit conditions make it difficult to finance working capital needs. Another less obvious risk of eschewing financial flexibility is the danger of permanently losing experienced skilled workers through temporary layoffs occasioned by recessions. Productivity suffers during the subsequent recovery as a consequence of laid-off skilled employees finding permanent jobs elsewhere. It may therefore be economical to continue to run plants, thereby deliberately building up inventory, to keep valued workers on the payroll. This strategy is difficult to implement without some capability of adjusting to a sudden increase in working capital financing requirements.

CONCLUSION

Over the past four decades, the statement of cash flows has become a valuable complement to the other statements. It is invaluable in many situations where the balance sheet and income statement provide only limited insight. For example, the income statement is a dubious measure of the success of a highly leveraged company that is being managed to minimize, rather than maximize, reported profits. Similarly, it is largely irrelevant whether the balance sheet of a company with an already substantially depleted net worth shows 10 percent lower equity in the current quarter than in the previous one. The primary concern of the investor or creditor at such times is whether the company can buy enough time to solve its operating problems by continuing to meet its near-term obligations.

The cash flow statement does more than enrich the analysis of companies encountering risks and opportunities that the income statement and balance sheet are not designed to portray. It also helps to identify the life cycle categories into which companies fit. At all stages of development, financial flexibility is essential to meeting the types of challenges that typically arise. The cash flow statement is the best tool for measuring flexibility, which, contrary to a widely held view, is not merely a security blanket for squeamish investors. In the hands of aggressive but prudent management, a cash flow cushion can enable a company to sustain essential long-term investment spending when competitors are forced to cut back.

Three

A Closer Look at Profits

What Is Profit?

Profits hold an exalted place in the business world and in economic theory. The necessity of producing profits imposes order and discipline on business organizations. It fosters cost-reducing innovations, which in turn promote the efficient use of scarce resources. The profit motive also encourages savings and risk taking, two indispensable elements of economic development. Finally, profitability is a yardstick by which businesspeople can measure their achievements and justify their claims to compensation.

In view of all these essential economic functions, one might suppose that users of financial statements would have long since devised a universally agreed-upon definition of profit. This is the case, however, only at the following, extremely rudimentary level:

$$Profit = Revenue - Costs$$

Defining profit in such a manner merely stirs up questions, however: What is revenue? Which costs count? Or, more precisely, which costs count now, and which count later? Because these questions can be answered in many different ways, countless definitions of profit are in common use. For analysts of financial statements, the most important distinction to understand is between bona fide profits and accounting profits.

BONA FIDE PROFITS VERSUS ACCOUNTING PROFITS

In defining **bona fide profits**, the simple formula, revenue minus costs, represents a useful starting point. When calculating this kind of profit, the analyst must take care to consider only genuine revenues and to deduct all relevant costs. A nonexhaustive list of costs includes labor, materials, occupancy, services purchased, depreciation of equipment, and taxes. No matter how meticulously the analyst carries out these computations, however, no calculation of profit can be satisfactory unless it passes a litmus test:

After a company earns a bona fide profit, its owners are wealthier than they were beforehand.

To underscore the point, there can be no bona fide profit without an increase in wealth. Bona fide profits are the only kind of profits that truly matter in financial analysis.

As for accounting profits, generally accepted accounting principles (GAAP) define voluminous rules for calculating them with extraordinary precision. For financial analysts, however, the practical definition of an *accounting profit* is simple:

An accounting profit is whatever the accounting rules say it is.

If, during a stated interval, a business adds nothing to its owners' wealth, but the accounting rules state that it has earned a profit, that is good enough. An accounting profit that reflects no genuine increase in wealth is certainly sufficient for many stock market investors. They cheerfully assign a price-earnings multiple to any number that a reputable accounting firm waves its magic wand over and declares to be a profit.

WHAT IS REVENUE?

Suppose, for example, that an entrepreneur launches a restaurant-franchising business. The fictitious Salsa Meister International does not operate any Salsa Meister restaurants. It merely sells franchises to other entrepreneurs and collects franchise fees.

The franchised restaurants, sad to say, consistently lose money. That fact has no bearing on Salsa Meister International's accounting profit, however. The restaurants' operations are not part of Salsa Meister International, their revenues are not its revenues, and their costs are not its costs. Salsa Meister International's income consists entirely of franchise fees, which it earns by rendering the franchisees such services as developing menus, providing accounting systems, training restaurant employees, and creating advertising campaigns.

An astute analyst will ask how money-losing franchisees come up with cash to pay fees. The diagram in Exhibit 5.1 answers this riddle. Salsa Meister International sells stock to the public and then lends the proceeds to the franchisees. The franchisees send the cash right back to Salsa Meister

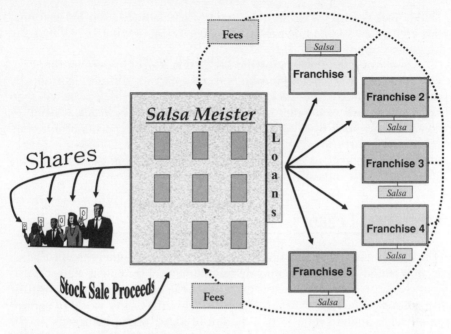

EXHIBIT 5.1 Turning Stock Market Proceeds into Revenue

International under the rubric of fees. Salsa Meister International gratefully accepts the fees, which exceed the modest costs of running a corporate headquarters, and renames them revenue.

According to GAAP, Salsa Meister International has earned a profit. Investors apply a price-earnings multiple to the accounting profit. On the strength of that valuation, the company goes forward with its next public stock offering. Once again, the proceeds finance the payment of fees by franchisees, whose numbers have meanwhile increased in connection with the Salsa Meister chain's expansion into new regions. Accounting profits rise, and the cycle of relabeling stock market proceeds, first as fees and finally as earnings, starts all over again.

The astute analyst is troubled, however. Cutting through the form of the transactions to the substance, it is clear that Salsa Meister International's wealth has not increased. Cash has simply traveled from the shareholders to the company, to the franchisees, and then back to the company, undergoing a few name changes along the way.

Merely circulating funds, it is clear, does not increase wealth. If Jack hands Jill a dollar, which she promptly hands right back to him, neither party is better off after the so-called transaction than before it. By definition, neither Jack nor Jill has earned a bona fide profit. Salsa Meister International has not earned a bona fide profit either, regardless of what GAAP may say about accounting profits.

Sooner or later, investors will come to this realization. When that happens, the company will lose its ability to manufacture accounting profits by raising new funds in the stock market. Salsa Meister's stock price will then fall to its intrinsic value—zero. Investors will suffer heavy losses, which they could have avoided by asking whether the company's reported profits truly reflected increases in wealth. Moreover, the investors will continue making similar mistakes unless they begin to understand that bona fide profits sometimes differ radically from accounting profits.

WHICH COSTS COUNT?

The willingness to take accounting profits at something other than face value is an essential element of genuinely useful financial statement analysis. It is likewise imperative that analysts exercise care in deciding what to substitute for a GAAP definition of profit. Once they leave the GAAP world of agreed-upon rules, analysts enter a free market of ideas, where numerous parties hawk competing versions of earnings.

Many of the variations hang on the question of which costs to deduct in deriving the most analytically informative definition of earnings. While some of the popular variants offer insight into knotty problems of financial statement analysis, others have the opposite effect of obscuring the facts. Many issuers of financial statements attempt to exploit dissatisfaction with GAAP by encouraging analysts to adopt earnings measures that make their own profits appear higher than either their accounting profits or their bona fide profits.

The archetype for most of today's alternative earnings measures is a version that adds back depreciation. As far back as 1930, an investment expert urged investors to ignore accounting-based earnings in the following words:

> Textbooks will advise the investor to look for earnings figures which give effect to depreciation charges. But depreciation, after all, is a purely accounting item, and can be adjusted, within limits, to show such net earnings as are desired. Therefore it would seem preferable for the investor to obtain, if possible, earnings before depreciation, and to make his own estimate of depreciation in arriving at approximate net earnings.[1]

Observe that the author does not dispute the relevance of depreciation to the calculation of earnings. Rather, he objects that they are too malleable.[2] The issuer of the statements can raise or lower its reported earnings simply by using its latitude to assume shorter or longer average lives for its depreciable assets.

It is fair to assume, in the case of financial statements that companies present to potential investors, that "such net earnings as are desired" are higher than the company's bona fide profits. Therefore, the necessary adjustment is to *increase* depreciation and thereby *reduce* earnings. The author agrees with today's boosters of alternative earnings measures that proper analysis requires adjustments to reported income, but he is very far from urging analysts to ignore depreciation altogether.

Promoters of many companies with negligible reported earnings, on the other hand, are not bashful about urging investors to disregard depreciation. This audacious assault on the very foundations of **accrual accounting** draws its inspiration from the world of privately owned real estate, where the logic of managing a public company is turned upside down. Instead of exploiting every bit of latitude in the accounting rules to maximize reported earnings, private owners of real estate strive to minimize reported income and, by extension, income taxes. Accordingly, when a private investor acquires a building (a depreciable asset) and the land that it sits on (which is not depreciable), she typically attributes as large a portion of the purchase price as possible to the building. That treatment maximizes the depreciation expense and minimizes the owner's taxes.

Let us suppose that annual rental revenue on the building offsets the landlord's out-of-pocket expenses, such as maintenance, repairs, property taxes, and interest on the property's mortgage. The owner, in other words, is breaking even, before taking into account the noncash expense of depreciation. Including depreciation, the property shows an annual loss, which reduces the owner's income tax bill. Let us also assume that after a few years, the owner sells the land and building. After paying off the mortgage balance, she walks away with more cash than she originally invested, thanks to the tendency of real estate values to rise over time.

Recapping the real estate investor's experience, she has sold the property for more than she paid. Her gain has not been reduced along the way by net cash outlays on operations. On the contrary, the tax savings produced by the noncash depreciation expense have contributed to the rise in her wealth. The key point is that the investor is wealthier than she was before she bought the building. According to our definition, she has realized a bona fide profit, despite reporting losses every single year. Adding to the paradox is the investor's success in selling the property for a gain. Economic theory states that an investment has value only because it produces profits. By extension, the value can increase only if the profits increase. In this instance, however, the property's value rose despite an uninterrupted flow of red ink.

Naturally, these curious events have a rational explanation. The rate at which the tax code allows owners to write off property overstates actual wear and tear. Over the typically very long life of a building, it may get depreciated several times over for tax purposes. The disparity between economic depreciation and tax-based depreciation may be viewed as a subsidy for socially productive investment. Alternatively, it can be seen as a testament to the real estate operators' influence over the legislators who write the tax code.

Either way, a conventional income statement provides a cockeyed view of the profitability of buying and selling buildings. A closer approximation of reality ignores the depreciation expense altogether and focuses on **cash-on cash-profit**. In the simplest terms, the owner lays out a sum at the beginning of the investment and takes out a bigger sum at the end, while also generating cash—through tax savings—during the period in which she owns the building.

HOW FAR CAN THE CONCEPT BE STRETCHED?

To a limited extent, a profitability analysis that ignores depreciation is applicable outside the world of real estate. In the broadcasting business, companies typically record depreciation and amortization expense that far exceeds physical wear and tear on assets. For example, when a company buys a radio or television station, the price reflects a comparatively small component of plant and equipment. The larger portion of the station's value derives from its exclusive right to utilize part of the broadcasting spectrum, a scarce resource that tends to become more valuable over time. Much as in the real estate illustration, the broadcaster may show perennial losses after depreciation, yet realize a handsome profit when it finally sells the station. Instead of analyzing broadcasters on the basis of conventional net income, it is appropriate for analysts to focus on **broadcast cash flow**, usually defined as:

operating income + depreciation and amortization + corporate overhead

(A more meticulous calculation of broadcast cash flow deducts cash outlays for acquisition of new programming while adding back the amortization of the cost of previously acquired programming; both items can be found on the statement of cash flows.)

Clearly, the deliberate neglect of depreciation is an analytical option that should be used with discretion. In many industries, fixed assets consist mainly of machines or vehicles that really do diminish in value through use. The major risk of analytical error does not arise from the possibility that reported depreciation expense will substantially exceed economic depreciation, but the reverse.

Through a false analogy with real estate and broadcasting, any marginally unprofitable company in a capital-intensive business can declare itself to be in the black. The trick is simply to proclaim that analysts should no longer consider depreciation. Supposed earnings generated in such fashion qualify as neither accounting profits nor bona fide profits, however.

CONCLUSION

Despite the critical importance of measuring profit, businesspeople cannot produce a definition that is satisfactory in every situation. Even the simple formula of revenue minus costs founders on the malleability of accounting-based revenues and costs. As Chapters 6 and 7 demonstrate, these basic measures of corporate performance are far too subject to manipulation and distortion to be taken at face value. Also, our brief discussions of real estate and leveraged buyouts show that net earnings can be calculated in perfect accordance with GAAP yet bear little relation to an investor's rate of return.

In light of such observations, financial analysts must walk a fine line. On the one hand, they must not lose touch with economic reality by hewing to accounting orthodoxy. On the other hand, they must not accept the version of reality that seekers of cheap capital would like to foist on them. Analysts should be skeptical of claims that a business's alleged costs are mere accounting conventions and that anyone who believes otherwise is a fuddy-duddy.

Revenue Recognition

Experience teaches that it can be dangerous to accept reported revenues at face value, even if they have been audited. Many corporations employ highly aggressive recognition practices that comply with GAAP yet distort the underlying economic reality. Sometimes, executives hell-bent on making their numbers will cross the line into fraudulent revenue recognition. Often, outward signs of exceptional success indicate, in reality, a high probability of downward revisions of previously reported revenues. Under intense pressure to maintain their stock prices, companies characterized by extremely rapid sales growth seem particularly prone to take liberties.

CHANNEL-STUFFING IN THE DRUG BUSINESS

On April 3, 2002, Bristol-Myers Squibb shares plummeted by as much as 14 percent in after-hours trading after the company said first-quarter earnings from operations would be $0.44 to $0.47 a share. Analysts surveyed by Thomson Financial/First Call had been expecting $0.56. For the full year, said the pharmaceutical producer, earnings would drop by at least 25 percent from 2001's $2.41 a share.

In the wake of the negative surprise, Chief Executive Officer Peter Dolan assumed direct responsibility for the worldwide medicines business. The previous head of the unit left the company. Two weeks later, the company announced that its chief financial officer would step down as well.

The explanation for the sudden drop in projected earnings was that in 2001 Bristol-Myers gave wholesalers discounts to induce them to buy its products at a much faster rate than necessary to fill prescriptions at pharmacies. That boosted revenues for certain drugs in 2001, as sales to wholesalers ran above end demand by consumers. In 2002, however, instead of reordering, wholesalers worked down their bloated inventories to supply their pharmacy customers. Bristol-Myers's sales to wholesalers consequently slackened. Dolan told analysts and investors that the company was cutting back shipments and that 2002 profits would depend on how quickly the wholesalers' inventory levels could be reduced.

Channel-stuffing is a security analysts' term for the financial reporting gimmick that Bristol-Myers employed to accelerate future revenues to the current period. Drug wholesalers were happy to hold more inventory than they needed, as long as the discounts they received were large enough to cover the related **carrying costs.** Expiration dates for the drugs they took into inventory were typically about two years in the future, so there was little risk that the products would lose their value while sitting in the wholesalers' warehouses. Furthermore, wholesalers that bought extra drugs at the current price stood to gain from subsequent increases in the retail price by the manufacturer. The price hikes would allow them to take higher markups on inventory purchased at the old price.

Why, though, would Bristol-Myers bother to stuff its wholesale distribution channels, especially considering that the discounts represented sales dollars forgone and never to be recovered? Wholesalers could absorb only so much redundant inventory. Sooner or later, the scheme would have to end, making it apparent that the company had overstated earnings by borrowing sales from future periods.

That is exactly what happened to Bristol-Myers. On March 10, 2003, the company restated its financial statements for 1999 through 2001 to correct "errors and inappropriate accounting." The company chopped earnings from continuing operations by about $900 million, partially offset by an upward revision for 2002. Earlier, the company had told investors that its planned restatement would merely shift reported revenues from earlier periods to 2002 and 2003. As it turned out, however, the company deleted $2.5 billion from the earlier years and booked only $1.9 billion in the later years, explaining that the disappearance of $0.6 billion was "primarily due to changes in accruals from sales returns, rebates,"[1] and accounting changes. Bristol-Myers stock, which had reached a peak of $70.37 at the end of 2000, closed at $22.51. Even after this damage to investors, Bristol-Myers was not done with its revisions. On March 16, 2004, the company restated its 1999 through 2002 earnings and its 2003 earnings upward.

Background of a Doomed Scheme

The stock's precipitous decline during 2001 and 2002 helped to explain why Bristol-Myers manipulated its earnings in a manner that was sure to prove unsustainable. Along with other pharmaceutical producers, Bristol-Myers was feeling profit pressures due to difficulties in developing new drugs to replace sales of products on which patent protection was expiring. The company had not generated a single major drug from billions of research dollars since the 1989 merger of Bristol-Myers and Squibb. Management's biggest hope, the hypertension drug Vanlev, failed to obtain Food and Drug Administration approval in 2000 after adverse side effects were discovered. In 2001, the company suffered embarrassment when it agreed to pay $2 billion for cancer drug Erbitux, a discovery of biotechnology company ImClone Systems that later failed to obtain Food and Drug Administration approval.

In 1996, then-CEO Charles Heimbold Jr. promised investors 12 percent annual earnings growth through 2000. That target proved elusive as industry competition escalated and a low-priced generic alternative threatened sales of a top-selling Bristol-Myers cancer drug. Following a late 1999 meeting, Heimbold replaced Donald Haydon Jr., the head of the medicines group. According to past and present company executives interviewed by the *Wall Street Journal*,[2] Haydon was known for speaking candidly about Bristol-Myers's declining sales prospects. Consequently, his reassignment was taken as a message that executives must meet their sales quotas at all costs. At that point, the medicines group began offering wholesalers discounts to induce them to order at higher levels than expected pharmacy prescriptions justified.

In addition, according to the interviewed executives, Bristol-Myers started to pump up the bottom line by taking into earnings portions of restructuring reserves created in earlier periods. This was contrary to Securities and Exchange Commission (SEC) accounting policy, reiterated in a 1999 bulletin, requiring that such reserves be used exclusively for specified purposes and prohibiting them from being taken into earnings in small amounts over time. Also suspect was Bristol-Myers's repeated practice of establishing restructuring reserves that exactly equaled gains on asset sales. In addition, the executives said, the company frequently added a penny or two to earnings per share (EPS) through gains on sales of small product lines, without reporting the divestments or highlighting them as one-time events. The SEC frowned on withholding information about such transactions on claims of immateriality and stated that even if one small transaction could be legitimately ignored, failing to disclose a number of them could be materially misleading. Finally, some of the interviewed executives contended that in mid-2001, Bristol-Myers overstated the portion of its $7.8 billion acquisition of DuPont's drug business that was attributable to in-process research and development and therefore qualified for immediate write-off under GAAP. The SEC had long claimed that companies were overvaluing in-process R&D to minimize the amount of goodwill that might cause a subsequent write-down. Executives interviewed by the *Wall Street Journal* contended that the company overstated the in-process R&D write-off to create the possibility of reversing portions of it in the future, as yet one more way to tweak reported earnings.

Company officials strenuously denied that its accounting policies were geared toward managing earnings or, by extension, maximizing the compensation of senior executives whose compensation was linked to the company's stock price. Bristol-Myers's March 10, 2003, write-down, however, came in the context of accelerating SEC and Federal Bureau of Investigation inquiries into senior management's role in the improper accounting.

In August 2004, Bristol-Myers agreed to pay $150 million to settle SEC charges of accounting fraud. This was followed in June 2005 by a $300 million settlement of Justice Department charges that also arose from inventory manipulation. The company further agreed that CEO Dolan would surrender the title of chairman and pledged to endow a chair in business ethics at Seton Hall University Law School. Christopher J. Christie, the U.S. attorney in Newark who was subsequently elected governor of New Jersey, said the scheme reflected a corporate culture that emphasized higher sales at all costs. "These people had knowledge which they should have disclosed to the investing public, which they did not," Christie commented. "It's not a channel-stuffing case. It's a failure-to-disclose case."[3]

Detecting Excessive Inventory

Not everyone was caught entirely off guard by Bristol-Myers's revelation of clogged-up distribution channels. Several days before the company's April 3, 2002, announcement, Merrill Lynch analyst Steven Tighe wrote that the inventory in the wholesale distribution chain for the company's top 10 core retail brands could total $500 million to $800 million.[4] That would approximate 2.42 times average weekly sales, an abnormally high level. Tighe estimated that the resulting sales deceleration would penalize Bristol-Myers earnings per share by $0.02 to $0.03 in 2002's first quarter.

The analyst derived his estimate of wholesale inventories for Bristol Myers's 10 major drugs, representing 50 percent of pharmaceutical revenues, from price and prescription statistics of IMS Health, a vendor of health care data. For example, IMS reported that pharmacy-level sales of Pravachol, a cholesterol-reducing drug, grew by 8 percent in 2001 and the retail price increased by 6 percent. Bristol-Myers reported a 21 percent sales gain for the year, implying a gap of 7 percent versus the sell-through at pharmacies.[5] The largest such sales disparity, amounting to $1.7 billion, involved Glucophage, an oral antidiabetic. According to IMS, prescriptions declined by 8 percent, offsetting an 8 percent retail price increase, yet Bristol-Myers recorded an 18 percent sales gain. Tighe reckoned that Glucophage wholesale inventories equaled a staggering 78 percent of his estimated 2002 sales for the brand.

It turned out that the inventory bloat and resulting earnings impact were even greater than Tighe's analysis suggested. Still, the detection of channel-stuffing was an alarm bell for the impending stock price decline. More impressively still, UBS Warburg analyst C. J. Sylvester warned of excess inventory on the order of $550 million in September 2001, half a year before the company dropped its bombshell.

Unfortunately for most users of financial statements, annual subscriptions to the data required for this sort of analysis, provided by companies such as IMS and NDCHealth, run into tens of thousands of dollars. The Bristol-Myers Squibb case study nevertheless illustrates the value of testing a company's reported earnings against independently provided information. Publicly available statistics for sales in certain industries, such as automobiles and casinos, can provide a helpful check.

A SECOND TAKE ON EARNINGS

What I like to do is get in the car and drive around and do drive-by shootings. You can haul someone out of their car and beat on them and steal their money and their car. It's kind of amusing that you have that ability.[6]

These are not the words of a career criminal, but of one of the many devotees of *Grand Theft Auto 3*, a video game produced by Take-Two Interactive Software. Another way that players score in the hugely popular game is to have sex with a prostitute, then murder her and steal her money. Other popular strategies consist of shooting random pedestrians and bludgeoning them with a baseball bat. Such features have earned *Grand Theft Auto 3* the distinction of being banned in Australia.

Less brutal, but nonimaginary, misdeeds won Take-Two a place in the annals of financial misrepresentation. The story began to unfold after the company's share price more than doubled in less than six months. Even at that, some experts considered the stock undervalued relative to industry peers such as Electronic Arts and Activision, giving rise to speculation that Take-Two might be an attractive candidate for acquisition by Microsoft.

Near-term dreams of continued upward momentum in the stock were shattered on December 14, 2001. Take-Two plunged by $4.72 to $10.33, a 31 percent drop, on rumors that the company might have to restate its earnings. The rumors proved on the mark. Take-Two announced on December 17 that it would restate its earnings for the first three quarters of the fiscal year ending October 31, 2001. According to management, the adjustment arose because the company recorded revenue on some games it sold to "certain independent third-party distributors" but which were later returned to or repurchased by Take-Two. The company estimated that earnings per share for fiscal 2000 would be restated from $0.88 to $0.75–$0.77.

Surprisingly to some observers, Take-Two's stock rose by $3.23 to $13.56, a 31 percent gain, on December 17. To short seller Marc Cohodes of Rocker Partners, the company's announcement was evidence that it was relying on accounting gimmickry. As he characterized it, Take-Two had been selling products to itself and including those sales in its revenues.[7] President Paul Eibeler, however, complained that the restatements were overshadowing Take-Two's "underlying strength"[8] and that the company's prospects for fiscal 2002 were strong. Some Wall Street analysts shared that view. Wedbush Morgan Securities' Miguel Iribarren reiterated his buy recommendation with a one-year price target of $25. Commerce Capital Markets' Richard Zimmerman confirmed his strong buy with a target of $20.

For the next few months, the financial reporting news got worse. On January 22, 2002, Take-Two announced that it would postpone the release of its fourth quarter and fiscal year-end results. The Nasdaq stock market promptly halted trading in Take-Two's shares. On February 12, the company restated its fiscal year 2001 earnings per share from $0.88 to $0.23, while also slightly reducing its reported per-share loss for the first nine months of fiscal 2002 from ($0.11) to ($0.09). In addition, Take-Two disclosed that the SEC had launched an investigation of its accounting. The following day, another classic red flag appeared, as the company's chief financial officer, Albert Pastino, resigned.

Despite these adverse developments, when trading in Take-Two shares resumed on February 15, some analysts remained upbeat. Morgan Keegan's Bob DeLean commented, "On the negative side, management has no credibility and you have historically aggressive accounting. But going forward, they are having success with a couple of big hits and the balance sheet is going to look a lot better."[9] He rated the stock outperform, with a six-month target of $30–$35. Rocker Partners' Cohodes remained the skeptic, arguing, "The numbers have been made up, that we know for sure. Everything else is speculation."[10]

In this instance, contrary to the lesson taught by many other cases of financial misreporting, it paid to accept the discredited management's assurances that the company's business prospects looked bright. Analyst Iribarren's target of $20 by December 2002 was achieved in April of that year, with the Standard & Poor's 500 Index nearly unchanged over the period. The lower end of DeLean's six-month target of $30–$35 by August 2002 was likewise reached, albeit tardily, in November 2002, notwithstanding a 15 percent drop in the S&P.

All this good news for shareholders came despite the fact that the revenue recognition misreporting ultimately turned out to be more extensive than the company disclosed in 2002. On January 31, 2004, Take-Two announced it would restate earnings back as far as fiscal 1999. The latest discrepancies involved the recording of reserves for price concessions.

On June 9, 2005, Take-Two agreed to a penalty of $7.5 million to settle SEC charges of accounting fraud. Former Chairman Ryan Brant consented to a penalty of $500,000 and disgorgement and prejudgment interest of $3.1 million, representing bonuses based on the originally reported earnings. Former Chief Operating Officer Larry Muller and former Chief Financial Officer James David Jr. also agreed to penalties and disgorgement of bonuses.

None of the parties admitted or denied the allegations in the SEC's complaint, but those allegations were as disturbing, in their own way, as descriptions of mayhem in *Grand Theft Auto 3*. The commission charged that Take-Two systematically booked revenue from approximately 180 separate so-called parking arrangements. At or around the end of fiscal years or quarters, the commission contended, the company shipped hundreds of thousands of video games to distributors who were under no obligation to pay for them, fraudulently booked the shipments as if they were sales, then accepted returns of the products in later periods. In many instances, the SEC claimed, management created fraudulent invoices to disguise the returns as "purchases of assorted product."[11] Furthermore, according to the complaint, Take-Two improperly recognized revenues on games that were still being manufactured and therefore could not be shipped. Finally, the SEC charged, the company accounted improperly for the acquisition of two video game publishers and failed to establish proper reserves for reductions in the retail prices of its games. Reminiscent of the treatment of innocent bystanders in the company's most notorious game, GAAP received the equivalent of a beating with a baseball bat at the hands of Take-Two's management.

An Income versus Cash Disparity

Encouragingly for users of financial statements, managers who improperly recognize revenues are often betrayed by the number trails they create. Consider how the financial statements of one computer manufacturer telegraphed future problems in this area. Shortly before Kendall Square Research's October 1993 revision of its previously reported earnings, a research service known as *Financial Statement Alert* warned that the company was recognizing revenues too early.

Kendall Square reported $45.4 million in revenue in the first six quarters after it went public in March 1992. Loren Kellogg, copublisher of *Financial*

Statement Alert, compared this income statement information with a figure from the company's statement of cash flows. Over the same 18-month period, Kendall Square's "cash received from customers" was just $25.7 million. Kellogg viewed the $19.7 million disparity between the two numbers as evidence that a large proportion of sales being booked by Kendall were dubious.

The warning proved prescient. Less than a month after Kellogg's analysis was reported in the *Wall Street Journal,* Kendall Square disclosed that its third-quarter 1993 revenues would be "substantially below" securities analysts' expectations. In lieu of earnings per share of $0.11 (the consensus forecast according to the forecast-tracking firm of Zacks Investment Research), the company said that it would report a loss. Additionally, Kendall Square delayed the release of its third-quarter earnings and announced the resignation of its senior vice president and treasurer, who had joined the company only a month earlier. All these developments, by the way, were classic indications of serious corporate problems.

Revenue recognition controversies were central to Kendall Square's difficulties. The company indicated that although third-quarter shipments were "generally in line with expectations," there was some question about the proper amount of revenue to recognize from the shipments. Jeffry Canin, an analyst at Salomon Brothers, speculated about a possible area of disagreement within the company. It was possible, he suggested, that some officials objected to counting as revenue rebates that might have been given to customers who agreed to upgrade to Kendall's next generation of computers. Smith Barney Shearson analyst Barry Bosak proposed the possibility that Kendall Square had been hurt by its reliance on sales to universities. A number of these institutions, which were in turn dependent on diminishing government funding, proved unable to pay. Indeed, some critics insinuated that Kendall Square had made research grants to educational institutions as quid pro quos for orders, a charge that management denied.

At any rate, Kendall Square's troubles continued, as auditor Price Waterhouse withdrew its clean opinion from the company's 1992 financial statements. Management revealed that the year's sales figure, originally reported as $20.5 million, included $4.2 million of "improperly recognized" revenue. Unaudited numbers for the first half of 1993 would also require restatement, the company added.

In the wake of these announcements, Kendall Square demoted and then fired its president, its chief financial officer, and the head of its technical products group. The company's acting chief executive officer announced that henceforth, Kendall Square would concentrate on building computers to order instead of creating inventories in anticipation of orders. That reform was likely to reduce problems associated with revenue recognition, but by the time it was introduced, the damage to users of financial statements was substantial. At $7^1/_2$, the company's stock price was down by about 70 percent from its peak three months earlier.[12]

ASTRAY ON LAYAWAY

On August 9, 2000, Wal-Mart Stores reported a 28 percent year-over-year increase in net income for its fiscal second quarter ending July 31. At $0.36, earnings per share (diluted) were up by 29 percent. Sales rose by a healthy 20 percent, climbing 5 percent at Wal-Mart units open for more than one year.

In light of these results, which one analyst characterized as "a very good quarter," the discount chain's share price might have been expected to rise. At the very least, investors would have expected the stock to hold steady, given that the EPS increase was in line with Wall Street analysts' consensus forecast, as reported by First Call/Thomson Financial. As it turned out, however, Wal-Mart's shares fell by $4.375 to $53.125. That represented an 8 percent decline on a day on which the Dow Jones Industrial Average changed only modestly (down 0.6 percent).

Both the *Wall Street Journal*[13] and the *Bloomberg* newswire[14] linked the paradoxical drop in Wal-Mart's stock to an accounting change that was expected to reduce the following (third) quarter's earnings. The retailer's management advised analysts to lower their earnings per share estimates for the August-to-October period by 1.5 to 2 cents, to reflect a shift in the company's method of accounting for layaway sales. In such transactions, customers reserve goods with down payments, then make additional payments over a specified period, receiving their merchandise when they have paid in full. Prior to the change in accounting practice, which Financial Accounting Standard (FAS) 101 made mandatory, Wal-Mart booked layaway sales as soon as it placed the merchandise on layaway. Under the new and more conservative method, the company began to recognize the sales only when customers completed the required payments and took possession of the goods.

According to one analyst, Wal-Mart's 8 percent stock price decline represented "somewhat of an overreaction." In reality, the price drop was an overreaction in its entirety. Changing the accounting method altered neither the amount of cash ultimately received by the retailer nor the timing of its receipt. The planned change in Wal-Mart's revenue recognition process therefore entailed no loss in time value of money. Lest anyone mistakenly continue to attribute economic significance to the timing of the revenue recognition, Wal-Mart explained that the small reduction in reported earnings in the third fiscal quarter would be made up in the fourth. On top of everything else, management had already announced the accounting change prior to its August 9 conference call.

An institutional portfolio manager spoke truly when he called the market's reaction to the supposed news "more confusion than anything else." If taken at face value, the press reports indicate that investors bid the shares down on so-called news that was both dated and irrelevant. Alternatively, investors may have had other reasons for driving down the shares. For one thing, store traffic declined in the three months ended July 31 from the preceding quarter's level. Additionally, German operations posted a larger loss than management had forecast. If these events were the true causes of Wal-Mart's slide, then the *Wall Street Journal* and the *Bloomberg* newswire erred in attributing the sell-off to an accounting change with no real economic impact. Either way, confusion reigned; the only question is whether it was the investors or the journalists who were confused.

RECOGNIZING MEMBERSHIP FEES

Bally Total Fitness provided another case in which questions about revenue recognition contributed to an unfavorable stock market reaction to seemingly upbeat earnings news. On July 30, 1998, the health club chain reported diluted earnings per share of $0.08, up from a year-earlier loss of $0.59. According to the *Wall Street Journal*,[15] the improved profits were "unexpectedly encouraging." They suggested that the success of the company's newer, more upscale clubs was bolstering overall performance. In the month following the earnings report, however, Bally's shares declined by 44 percent. The Dow Jones Industrial Average fell by a less severe 16 percent over the same period. In the wake of Bally's report, moreover, short sales (representing bets that the price would fall) accounted for 15 percent of all outstanding shares. During the first quarter of 1998, the company's **short interest ratio** fluctuated in a range of 3 percent to 5 percent.

Investors were unwilling to accept Bally's earnings increase at face value because of the company's growing reliance on memberships that it financed, as opposed to selling for cash. Bally's financed customers' initial membership fees, which ranged from $600 to $1,400, for up to 36 months, charging annual interest rates of 16 percent to 18 percent.[16] (Ongoing dues represented just 27.9 percent of net revenues, with approximately 90 percent of members paying an average of only about $7 a month in 1998.) On the whole, the company's reported profit margins benefited from the increase in financed memberships as a percentage of total revenues. The reported earnings, however, rested on assumptions regarding the percentage of customers who would ultimately fail to make all of the scheduled installments.

Even under the best of circumstances, a considerable portion of any health club's new members let their memberships lapse, despite paying an initial fee. As New York University accounting professor Paul Brown notes, "People have little to lose from walking away from a health-club membership. It's not a health-care plan we're talking about, or even a car, which they might need for transportation."[17]

To be sure, Bally set aside reserves for uncollectible amounts, consistent with good accounting practice. The size of the reserves, however, required judgment about the credit quality of the new members. Because financed memberships were not entirely new to Bally, management had some experience on which to base its assumptions. In addition, the company had succeeded in increasing the use of an electronic funds transfer payment option in recent years. Collection rates were higher for members whose credit cards or bank accounts were automatically charged for fees than for those billed through monthly statements. There were risks, though, in stepping up reliance on customers who needed to borrow in order to join. As in any sales situation, aggressive pursuit of new business could result in acceptance of more marginally qualified customers. On average, the newer members might prove to be less financially capable or less committed to physical fitness than the previous purchasers of financed memberships. If more members failed on their payments than management assumed, Bally would prove in hindsight to have been too aggressive in recognizing revenue and would have to rescind previously reported income.

By taking the second-quarter 1998 earnings with a grain of salt, users of financial statements were not necessarily casting aspersions on Bally's management. Rather, they were understandably applying caution in evaluating a company in a service industry historically identified with questionable revenue recognition practices. Some analysts sprang to Bally's defense following the *Wall Street Journal*'s critical article by highlighting the company's adoption of a conservative practice at the Securities and Exchange Commission staff's behest in July 1997. Previously, Bally had fully recognized initial membership fees at the time that the memberships were sold. A health club operator could abuse this approach by using high-pressure tactics to book financed memberships for individuals who were highly unlikely to keep up their payments. Outsiders relying on the financial statements would perceive a growth in revenues that must, in time, prove unsustainable. Under the new accounting treatment, Bally spread the revenues from the initial fees over the expected membership lives—36 months for sales made for cash on the barrelhead and 22 months for financed sales.

The SEC's urging of Bally to spread out its recognition of membership fees was part of a broader effort extending beyond the health club industry. There was no change in the accounting principle, namely, the matching concept. In the case of a health club, members' up-front fees represent payments for services received over the term of their membership. Club operators should therefore recognize the revenue over the period in which they render the service. During the late 1990s, the underlying theory underwent no change, but the SEC intensified its focus on membership fees after determining that some companies were interpreting the rules too liberally. Among the industries that came under increased scrutiny were the membership club retailers. In this type of operation, consumers pay up-front fees for the privilege of shopping at stores that sell discounted merchandise.

On October 19, 1998, BJ's Wholesale Club switched from immediate recognition of its annual membership fee (typically $35 for two family members) to incremental recognition of the fee over the full membership term, generally 12 months. In conjunction with the change in accounting policy, BJ's restated its net income for the fiscal first half ending August 1 to $10.4 million. That was down 64 percent from the previously reported $28.6 million. The restatement reflected a one-time charge for the accounting change's cumulative effect on preceding years, as well as a $1.1 million after-tax charge arising from a change to more conservative accounting for new-store preopening expenses.

Just a month and a half before these events, BJ's had issued a press release asserting that its practice of immediately recognizing annual membership fees was consistent with GAAP.[18] Management had also argued that no deferral was required, on the grounds that BJ's offered its members the right to cancel and receive refunds for only 90 days after enrollment. A mere 0.5 percent of members actually requested refunds. In contrast to the situation at Bally Total Fitness, moreover, membership fees represented a minor portion of BJ's revenues, 98 percent of which derived from merchandise sales.

Under GAAP, however, the general requirement was to spread membership fees over the full membership period. If a company offered refunds, it could not book *any* of the revenue until the refund period expired, unless there was a sufficiently long history to enable management to estimate future experience with reasonable confidence. At most, BJ's refund record might have entitled the company to begin booking the fees on the date that members enrolled. Spreading the revenue recognition over the membership period would have been mandatory in any case.[19]

In December 1999, the SEC staff clarified the point by issuing "Staff Accounting Bulletin No. 101—Revenue Recognition in Financial Statements" (SAB 101). The staff stated its preference that companies not book membership fees until refund privileges expired. MemberWorks, a provider of membership programs offering services and discounts in a wide range of fields including health care, personal finance, and travel, altered its accounting in response to SAB 101, effective July 1, 2000. A one-time noncash charge of $25.7 million resulted, reflecting the deferral of previously recognized membership fees.[20]

A POTPOURRI OF LIBERAL REVENUE RECOGNITION TECHNIQUES

By intensifying its enforcement of established revenue recognition rules in SAB 101, the SEC put a stop to techniques that the staff considered overly aggressive. Professional Detailing, a recruiter and manager of sales staff for pharmaceutical companies, had to stop including in revenues the reimbursements that it received from clients for placing help-wanted ads. Within a month, the company's share price fell by 31 percent. Physician & Hospital Systems & Services, a unit of National Data Corporation, abandoned its long-standing policy of booking revenues for its back-office services not merely before it completed the work, but before it mailed out bills. National Data ended the practice and took a $13.8 million one-time charge to correct the previous pumping up of revenues. First American Financial took a cumulative $55.6 million charge when it embraced the matching principle by beginning to book revenues for loan services over the loan's duration, rather than immediately.[21]

Percentage-of-Completion Method

Under certain circumstances, a company engaged in long-term contract work can book revenue before billing its customer. This result arises from GAAP's solution to a mismatch commonly observed at construction firms. A variety of service companies, defense contractors, and capital goods manufacturers come up against the same accounting issue.

Typically, the company agrees to bill its customers in several installments over the life of the contract. The billing may lag behind the company's incurring of expenses to fulfill its obligations. Without some means of correcting this mismatch, reported profit will be inappropriately high in the contract's early stages and inappropriately low in the late stages.

The percentage-of-completion method is how GAAP addresses the problem. It permits the company to recognize revenue in proportion to the amount of work completed, rather than in line with its billing. The percentage-of-completion method can rectify the mismatch but may also entail considerable subjectivity. This is particularly so when the company specializes in finding creative solutions to particular companies' unique problems, a sort of work that cannot be readily measured by engineering standards. Management can speed up revenue recognition on such contracts by making assumptions that are liberal yet difficult for the auditors to reject on objective grounds. As is generally the case with artificial acceleration, taking liberties with the percentage of completion borrows future revenues, making a surprise shortfall inevitable at some point.

Crossing the Line

In the foregoing cases, the regulators merely complained that the companies' existing revenue recognition policies painted too rosy a picture, but in other instances, management has been accused of misrepresentation. For example, in 1996, the SEC claimed that computer manufacturer Sequoia Systems and four former executives engaged in a "fraudulent scheme" aimed at inflating the company's revenue and income. According to the complaint filed in U.S. District Court in Washington, the ex-chairman and three other officials booked letters of intent as revenue, backdated some purchase orders, and granted customers special terms that Sequoia never disclosed. Furthermore, charged the SEC, the executives profited from the scheme by selling stock before a true picture of the company's financial condition emerged. The company and its former officials settled the SEC's civil charges without admitting or denying guilt.[22]

FATTENING EARNINGS WITH EMPTY CALORIES

Doughnut maker Krispy Kreme went public at $21 a share in April 2000. Its stock soared by 76 percent to $37 on the first day of trading. That put its price-earnings ratio at 78 times, more than triple the multiple on the Standard & Poor's Food Index of around 23 times.

Notwithstanding the undeniably addictive quality of its doughnuts, some analysts thought Krispy Kreme's shares had risen too high. Investors were encouraged, however, by a growth rate far in excess of the typical food company. **Same-store sales** had jumped by 14 percent in fiscal 2000 (ended January 30). The number of stores had vaulted 20 percent to 144—58 company-owned and 86 franchised—since the end of fiscal 1998. Whenever a new store was slated to launch, eager customers lined up in droves to satisfy their cravings the instant the doors opened. Propelled by consumers' sugar high, Krispy Kreme shares continued to surge, reaching $108.50 in November 2000.

The mania could not last forever. In 2003, the pace of new store openings slackened, throwing into question Krispy Kreme's valuation as a super growth stock. At this point, according to a Securities and Exchange Commission complaint released in 2009, Krispy Kreme revised its senior executive compensation plan.[23] Henceforth, officers would receive no bonuses unless the company reported earnings in each quarter that exceeded its earnings per share **guidance** by at least $0.01.

To continue to clear the bar that it set for itself, the SEC said, management began to manipulate certain expense accruals to produce EPS at least one penny above the guidance. Ultimately, Krispy Kreme strung together 13 consecutive quarters in which it exceeded that threshold. In addition, said the SEC, Krispy Kreme improperly recorded questionable transactions involving company purchases of franchised stores.

The Long Slide Begins

On May 7, 2004, the company issued a first-ever profit warning, telling investors that its earnings would be 10 percent lower than it previously expected. Krispy Kreme blamed its faltering profits on the new popularity of low-carbohydrate diets, but some analysts suspected that the real problem was overexpansion. They noted that there was no sign of carb consciousness hurting business at rival Dunkin' Donuts. Krispy Kreme shares, which had split twice in 2001, suffered a one-day, 29 percent decline on the news. Later that month, the *Wall Street Journal* detailed questionable aspects of the franchise repurchases, based on information by a person familiar with the transactions.[24]

In 2003, according to the account, Krispy Kreme began a negotiation to buy back its struggling seven-store Michigan franchise. Dough-Re-Mi reportedly owed Krispy Kreme several million dollars for franchise fees, equipment, and ingredients and was delinquent on its payments. The *Journal* reported that the parties reached a preliminary agreement in which Krispy Kreme asked its franchisee to absorb the cost of closing down two underperforming stores and to repay past-due interest. Then, according to the *Journal*'s informant, Krispy Kreme agreed to increase the purchase price by the amount of these additional costs.

Why would Krispy Kreme try to recover the store-closing costs and overdue interest, only to pay it right back? The motivation might have been to increase reported earnings. If the transaction was structured as the *Journal* stated, the extra money paid out to Dough-Re-Mi became part of an intangible asset, reacquired franchise rights, which would not amortize. That is, no scheduled, bit-by-bit write-down would reduce future earnings. On the other hand, when the very same dollars came back to Krispy Kreme, they would be recorded as interest income. In essence, according to the *Wall Street Journal*'s story, Krispy Kreme manufactured earnings by taking money out of one pocket and putting it into another.

The money given to Dough-Re-Mi to cover the closing costs also became an intangible asset, again assuming the *Journal*'s account was accurate. Had Krispy Kreme instead repurchased the franchises and then closed the stores, it would have incurred an expense. The catch is that an asset is supposed to be something that creates future economic value. Terminated stores would not seem to satisfy that definition.

Krispy Kreme's defense of its accounting was a classic of the genre. To begin with, said the company, the auditor approved its handling of the items. This was not a strong justification, judging by the many border-line actions that corporations' auditors approve every year. Second, argued Krispy Kreme, Dough-Re-Mi's interest payment was unrelated to the ac-quisition. By a remarkable coincidence, however, it occurred on the very same day, and it was deducted from Krispy Kreme's final remittance to the franchise seller.

There was yet another strange aspect to the deal. Originally, Krispy Kreme said it would pay the equivalent of $24.5 million for the Michigan franchise. Later on, the price jumped by 26 percent to $32.1 million. The company's chief financial officer claimed that the disparity arose from an ini-tially incomplete assessment of the costs of the transaction. Krispy Kreme, he said, should have included in the price the potential added costs of a promis-sory note that Dough-Re-Mi's top executive and major shareholder took in exchange for agreeing to defer his portion of the purchase price while he stayed on as a Krispy Kreme employee. Krispy Kreme, however, dismissed the executive soon after the transaction closed, triggering a payment $5 mil-lion greater than the amount originally attributed to the promissory note. This extra money, too, became part of the nonamortizing, intangible asset known as reacquired franchise rights. The shortness of the interval between the transaction and the increased payment raised the question whether at least a portion of the disbursement was in substance a severance payment to the executive. If it had been booked that way, Krispy Kreme would have realized an immediate expense. Krispy Kreme's dubious rebuttal was that the payment was not severance because it went to Dough-Re-Mi, rather than directly to the executive.

Further undercutting Krispy Kreme's credibility were details of a second franchise repurchase, in northern California. The 10-K filed in May 2002 reported that as of January 2001 CEO Scott Livengood held a 3 percent share of the franchise. In reality, his stake amounted to 6 percent, but in August 2001 he ceded 3 percent to his wife as part of a separation agreement. The couple divorced in June 2002. A Krispy Kreme spokeswoman blamed the 10-K discrepancy on a proofreading error, but the company had a potential motive for wanting to state as low a figure as possible. Allowing executives to hold nontrivial stakes in franchises was unusual. Some other franchised food companies prohibited the practice, viewing it as a conflict of interest.

On July 29, 2004, Krispy Kreme disclosed that the SEC had opened an informal inquiry into its accounting practices. The company's stock plunged by 16 percent on the news. One focus of the investigation was franchise repurchases. Camelback Research Alliance noted that Krispy Kreme's practice of not amortizing the reacquired rights was nonstandard in the franchising industry. The company parried that it believed the franchise rights had indefinite lives and therefore should not be written off over time.

Camelback co-founder Donn W. Vickrey also suggested that Krispy Kreme had paid inflated prices in some franchise repurchases.[25] He noted that in 2003 the company paid $67.5 million for franchises in Dallas and Shreveport owned by two former directors. The assets included five stores and one commissary, a production facility that served off-premises customers. At the same time, Krispy Kreme was declining to buy back a southern California franchise that was for sale for a reported $80 million and held 22 stores. Vickrey questioned whether the California stores could truly be so much less valuable. The questions about valuation of the franchise repurchases raised the specter of questionable transactions with related parties. Taking into account all of Krispy Kreme's accounting practices, Camelback gave the company an F for earnings quality, a designation the research firm customarily awarded only to companies with three characteristics:

1. Flat or declining fundamentals, providing a motivation to prettify the financials.
2. Visible evidence of unusual or improper accounting or transactions.
3. Evidence of weak corporate governance.

The Heat Goes Up

Vickrey's criticisms proved astute. Krispy Kreme's chief operating officer resigned less than a month later, a top-level executive change that analyst Skip Carpenter of Thomas Weisel Partners viewed as a sign of more problems to come.[26] A major earnings disappointment followed later the same month. The company declined to provide earnings guidance, which is usually a reason to worry. David Rocker of Rocker Partners further noted that most, if not all, of the cash on Krispy Kreme's balance sheet appeared to have come from a sale-and-leaseback transaction, rather than from operations.[27] On September 12, 2004, auditor PricewaterhouseCoopers refused to complete its review of the latest quarter's financial statements until an outside law firm hired by the board completed certain procedures that the auditor requested.

On October 8, 2004, the SEC upgraded its inquiry to a formal investigation of Krispy Kreme's financial reporting practices. Less than a week later, two former directors were slapped with a lawsuit alleging that they pumped up the price Krispy Kreme agreed to pay for the Dallas-Shreveport franchise, which they owned, by obtaining an outside bid that they never seriously considered. On November 22, 2004, Krispy Kreme stock fell 16 percent to $9.64 as the company announced its first-ever loss as a public company. That was down from an August 2003 peak, adjusted for splits, of $49.74. Among other depressing statistics, same-store sales declined by more than 6 percent, and it cost the company $3 million to deal with the SEC probe and pending litigation. Departing from customary practice for earnings calls, management declined to answer any questions and withdrew its previous projection of 15 percent sales growth in 2005.

Krispy Kreme could no longer pin its troubles on the low-carbohydrate diet fad, which appeared to be fading. A Legg Mason analyst charged the company with carelessness in selecting new store locations and failure to train new franchisees properly. In addition, the company had saturated the market by selling its goodies in supermarkets and convenience stores. Instead of a long line of customers camped out in sleeping bags, the manager of a new Krispy Kreme store in San Antonio found only his employees waiting for him when he arrived to open up. The city already had three other Krispy Kreme outlets, and its doughnuts were being sold in Albertsons and H-E-B supermarkets. There were also possible signs of strain among franchisees. A Midwestern franchisee exercised an option to sell 11 percent of its shares back to the company, and Krispy Kreme disclosed a $2 million charge for doubtful accounts from two franchisees.

On December 16, 2004, Krispy Kreme conceded that some of the payment to Dough-Re-Mi's former owner should have been treated as compensation expense. Lawyers hired by the board, however, found no intentionally improper conduct in the incident. Management also acknowledged errors in its accounting for the acquisition of a California franchise. Krispy Kreme stock rose by 8.7 percent on the news, as analysts rejoiced that the disclosures were not worse. PricewaterhouseCoopers, however, continued to refuse to complete its review of results for two prior quarters, pending completion of the ongoing investigation by a special committee of the board and the outside law firm.

It quickly became clear that the company was not yet out of the woods. On January 4, 2005, Krispy Kreme said it would reduce its previous year's reported profit and that it would be in default on its $150 million bank credit line due to its failure to file financial statements and probably also as a result of its earnings decline. Without the ability to draw further on its bank line, said Krispy Kreme, it would be unable to honor its guarantees of franchisees' debts, of which $16.7 million was in default. In February, the company said that it needed additional credit by the end of March to remain in business. By this time, more than a dozen shareholder lawsuits had piled up, including one alleging that Krispy Kreme had tried to meet investors' expectations for earnings growth by ordering some employees to ship more doughnuts than wholesale customers had ordered.

In response to its deteriorating situation, Krispy Kreme replaced chief executive Scott Livengood with a turnaround specialist. On February 24, 2005, the U.S. attorney's office for the Southern District of New York launched an investigation on top of the SEC's ongoing probe. Several new elements entered the disclosures of financial reporting problems on April 9, 2005, when Krispy Kreme increased the size of the corrections to its fiscal 2004 results from the $3.8 million to $4.9 million range to a range of $5.2 million to $6.2 million. The previously undisclosed problems involved derivatives transactions, errors in accounting for leases and improvements related to leases, and reversal of income related to equipment sold to a franchisee before Krispy Kreme bought that operation. Management said further restatements probably would be needed on the last item, as the basis for recognizing the revenue would be changed to the installation date of the equipment, rather than the shipping or delivery date.

The Resolution

After 10 months, the board special committee submitted a report of its investigation. The carefully worded document indicated that although all employees and franchisees who were interviewed denied deliberately distorting Krispy Kreme's earnings or being ordered to do so, "the number, nature, and timing of the accounting errors strongly suggest that they resulted from an intent to manage earnings."[28] The report criticized "round-trip transactions" in which money flowed out to franchise sellers, then flowed back in and was booked as revenue, enabling management to achieve its bogey of $0.01 above guidance.

The denouement came in 2009, when former CEO Livengood and former CFOs John Tate and Randy Casstevens settled SEC charges that they were instrumental in inflating Krispy Kreme's earnings in an alleged scheme to increase their compensation. They did not admit or deny the allegations but agreed to surrender money the SEC said they earned illegally, pay civil penalties, and be permanently enjoined from committing future violations. The SEC complaint also alleged that Krispy Kreme management conducted misleading conference calls with securities analysts, helping to keep the stock price higher than it would have been without the alleged financial manipulation, which the SEC said the executives knew about but failed to disclose. Livengood, Tate, and Casstevens collectively sold approximately 324,000 shares of stock in August 2003, close to the price peak.

Learning Lessons from Doughnuts

Krispy Kreme was not a case of massively fictitious earnings. Rather, the SEC complaint depicted a process of nickel-and-diming, through a wide range of financial statement items, to beat earnings guidance by $0.01 in every single quarter. Security analysts found no clear-cut evidence within the reported numbers that stated profits were inaccurate. Still, users of financial statements can draw some lessons for future reference.

To begin with, an exceptionally long record of beating guidance or posting year-over-year gains in quarterly earnings is a reason to suspect earnings management. Businesses tend to grow unevenly over time, reflecting such factors as the business cycle, waxing and waning of competitive pressures, and fluctuations in input costs. A second lesson of the Krispy Kreme case is that related-party transactions and deceptive financial reporting often go hand in hand. Finally, when management offers an excuse for deteriorating earnings that does not stand up to scrutiny, as Krispy Kreme did by citing the low-carb craze, it may be using financial reporting tricks to try to conceal the true causes.

TARDY DISCLOSURE AT HALLIBURTON

In 2002, the *New York Times* reported on a 1998 change in accounting policies by the Halliburton Corporation that enabled the industrial construction company to book more than $100 million of disputed costs as revenue.[29] Halliburton did not disclose the change in its treatment of cost overruns until more than a year later. Apparently in response to the *Times* article, the Securities and Exchange Commission initiated an investigation that eventually led to charges of filing materially misleading financial reports.

The Halliburton affair probably attracted disproportionate attention for an accounting controversy of less than gargantuan proportions because of the identity of the chief executive officer on whose watch it occurred. By the time Halliburton's tardy disclosure became public knowledge, CEO Dick Cheney had moved on to become vice president of the United States. Inconveniently for the White House, a shareholder lawsuit alleging a massive scheme to defraud investors was filed against Cheney and other Halliburton executives on the day after President George W. Bush called for a crackdown on accounting abuses. Bush advocated tougher prison sentences for corporate officials engaging in fraud and a strengthening of the SEC's ability to uncover financial reporting scams.

Additional embarrassment for the administration arose from Cheney's close ties to Arthur Andersen, which incurred massive criticism for its auditing of Enron and ultimately went out of business. In a 2000 memo to his colleagues, Arthur Andersen's Terry Hatchett boasted that his relationship with Cheney was so tight that he remained lead partner on the Halliburton account even after leaving the Dallas office to head Asian operations.

Additionally, Cheney appeared in a marketing video hailing Arthur Andersen's capabilities.

The Accounting Issues

The accounting issues involved cost overruns incurred in construction projects. Depending on the terms of the contract and the nature of the overrun, Halliburton could potentially recover the associated cost from a customer. Prior to 1998, the company recognized income from recovery of overrun costs in the quarter in which it resolved the claim. Beginning in the second quarter of 1998, however, Halliburton departed from its traditional practice and began recognizing revenues by offsetting its losses on certain projects with estimated probable recoveries on claims that it had not yet resolved.

Both the old and the new accounting treatment were acceptable under GAAP. The new treatment, however, boosted reported pretax income by $200 million between the second quarter of 1998 and the third quarter of 1999. In the fourth quarter of 1998, the change in accounting policy raised reported pretax profits by 46 percent. The numbers that investors saw during this period were not comparable to those reported for earlier periods, meaning they did not obtain an accurate picture of Halliburton's profit trend. Not until March 2000 did the company reveal, in its 1999 Form 10-K filing, that it had changed its accounting policy.

In 2001, Halliburton adopted an even more aggressive approach to recognizing revenue. For some projects, Halliburton began reporting sales months before billing customers for the work. Previously, the policy was to book revenues only if the company expected to bill clients within one month. In addition, the company began keeping some disputed bills on the books for over a year instead of writing them off and reporting losses. The previous policy was to refrain from a write-off only if it believed it would collect most of the claim within one year. As a result of this change, disputed claims doubled from $113 million in 2000 to $234 million in 2001.

Chief Financial Officer Doug Foshee said he could not imagine that Cheney had specifically approved the 1998 change in accounting policy. He characterized it as a routine business decision prompted by a shift in the company's business mix. Up until the late 1990s, Halliburton worked mostly under cost-plus contracts, in which it was guaranteed a profit over whatever costs it incurred. By 1998, most contracts were on a fixed-price basis. Under this arrangement, the company had to complete the work for a predetermined fee or else negotiate repayment for cost overruns and for costs arising from changes in specifications of the work.

Those changed circumstances may well have affected Halliburton's accounting policies, but the adoption of a more liberal revenue recognition policy occurred in the context of pressure on the company's stock price due to its 1998 merger with Dresser Industries. Dresser faced potentially large legal liabilities from asbestos-related litigation. Furthermore, conditions were difficult in Halliburton's energy services business. Corporate-wide sales and profits fell in the fourth quarter of 1998 from the year-earlier period.

Halliburton's financial statements provided further hints that in response to these pressures the company took liberties to present its results in a favorable light. When Cheney became CEO in October 1995, the company had about $0.95 of receivables for each dollar of quarterly revenues. At the end of his tenure, in July 2000, the figure stood at $1.20. This increase did not appear to reflect a general change in industry conditions. Over that same span, the average ratio of receivables to sales at five major competitors declined from $0.92 to $0.86. On the face of it, Halliburton became more aggressive about booking revenues before getting paid, a classic technique for pumping up reported earnings.[30]

The Resolution

On August 3, 2004, the SEC announced that Halliburton and its former controller, Robert C. Muchmore Jr., had agreed to settle charges of filing materially misleading financial statements by paying penalties of $7.5 million and $50,000, respectively. The administrator of the commission's Fort Worth office, Harold F. Degenhardt, commented, "The SEC's action today emphasizes the importance of complete transparency in a company's financial disclosures. Important information bearing on a company's results should be clearly and timely disclosed, even if those results are calculated in accordance with Generally Accepted Accounting Principles (GAAP)."[31]

The company and Muchmore neither admitted to nor denied the SEC charges. Vice President Cheney's attorney noted that the SEC had investigated the matter very thoroughly and had found no responsibility for nondisclosure on the part of either the board or the CEO. He declined to answer a question about whether Cheney knew of the effect of the accounting change on Halliburton's profits.

Lessons from Halliburton

An auditor's seal of approval does not guarantee that a company's financial reporting is reliable. Arthur Andersen went along with Halliburton's decision not to disclose an important change in accounting policies in the year in which it was made. Immateriality is a common rationale for such a decision, yet in the fourth quarter of 1998, the change in accounting for cost overruns produced nearly a 50 percent overstatement of pretax earnings. By the by, Halliburton fired Arthur Andersen in April 2002, the month before the *New York Times* raised questions about the company's accounting practices.

Neither should users of financial statements be complacent just because a prestigious individual has ultimate responsibility for the integrity of the numbers. Halliburton CEO Dick Cheney was a former congressman, White House chief of staff, and secretary of defense. By some accounts, he was a hands-off manager who would not have concerned himself with the accounting decision that eventually resulted in a settlement with the Securities and Exchange Commission. On the other hand, he evidently felt familiar enough with accounting matters to praise Arthur Andersen's work in a marketing video. In any case, if earnings look suspiciously strong during a rough patch for the company's industry, users of financial statements should never automatically rule out the possibility that manipulative accounting explains the disparity.

MANAGING EARNINGS WITH RAINY DAY RESERVES

Overstating near-term reported earnings by recognizing sales prematurely is the revenue-related abuse that creates the greatest notoriety. Analysts must also watch out for the opposite sort of finagling, however. Sometimes, management *delays* revenue recognition to *understate* short-run profits. The motive for this paradoxical behavior is a desire to report the sort of smooth year-to-year earnings growth that equity investors reward with high price-earnings multiples (see Chapter 14).

Steady earnings growth rarely occurs naturally. A company can produce it artificially, however, by creating a rainy day reserve. When net profit happens to be running above expectations, management stows part of it in a rainy day reserve. Later on, when the income is needed to boost results to targeted levels, management pulls the earnings out of storage. Smoothing the bottom line is not uncommon, but companies are touchy about the subject.

Chemical producer W. R. Grace reacted with indignation when it was accused of managing its earnings through improper reserves. On December 22, 1998, the Securities and Exchange Commission charged the company and six of its former executives with falsely reporting earnings over the preceding five years by improperly shifting revenue. Grace followed the standard script, declaring that it would "vigorously contest"[32] the charges, stating its belief that its financial reporting was proper and pointing out that its outside auditors had raised no objections to the accounting. An attorney for former Grace Chief Executive Officer J. P. Bolduc, who was among the accused executives, said that his client would fight the charges and expected to be vindicated. The SEC, complained the lawyer, was trying to punish Bolduc for carrying out his duties exactly as he should have.

The SEC specifically alleged that Grace had declined to report $10 million to $20 million of revenue that its kidney dialysis services subsidiary, National Medical Care (NMC), received in the early 1990s as the result of a change in Medicare reimbursement rules. According to the commission's enforcement division, the Grace executives reckoned that with earnings already meeting Wall Street analysts' forecasts, the windfall would not help the company's stock price. Such an inference would have been consistent with investors' customary downplaying of profits and losses that they perceive to be generated by one-time events (see Chapter 3). In fact, it was possible that the unexpected revenue would actually hurt the stock price down the road by causing NMC's profits to increase by 30 percent, an above-target and unsustainable level.

To solve the perceived problem of excessively high profits at NMC, Grace's management allegedly placed the extra revenue in another account, which it later drew on to increase the health care group's reported revenues between 1993 and 1995. As an example, claimed the SEC, senior managers of Grace asked NMC's managers to report an extra $1.5 million of income in the fourth quarter of 1994, when corporate earnings needed a boost.

Brian J. Smith, who was Grace's chief financial officer until July 1995, testified in a deposition that because the kidney dialysis unit could not maintain its pace of earnings increases, "We believed that it was prudent to reduce the growth rates."[33] His attorney denied, however, that the goal was to please Wall Street analysts by keeping reported earnings smooth, as former Grace and NMC employees asserted. Smith had bona fide liabilities in mind, claimed the attorney.

A senior partner at Grace's auditing firm, Price Waterhouse, did not agree that the additions to reserves were appropriate. Eugene Gaughan testified that in 1991, he pointed out that the accounting rules clearly stated that profits could be set aside only for foreseeable and quantifiable liabilities; GAAP did not give companies discretion to create rainy day funds.

In its year-end audit, Price Waterhouse proposed reversing the reserves, but management refused. According to the auditing firm's records, the Grace executives said that they wanted a "cushion for *unforeseen* future events"[34] (italics added). Eventually, Price Waterhouse allowed the additions to reserves to stand. The auditors' decision reflected a finding that the amount placed in the reserve was not material from Grace's corporate-wide standpoint, although it would be if NMC were a stand-alone company. (At the time, auditors generally judged an item material if it affected earnings by

5 percent or 10 percent. The Securities and Exchange Commission later established the criterion that an event was material if it would affect an investor's decision.)

According to Gaughan, Price Waterhouse objected again around the end of 1992, after seeing a memo that described Grace's use of reserves to influence reported growth in profits, while gearing NMC executives' incentive compensation to "actual results." Another Price Waterhouse partner, Thomas Scanlon, said that he told Grace CEO Bolduc that stockpiling reserves was wrong and would have to stop. By that time, the contents of the rainy day reserve had grown to about $55 million.

It appears, in short, that Grace's 1998 statement that its auditors had raised no objections to its accounting for the Medicare reimbursement windfall was true only in the technical sense that Price Waterhouse issued clean financials, based on materiality considerations. As a spokeswoman for the auditing firm pointed out, such an opinion does not imply agreement with everything in the statements. As late as April 1999, however, Grace was still insisting that Price Waterhouse had approved its accounting "without reservation."[35]

On June 30, 1999, Grace settled the case without admitting or denying the SEC's charges. The company agreed to cease and desist from further securities law violations and also to set up a $1 million education fund to promote awareness of and education about financial statements and generally accepted accounting principles. Adhering again to the standard script, the corporation explained that it settled the case "because we think it is in the best interests of our employees and shareholders to put this matter behind us and move forward."[36]

The Grace affair serves as a reminder that almost invariably, an allegation of irregularities in corporate financial reporting is followed by a vehement, formulaic denial. No matter how offended the company purports to be about having its integrity questioned, analysts should take the protests of innocence with a grain of salt. The record does not suggest that the companies that bray loudest in defending their accounting practices are sure to be vindicated in the end.

FUDGING THE NUMBERS: A SYSTEMATIC PROBLEM

As the preceding examples demonstrate, manipulation of reported revenue is distressingly common. Readers may nevertheless wonder whether this discussion presents too bleak a picture of human nature. Are not most people basically honest, after all? To a novice analyst who has never been blindsided by revisions of previously reported sales figures that proved misleading or fraudulent, it may seem paranoid to view every company's income statement with suspicion.

Harvard Business School Professor Emeritus Michael C. Jensen observes, however, that misrepresenting revenues is the inevitable consequence of using budget targets in employee compensation formulas.[37] "Tell a manager that he will get a bonus when targets are realized and two things will happen," writes Jensen. "First, managers will attempt to set easy targets, and, second, once these are set, they will do their best to see that they are met even if it damages the company." He cites real-life examples of managers who "did their best" through such stratagems as:

- Shipping fruit baskets that weighed exactly the same amount as their product and booking them as sales.
- Announcing a price increase, effective January 2, to induce customers to order before year-end and thereby help managers achieve their sales targets. The price hike put the company out of line with the competition.
- Shipping unfinished heavy equipment from a plant in England (resulting in revenue recognition in the desired quarter) to the Netherlands. At considerable cost and inconvenience, the manufacturer then completed the assembly in a warehouse located near its customer.

Compounding the problem of managers who play games with their revenues is the willingness of some corporate customers to play along. "All too often, companies wouldn't be able to accomplish the frauds without the assistance of their customers," observes Helane L. Morrison, a district administrator for the Securities and Exchange Commission.[38] For example, one-third of wireless communications provider Hybrid Networks' revenue in the fourth quarter of 1997 consisted of a sale made on the final day of the reporting period to a distributor, Ikon Office Solutions. Ikon agreed to purchase $1.5 million worth of modems from Hybrid, despite knowing that it had no customers for the equipment. Hybrid closed the sale by providing a side letter essentially permitting Ikon to return the modems without paying for them. Ikon exercised that option in 1998, yet Ronald Davies, the Ikon executive who handled the purchase, sent an e-mail to Hybrid denying any knowledge of the side letter. Unfortunately, Hybrid later gave a copy of the side letter to its auditors. The SEC then sued Hybrid, which was forced to restate its revenues to eliminate the nonfinal sale of modems to Ikon. Furthermore, Davies received a cease-and-desist order to refrain from further violations of the securities laws. In certain other enforcement actions alleging improper recognition of sales as well, the SEC has charged executives of corporate customers with collusion.

How widespread are revenue recognition gambits that enrich managers but impair bona fide profits? According to Ikon executive Davies, "It's very common for a manufacturer to call you up and say, 'I need to hit my quarterly number, would you mind giving me a purchase order for $100,000?'"[39] In the litigation surrounding W. R. Grace's alleged delay of revenue recognition to smooth earnings, the chief financial officer's attorney defended his client's action by arguing, "Any CFO anywhere has managed earnings in a way the SEC is now jumping up and down and calling fraud."[40] Michael Jensen chimes in, "Almost every company uses a budget system that rewards employees for lying and punishes them for telling the truth." He proposes reforming the system by severing the link between budget targets and compensation. Realistically, however, radical reforms are not likely to occur any time soon.

Analysts therefore need to scrutinize carefully the revenues of every company they examine. Even in the case of the bluest of the blue chips, watching for rising levels of accounts receivable or inventory, relative to sales, should be standard operating procedure. Regardless of management's programmed reassurances, conspicuous surges in unbilled receivables and deferred income are telltale danger signals. It is imperative that analysts raise a red flag when a membership-based company's registrations deviate from their customary relationship with reported sales. "Budget-gaming is rife," says Jensen, and "in most corporate cultures, much of this is expected, even praised." Let the analyst beware.

Restatements of revenues and earnings arise in a wide range of circumstances. Many well-publicized cases involve young companies in comparatively new industries. Until the potential abuses have been demonstrated, management may be able to take greater liberties than the auditors will countenance at a later point. On the other hand, major, long-established corporations are sometimes overzealous in booking sales. Mature companies may pump up revenues out of a desire to meet high expectations created by earlier rapid growth.

After the fact, companies variously attribute excesses in reporting to misjudgment, bookkeeping errors, deliberate misrepresentation by rogue managers, or some combination of the three. Seasoned analysts, having been burned on many occasions by revenue revisions, tend to doubt that overstatements are ever innocent mistakes. To gain some of the veterans' perspective, if not necessarily their jaundiced view of human nature, it is worthwhile to review a few case histories of misstated revenues.

In November 2002, Enterasys Networks restated its revenue downward by 11 percent for a 19-month period in 2000 and 2001, blaming accounting mistakes. The network equipment maker's net loss for the period rose by the same amount. (A change in the fiscal year accounted for the unusual

19-month interval.) The purported mistakes that contributed to the elimination of $153 million of sales included revenues booked in the wrong periods, inflated valuations of stock received as payment for products, and expected payments that were booked as revenues but failed to materialize during the 19-month interval. Enterasys was the major surviving subsidiary of Cabletron Systems, cofounded by Craig Benson, who had just been elected governor of New Hampshire when the revisions were announced. The *Wall Street Journal* received no response to its call to a spokesman for the transition team of governor-elect Benson, who had served on the Enterasys audit committee since June 2000.

Cincinnati Milacron credited an anonymous tip for its uncovering of a $2.3 million overstatement of sales in the first half of 1993. The "isolated" incident, said the company, involved a failure by the Sano plastic machinery unit to observe the "sales cutoff" rule. Contrary to Cincinnati Milacron's policy, Sano had counted in sales units that had not been shipped. The obligatory firing centered on a senior manager, while others escaped with reprimands.[41]

First Financial Management blamed accounting errors, rather than policy violations, for its restatement of revenues for the first nine months of 1991. (Some of the employees at fault were fired, all the same.) The problem arose in the Basis Information Technologies subsidiary, a unit that First Financial had formed by consolidating 19 separate companies. Basis Information Technologies reportedly lost track of certain accruals of revenue, which should have been reduced as contracts expired. While uncovering the mess, First Financial also found that certain acquisition-related expenses had been amortized improperly.[42]

In a June 2003 interview with *Fortune,* Lucent Technologies' outside counsel commented on the company's booking of $125 million of revenue in a deal that the Securities and Exchange Commission had questioned. Paul Sanders of Cravath, Swaine & Moore characterized the telecommunications equipment manufacturer's handling of the transaction with Winstar as a "failure of communication," rather than as accounting fraud. Asked if the failure was intentional, Sanders replied, "I don't know. I don't think so."[43] One month later, Lucent was forced to publish a retraction in which it acknowledged that Sanders's comments were inaccurate and that it had falsified documents. On May 17, 2004, Lucent and three former executives agreed to settle, without admitting or denying the allegations, SEC charges that the company fraudulently and improperly recognized about $1.148 billion of revenue and $470 million in pretax earnings during fiscal 2000. The SEC complaint asserted that nine current and former Lucent executives improperly granted or failed to disclose side agreements and other incentives to induce customers to buy the company's products, all in order to meet internal sales targets and obtain sales-based bonuses. Furthermore, the SEC charged, the executives violated internal accounting controls and misled corporate finance and accounting personnel about the existence of extracontractual commitments. This case did not result in a restatement of financial results, but the SEC fined Lucent $25 million for not cooperating with its investigation.

CONCLUSION

Motivational speakers assure their audiences that if they visualize success, success will follow. Some of the corporate executives who live by the self-help creed take this advice a bit too literally. Seeing conditional sales and dubious memberships, they visualize GAAP revenues, believing that reality will follow. They transfer their own mirage to the financial statements, pumping up their companies' perceived market value and credit quality. When the revenues derived from wishful thinking fail to materialize, the managers may resort to fraud to maintain the illusion. The positive mental attitude that overstates revenues in the early stage is no less damaging, however, than the fraud responsible at a later point. When evidence of overly aggressive revenue recognition appears, analysts must act swiftly and decisively, lest they become infected by the managers' dangerous optimism.

Expense Recognition

As Chapter 6 illustrated, companies can grossly distort their earnings through aggressive revenue recognition. Analysts who arm themselves with appropriate skepticism about financial statements are bound to wonder whether companies also pump up the bottom line by taking liberties in booking expenses. The answer is resoundingly affirmative. Corporate managers are just as creative in minimizing and slowing down the recognition of expenses as they are in maximizing and speeding up the recognition of revenues.

NORTEL'S DEFERRED PROFIT PLAN

Nortel Networks illustrated the distorting power of accruals, one of the most abused features of financial reporting. Founded in 1882 as the Bell Telephone Company of Canada's department for manufacturing telephones and telephone equipment, the unit was spun off as the Northern Electric and Manufacturing Company Limited in 1895. It went through various ownership and name changes, eventually becoming known as Nortel Networks to signify the company's quest to dominate the global market for public and private telecommunications networks.

Nortel grew into North America's largest telecommunications equipment manufacturer and rode the late-1990s boom in fiber optics equipment. From the mid-1990s until mid-2000, its market capitalization soared more than tenfold, and the company shelled out $30 billion for acquisitions. Nortel's showy advertisements featured celebrities such as Elton John.

The Tech Wreck brought those heady days to an end in 2000. It became apparent that like many of its high-tech peers, the showpiece of Canadian industry had paid exorbitant prices for ill-considered acquisitions, extended credit to customers on unsound terms, and made overly optimistic earnings forecasts. Between September 2000 and August 2002, Nortel's market capitalization sank by 99 percent, devastating Canadian pension plans that were heavily invested in its shares.

First Indications of Accounting Discrepancies

New CEO Frank Dunn moved aggressively to stabilize the company, slashing the workforce from 95,000 to 35,000 and exiting several major businesses. The turnaround ran into a snag on October 23, 2003, however. Nortel announced that it had made accounting "mistakes" that required a reduction of previously stated losses totaling $740 million for 2000, 2001, 2002, and the first half of 2003. A review found that the company's balance sheet overstated liabilities by $900 million for the period in question, with the associated losses partly offset by $160 million in corresponding tax benefits. In addition, the company's second look at its books revealed that $92 million in revenues from the three-and-a-half-year span should have been deferred to later periods.

Dunn, who had been chief financial officer in 2000 and much of 2001, explained that the errors were made during a volatile period for the high-tech industry. "I want to assure Nortel Networks stakeholders that we are committed to working to identify the causes of the mistakes," said Dunn, "and to implement the appropriate measures to ensure that the problems will not recur in the future."[1] Shareholders were not entirely reassured, as Nortel's shares fell by 6 percent in after-hours trading. On the whole, though, investors concluded that because the planned restatements were modest and would reduce previous losses, the news was not all that bad.

Three months later, Nortel and its CEO appeared to have regained any lost ground with investors as the company announced its first annual profit in six years. "Great execution," exulted one Wall Street analyst. "The numbers look really good."[2]

Unfortunately, the numbers proved not to be as good as they looked. On March 10, 2004, Nortel disclosed that an investigation by its audit committee was likely to necessitate another revision of past earnings. As a result, the company had to wave a classic red flag with respect to the credibility of its financial statements by delaying the filing of its 2003 financial reports. The following week, Nortel placed Chief Financial Officer Douglas C. Beatty and Controller Michael J. Gollogly on indefinite paid leaves of absence. Based on the unusual procedure of putting the executives on leave, rather than firing them, accounting experts suspected the company's problems were acute and might involve a disagreement with auditor Deloitte & Touche.

Some brokerage house analysts, however, continued to express confidence in the company's outlook. "In my opinion Nortel has made mistakes in the past, but I'd like to believe that they learned their lesson,"[3] commented one analyst who maintained his buy recommendation. An analyst at an independent equities research firm acknowledged there was an issue of trust in management but expressed hope that the accounting changes would be minor and have little impact on Nortel's share price. "When you're adjusting prior year numbers, who cares, I'm buying the stock today,"[4] the analyst said.

That remark would prove misguided by a long shot. More skeptical observers were apt to wonder whether the latest accounting inaccuracies were truly inadvertent errors. In 2003, Nortel had introduced a special bonus scheme. Senior executives' bonuses were tied to profits, and according to Toronto's *Globe and Mail*, 16 executives had collected a total of $43.6 million under the plan. Dunn and Beatty had reportedly received $2.15 million and $831,000, respectively.[5]

From Bad to Worse

Nortel was the most heavily traded stock on the New York Stock Exchange on March 5, 2004, falling by 3.7 percent, as the U.S. Securities and Exchange Commission (SEC) announced that it had upgraded its inquiry into the company's accounting to a formal investigation. John Gavin, president of the regulatory research firm SEC Insight Inc., commented that the SEC's upgrading of its probe, which empowered the commission to issue subpoenas, might indicate that Nortel was "not cooperating as much as they say they are."[6] The Ontario Securities Commission also was looking into Nortel's financial reporting, and an inquiry by the Royal Canadian Mounted Police later evolved into a criminal investigation.

Analysts who had downplayed the significance of the accounting revelations were dealt a blow on April 28, 2004. Nortel dropped a bombshell in the form of a 50 percent cut in its previously announced 2003 earnings of $732 million. The company said some of those profits would be shifted to earlier years, for which it reported losses. Nortel also delayed the reporting of its results for the first quarter of 2003, further damaging its credibility.

In addition to dashing hopes that the new round of accounting statements would be minor, Nortel rattled the market by firing CEO Dunn, CFO Beatty, and controller Gollogly. They were terminated for cause, but under Canadian law that phrase included incompetence, so the dismissal did not necessarily imply any criminal acts. Nortel also placed the finance chiefs of its four operating divisions on paid leave. The company's stock price dropped by 28 percent, and Standard & Poor's downgraded its corporate credit rating from B to B–.

Some observers suggested that the senior executives were scapegoats for the board's failure to police the company's accounting practices. Dunn continued to receive high marks for his response to the 2001 business downturn. Furthermore, industry experts considered the company well positioned from a technological standpoint.

Notwithstanding these purported operational strengths, the credibility of Nortel's financial reporting continued to deteriorate. On June 2, 2004, the company indicated that the 50 percent cut in its 2003 earnings would not necessarily be the last revision. The possibility of further restatements arose as Nortel turned its attention to its reporting for the second half of 2003.

Management's credibility continued to shrink as the company kept pushing back its target date for producing definitive earnings restatements. Nortel had 650 employees devoted to the task, augmented by a host of outside auditors and consultants. By August 2004, their efforts had produced only "estimated limited preliminary unaudited" numbers.[7]

Three months later, the company still had not reported any results for 2004, and it once again delayed the release of its financials. On August 11, 2004, a new chapter opened. Nortel's investigation, which previously had focused on accruals and provisions, had turned to revenue recognition. The company said that $250 million of the $2.5 billion in 2000 revenue that had been slated for shifting to later years would be eliminated altogether. Incorrect recognition of that amount resulted from a combination of nontransfer of legal title to customers, failure to meet criteria for recognizing revenue prior to shipment, the collectibility questions, and other incorrect steps. Duncan Stewart, a fund manager with Terra Capital in Toronto, said Nortel's senior managers were "looking like clowns"[8] for failing to meet self-imposed deadlines for filing financial statements and for announcing major new financial reporting problems after many months of investigating.

On January 10, 2005, Nortel finally filed its 2003 financial statements. Reflecting the heavy criticism of the board's oversight of the company's accounting, five directors said they would not seek reelection, although they were not charged with any wrongdoing. In a highly unusual step, 12 senior executives agreed to return $8.6 million in bonuses they received based on erroneous accounting.

Nortel settled SEC civil charges of accounting fraud for $35 million, but rumors of poor financial condition persisted. The company was unable to obtain governmental financial assistance, and the recession of the late 2000s struck a further blow. On January 19, 2009, Nortel filed for bankruptcy in the United States, Canada, and the United Kingdom. The company initially hoped to reorganize and emerge from bankruptcy, but in June 2009 announced that it would instead liquidate all of its assets.

Lessons from Nortel

Nortel followed a time-honored (albeit not honorable) strategy of taking a big bath in its money-losing period of 2001–2002. Overstating losses created cookie-jar reserves that could be taken into profits later years. The big bath strategy is premised on the belief that magnifying an annual loss will not hurt the stock price as much as magnifying an annual profit will help it in a subsequent year.

Perhaps even more important in Nortel's case was the impact on bonuses that were paid as a function of returning to profitability. This was the arrangement for most Nortel employees even before the new plan for senior executives was adopted in 2003. In this sort of scheme, current bonuses are not reduced from zero if a reported loss is pumped up through unjustified accruals, but future bonuses are increased if those accruals are taken into profits later on, in a profitable year.

Based on past examples of big baths and cookie jar reserves, investors' muted reaction to the October 2003 announcement of a restatement, on the grounds that it lowered previously reported losses, was naive. Nortel's experience shows that if a company uses accruals to understate profits, it will have no compunction about overstating profits through aggressive revenue recognition. Instead of blowing over, the 2003 announcement proved to be the beginning of a situation that kept getting worse and worse.

The accruals that Nortel abused arose from contractual liabilities. For example, suppose the company missed a deadline on a $5 million contract and reasonably estimated the failure would cost it $500,000 through a customer refund. The amount of the expected refund would be booked as an expense, reducing current-year profits, and would be recorded as a liability until it was paid. If the customer subsequently agreed to accept a refund of only $300,000, the remaining $200,000 would be recognized as a profit in the period in which the refund was paid. The investigation by Nortel's board found that in 2003 management raided the cookie jar, taking reserves off its balance sheet without legitimate triggers for doing so. Furthermore, management overstated the reserves to create a bigger cookie jar into which it could dip.

Abuse of accruals was deeply embedded in Nortel's culture. Executives used the term *hardness* to describe the state of having ample reserves in place to draw on later as a means of managing earnings. The *Wall Street Journal* got access to an internal company document showing quarterly earnings targets. During the first half of 2003, the profit line kept rising as another number labeled *balance sheet* also kept changing, suggesting that management was generating the earnings increases by drawing on reserves.[9]

For internal purposes that included calculation of bonuses, Nortel used a figure it called "pro forma income." Its initial, publicly reported net income for the first quarter of 2003 was $54 million. The internal figure, on the other hand, included approximately $361 million in reserves, of which roughly $160 million was inappropriately reversed, according to the board's investigation. In the second quarter, Nortel publicly reported a $14 million loss, but the pro forma profit was $34 million, triggering bonuses of 10 to 25 percent of annual salary for most employees and two to four times salary for top managers, once four quarters of cumulative profits were recorded. Ultimately, the scheme unraveled when the board ordered management to clean up the company's balance after years of accumulated reserve accounting that gave rise to confusion.

An important takeaway from the Nortel case is that seemingly small items can prove highly significant. Investors paid little attention to a few hundred million dollars of reserve-related losses in the context of a total of $34 billion of losses recorded from 2000 to 2004. Those additions to reserves, however, added to accrued liabilities that grew to $5 billion by the summer of 2002, giving management a vast opportunity to manipulate earnings to enhance its bonuses.

GRASPING FOR EARNINGS AT GENERAL MOTORS

Rebates are another frequently abused element of expense recognition. General Motors's fiddling with this device shows the important role of corporate culture in the integrity of financial reporting. The corporate culture problem more familiar to many users of financial statements is the casual attitude toward the niceties of generally accepted accounting principles (GAAP) that characterizes many young, fast-growing companies with soaring stock prices. Sticking with blue chips, however, is no guarantee that the books are immaculate. A long-established company with a strong balance sheet and a lengthy record of stable earnings may have a corporate culture that includes going by the book on accounting matters, but that culture may change if profitability starts to erode.

General Motors (GM) illustrated this pathology as its fortunes deteriorated in the early 2000s.[10] During its long reign as the world's largest automaker, GM displayed all the insignia of a blue chip. When it was first rated by Moody's and Standard & Poor's in 1953, the company achieved the top ranking of Triple-A. Far from cutting corners in its financial reporting,

GM in its heyday exceeded the requirements, providing investors audited financial statements before it became mandatory under the Securities Act of 1933.

Over time, however, GM lost its commanding position in the auto industry. This was partly because foreign manufacturers captured market share by catering to changes in consumer preferences to which U.S. producers GM, Ford, and Chrysler were slow to respond. By 1981, GM's Triple-A ratings were gone, and its attitude toward financial reporting began to shift. The company liberalized some of its policies in 1982 and soon became a regular proponent of looser accounting standards at hearings of the Financial Accounting Standards Board.

By 2005, GM's bond ratings had slid all the way to the speculative grade category, at Double-B. In the same year, disturbing signs began to surface that an aggressive approach to financial reporting had become embedded in GM's corporate culture. On October 26, 2005, the company disclosed that the Securities and Exchange Commission was investigating various aspects of its accounting. The probe, replete with subpoenas, addressed accounting for retirement benefits; certain transactions with Delphi, a bankrupt supplier that was formerly a division of GM; and the treatment of recovery of recall costs from suppliers.

On November 9, 2005, GM announced that it would have to restate its financial results for 2001 and possibly for subsequent years. The company said it had "erroneously" booked credits from suppliers, resulting in an overstatement of 2001 income by $300 million to $400 million.[11] That represented a hefty chunk of the $601 million in net income that the automaker originally showed in its 2001 annual report. The figure was down from $4.45 billion in 2000, underscoring the intense earnings pressure that GM was feeling.

At issue in GM's restatement was the recording of rebates and other credits from suppliers. The accounting rules stated that if the rebates involved not only current business but were upfront inducements to place large orders over several years, they should be taken into earnings over time, rather than booked immediately. In March 2005, Chief Financial Officer John Devine had stated that GM's "very clear" policy was to take no rebates from suppliers. In conjunction with the announcement of a coming restatement, however, spokeswoman Toni Simonetti backtracked on that claim. "I will say that some years ago we did say that we would generally discontinue this practice and generally we have," she explained. "I'm not sure if it's been stopped completely across the board."[12]

Judging by the range of accounting practices that the SEC was looking into, it appeared that the inappropriate handling of rebates was not an isolated incident, but symptomatic of widespread aggressiveness in GM's reporting. Coincident with its November 9, 2005, restatement announcement, the company disclosed that it had evaluated the effectiveness of its controls and procedures for determining whether assets should be deemed impaired and written off. Chairman Rick Wagoner said that he and CFO Devine had concluded that the company's controls were not effective at the SEC-defined "reasonable assurance level." As a result, GM had failed to reduce the value of its investment in Fuji Heavy Industries, the producer of Subaru cars, in a timely manner.

Yet another blow to the credibility of GM's financial reporting arrived on March 16, 2006. The company said that some cash flows from its mortgage subsidiary that should have been classified among its investing activities were instead booked as operating activities. This revelation puzzled accounting experts because the applicable rules were unambiguous. Extending a loan or receiving repayment fell into investing activities; interest payments were included in operating cash flow. It was difficult to see how an error could arise.

Similarly troubling was GM's revelation that in 2000 it booked a $27 million gain on the sale of precious metals in its inventory, even though it had agreed to repurchase the metals the following year. The repurchase agreement made the transaction a financing, rather than a sale, so the company should have recorded no income. Running afoul of such a fundamental accounting principle did not sound like an honest mistake. Rather, it had the scent of a transaction concocted for no economic purpose but rather to generate reported earnings at a company desperate to appear profitable.

It further developed that GM's aggressive accounting had not ended in 2000–2001. The company told investors that it had understated its loss in 2005's first quarter by $149 million. Management said it had prematurely increased the value of vehicles it was leasing to car-rental companies, assuming they would be worth more after those companies were through with them.

In the wake of the latest accounting-related disclosures, GM delayed the filing of its 10-K annual report to the SEC, a classic warning sign of financial distress. Another such indication had already come in December 2005 with an abrupt senior management change. Chief Financial Officer John Devine was replaced by Frederick "Fritz" Henderson, who later succeeded Wagoner as chief executive officer.

These telltale events did not turn out to be false warnings. On June 1, 2009, General Motors filed for bankruptcy. By then, the company's stock price had plummeted to $0.75 from its year-end 2005 level of $19.42. Even as late as 2005–2006, many investors found it hard to imagine a bankruptcy filing by a company once regarded as the bluest of blue chips. To close watchers of financial reporting, however, that outcome was by no means inconceivable. The mounting evidence of aggressive accounting strongly suggested that GM's corporate culture was deteriorating as its ability to generate bona fide profits waned.

TIME-SHIFTING AT FREDDIE MAC

Ordinarily, a company's stock price rises when its reported earnings unexpectedly increase. The opposite occurred, however, after Freddie Mac announced on January 22, 2003, that it would revise upward its earnings for previous years. Between January 21 and January 23, the mortgage finance company's shares fell nearly 5 percent while the S&P 500 Index was essentially unchanged.

The explanation of this seemingly strange response was the concern that the announcement raised among investors about the reliability of the financial statements of the government-sponsored enterprise (GSE) officially known as the Federal Home Loan Mortgage Corporation. Even before the news, investors were apprehensive about the complexity of Freddie Mac's accounting. Anxiety increased when the company's auditor, Pricewaterhouse-Coopers (PwC), raised questions about the way the company treated past accounting for certain hedging transactions. After Arthur Andersen surrendered its licenses to audit public companies following its conviction on criminal charges relating to its handling of Enron's audit (see Chapter 11), PwC had taken over as Freddie Mac's auditor. When PwC reviewed the 2002 results, it questioned company accounting decisions that Arthur Andersen had approved, raising the possibility that further problems would emerge.

Freddie Mac steadfastly denied that its handling of derivatives was aimed at smoothing its earnings. That is, the company contended that it did not deliberately hold down its reported profits during good times, making it easier later on to post the steady earnings increases that security analysts craved. On June 25, 2003, however, Freddie Mac admitted that in some instances it manipulated its earnings to match Wall Street earnings forecasts. Management nevertheless claimed that most of the understatement of net income for 2000 through 2002, which it estimated at $1.5 billion to $4.5 billion, was accidental. (The figure rose to nearly $5 billion by the time a review of the company's financial reporting was completed in November 2003.)

Even if it was true that intentional misrepresentations were the lesser part of the earnings understatement, the company's questionable practices had a huge impact that even conscientious analysts could not detect from the outside. Freddie Mac time-shifted $420 million of pro forma profits (the measure the company was then urging investors to focus on) through linked swaps. In these transactions, the company bet on a rise in interest rates at the same time that it bet on a decline in interest rates. The net economic benefit was nil, and there was minimal business justification for the swaps, other than altering the timing of profits. Freddie Mac structured the swaps such that it made its payments in one month and received payment for the offsetting trade in the following month. That reduced net income in one year and raised it in the next.

Freddie Mac's noneconomically driven financial engineering also displayed a characteristic frequently observed in accounting manipulation, namely, snowballing misrepresentation. The company initiated its use of linked swaps in 2001 because falling interest rates were creating an earnings blizzard. If interest rates had leveled off, bringing profits down to a more normal growth rate, Freddie Mac could have begun working down the earnings reserve it had created. Instead, rates continued to fall. To keep the game going and avoid reporting an unwanted earnings spike, management had to undertake bigger and bigger linked-rate swaps. The final swap shifted more income than the first eight combined.[13]

Freddie Mac's manipulation did not end there. Another ploy to hide earnings consisted of ceasing to use market prices for certain derivatives. Outside investigators labeled this action "results-oriented, reverse engineered, and opportunistic."[14] Incredibly, it turned out that after all of management's maneuvers were stripped away, the net effect was that the company *overstated* its 2001 earnings by almost $1 billion.

Encouragingly, from the standpoint of dissuading future abusers of GAAP, Freddie Mac's misdeeds brought retribution. The board fired the company's president and obtained the resignations of its chief executive officer and chief financial officer. The CEO was succeeded by the former chief investment officer, but he, too, eventually lost his job after his role in the linked-rate swaps came to light. In addition, the company paid a $125 million fine in a settlement with the Office of Federal Enterprise Oversight. The regulator's report traced the origins of Freddie Mac's inappropriate practices back to the mid-1990s.

Furthermore, the revelations about Freddie Mac's accounting practices lent fuel to politicians' intent on reining in Freddie Mac and its fellow GSE, Fannie Mae. The two companies later became central figures in the financial crisis of 2008 and were placed under government conservatorship. Financial reporting issues were not the immediate cause of their fall from grace, but they were symptomatic of unhealthy corporate cultures that led to unsound financial practices.

CONCLUSION

Just as companies have myriad ways of exaggerating revenues, they follow a variety of approaches in downplaying expenses. Corporate managers make liberal assumptions about costs that may be capitalized, pile up unjustified accruals, dilute expenses with one-time gains, and jump the gun in booking rebates from suppliers. These gambits are often exceedingly difficult to detect in companies' public financial statements, but seemingly minor yet unprecedented or unconventional entries can foreshadow major restatements. To pick up such clues, analysts must be disciplined enough to disbelieve the innocent explanations that companies routinely provide for abnormalities that point to trouble down the road.

The Applications
and Limitations
of EBITDA

As noted in Chapter 3, corporations have attempted in recent years to break free from the focus on after-tax earnings that has traditionally dominated their valuation. The impetus for trying to redirect investors' focus to operating income or other variants has been the minimal net profits recorded by many New Economy companies. Conventionally calculated price-earnings (P/E) multiples of such companies, most inconveniently, make their stocks look expensive. Old Economy companies generally have larger denominators (the E in P/E), so their multiples look extremely reasonable by comparison.

Long before the dot-com companies began seeking alternatives to net income, users of financial statements had discovered certain limitations in net income as a valuation tool. They observed that two companies in the same industry could report similar income yet have substantially different **total enterprise values**. Similarly, credit analysts realized that in a given year, two companies could generate similar levels of income to cover similar levels of interest expense yet represent highly dissimilar risks of defaulting on their debt in the future.

Net income was not, to the disappointment of analysts, a standard by which every company's value and risk could be compared. Had they thought deeply about the problem, they might have hypothesized that *no* single measure could capture financial performance comprehensively enough to fulfill such a role. Instead, they set off in quest of the correct single measure of corporate profitability, believing in its existence as resolutely as the conquistadors who went in search of El Dorado.

EBIT, EBITDA, AND TOTAL ENTERPRISE VALUE

The fictitious case of Deep Hock and Breathing Room (Exhibit 8.1) illustrates the problems of relating net income to total enterprise value. Both companies compete within the thingmabob industry. Their net profits for the latest year are $28.6 million and $33.0 million, respectively.

When Breathing Room announces an agreement to be acquired by a multinational thingmabob producer for $666 million, Deep Hock's founder and controlling shareholder, Philip Atlee, realizes that his company is a hot item in the mergers-and-acquisitions (M&A) market. Trusting his own skills as a negotiator, he dispenses with M&A advisers and directly contacts an investor group that has previously approached him about buying Deep Hock. With thingmabob makers in strong demand, Atlee reasons, now is the time to sell.

Breathing Room's selling price represented a multiple of 20 times its $33.0 million net income, in line with levels paid in other recent thingmabob acquisitions. On that basis, Atlee sets his sights on a price of 20 times Deep Hock's $28.6 million of net income, or $572 million. He starts the negotiations at a higher level and, after some haggling, accepts a $572 million offer. After popping open the champagne, Atlee begins shopping for a yacht.

One month later, Atlee's quiet retirement is rudely disturbed by news that the investors who bought Deep Hock have quickly resold it to a large industrial corporation for $666 million. The ex-CEO realizes, to his dismay,

EXHIBIT 8.1 Comparative Financial Data ($000 omitted) Year Ended December 31, 2010

	Deep Hock Corporation	Breathing Room, Inc.
Total debt	$ 67.0	$ 0.0
Shareholders' equity	133.0	200.0
Sales	$500.0	$500.0
Cost of sales	415.0	415.0
Depreciation and amortization	25.0	25.0
Selling, general, and administrative expense	10.0	10.0
Operating income	50.0	50.0
Interest expense	6.7	0.0
Income before income taxes	43.3	50.0
Provision for income taxes	14.7	17.0
Net income	$ 28.6	$ 33.0

that he apparently left $94 million on the table. Dumbfounded by the turn of events, Atlee wonders why anyone would pay $666 million for Deep Hock. That is equivalent to the price paid for Breathing Room, a company with net income 15 percent higher. Surely, the investment group that paid $572 million for Deep Hock could not have boosted its profits materially in the space of a month. Neither have price-earnings ratios on thingmabob companies risen from 20 times in the interim.

Determined to solve the mystery, Atlee seeks an explanation from his niece, Alana, an intern at an investment management firm. Drawing on her experience in analyzing financial statements, she obliges by pointing out that Deep Hock's income from operations, at $50.0 million, is equivalent to Breathing Room's. The difference at the bottom line arises because Breathing Room, with a debt-free balance sheet, has no interest expense.

"If I had bought your company, Uncle Phil," Alana explains, "I would have immediately created pro forma financials showing what Deep Hock's net income would be if all of its debt were paid off. Without the $6.7 million of interest expense, its income before income taxes would be $50.0 million, just like Breathing Room's. At the company's effective tax rate of 34 percent, the tax bill would be higher ($17.0 million versus $14.7 million), but net income would rise from $28.6 million to $33.0 million, the same as at Breathing Room. Then I would put the company up for sale at 20 times earnings, or $666 million. That's probably what that group of investors did after they bought Deep Hock from you."

Pausing for effect, Alana adds a detail concerning the transaction. "In order to raise Deep Hock's earnings from $28.6 million to $33.0 million on an actual, as opposed to a pro forma basis, somebody has to retire the $67 million of debt. Assuming the investor group paid off the borrowings and sold the company debt-free, its net gain wasn't $94 million, as you assumed, but only $27 million. I mention that, just in case it's any consolation to you. An alternative way to structure the deal would have been to make the $67 million debt assumption part of the $666 million purchase price. Either way, the net cash proceeds to the seller come to $599 million, for a quick profit of $27 million."

Still unhappy about failing to get top dollar but intrigued by his niece's insights into financial statement analysis, Atlee asks a follow-up question. "I see now that applying a multiple to net income is not a good way to compare the total enterprise values of companies with dissimilar capital structures. This kind of situation must arise frequently. Is there a simple, direct valuation method that would have shown us what our company was truly worth, even if we weren't clever enough to think of increasing the earnings by eliminating the debt?"

"Yes," answers Alana. "Instead of calculating a multiple of net income on the comparable transaction, that is, the sale of Breathing Room, you should have calculated a multiple of **EBIT**. That stands for 'earnings before interest and taxes.' Add Breathing Room's net income, income taxes, and interest expense to get the denominator. The numerator is the sale price:

$$\frac{\text{Total Enterprise Value}}{\text{Net Income} + \text{Income Taxes} + \text{Interest Expense}} = \frac{\$666}{\$33.0 + 17.0 + 0.0}$$

$$= 13.32\text{X}$$

"Let's apply that same EBIT multiple of 13.32 to the comparable data from Deep Hock's income statement," Alana continues.

$$\text{Net Income} + \text{Income Taxes} + \text{Interest Expense} = \$28.6 + 14.7 + 6.7$$

$$= \$50.0$$

$$\$50.0 \times 13.32 = \$666.0$$

"So that's how the pros ensure that valuation multiples will be consistent between companies with similar operating characteristics but different financial strategies?" asks the sadder but wiser ex-CEO of Deep Hock.

"Actually, Uncle Phil," Alana replies, "there's one more comparability issue that we need to address. As you know, the accounting standards leave companies considerable discretion regarding the depreciable lives they assign to their property, plant, and equipment. The same applies to amortization schedules for intangible assets. Now, let's imagine for a moment that Breathing Room's managers had been writing off its assets not at a rate of $25 million a year, but only $20 million a year. That means that they would have been depreciating assets more slowly than you were, since the two companies' rates of depreciation were identical. Here's Breathing Room's income statement, revised for this hypothetical change in depreciation rates" (Exhibit 8.2).

"Let's calculate EBIT from this statement and apply the EBIT multiple that, according to our previous analysis, represents the value being assigned to thingmabob companies currently:

$$\text{Net Income} + \text{Income Taxes} + \text{Interest Expense} = \$36.3 + 18.7 + 0.0$$

$$= \$55.0$$

$$\$55.0 \times 13.32 = \$732.6 \text{ million}$$

EXHIBIT 8.2   Breathing Room, Inc.

Statement of Consolidated Income
Year Ended December 31, 2010
($000 omitted)

Sales	$500.0
Cost of sales	415.0
Depreciation and amortization	20.0
Selling, general, and administrative expense	10.0
Operating income	55.0
Interest expense	0.0
Income before income taxes	55.0
Provision for income taxes	18.7
Net Income	$ 36.3

"It appears that simply by stretching out the depreciable lives of its assets, Breathing Room has boosted its value from $666 million to $732.6 million. But that can't be correct. Depreciation is an accrual, rather than a cash expense. Changing the depreciation rate for financial reporting purposes is therefore nothing but an alteration of a bookkeeping entry. It doesn't increase or decrease the number of dollars actually flowing into the company. If management had changed the depreciation rate for tax reporting purposes, then the actual tax payments would decline. In that case, more dollars *would* flow into Breathing Room. But that's another matter. What we're concerned about is that Breathing Room might fetch a higher price than Deep Hock, merely because of a difference in accounting policy that represents no difference in economic value.

"To prevent this sort of distortion, we calculate a multiple on a base that's even better than EBIT. It's called EBITDA. That stands for 'earnings before interest, taxes, depreciation, and amortization.' (Yes, I know that on the income statement, the correct order, moving from top to bottom, is EBDAIT. But the convention is to use the acronym EBITDA, pronounced 'eebit-dah.') Breathing Room's EBITDA multiple is the same, whether it depreciates its assets at the rate of $25 million a year or $20 million a year:

$$\text{EBITDA Multiple} = \frac{\text{Total Enterprise Value}}{\substack{\text{Net Income} + \text{Income Taxes} + \text{Interest Expense} \\ + \text{Depreciation} + \text{Amortization}}}$$

"Original depreciation schedule:

$$\frac{\$666}{\$33 + 17.0 + 0.0 + 25.0} = \frac{\$666}{75} = 8.88X$$

"Decelerated depreciation schedule:

$$\frac{\$666}{\$36.3 + 18.7 + 0.0 + 20.0} = \frac{\$666}{75} = 8.88X$$

"If we calculate Deep Hock's EBITDA and apply that same multiple of 8.88X, we get the correct total enterprise value of $666 million, meaning that we've achieved comparability with respect to both capital structure and depreciation policy:

$$\text{Net Income + Income Taxes + Interest Expense} \atop + \text{Depreciation + Amortization} = \$28.6 + 14.7 + 6.7 + 25.0$$

$$= \$75.0$$

$$\$75.0 \times 8.88 = \$666.0$$

"In summary, Uncle Phil, it's much smarter to calculate total enterprise value as a multiple of EBITDA than to use net income. But the most important lesson is that if you decide to come out of retirement and start another company, be sure to hire me as your financial adviser."

Atlee grins. "I guess you're never too old to learn new and better approaches to financial statement analysis."

THE ROLE OF EBITDA IN CREDIT ANALYSIS

The dialogue between Phil Atlee and his niece shows that similar companies with similar net income can have substantially different total enterprise values. Much in the same way, companies with similar interest coverage can have substantially different default risk. In credit analysis, as in valuing businesses, EBITDA can discriminate among companies that look similar when judged in terms of EBIT. Consider the fictitious examples of Rock Solid Corporation and Hollowman, Inc. (Exhibit 8.3).

Measured by conventional fixed charge coverage (Chapter 13), the two companies look equally risky, with ratios of 2.10X and 2.11X, respectively:

Fixed charge coverage:

$$\text{Net Income + Income Taxes + Interest Expense}$$

Interest expense:

$$\text{Rock Solid Corp.:} \quad \frac{\$73.0 + 37.0 + 100.0}{\$100.0} = 2.10X$$

$$\text{Hollowman, Inc.:} \quad \frac{\$66.0 + 34.0 + 90.0}{\$90.0} = 2.11X$$

EXHIBIT 8.3 Comparative Financial Data ($000 omitted) Year Ended December 31, 2010

	Rock Solid Corporation	Hollowman, Inc.
Total debt	$ 950.0	$ 875.0
Shareholders' equity	750.0	675.0
Total capital	1,700.0	1,550.0
Sales	2,000.0	1,750.0
Cost of sales	1,600.0	1,400.0
Depreciation and amortization	75.0	30.0
Selling, general, and administrative expense	115.0	130.0
Operating income	210.0	190.0
Interest expense	100.0	90.0
Income before income taxes	110.0	100.0
Provision for income taxes	37.0	34.0
Net income	$ 73.0	$ 66.0

(For convenience of exposition, we refer to this standard credit measure as the EBIT-based coverage ratio. Note that for some companies, the sum of net income, income taxes, and interest expense is not equivalent to EBIT, reflecting the presence of such factors as extraordinary items and minority interest below the pretax income line.)

As it happens, Hollowman and Rock Solid are almost perfectly matched on **financial leverage**, another standard measure of credit risk. (For a discussion of calculating the total-debt-to-total-capital ratio in more complex cases, see Chapter 13.)

Total-debt-to-total-capital ratio:

$$\frac{\text{Total Debt}}{\text{Total Debt} + \text{Equity}}$$

$$\text{Rock Solid Corp.:} \quad \frac{\$950.00}{\$950.0 + 750.0} = 55.9\%$$

$$\text{Hollowman, Inc.:} \quad \frac{\$875.0}{\$875.0 + 675.0} = 56.5\%$$

By these criteria, lending to Hollowman, Inc. is as safe a proposition as lending to Rock Solid Corp. Bringing EBITDA into the analysis, however, reveals that Rock Solid is better able to keep up its interest payments in the event of a business downturn.

In the current year, Rock Solid's gross profit—sales less cost of goods sold—is $400 million. Suppose that through a combination of reduced

EXHIBIT 8.4 Statements of Income ($000 omitted) Year Ended December 31, 2010

	Rock Solid Corporation	Hollowman, Inc.
Sales	$1,800.0	$1,575.0
Cost of sales	1,560.0	1,365.0
Depreciation and amortization	75.0	30.0
Selling, general, and administrative expense	115.0	130.0
Operating income	50.0	50.0
Interest expense	100.0	90.0
Income (loss) before income taxes	(50.0)	(40.0)
Provision (credit) for income taxes	(17.0)	(14.0)
Net income (loss)	$ (33.0)	$ (26.0)

revenue and margin deterioration, the figure drops by 40 percent to $240 million, while other operating expenses remain constant (Exhibit 8.4). Operating income now totals only $50 million, just half of the $100 million interest expense. Fixed charge coverage falls to 0.50X from the previously calculated 2.10X.

Is Rock Solid truly unable to pay the interest on its debt? No, because the $75.0 million of depreciation and amortization charged against income is an accounting entry, rather than a current-year outlay of cash. Adding back these noncash charges shows that the company keeps its head above water, covering its interest by a margin of 1.25X:

EBITDA coverage of interest:

$$\frac{\text{Net Income} + \text{Income Taxes} + \text{Interest Expense} + \text{Depreciation} + \text{Amortization}}{} = \text{Interest Expense}$$

$$\frac{(\$33.0) + (17.0) + 100.0 + 75.0}{100.0} = 1.25\text{X}$$

By contrast, if Hollowman's gross profit falls by 40 percent, as also shown in Exhibit 8.4, its interest coverage is below 1.0 times, even on an EBITDA basis:

$$\frac{(\$26.0) + (14.0) + 90.0 + 30.0}{90.0} = 0.89\text{X}$$

Rock Solid can sustain a larger decline in gross margin than Hollowman can before it will cease to generate sufficient cash to pay its interest in full.

The reason is that noncash depreciation charges represent a larger portion of Rock Solid's total operating expenses—4.2 percent of $1.790 billion, versus 1.9 percent of $1.560 billion for Hollowman (Exhibit 8.3). This difference, in turn, indicates that Rock Solid's business is more capital-intensive than Hollowman's. Further examination of the companies' financial statements would probably show Rock Solid to have a larger percentage of total assets concentrated in property, plant, and equipment.

In summary, conventionally measured fixed charge coverage is nearly identical for the two companies, yet they differ significantly in their probability of defaulting on interest payments. Taking EBITDA into account enables analysts to discriminate between the two similar-looking credit risks. This is a second major reason for the ratio's popularity, along with its usefulness in ensuring comparability of companies with dissimilar depreciation policies, when estimating the total enterprise values.

ABUSING EBITDA

Like many other financial ratios, EBITDA can provide valuable insight when used properly. It is potentially misleading, however, when applied in the wrong context. A tip-off to the possibility of abuse is apparent from the preceding illustration. By adding depreciation to the numerator, management can emphasize (legitimately, in this case) that although Rock Solid's operating profits suffice to pay only 50 percent of its 2001 interest bill, the company is generating 125 percent as much cash as it needs for that purpose. Lenders derive a certain amount of comfort simply from focusing on a ratio that exceeds 1.0X, rather than one that falls below that threshold.

In their perennial quest for cheap capital, sponsors of leveraged buyouts have noted with interest the comfort that lenders derive from a coverage ratio greater than 1.0X, regardless of the means by which it is achieved. To exploit the effect as fully as possible, the sponsors endeavor to steer analysts' focus away from traditional fixed charge coverage and toward EBITDA coverage of interest. Shifting investors' attention was particularly beneficial during the 1980s, when some buyouts were so highly leveraged that projected EBIT would not cover pro forma interest expense even in a good year. The sponsors reassured nervous investors by ballyhooing EBITDA coverage ratios that exceeded the psychologically critical threshold of 1.0 times. Meanwhile, the sponsors' investment bankers insinuated that traditionalists who fixated on sub-1.0X EBIT coverage ratios were hopelessly antiquated and unreasonably conservative in their analysis.

In truth, a bit of caution is advisable in the matter of counting depreciation toward interest coverage. The argument for favoring the EBITDA-based over EBIT-based fixed charge coverage rests on a hidden assumption. Adding depreciation to the numerator is appropriate only for the period over which a company can put off a substantial portion of its capital spending without impairing its future competitiveness.

Over a full operating cycle, the capital expenditures reported in a company's statement of cash flows are ordinarily at least as great as the depreciation charges shown on its income statement. The company must repair the physical wear and tear on its equipment. Additional outlays are required for the replacement of obsolete equipment. If anything, capital spending is likely to exceed depreciation over time, as the company expands its productive capacity to accommodate rising demand. Another reason that capital spending may run higher than depreciation is that newly acquired equipment may be costlier than the old equipment being written off, as a function of inflation.

In view of the ongoing need to replace and add to productive capacity, the cash flow represented by depreciation is not truly available for paying interest, at least not on any permanent basis. Rather, the D in EBITDA is a safety valve that the corporate treasurer can use if EBIT falls below I for a short time. Under such conditions, the company can temporarily reduce its capital spending, freeing up some of its depreciation cash flow for interest payments. Delaying equipment purchases and repairs that are essential, but not urgent, should inflict no lasting damage on the company's operations, provided the profit slump lasts for only a few quarters. Most companies, however, would lose their competitive edge if they spent only the bare minimum on property, plant, and equipment, year after year. It was disingenuous for sponsors of the most highly leveraged buyouts of the 1980s to suggest that their companies could remain healthy while paying interest substantially greater than EBIT over extended periods.

Naturally, the sponsors were prepared with glib answers to this objection. Prior to the buyout, they claimed, management had been overspending on plant and equipment. The now-deposed chief executives allegedly had wasted billions on projects that were monuments to their egos, rather than economically sound corporate investments. In fact, the story went, investments in low-return projects were the cause of the stock becoming cheap enough to make the company vulnerable to takeover. Investors ought to be pleased, rather than alarmed, to see capital expenditures fall precipitously after the buyout. Naturally, this line of reasoning was less persuasive in cases where the sponsors teamed up with the incumbent CEO in a management-led buyout.

Investors in many of the 1980s transactions were advised to take comfort as well from the fact that a portion of the annual interest expense consisted of accretion on zero-coupon bonds, rather than conventional cash coupons (interest payments). By way of explanation, investors buy a zero-coupon issue in its initial distribution at a steep discount—say, 50 percent—to its face value. Instead of receiving periodic interest payments, the purchasers earn a return on their investment through a gradual rise in the bond's price. At the bond's maturity, the obligor must redeem the security at 100 percent of its face value.

By using zero-coupon financing along with conventional debt, LBO sponsors could generate financial projections that showed all interest being paid on schedule, while at the same time making capital expenditures large enough to keep the company competitive. Often, the projections optimistically assumed that the huge debt repayment obligations would be financed with the proceeds of asset sales. The sponsors declared that they would raise immense quantities of cash by unloading supposedly nonessential assets.

With the benefit of hindsight, the assumptions behind many of the LBOs' financial projections were extremely aggressive. Still, the sponsors' arguments were not entirely unfounded. At least some of the vast, diversified corporations that undertook leveraged buyouts during the 1980s had capital projects that deserved to be canceled. Some of the bloated conglomerates owned deadweight assets that were well worth shedding.

The subsequent wave of LBO-related bond defaults,[1] however, vindicated analysts who had voiced skepticism about the new-styled corporate finance. Depreciation was not, after all, available as a long-run source of cash for interest payments. This was a lesson applicable not only to the extremely leveraged deals of the 1980s but also to the more conservatively capitalized transactions of later years.

A MORE COMPREHENSIVE CASH FLOW MEASURE

Despite its limitations as a tool for quantifying credit risk, EBITDA has become a fixture in securities analysis. Many practitioners now consider the ratio synonymous with cash flow or, more formally, operating cash flow (OCF). The interchangeability of EBITDA and OCF in analysts' minds is extremely significant in light of a long tradition of empirical research linking cash flow and bankruptcy risk.

In an influential 1966 study,[2] William H. Beaver tested various financial ratios as predictors of corporate bankruptcy. Among the ratios he tested was a definition of cash flow still widely used today. Cash flow (as defined by Beaver, 1966) is:

Net Income + Depreciation, Depletion, and Amortization

(Depletion, a noncash expense applied to natural resource assets, is ordinarily taken to be implicit in depreciation and amortization, hence the use of the acronym EBITDA, rather than EBITDDA.)

Beaver found that of all the ratios he tested, the best single predictor of bankruptcy was a declining trend in the ratio of cash flow to total debt. This relationship made intuitive sense. Practitioners reasoned that bankruptcy risk was likely to increase if net income declined or total debt increased, either of which would reduce the cash-flow-to-total-debt ratio. The empirical evidence indicated that by adding depreciation to the numerator, analysts improved their ability to predict which companies would go bust, relative to comparing total debt with net income alone.

Note that Beaver's definition of cash flow was more stringent than EBITDA, since he did not add back either taxes or interest to net income. Even so, bond analysts have developed a tradition of telescoping default risk into the single ratio of cash flow (meaning EBITDA) as a percentage of total debt, all based ultimately on Beaver's 1966 finding.[3] In so doing, practitioners have institutionalized a method that Beaver never advocated and that subsequent experience has shown to be fatally flawed.

Beaver did not conclude that analysts should rely solely on the ratio of cash flow to debt ratio, but merely that it was the single best bankruptcy predictor. As he noted in his study, other academic researchers were already attempting to build bankruptcy models with greater predictive power by combining ratios into a **multivariate** analysis. As of 1966, no one had yet succeeded, but just two years later, Edward I. Altman introduced a multivariate model composed of five ratios[4] (see Chapter 13). The development of Altman's Z-Score and other multivariate models has demonstrated that no single financial ratio predicts bankruptcy as accurately as a properly selected combination of ratios.

Since 1968, there has been no excuse for reducing bankruptcy risk to the sole measure of EBITDA to total debt. Nevertheless, that procedure remains a common practice. Similarly unjustifiable, on the basis of empirical evidence, is the widely used one-variable approach of ranking a sample of corporate borrowers according to their EBITDA coverage of interest.

Bizarrely, investment managers sometimes ask bond analysts to provide rankings of companies by their "actual credit risk," as opposed to Moody's and Standard & Poor's ratings. Asked to elaborate on this request, the investment managers reply that actual risk *obviously* means EBITDA coverage. Apparently, they consider it self-evident that the single ratio of cash flow (as they define it) to fixed charges predicts bankruptcy better than all of the rating agencies' quantitative and qualitative considerations combined. Little do the investment managers realize that they are setting credit analysis back by more than 30 years!

Nearly as outmoded as exclusive reliance on a single EBITDA-based ratio is analysts' belief that they can derive a satisfactory measure of cash flow by simply selecting some version of earnings and adding back depreciation. It became apparent that neither EBITDA nor net income plus depreciation was a valid proxy for cash flow at least as far back as 1975, when W. T. Grant filed for bankruptcy. The department store chain's collapse showed that reliance on an earnings-plus-depreciation measure could cause analysts to overlook weakness at a company with substantial working capital needs. Many subsequent failures in the retailing and apparel industries have corroborated that finding.

At the time of its bankruptcy filing, W. T. Grant was the largest retailer in the United States. Up until two years before it went belly-up, the company reported positive net income (see Exhibit 8.5). Moreover, the department store chain enjoyed positive and stable cash flow (as defined by Beaver, in other words, net income plus depreciation). Bankruptcy therefore seemed a remote prospect, even though the company's net income failed to grow between the late 1960s and early 1970s. In 1973, W. T. Grant's stock traded at 20 times earnings, indicating strong investor confidence in the company's

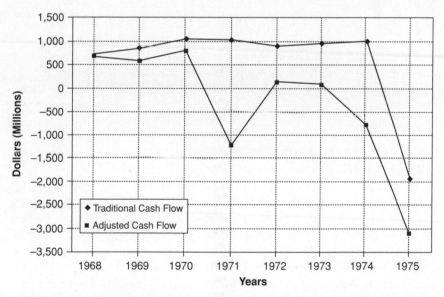

EXHIBIT 8.5 W. T. Grant Alternative Cash Flow Measures 1967–1975
Sources: Clyde P. Stickney and Paul R. Brown, *Financial Reporting and Statement Analysis: A Strategic Perspective,* 4th ed. (Orlando, FL: Dryden), 106–123; James Largay, "Cash Flows, Ratio Analysis and the W. T. Grant Company Bankruptcy," *Financial Analysts Journal,* July–August 1980, 51–55.

future. The board of directors reinforced that confidence by continuing to authorize dividends until mid-1974.

Investors would have been less sanguine if they had looked beyond the cash sources (earnings and depreciation) and uses (interest and dividends) shown on the income statement. It was imperative to investigate whether two balance sheet items, inventories and accounts receivable, were tying up increasing amounts of cash. If so, it became vital to determine whether the company could generate an offsetting amount of cash by expanding its accounts payable. Recognizing the need for this added level of analysis, the Financial Accounting Standards Board (FASB) eventually prescribed a more comprehensive definition of *operating cash flow,* as defined in SFAS 95, "Statement of Cash Flows."

Operating cash flow (as defined by FASB, 1987):

Net Income + Depreciation − Changes in Working Capital Requirements

Where

$$\text{Working Capital Requirements} = \text{Accounts Receivable} + \text{Inventory} - \text{Accounts Payable}$$

Note that this definition focuses on the elements of working capital that ordinarily grow roughly in proportion with the scale of operations. The FASB formulation excludes cash and marketable securities, as well as short-term debt.

WORKING CAPITAL ADDS PUNCH TO CASH FLOW ANALYSIS

Adding working capital to cash flow analysis frequently reveals problems that may not be apparent from observing the trend of EBITDA or net income plus depreciation. In fact, reported earnings often exceed true economic profits specifically as a function of gambits involving inventories or accounts receivable. Fortunately, such ploys leave telltale signs of earnings manipulation. Aside from seasonal variations, the amount of working capital needed to run a business represents a fairly constant percentage of a company's sales. Therefore, if inventories or receivables increase materially as a percentage of sales, analysts should strongly suspect that the earnings are overstated, even though management will invariably offer a more benign explanation.

Consider, for example, an apparel manufacturer that must produce its garments before knowing which new styles will catch the fancy of shoppers in the season ahead. Suppose that management guesses wrong about the fashion trend. The company now holds inventory that can be sold, if at all, only at knockdown prices. Instead of selling the unfashionable garments, which would force the manufacturer to recognize the loss in value, management may decide to retain them in its finished goods inventory. Accounting theory states that the company should nevertheless recognize the loss by writing down the merchandise. In practice, though, management may persuade its auditors that no loss of value has occurred. After all, judging what is fashionable is a subjective process. Moreover, management can always argue that the goods remain in its warehouse only because of a temporary slowdown in orders. If the auditors buy the story, it will not alter the fact that the company has suffered an economic loss. Analysts focusing exclusively on EBITDA will have no inkling that earnings are down or that the company' cash resources may be starting to strain.

In contrast, analysts will recognize that something is amiss if they monitor a cash flow measure that includes working capital in addition to net income and depreciation. While the current season's goods remain in inventory, the company is producing clothing for the next season. Observe what happens to working capital requirements, bearing in mind the FASB 95 definition, as the new production enters inventory:

$$\text{Working Capital Requirements} = \text{Accounts Receivable} + \text{Inventory} - \text{Accounts Payable}$$

Inventory increases, causing working capital requirements to increase. According to the FASB definition, a rise in working capital requirements reduces operating cash flow. Analysts receive a danger signal, even though net income plus depreciation advances steadily.

A surge in accounts receivable, similarly, would reduce operating cash flow. The buildup in receivables could signal either of two types of underlying problems. On the one hand, management may be trying to prop up sales by liberalizing credit terms to its existing customers. Specifically, the company may be carrying financially strained businesses by giving them more time to pay up their accounts. If so, average accounts receivable will be higher than in the past. That will soak up more cash and force the company to absorb financing costs formerly borne by its customers. Alternately, a buildup in receivables may result from extension of credit to new, less creditworthy customers that pay their bills comparatively slowly. To reflect the greater propensity of such customers to fail on their obligations, the company ought to increase its reserve for bad debts. Current-period reported income would then decline. Unfortunately, companies do not invariably do what they ought to do, according to good accounting practice. If they do not, a cash flow measure that includes working capital requirements will reveal a weakness not detected by net income plus depreciation or EBITDA.

To be sure, management may attempt to mask problems related to inventory or receivables by pumping up the third component of working capital requirements, accounts payable. If the company takes longer to pay its own bills, the resulting rise in payables may offset the increase on the asset side. Fortunately for analysts, companies think twice before playing this card, because of potential repercussions on operations. The company's suppliers might view a slowdown in payments as a sign of financial weakness. Vital trade credit could dry up as a consequence.

In any case, analysts should use operating cash flow as one of many diagnostic tools. They should not rely on it exclusively, any more than they should limit their surveillance solely to tracking EBITDA. If a company resorts to stretching out its payables, other ratios detailed in Chapter 13 (receivables to sales and inventories to cost of goods sold) will nevertheless send out warning signals. Note, as well, that if the company does not finance the bulge in inventories and receivables by extending its payables or drawing down cash, it must add to its borrowings. Accordingly, a rising debt-to-capital ratio (see Chapter 13) can confirm an adverse credit trend revealed by operating cash flow.

CONCLUSION

Despite repeated demonstrations of the truism that no single measure encapsulates all of a company's pertinent financial traits, investors continue to search for the silver bullet. If a company's value is not a direct function of its net income, they tell themselves, the problem must be that net income is too greatly affected by incidental factors such as tax rates and financial leverage. The answer must be to move up the income statement to a measure that puts companies on a more even plane with one another. As former Merrill Lynch investment strategist Richard Bernstein points out,[5] operating earnings tend to be stabler than reported earnings, EBIT tends to be stabler than operating earnings, and EBITDA tends to be stabler than EBIT. Companies welcome analytical migration toward less variable measures of performance, because investors reward stability with high price-earnings multiples. The trend of moving up the income statement reached its logical conclusion during the technology stock boom of the late 1990s. Investors latched onto the highest, most stable figure of all by valuing stocks on price-sales ratios. (To obscure what was going on, some companies actually resorted to discussing their earnings before expenses, or EBE.)

Strategist Bernstein found that by attempting to filter out the volatility inherent in companies' earnings, investors reduced the effectiveness of their stock selection. In a study spanning the period 1986 to July 2001, he compared the performance of portfolios of stocks based on low ratios of price to earnings with alternative portfolios of stocks priced at low multiples of EBITDA, cash flow, book value, and sales. The good old-fashioned low P/E criterion produced the highest average return (16.7 percent) of any of the strategies. Stocks chosen on the basis of low total enterprise value[6] to EBITDA produced the lowest average return, 12.3 percent. Adjusted for risk, as well, investors achieved far better results by relying on the bottom line, net income, instead of moving up the income statement to EBITDA. Bernstein's findings reinforced the message that instead of seeking an alternative to net income that summarizes corporate performance in its entirety, analysts of financial statements should examine a variety of measures to derive maximum insight.

The Reliability of Disclosure and Audits

A naive observer might consider it overkill to scrutinize a company's financial statements for signs that management is presenting anything less than a candid picture. After all, extensive regulations compel publicly traded corporations to disclose material events affecting the value of their securities. Even if a company's management is inclined to finagle, investors have a second line of defense in the form of mandatory annual certification of the financials by highly trained auditors. The Securities and Exchange Commission's (SEC) Corporation Finance and Enforcement divisions provide an additional line of defense.

These arguments accurately portray how the system is supposed to work for the benefit of the users of financial statements. As in so many other situations, however, the gap between theory and practice is substantial when it comes to relying on legal mechanisms to protect shareholders and lenders. Up to a point, it is true, fear of the consequences of breaking the law keeps corporate managers in line. *Bending* the law is another matter, though, in the minds of many executives. If their bonuses depend on presenting results in an unfairly favorable light, they can usually see their way clear to adopting that course.

Getting the job done, in the corporate world's success-manual jargon, most definitely includes hard-nosed negotiating with auditors over the limits to which the accounting standards may be stretched. Technically, the board of directors appoints the auditing firm, but management is the point of contact in hashing out the details of presenting financial events for external consumption. A tension necessarily exists between standards of professional excellence (which, it must be acknowledged, matter a great deal to most accountants) and fear of the consequences of losing a client.

At some point, resigning the account becomes a moral imperative, but in the real world, accounting firms must be pushed rather far to reach that point. As a part of the seasoning process leading to a managerial role, accountants become reconciled to certain discontinuities between the bright, white lines drawn in college accounting courses and the fuzzy boundaries for applying the rules. Consequently, it is common for frontline auditors to balk at an aggressive accounting treatment proposed by a company's managers, only to be overruled by their senior colleagues.

Even if the auditors hold their ground against corporate managers who believe that everything in life is a negotiation, the outcome of the haggling will not necessarily be a fair picture of the company's financial performance. At the extreme, executives may falsify their results. Fraud is an unambiguous violation of accounting standards, but audits do not invariably catch it. Cost considerations preclude reviewing every transaction or examining every bin to see whether it actually contains the inventory attributed to it. Instead, auditors rely on sampling. If they happen to inspect the wrong items, falsified data will go undetected. Extremely clever scamsters may even succeed in undermining the auditors' efforts to select their samples at random, a procedure designed to foil concealment of fraud.

When challenged on inconsistencies in their numbers, companies sometimes blame error, rather than any intention to mislead the users of financial statements. On April 16, 2001, Computer Associates International preliminarily reported operating earnings of $0.40 a share for the fiscal year ended March 31. On May 4, the software producer put the figure at $0.16. The discrepancy, said management, resulted from a typographical error. According to the company, an employee transcribed a number incorrectly in preparing a news release.[1]

Investors might have been excused for reacting skeptically. Shortly before the May 4 announcement, Computer Associates' accounting practices had come under attack in the press. Besides, seasoned followers of the corporate scene realize that companies are not always as forthcoming as investors might reasonably expect. The following examples from the casino business illustrate the point.

AN ARTFUL DEAL

On October 25, 1999, Trump Hotels & Casino Resorts reported a year-over-year rise in its third-quarter earnings per share, from $0.24 to $0.63, excluding a one-time charge related to the closing of the Trump World's Fair Casino Hotel. The net exceeded analysts' consensus forecast of $0.54 a share,[2] resulting in a jump in Trump's share price from $4 to $4 5/16. Also up on the day were the bonds of one of the company's casinos, Trump Atlantic City, which climbed about one point to 84 1/4.

"Our focus in 1999 was threefold," said President and Chief Executive Officer Nicholas Ribis, in explaining the profit surge, which surprised industry analysts. "First, to increase our operating margins at each operating entity; second, to decrease our marketing costs; and third, to increase our cash sales from our non-casino operations. We have succeeded in achieving positive results in each of these three categories."[3]

The company's self-congratulatory press release contained no mention of another important contributor to the third-quarter surge in revenues and, by extension, net income. As the subsequently filed quarterly report on Form 10-Q finally acknowledged, $17.2 million of the period's revenue arose from bankrupt restaurant operator Planet Hollywood's abandonment of its lease on the All Star Café at Trump's Taj Mahal casino. With the termination of the lease, all improvements and alterations, along with certain other assets, became the property of Trump, which took over the restaurant's operation. An independent appraisal valued the assets received by Trump at $17.2 million. Without that boost, the company's revenues would have declined, year over year, and net income would have undershot, rather than exceeded, analysts' expectations.

The discrepancy between the October 25 disclosure and the fuller accounting in the 10-Q "became an embarrassment" to Trump Hotels & Casino Resorts, according to the *Wall Street Journal*.[4] Moreover, the timing was unfortunate. The incident occurred as management was making a round of investor presentations aimed at generating support for its plans to develop a new resort on the Atlantic City, New Jersey, site of the shuttered World's Fair casino.

Worse yet, from the company's standpoint, the fact that Trump had omitted some rather useful information was detectable. Bear, Stearns & Co. bond analyst Tom Shandell noticed that the company's press release reported mysteriously large revenues for the Trump Taj Mahal. The unit's revenues increased by $4.9 million over the comparable 1998 quarter, even though the New Jersey Casino Control Commission reported a $12.1 million decline in the Taj Mahal's *casino* revenues. Shandell was correct in suspecting that some other large, unspecified item was buried in the numbers; the difference between the purported $4.9 million increase and the commission's reported decline of $12.1 million was essentially identical to the $17.2 million of All Star Café assets that later came to light. No such inference or backing out of numbers would have been required if Trump's third-quarter 1999 press release had provided as much detail on the Taj Mahal's operations as the corresponding 1998 release. That was not the case, however, as Exhibit 9.1 demonstrates.

Was the drastic cutback in disclosure in Trump's third-quarter 1999 earnings release part of a deliberate attempt to conceal the fact that the

EXHIBIT 9.1   Disclosure of Trump Taj Mahal Results in Trump
Hotels and Casino Resorts Earnings Release Three Months
Ended September 30, 1998 ($000 omitted)

Revenues		
Casino	$148,011	
Number of slots	4,137	
Win per slot/day	277	
Slot win		$ 82,456
Number of tables	157	
Win per table/day	$ 4,160	
Table win	$ 60,087	
Table drop	$328,456	
Hold %		18.3%
Poker, keno, race win		$ 5,468
Rooms	$ 11,410	
Number of rooms sold	112,875	
Average room rates		$ 101.09
Occupancy %		98.2%
Food and beverage	$ 15,034	
Other	5,667	
Promotional allowances		(18,018)
Net revenues		$162,104
Costs and expenses Gaming	83,711	
Rooms		3,752
Food and beverage	4,844	
General and administrative	23,785	
Total expenses	116,092	
EBITDA*	$ 46,012	

*EBITDA reflects earnings before depreciation, interest, taxes,
Casino Reinvestment Development Authority writedown, and
nonoperating income.

Three Months Ended September 30, 1999 ($000 omitted)

Revenues	$167.7	
Operating profit		41.4
EBITDA	51.0	
Margin	30.4%	

Sources: Trump Hotels and Casino Resorts Press Releases dated
October 7, 1998, and October 25, 1999.

year-over-year revenue gain was solely attributable to a nonrecurring event? Not to hear the company's president tell it. "It was never hidden," Ribis insisted. "When there was a specific question about it, we broke it out."[5] The gain on the All Star Café simply got lost in the shuffle, he maintained, when the lawyers pressed him to put out third-quarter earnings before commencing the road show for the proposed new casino. "As soon as I learned of the accounting treatment we spoke with all of our investors and analysts," added Ribis.[6]

By apparently claiming that he discovered the true source of his company's year-over-year earnings increase only after the quarterly results had been released, Ribis did not burnish his reputation as a details man. That professed shortcoming may not explain why, seven months later, Trump Hotels & Casino Resorts decided not to renew Ribis's expiring contract as CEO. Perhaps it had more to do with the 56 percent drop in Trump's stock price in the 12 months ending May 2000. One thing is certain, however. Investors who relied solely on the company's disclosure were burned if they bought into the rally that followed the bullish-sounding press release. After analyst Shandell's inquiries uncovered the All Star Café's contribution to third-quarter results, the stock promptly sagged from \$4 5/16 to \$3 7/8, while the Trump Atlantic City bonds slid from 84 1/4 to 80. On January 16, 2002, Trump Hotels and Casinos agreed to settle SEC charges that it "recklessly" misled investors in this incident, without admitting or denying the commission's findings.[7]

DEATH DUTIES

In roughly the same period in which the Trump Hotels & Casino Resorts controversy arose, the gambling industry provided another example of the hazards of relying on company disclosures. Arthur Goldberg, chief executive officer of Park Place Entertainment, entered the hospital in June 1999. The company attributed his confinement to a respiratory infection, but rumors began to circulate that he was gravely ill.[8] By the time Goldberg was released from the hospital on July 7, Park Place's stock had fallen by 6 percent. Over the same period, the 12 stocks constituting the Chicago Board Options Exchange Gaming Index rose by an average of 8 percent.

As late as September 2000, Park Place denied a report that Goldberg planned to step down as CEO the following year.[9] Asked about his health, the 58-year-old casino king tersely replied, "It's okay. Things wear out as you get older."[10] On October 19, 2000, Goldberg died of complications of bone marrow failure—decidedly not a condition that develops suddenly.

The stock market's reaction to Goldberg's death was surprising, in view of his reputation as "the driving force behind Park Place Entertainment, the man who in just ten years turned a failing casino company into a powerhouse that dominated the industry."[11] After dropping initially, the stock finished up a quarter-point on the day. Analysts credited the shares' resilience to Goldberg's success in assembling a strong management team. Be that as it may, investors who relied on the company's disclosures during Goldberg's 1999 hospitalization, while ignoring rumors of a potentially fatal illness, failed to capitalize on information that influenced the stock and ultimately proved to be correct.

Park Place Entertainment might be criticized for tardiness in divulging Goldberg's health problems, but at least its disclosure was more punctual than that of Sun City Industries under similar circumstances. On May 29, 1997, the food-service distributor announced with deepest regret the death of its president, Gustave Minkin. This initial disclosure of Minkin's passing came four days after the event. For investors who have noticed that senior-level personnel changes often affect the value of a stock, somewhat prompter reporting is desirable.

SYSTEMATIC PROBLEMS IN AUDITING

No system for auditing companies' books will ever work perfectly. Updating of accounting standards will inevitably lag business innovations that generate new types of transactions, giving companies leeway in how they are to be reported. Indeed, companies devote vast energy specifically to finding gray areas and loopholes in existing standards. Moreover, even crystal-clear accounting rules cannot fully protect the users of financial statements from corporate executives who violate them. Regrettably, the most respected auditing firms are bound to have a few bad apples (i.e., individuals willing to accept bribes to facilitate management's misrepresentations rather than faithfully fulfill their role as protectors of financial statement users). As with other types of crime, it is not feasible for the government to devote enough resources to law enforcement to deter would-be perpetrators through near certainty of getting caught.

To say that no perfect system can be designed, however, is quite different from saying that existing provisions for issuing financial accounting standards, conducting audits, and policing fraud are as good as real-world conditions permit. The present system is not the product of objective analysis by panels of experts driven solely by a desire to provide accurate and transparent financial statements to the public. On the contrary, the design of the rule-making bodies and the rules they issue are outcomes of fierce political struggles. Auditing firms are profit-maximizing businesses that face unavoidable conflicts between upholding professional standards, on the one hand, and retaining clients and controlling costs, on the other. Given these facts, individual cases of audit failure cannot be viewed as isolated incidents. A systematic component perpetuates financial misreporting, despite reforms that periodically emerge in reaction to exceptionally shocking accounting scandals.

The system's response to the financial reporting megascandals of 2001–2002, involving prominent companies such as Enron, Global Crossing, Tyco International, and WorldCom, illustrates the intractability of the problem. Critics of the accounting profession highlighted the conflict of interest that had grown over the years between the provision of audits and the sale of consulting services to the same clients. Was an auditor likely to stand firm in a dispute over accounting policy, they asked, if the company's management could dangle lucrative consulting contracts as an inducement to back down?

Popular outrage over the post–Tech Wreck accounting scandals created political momentum to eliminate the auditing-consulting conflict. A *Wall Street Journal* analysis of the companies constituting the Dow Jones Industrial Average[12] found, however, that two years after the Securities and Exchange Commission began to crack down on the practice, 62 percent of fees paid to auditors were for nonauditing services. Furthermore, the decline from 75 percent in the preceding year (2001) was overstated. The new rules on auditor independence expanded the definition of what could be considered part of the audit fee. Services that were reclassified from nonauditing to auditing included statutory audits, reviews of documents filed with the Securities and Exchange Commission, and consultations on taxes and accounting to the extent they were needed to comply with generally accepted auditing standards. To some extent as well, the relative decline in the auditing-related portion of total fees reflected an average 10 percent to 15 percent year-over-year increase in the cost of audits, reflecting the increased complexity of accounting standards and expanded use of specialists to deal with derivatives contracts. According to Barbara Roper, director of investor protection at the Consumer Federation of America, "The conflict looks less without anything having changed."[13]

The response to the 2001–2002 accounting scandals illustrates the way lobbyists for reporting companies and their auditors can block more thoroughgoing reforms. Advocates for the users of financial statements, such as the Chartered Financial Analysts Institute, are outgunned by corporate and auditing interests. Those groups commit substantial resources to participating in hearings and requests for comments that influence the deliberations of the Financial Accounting Standards Board and the SEC. As the reform process drags on, popular anger over accounting issues tends to subside, as the public's attention shifts to new controversies in other areas of legislation and regulation. With attention diverted from reform of the accounting system, persistent lobbying by corporations and auditors waters down the original sweeping proposals.

Systematic problems in the audit process arise not only from the regulatory structure but also from the business strategies of profit-maximizing accounting firms.[14] The problem dates back to the 1970s, when the American Institute of Certified Public Accountants lifted a ban on auditors advertising their services, soliciting rival firms' clients unless invited, and participating in competitive bids for business. This change resulted from a federal government crackdown on such rules within professions, deeming them anticompetitive and threatening to launch antitrust suits to abolish them. Bidding wars resulted, and over time, audits became a service that accounting firms offered at a knockdown rate to compete for the more profitable consulting business. Increasingly, auditing was offered at a flat fee, making it imperative to hold down costs. Under pressure to limit the hours devoted to an audit, firms were not consistently able to devote the resources needed to uncover improper reporting.

In the 1990s, risk-based audits emerged as a means of keeping a lid on costs. Firms abandoned their traditional bottom-up approach of examining all components of the financial statements. Instead of focusing on details of individual transactions, they identified the areas that in their judgment presented the greatest risk of error or fraud, such as complex derivatives. Incredibly, these judgments in some cases were based on management's advice. For instance, when Ernst & Young audited the 2002 accounts of HealthSouth (see Chapter 11 for details of that company's massive accounting fraud), the audit team asked the company's executives whether they were aware of any significant instances of fraud, to which the executives naturally answered no. The auditors accepted management's assertion on the grounds that they considered HealthSouth's management ethical and its system for generating financial data reliable. On that basis, the Ernst & Young audit team performed many fewer tests of HealthSouth's numbers than they would have at a company they deemed to have a higher risk of improper accounting.

The detrimental impact of the shift toward risk-based audits was also apparent in the accounting fraud of telecommunications giant WorldCom. For a period during 2002, investors seriously wondered if any company's financial statements were reliable, considering what lay beneath the WorldCom financials that, according to Arthur Andersen, were prepared in accordance with generally accepted accounting principles (GAAP). All told, WorldCom racked up $10.6 billion of fraudulent profits on the way to becoming, in 2002, the largest corporate bankruptcy up to that time.

In WorldCom's early days, Arthur Andersen audited the company in a meticulous, bottom-up way. It reviewed thousands of individual transactions and confirmed them in the company's general ledger. As the company grew, however, Andersen migrated toward a risk-based process. The auditors used sophisticated software to analyze WorldCom's statements and met to brainstorm about ways in which management might be fudging the numbers. Once they identified an area of high risk, they assessed the adequacy of the internal controls by reviewing procedures with employees and running sample tests to determine whether the procedures were being followed.

If a question arose about controls or procedures, Andersen relied on the answers provided by management. This was problematic for two reasons. First, Andersen's software had identified WorldCom as a maximum-risk client. Second, the relationship between Andersen and WorldCom's management was not conducive to asking tough questions or being skeptical about the answers. In its proposal to the company for the 2000 audit, Andersen characterized itself as "a committed member of [WorldCom's] team."[15] Imagine a football referee calling himself a member of a team in a game at which he was officiating!

Andersen's auditors regularly asked WorldCom managers whether they had made any unusual top-side adjustments (i.e., general ledger accounting entries that were recorded after the books had closed for the quarter). The executives consistently replied that they had not, and according to a report by the company's bankruptcy examiner, Andersen did no tests to confirm their claims. As a supposed safeguard, the auditors looked for large swings in items on WorldCom's consolidated balance sheet. Finding none, they concluded that no follow-up procedures were needed. As it turned out, however, management had manipulated the statements precisely to ensure that there would be no unusual variances. WorldCom's top-side adjustments reversed liabilities and reclassified expenses as assets to delay the recognition of costs. If Andersen's people had drilled down to specific journal entries in the old-fashioned way, they would have discovered hundreds of large entries of suspiciously round numbers and no supporting documentation. One post-quarter-end entry for $239 million was documented solely by a sticky note showing the number "$239,000,000."

Going to the trouble of checking such items, however, would have added to the cost of auditing WorldCom. That was not something Arthur Andersen was keen on, given that it had already spent more on the company's audit than it had billed. As a result of competitive pressures, the audit had become a loss leader that Andersen used to obtain profitable consulting business from WorldCom.

Obsessive cost control similarly hamstrung the auditors' backup to protecting users of financial statements, the Securities and Exchange

Commission.[16] Congress was stingy in funding the SEC's efforts to check filings such as 10-Ks, 10-Qs, and initial public offering prospectuses. Between 1981 and 2001, the number of filings that the commission's Corporation Finance Division was called on to review grew by 81 percent, but the staff expanded by only 29 percent. A report by management consultant McKinsey & Co. found that to meet numerical targets for reviewing filings, the overstretched Corporation Finance employees gamed the system, selecting smaller, easy-to-review filings and avoiding more complex ones. Furthermore, the emphasis on volume deterred the surveillance people from exercising their option of ordering deeper reviews. A further indication of tightfistedness in funding the SEC was loss of staff, as salaries fell behind private-sector pay levels. In 1999 and 2000, SEC personnel quit at twice the average rate within the federal government.

Congress's unwillingness to give the SEC the resources it needed to do its job reflected more than competing claims on the federal budget. From an ideological standpoint, many members of Congress opposed strict controls on business. One manifestation of this attitude was a 1995 proposal for a five-year freeze on the SEC's budget, a cutback in the number of commissioners from five to three, and a requirement that the agency justify the cost of any regulatory change. Fortunately for users of financial statements, these proposals were not accepted. In October 2000, SEC Chairman Arthur Levitt and enforcement chief Richard Walker presented evidence of auditors agreeing to turn a blind eye to accounting irregularities rather than risk losing profitable consulting business. Levitt wanted to restrict firms' ability to provide auditing and consulting to the same clients, but Senate Banking Committee Chairman Phil Gramm denounced the plan as "too draconian."[17] The SEC had to settle for merely requiring companies to disclose the amounts they paid auditors for consulting work.

Lynn Turner, former chief accountant at the SEC, said that the relentless assault from Congress affected the commission's agenda and reforms. In addition, Congress's tight rein on the purse strings had an adverse effect at the ground level of enforcement. Between 1991 and 2001, the cases opened by the Enforcement Division grew by 65 percent while the staff expanded by only 27 percent. According to former SEC official Richard Sauer, resources were too stretched to leave time to prospect for new infractions. There was already a backlog of items that clearly constituted violations. These constraints signaled to corporate management that there was a good chance that cheating would go undetected.

As a demonstration of the impact of Congress's frugality, in 1999, the enforcement staff followed up on an investment newsletter tip regarding financial misreporting at Tyco International (see Chapter 10). Responding to a request for documents, Tyco submitted pages that blacked out entries related to Chairman Dennis Kozlowski's borrowings under an employee loan program, saying those items were irrelevant to the SEC's request. It later turned out that Kozlowski had borrowed extensively for personal expenses, even though the program was intended to help executives cover taxes on stock grants. Fearful that a wider probe would absorb too much of their limited resources, SEC personnel did not question the blackouts or request the full company ledger. They shut down their investigation with no action. New York State prosecutors later charged Kozlowski with looting $600 million from Tyco.

One final line of defense for users of a company's financial statements is the audit committee of its board of directors. This protection has not proven infallible over the years. In a study of financial frauds that came to light between 1987 and 1997, the Securities and Exchange Commission found that the audit committees of many of the companies involved met only once a year or so. Some had no audit committees. In one of the few encouraging notes of recent years, the SEC has imposed a financial literacy requirement on audit committee members. This might seem too obvious a criterion to necessitate a specific regulation, but readers should bear in mind that former football star and convicted armed robber O. J. Simpson once served on the audit committee of Infinity Broadcasting Corporation.[18]

CONCLUSION

If the horror stories recounted in this chapter were isolated incidents, it might be valid to argue that in most cases, the combined impact of corporate disclosure requirements, external audits, and regulatory backup ensures a high level of reliability in financial statements. Intense analysis of the statements by the users would then seem superfluous. Many companies, however, are either stingy with information or slippery about the way they present it. Rather than laying down the law (or GAAP), auditors typically wind up negotiating with management to arrive at a point where they can convince themselves that the bare minimum requirements of good practice have been satisfied. Taking a harder line may not produce fuller disclosure for investors but merely mean sacrificing the auditing contract to another firm with a more accommodating policy. Given the observed gap between theory and practice in financial reporting, users of financial statements must provide themselves with an additional layer of protection through tough scrutiny of the numbers.

Mergers-and-Acquisitions Accounting

The accounting treatment of a merger or acquisition does not affect the combined companies' subsequent competitive strength or ability to generate cash. Discretionary accounting choices in mergers-and-acquisitions (M&A) activity can, however, have a substantial impact on reported earnings. Intentionally opaque accounting makes it difficult for users of financial reporting to tell whether a highly acquisitive company is achieving **organic growth** or creating an illusion of dynamism through business combinations that generate no economic benefits.

MAXIMIZING POSTACQUISITION REPORTED EARNINGS

The conglomerate Tyco International devised an ingenious means of dressing up postacquisition performance in its 1998 acquisition of United States Surgical. Shortly before closing its deal with Tyco, the acquiree took a $190 million write-off, reducing future depreciation charges and thereby boosting future earnings. United States Surgical filed no further financial statements after taking the write-off, however. The reduction in asset values was consequently never reported to investors. After the renowned short seller James Chanos drew journalist Floyd Norris's attention to the issue, Tyco's chief financial officer provided more details than the *New York Times* columnist had managed to back out of Tyco's Securities and Exchange Commission (SEC) filings. Norris commented that the unreported write-off was significant for the light it shed on Tyco's reputation for improving the operations of companies it acquired.[1] Legitimately spurring its subsidiaries to greater achievements was no easy task, with operations scattered across such diverse businesses as medical supplies, leasing, home-security and fire-alarm systems, underwater cable, and electronic components. (The company had no connection with toy manufacturer Tyco.)

Helping to draw attention to Tyco's questionable M&A accounting in 1999 was Albert Meyer of David W. Tice Associates. In a detailed, nine-page report, Meyer highlighted the large number of one-time charges taken by the company after many acquisitions. "You have to believe all these restructuring charges have no meaning to believe this thing is really growing at double-digit rates."[2]

Meyer emphasized that he was not accusing Tyco of fraud, but merely of aggressive accounting. Nevertheless, the diversified manufacturer responded in the classic manner of a company criticized for tricky financial reporting. Tyco angrily denounced Meyer's report, stating that "rumors relating to the company are false, unfounded, and malicious." Chairman Dennis Kozlowski insisted in a conference call that there were "no restatements, no irregularities, and no investigations" involving Tyco's financial statements.[3] Predictably, as well, Tyco received moral support from Wall Street securities analysts, almost all of whom had buy recommendations on the stock. An analyst from one of the leading firms said that as a result of hearing Tyco's conference call, "we were convinced there are no accounting issues."[4]

The Securities and Exchange Commission, however, was not convinced. On December 9, 1999, Tyco disclosed that the securities watchdog had launched an informal inquiry into special charges and reserves taken in connection with 120 acquisitions over the preceding six years. Tyco's share price plummeted by 23 percent on the news. The company continued to insist that the criticisms of its financial reporting were all unfounded. Another leading Wall Street firm's analyst chimed in: "While this investigation puts a further cloud on the stock, we believe that the company will receive a clean bill of health from the SEC regarding its accounting policies, which could put an end to all the rumors and accusations."[5]

This analyst was later fired by his firm and fined by the National Association of Securities Dealers for such misdeeds as being excessively chummy with Tyco's Kozlowski and publishing research reports containing misleading statements and exaggerated claims. He was not alone in defending Tyco's financial reporting. One prominent analyst, who claimed to have followed the company's accounting closely, dismissed the issues raised by Chanos and Meyer as "bogus" and nothing but "noise." Still, a nearly 50 percent cumulative drop in Tyco's stock in the weeks following Meyer's report made some of the company's sell-side boosters nervous. "Most of us are doing fine," joked one analyst, "except for a few who are on suicide watch."[6]

No such desperate acts were warranted by the outcome of the SEC inquiry, announced on June 26, 2000. Tyco was required to restate its results to reverse merger reserves that the commission said should never have been set up or should have been reversed earlier, but the restatement shifted a paltry $0.02 a share from one quarter to another. Tyco's stock jumped by 13 percent on the news. A leading Wall Street firm's accounting analyst commented, "To see these items come out of what, by all indications, was an exhaustive SEC review, is a testament to the integrity of Tyco's accounting practices."[7] An analyst at a prominent money management firm that held about 12 million Tyco shares added that the results of the SEC inquiry "put to rest any lurking fears about the company's accounting and the credibility of its management."[8]

Nevertheless, the issue of Tyco's merger accounting continued to lurk. Two-and-a-half years later, Tyco shares fell by 19 percent after the *Wall Street Journal* reported that the company had spent more than $8 billion in the preceding three years on more than 700 undisclosed acquisitions. Alert analysts had suspected something was going on behind the scenes. They questioned why, in the most recent fiscal year, debt attributable to Tyco's industrial businesses doubled to $21.6 billion even though the company reported $4.8 billion in **free cash flow.**

Tyco Chief Financial Officer Mark Swartz defended the company's disclosures on the grounds that the numerous small acquisitions were not individually material relative to Tyco's huge size. This was a case of meeting the letter of generally accepted accounting practices (GAAP) but violating the spirit by concealing acquisitions that were collectively material. Swartz acknowledged that the amount spent on unannounced deals was not determinable from Tyco's financial statements because it reported acquisition expenditures net of cash on the acquired companies' balance sheets and did not disclose the aggregate amount of that cash.

Lurking concerns about Tyco's acquisition accounting surfaced again when an April 1, 2002, *Fortune* article[9] published allegations of deceptive accounting in connection with the 1999 acquisition of electronics manufacturer Raychem. In its last year as an independent company, Raychem reported earnings of $179 million, down from 1997's $253 million. Five former financial employees and a former consultant to Raychem said that between the May 1999 announcement of the deal and the August 1999 closing, they were asked to accelerate payment of expenses, hold back postings of payments received, and overstate reserves. *Fortune* published an excerpt from a July 30, 1999, memo by Raychem Treasurer Lars Larson on the subject of "accelerating cash outflow." Larson wrote, "At Tyco's request, all major Raychem sites will pay all pending payables, whether they are due or not." He went on to say that he understood Raychem's chief financial officer had agreed to the policy, "even though we will be spending the money for no tangible benefit either to Raychem or Tyco." On August 3, Larson wrote, "The purpose of this effort is, at Tyco's request, to cause cash flows to be negative in the 'old' Raychem, and more positive in the new company."[10]

Separately, the head of an outsourcing firm responsible for managing Raychem inventory reported that Tyco took a 100 percent reserve on $5 million of inventory that supposedly might have no remaining useful life following the acquisition. Considering that the inventory included such items as gloves and light bulbs, which would have useful lives of many years, the outsourcing firm had recommended a 30 percent reserve, while allowing that a 36 percent reserve would be defensible. All in all, it appeared that Chanos and Meyer had been on the right track in 1999 and that the "exhaustive SEC review" concluded the following year had left some stones unturned.

Two months after the *Fortune* exposé appeared, Tyco CEO Kozlowski resigned for the proverbial personal reasons, although the *New York Times* reported that he was under criminal investigation. Tyco's stock plunged by 20 percent on the news. The SEC opened a new investigation of Tyco's financial statements, including those as far back as 1999, and questioned whether the company had withheld important information during its earlier probe.

Under Kozlowski's successor, the company initiated an internal review of its past financial reporting. The investigators concluded that Tyco repeatedly used aggressive, albeit legal, accounting gimmicks, including depressing the reported profits of acquired companies immediately before acquisition, in order to generate profit surges in the first quarter after closing. Company officials referred to such practices as "financial engineering" and ordered employees to "create stories" to justify accounting changes that would hype Tyco's reported earnings. One document related to these practices included a handwritten notation: "I would strongly recommend Never to put this in writing!!"[11] Andrew Ross Sorkin of the *New York Times* concluded:

> *The new Tyco, though still viable, is what skeptics always thought it was: a hodgepodge of consistently profitable but unconnected, slow-growth businesses. . . . Without a steady stream of acquisitions—and the artificially inflated earnings boost that Tyco engineered for the first couple of quarters after each deal was completed—the consistent growth that made Tyco a highflying stock in the last couple of years is over.*[12]

Aside from its tricks for boosting reported earnings by holding down acquired companies' preacquisition profits, Tyco's financial reporting aggressiveness involved distortion of reported free cash flow through a nonstandard definition of the term. Tyco excluded cash received from sales of receivables and cash outlays for the purchase of customer accounts for its ADT security-alarm business, labeling the latter "acquisitions." Separate from the company's assorted accounting issues were charges of looting the company of $600 million, which led to Dennis Kozlowski's 2005 conviction and sentencing to $8^1/_3$ to 25 years in prison. His trial was a spectacle that featured a videotape of a $2 million birthday party for Kozlowski's wife, half of which was paid for by Tyco, replete with togas and gladiator costumes, an ice sculpture of Michelangelo's *David,* a birthday cake in the shape of a woman's body, and entertainment by Jimmy Buffett. As for Albert Meyer, whose scrutiny of Tyco's financial statements helped attentive investors avoid huge losses in the company's stock, the pleasure of the media recognition he received for his diligence was somewhat offset by an angry call from a Tyco shareholder in 1999, excoriating him for "bringing a good company down."[13]

MANAGING ACQUISITION DATES AND AVOIDING RESTATEMENTS

Companies have developed a number of subtle strategies for exploiting the discretion afforded by the rules for acquisition accounting. Maximizing reported earnings in the postacquisition period remains a key objective. For example, one M&A-related gambit entails the GAAP-sanctioned use, for financial reporting purposes, of an acquisition date other than the actual date on which a transaction is consummated. Typically, companies use this discretion to simplify closing their books at month- or quarter-end. For example, if an acquisition agreement is completed on May 27, the acquirer may begin reporting the acquired company's results in its own figures as of May 31.

In 1999, Navigant Consulting (formerly known as Metzler Group and unrelated to the travel management company Navigant International) exploited the acquisition date leeway in an unusually aggressive fashion. The utilities consulting company acquired Penta Advisory Services in mid-September, but designated July 1 as the acquisition date. Following standard practice under purchase accounting rules, Navigant included Penta's revenues in its own totals from the acquisition date forward. Navigant's revenue therefore received a boost for the entire third quarter, even though Penta entered the corporate fold only at the tail end of the period.

To be sure, the numbers involved were small. Penta's trailing-12-months revenues were in the range of $5 million to $6 million, while Navigant's 1998 sales were $348 million. Nevertheless, Merrill Lynch analyst Thatcher Thompson took management to task for shifting the acquisition date by $2^1/_2$ months. It was a more aggressive approach, he wrote, than he had ever previously observed under comparable circumstances.[14]

Thompson was not the only commentator with qualms about Navigant's merger accounting, notwithstanding its number three ranking, at the time, on the *Forbes* list of Best Small Companies in America. Other critics focused on management's exploitation of the standards (later tightened up) governing the classification of acquisitions as material to overall financial results. Under Securities and Exchange Commission rules, companies did not have to restate previous statements to reflect the revenues and earnings of acquired businesses deemed immaterial in size. Navigant grew rapidly after going public in 1996 by making many moderate-size acquisitions. Individually, the acquired consulting businesses were immaterial under GAAP, but collectively, they had a large impact on the company's results.

Barron's columnist Barry Henderson estimated revenues for Navigant's 1998 acquisitions for the final three quarters of 1998 by tracing the increase in shares outstanding, quarter by quarter.[15] He deducted the number of shares representing exercise of management stock options to estimate how many shares were issued to pay for acquisitions. Multiplying this figure by the share price gave the estimated dollar amount paid for acquisitions during the quarter. (To be conservative, the journalist used the minimum stock price for the period.) Next, Henderson divided the estimated aggregate acquisition price by 2.2, the multiple of trailing-12-months revenue that Navigant said it usually paid for consulting businesses. The answer represented a reasonable estimate of the revenues produced by the supposedly immaterial companies acquired during the second through fourth quarters of 1998. If Navigant had been required to restate its 1998 first-quarter results for these transactions, Henderson concluded, revenue would have been $83 million to $84 million, instead of the $79 million reported. That would have reduced first-quarter 1999 year-over-year revenue growth to around 16 percent from the sexier 22 percent generally cited by securities analysts.

As it turned out, investors were wise to react to the red flag raised by Navigant's liberal accounting for acquisitions. On November 22, Chairman and Chief Executive Officer Robert P. Maher resigned under pressure, touching off a 48 percent plunge in Navigant's stock. The company's directors had uncovered evidence that Maher and two other senior officials were involved in "inappropriate" stock purchases.

In brief, Maher borrowed $10 million from the company in August 1999, saying it was for a real estate investment.[16] Navigant's board subsequently came to believe that he in fact advanced the funds to Stephen Denari, the company's vice president of corporate development. Denari had borrowed a like amount to purchase Navigant shares at $28.39[17] from the former owner of a company that Navigant had acquired for stock. A short while later, the shares soared to $54.25 when Navigant hired a financial adviser to explore strategic options, including a possible sale of the company.[18]

CONCLUSION

A highly acquisitive company can stay within the boundaries of GAAP yet present an earnings record that grossly misleads outside users of its financial statements. The Tyco and Navigant cases show that none of the following constitutes assurance that a serial acquirer is not monkeying around with its financial reporting:

- Inclusion of the corporation in a business magazine's best companies list.
- A vote of confidence in the company's accounting by famous Wall Street securities analysts, even if the analyst does not follow companies but instead concentrates entirely on accounting issues.
- A finding of only minor accounting issues after an exhaustive review of the company's financials by the Securities and Exchange Commission.
- Heated denials by management that it has misrepresented its results.

Recognizing that such safeguards cannot be relied on, users of financial statements must cast a skeptical eye on companies that report remarkable but difficult-to-explain earnings increases. Clues to hanky-panky may include an unusually large number of special items, a mysterious buildup of cash despite large reported free cash flow, and, if an acquired company was a public reporter prior to its acquisition, a drop in earnings just prior to closing. Sadly, many M&A transactions produce more of this sort of accounting trickery than bona fide synergies or operating improvements in the acquired companies.

Is Fraud Detectable?

This chapter addresses the most difficult challenge to an analyst of financial statements. It is the case of a company that does not merely bend the rules, but intentionally breaks them. Often, the auditor actively participates in the fraud, thereby disabling one of the analyst's key defenses against deception. Analysts who uncover a major, flagrant violation of financial reporting standards can avert huge investment losses or produce large gains through selling short. They also can make their reputations in the process.

The discussion begins with "Telltale Signs of Manipulation," the findings of systematic studies of financial statements of companies that misrepresented their results. Three case studies of fraudulent reporting follow, involving Enron, HealthSouth, and Parmalat. These studies explain how the frauds were perpetrated and also explore the extent to which analysts succeeded in detecting the wrongdoing.

TELLTALE SIGNS OF MANIPULATION

The aggressive accounting practices detailed in the preceding chapters may not win awards for candor, but neither will most of them land corporate managers in the penitentiary. There are many ways for companies to pull the wool over investors' eyes without fear of legal retribution. Sometimes, however, corporate executives step over the line into illegality.

Outright misrepresentation falls into a category entirely separate from the mere exploitation of financial reporting loopholes. Moreover, the gravity of such misconduct is not solely a matter of temporal law. In 1992, the Roman Catholic Church officially classified fraudulent accounting as a sin. A catechism unveiled in that year listed cooking the books in a series of so-called new transgressions, that is, offenses not known in 1566, the time of the last previous overhaul of church teachings.

Neither fear of prosecution nor concern for spiritual well-being, however, entirely deters dishonest presenters of financial information. Audits, even when conducted in good faith, sometimes fail to uncover dangerous fictions. Financial analysts must therefore strive to protect themselves from the consequences of fraud.

No method is guaranteed to uncover malfeasance in financial reporting, but neither are analysts obliged to accept an auditor's clean opinion as final. Even without the resources that are available to a major accounting firm, it is feasible to find valuable clues about the integrity of financial statements.

Messod Daniel Beneish, professor of accounting and information systems at the Kelley School of Business at Indiana University, has developed a model for identifying companies that are likely to manipulate their earnings, based on numbers reported in their financial statements.[1] (Beneish defines *manipulation* to include both actual fraud and the management of earnings or disclosure within generally accepted accounting practices [GAAP]. In either case, his definition specifies that the company subsequently must have been required to restate results, write off assets, or change its accounting estimates or policies at the behest of its auditors, an internal investigation, or a Securities and Exchange Commission [SEC] probe.) Beneish finds, by statistical analysis, that the presence of any of the following five factors increases the probability of earnings manipulation:

1. Increasing days' sales in receivables.
2. Deteriorating gross margins.
3. Decreasing rates of depreciation.
4. Decreasing asset quality (defined as an increase in the ratio of noncurrent assets other than property, plant, and equipment to total assets).
5. Growing sales.

Note that Beneish does not characterize these indicators as irrefutable evidence of accounting malfeasance. Indeed, it would be disheartening if every company registering high sales growth were shown to be achieving its results artificially. Nevertheless, Beneish's data suggest a strong association between the phenomena he lists and earnings manipulation.

Evidence of financial reporting manipulation can also be found outside the financial statements. A paper published by the Rock Center for Corporate Governance[2] focuses on the conference calls that corporate senior executives make in connection with quarterly earnings releases. Professor David F. Larcker and doctoral candidate Anastasia A. Zakolyukina of the Stanford Graduate School of Business identified verbal cues of financial reporting hanky-panky by analyzing the question-and-answer sections of the transcripts of 29,663 conference calls.

Based on which companies subsequently restated their results, as well as a set of criteria for identifying especially serious accounting problems, Larcker and Zakolyukina label each Q&A section "truthful" or "deceptive." Their methodology is significantly better than random, classifying 50 percent to 65 percent of the Q&A sections correctly. They also find that judgments based on the words used by chief executive officers and chief financial officers are more accurate than a model based on discretionary accruals.

Relative to the answers given by truthful executives, the replies of deceptive executives contain more references to general knowledge (such as the phrase "you know"), fewer nonextreme positive emotions ("solid" or "respectable"), and fewer references to shareholder value and creating value. Furthermore, deceptive CEOs make fewer references to themselves and more to impersonal third parties, saying "the team" or "the company," rather than "I." They use more extreme positive emotions ("fantastic," for example) and fewer extreme negative emotions, as well as fewer certainty and hesitation words.

FRAUDSTERS KNOW FEW LIMITS

Companies that cross the line from earnings management to outright fraud sometimes go to great lengths to cover their tracks. This may include enlisting the auditors to be coconspirators against, rather than protectors of, the users of financial statements. The evidence of criminal misrepresentation often appears obvious after the fact, but not even the most skilled analysts definitively identified some of the most famous frauds until the schemes became unsustainable and the companies collapsed.

The three following case studies, Enron, HealthSouth, and Parmalat, are cautionary tales. What appears to be a run-of-the-mill instance of aggressive reporting may prove to be something much more malevolent. It may turn out to be a case of almost no bona fide assets supporting the claims of creditors and shareholders. In studying these notorious frauds, readers should pay close attention not only to the suspicious financial statement items but also to the behavior of senior managers as the validity of their stated profits is challenged.

ENRON: A MEDIA SENSATION

In October 2000, *Fortune* published a list of the world's most admired companies, based on evaluations by executives and securities analysts. The business magazine wrote about one of these elite corporations, "No company illustrates the transformative power of innovation more dramatically than Enron."[3] Over the preceding decade, *Fortune* continued, Enron had transformed itself from an Old Economy pipeline operator to a New Economy trading powerhouse and increased its revenues from $200 million to $40 billion by inventing entirely new businesses. As it turned out, Enron's inventing had more to do with its reported earnings. The company filed for bankruptcy on December 2, 2001, only a little more than a year after being ranked among the 25 most admired companies in the world.

Enron's spectacular fall was an extraordinary media event. For more than a year, newspaper headlines dealt with a single company's accounting practices, a subject rarely given such attention. The affair spawned a best-selling book, *The Smartest Guys in the Room,* by Bethany McLean and Peter Elkind, which was adapted into a film directed by Alex Gibney. Lucy Prebble's satirical play, *Enron,* was a runaway hit in London, but the New York production closed after just three weeks, adding the backers' $3.6 million to the collateral damage from the company's sorry history.[4]

More important from the standpoint of investors and lenders, Enron raised the bar for financial statement analysts. The company did not merely take liberties with accounting standards in ways that standard ratio analysis would reveal. Instead, the secretive management kept many of the most important sources of reported earnings off the balance sheet and did its best to intimidate anyone who complained about inadequate disclosure. As a result, some portfolio managers and analysts came to mistrust management long before any serious misrepresentation came to light. Outsiders' inability to model the company's earnings added to their discomfort. Restatements announced in late 2001 covered annual reports beginning in 1997, but not until a few days before Enron's collapse did security analysts openly proclaim that the company's financial statements were unreliable.

Company Background

Enron was the product of the 1979 acquisition of Houston Natural Gas by InterNorth, the holding company for Northern Natural Gas, founded in Omaha, Nebraska, in 1932. Shortly after the formation of HNG/InterNorth, former HNG Chief Executive Officer Kenneth Lay became CEO and renamed the company Enteron. After business cards and stationery were printed, management learned that the new name closely resembled the Greek word for intestines, so Enron was substituted.

Lay took Enron far beyond its original activities, natural gas pipelines and the generation and distribution of electricity and natural gas. He developed a vast trading business dealing in diverse products that included oil transportation, electric power, steel, paper, broadband, weather, and wastewater, as well as a variety of commodity futures. In 1999, the company launched an Internet-based trading business, EnronOnline. President and Chief Operating Officer Jeffrey Skilling built this operation into America's leading gas and electricity wholesaler and succeeded Lay as CEO.

Enron rode high on the trend of energy deregulation. In 2000, revenues more than doubled, earnings soared by 25 percent, and the company's share price rose by 89 percent. In 2001, however, everything began to unravel. In August, Skilling suddenly stepped down as CEO, forcing Lay, who had continued as chairman, to take back the reins. Lay commented, "I can honestly say the company is in the strongest shape it's ever been in."[5] Unexpected turnover in senior management is a classic warning sign of financial misrepresentation, and trouble was signaled again with the departure of Chief Financial Officer Andrew Fastow in October.

At the same time that he was a senior executive of Enron, Fastow had been the managing member of LJM Cayman, a private investment partnership that engaged in derivatives transactions ostensibly designed to manage Enron's trading risk. Shareholders saw a conflict of interest in Fastow's dual role and worried about the vagueness of disclosure regarding LJM and related partnerships. In response to this criticism, Enron terminated its relationship with the partnerships. The associated write-down of a promissory note produced a $1.2 billion decline in shareholders' equity, which Enron did not even mention in its earnings release for the quarter ending September 30, 2001.

When CEO Lay later alluded to the write-down in a conference call with analysts, investors became alarmed about the lack of clarity regarding the partnerships. They feared that Enron might have used them to hide losses in its core trading business. Investors were not alone in their confusion. In August, when asked about details of Fastow's complex transactions, Lay had replied that the questions were getting way over his head. Now, the two individuals who did appear to understand the deals—Skilling and Fastow—were gone from the company. Investor anxiety mounted as the Securities and Exchange Commission launched an investigation into Enron's financial reporting.

Ominously as well, the supposedly highly profitable company was facing a possible cash squeeze. Enron drew down a $3.3 billion bank line of credit and faced the possibility that its debt would be downgraded to speculative grade. Already, Enron's bonds were trading at yields comparable to others in that category. The company faced the problem that a fall to speculative grade might compel it to issue tens of millions of shares of stock to cover the $3.3 billion of loans it had guaranteed, driving down its share price through **dilution**. Downgrading could also cripple Enron's trading business by inducing other traders to cease doing business with it.

As the situation deteriorated, Enron struck a deal to be acquired by Dynegy for stock of the rival energy trader worth $9.80 per Enron share. A year earlier, Enron had traded at $83. The transaction, which included a cash infusion by Dynegy's 27 percent owner, ChevronTexaco, hinged on Enron avoiding a downgrade to speculative grade.

Enron's case for remaining investment grade was not helped by a $591 million downward restatement of earnings for the period 1997 through 2001. Most of the revision arose from including in earnings the results of two special purpose partnerships formerly treated as independent and of a subsidiary of the LJM partnership previously run by Fastow. The remainder, $92 million, consisted of changes that Enron's auditor, Arthur Andersen, had recommended but backed down on, accepting the company's argument that the amounts involved were immaterial.

A spokesman for Arthur Andersen called it "an unfortunate situation."[6] This proved to be a massive understatement. The firm, one of the nation's five largest auditors, was forced out of the accounting business after being convicted of obstruction of justice for shredding documents related to the Enron audit.

Enron at long last conceded that it was overly indebted. Management tried to restructure existing debt, arrange additional borrowings, obtain equity infusions, and raise cash by selling overseas assets. On November 19, 2001, the company told investors that it had $9.15 billion in debt coming due by the end of 2002 and only about $1.75 billion of cash and credit lines available. This disclosure came in the 10-Q for the quarter ending September 30, which was filed five days late—another classic warning sign of financial reporting malfeasance.

On November 21, Fitch stated that its Enron rating of BBB–, the lowest in the investment grade tier, depended on the Dynegy acquisition being consummated. The rating agency warned that if the deal broke down, a bankruptcy filing was highly possible. For the next few days, Standard & Poor's, Moody's Investors Service, and Fitch kept their ratings in the investment grade category as the company attempted to negotiate a restructuring of its bank debt. On November 28, the talks broke down, and all three agencies lowered Enron to speculative grade. Dynegy terminated its proposed acquisition, and on December 2, Enron became, by a wide margin, the biggest corporate bankruptcy ever, up to that time.

In congressional hearings on December 12, Arthur Andersen CEO Joseph P. Berardino suggested that Enron might have violated securities laws. Fastow pleaded guilty to wire and securities fraud. Lay and Skilling were convicted of fraud and conspiracy, although Lay's conviction was rescinded when he died shortly before he was to begin his prison sentence.

How Enron Misled Investors

One key to Enron's concealment of its true financial condition was simply a lack of forthrightness. Many of Enron's disclosures met the letter of the law, but according to a *Wall Street Journal* article, some top-flight professors of accounting said they could not make heads or tails of Enron's transactions with Fastow or the company's reasons for entering into them. Another article in the same publication stated that most securities analysts readily conceded that they did not know how Enron made money.

The company's description of its business shed no light and instead spread confusion. Enron derived more than 90 percent of its reported revenue from trading, which it called "wholesale services." It explained that business as follows:

> *Enron builds wholesale businesses through the creation of networks involving selective asset ownership, contractual access to third-party assets, and market-making activities.*

This statement, wrote Dan Ackman of *Forbes.com*, read "like something written in German, translated to Chinese and back to English by way of Polish."[7]

Enron also misled investors by aggressively exploiting wiggle room in the accounting rules. The company booked revenue from its energy-related derivatives contracts on the basis of gross value, rather than net value, as is the norm for other securities transactions. For instance, if a brokerage firm trades 10,000 shares of a $50 stock for a customer, it books as revenue either its commission or the spread between the bid and asked price, which might total $500. Trading an energy contract with the same gross value of $500,000 and a similarly small commission or spread, Enron booked revenue of $500,000—a thousand times what a brokerage firm would record. This accounting treatment enabled Enron to double its reported revenue in 2000, leapfrogging companies with far greater economic impact to call itself the "seventh largest company in America."

Excessive liberties with **mark-to-market accounting** rules constituted yet one more element of Enron's misrepresentation. Under GAAP, it was legitimate to include in current earnings the profits on energy-related contracts and other derivatives that it expected to earn over future periods that could be as long as 20 years. At the end of each quarter, the company estimated the fair value of each open contract to buy or sell electricity or natural gas at a stated price. A subsequent change in the value of a contract would be added to or subtracted from earnings. The potential for abuse arose from the fact that quoted market prices were available only for contracts extending out a few years. No such independent basis for valuation existed for longer-dated contracts. In such cases, Enron was allowed to generate its own valuations, using undisclosed assumptions and pricing models.

Naturally, Enron Chief Accounting Officer Richard Causey assured investors that the company's valuation estimates were conservative. He also maintained that the unrealized gains were not heavily concentrated in long-term contracts, where uncertainty regarding valuation was greatest. Analysts nevertheless worried about Enron's disclosure that it booked $747 million in unrealized gains in the second quarter of 2001. That figure exceeded the company's EBITDA of $609 million. (For competitors that did not disclose a comparable number, analysts made quarterly comparisons of the changes in values of net assets from risk management activities.)

President Jeffrey Skilling went further than Causey in discouraging skepticism about the veracity of Enron's reported earnings, venturing into outright intimidation. On a conference call dealing with Enron's earnings, analyst Richard Grubman complained that the company was unique in refusing to include a balance sheet in its earnings release. Skilling replied, "Well thank you very much, we appreciate that . . . [obscene epithet]."[8]

Another hint about Enron's deceptive methods emerged as the company was attempting to save itself through a sale to Dynegy. Floyd Norris of the *New York Times* reported that on October 23, 2001, the day before the company forced out Chief Financial Officer Andrew Fastow, the Financial Accounting Standards Board's (FASB) Emerging Issues Task Force received a rush question: A hypothetical "Big Energy Corporation" has a natural gas pipeline subsidiary and an energy trading subsidiary. May the company report profits earned in one subsidiary but not report losses incurred at the other?

Just as Enron's income statement concealed the nature of its reported earnings, its balance sheet misrepresented the reality of its financial position. From the outset of Ken Lay's transformation of a trading natural gas utility into a trading powerhouse, massive amounts of debt had been required. Off-balance-sheet entities kept debt off the company's books, based on accounting rules under which Enron could assert that it did not exert control. Experienced credit analysts ignored the accounting technicalities and added back Enron's proportionate share of the off-balance-sheet entities' debt. Still, the off-balance-sheet vehicles, combined with nontransparent disclosures, enabled the company to make itself look less debt-laden than it really was. From heavy reliance on off-balance-sheet financing, it was not a wholly surprising progression to Fastow's lucrative and conflicted partnerships.

Enron also disguised the magnitude of its debt burden by extensive use of a derivatives trade called a "prepaid swap." Unlike an ordinary swap, this transaction required Enron's counterparty to make its payments up-front, while Enron's payments were spread over a multiyear period. The spokesman for one bank that engaged in a prepaid swap noted that the cash flows replicated a floating-rate loan. Therefore, he said, the bank booked the transaction as a loan. Enron, in contrast, treated it as a swap.

While Enron grossly misled investors by stretching the rules, a large part of its deception consisted of outright violation of basic accounting standards, with the acquiescence of its auditor. Among the objections that Arthur Andersen agreed to waive on grounds of immateriality was a $172 million addition to shareholders' equity in 2000. The amount represented a note receivable that the company received in exchange for shares of stock that it issued to four special purpose entities. Under GAAP, when a company issues stock, it can record equity only when it receives cash. When Enron revised its financial statements in October 2001, it blithely labeled this violation of GAAP an accounting error.

Another violation of GAAP improperly enabled Enron to keep debt of an affiliate off its balance sheet. In testimony before Congress, Arthur Andersen CEO Berardino said that Enron failed to disclose to its auditor that it had guaranteed half of a 3 percent investment by a financial institution in its special purpose entity, Chewco Investments. Under GAAP, that arrangement meant Enron failed to meet a test for avoiding consolidation of Chewco.

As the Enron scandal continued to generate headlines, reports emerged of grossly fraudulent activities. Employees claimed that in 1998, management took them to an empty trading floor and had them pretend to be salespeople busily engaged in selling energy contracts, all to impress visiting securities analysts. Equally crude was a scheme in which Enron reportedly borrowed $500 million from a bank and bought Treasury bills. A few days later, it sold the Treasury bills and repaid the bank, reporting the proceeds from the meaningless transaction as operating cash flow.

Did Analysts Detect the Fraud?

The high profile of Enron's collapse spelled fame and fortune for anyone who could legitimately claim to have spotted the fraud in advance. Investors were sure to flock to anyone with a methodology deemed likely to uncover future faked profits. The record indicates, however, that not even diligent scrutinizers of Enron's financial statements recognized the depths of the fraud. Management successfully concealed the worst of its misdeeds until most of the investors' money had been lost.

To be sure, the lack of transparency in Enron's financial statements attracted notice well before the debacle. On September 20, 2000, the *Wall*

Street Journal raised concerns about the year-to-date near-doubling of Enron's share price to $84.875, some 60 times earnings. The article drew attention to the major contribution of unrealized, noncash gains to the reported earnings of Enron and other companies with large energy-trading units. "There could be a quality-of-earnings issue," said Michigan State University accounting professor Tom Linsmeier. "There certainly might be great volatility that could cause what now looks like a winning, locked-in gain to not arise sometime in the future."[9] The opacity of Enron's fair value assumptions was a major concern. "Ultimately they're telling you what they think the answer is, but they're not telling you how they got to that answer," Business Valuation Services analyst Stephen Campbell complained. "That is essentially saying 'trust me.'"[10]

The *Wall Street Journal*'s detailed discussion of the mark-to-market accounting issue alerted short seller James Chanos of Kynikos Associates to the potential downside in Enron's stock. Renowned for his skill as a dissector of financial statements, Chanos was modest about his discoveries when he later discussed Enron's fall. Up until the summer of 2001, Chanos stated, he suspected nothing worse than a case of overstated earnings. "That is all you could tell from [Enron's] documents," he said.[11] Chanos thought that the stock price would decline but not that it would plunge to pennies a share.

Others who pored over the financials achieved similar results. For instance, in May 2001, Off Wall Street Consulting recommended a short sale of Enron, then trading around $59. The analytical firm cited two factors identifiable from the financial statements, namely, the mark-to-market on nontraded assets and related-party transactions with private partnerships. When Enron fell to $26, a little below Off Wall Street Consulting's $30 target price, the firm removed its sell recommendation. That proved astute in the short run, as the stock rallied to $36 before entering its final death spiral. If Off Wall Street had known the full scope of Enron's deception, however, it presumably would have set a target price well below $30.

In August 2001, BNP Paribas analyst Daniel Scotto issued a report titled "All Stressed Up and No Place to Go," which urged investors to sell Enron's stock and bonds no matter what. Ten months earlier, Scotto suspended his ratings on all companies conducting business in California, including Enron. That action, however, was based on his concern that the companies would not be fully compensated by regulators for deferred energy accounts under the state's deregulation plan. In short, Scotto deserved credit for advising investors to bail out before some of the biggest losses, but his warning came long after the $90 peak of August 2000.

Another purported instance of advance detection of Enron's misreporting involved the Cayuga Fund, managed with the assistance of students at the

Cornell University Johnson Graduate School of Management. On December 1, 2000, a year and a day before the bankruptcy filing, the fund liquidated its entire Enron position at $67.38. That enabled the fund to book a return of 129 percent on shares it had purchased much more cheaply.

Feidhlim Boyle and Tyger Park, the students who advocated a 100 percent sale, noted that the Beneish financial model indicated a possibility of earnings manipulation. In addition, the student-analysts observed a lack of clarity in the earnings generated by the energy trading business. Finally, they could not understand the footnotes in the annual report, and their professor likewise found them obscure. Park recalled a remark by master investor Warren Buffett that if you cannot understand the footnotes, it is because management does not want you to.

The Cornell students did not detect Enron's fraud, however. In fact, they downplayed the importance of the Beneish model's signal. The students recommended a sale based on the stock's prevailing price but rated Enron neutral over the long term, which they surely would not have done if they suspected massive falsification.

McCullough Research did an excellent job of spotting inconsistencies in Enron's financials. Enron Online's quarterly earnings report for the nine months ending September 30, 2001, claimed $544 billion of notional revenue (representing electricity and gas transmitted), yet its Federal Energy Regulatory Commission filing for the same period showed only $693 *million* of energy purchases and sales. McCullough also found a discrepancy between reported earnings less dividends and additions to retained earnings. Finally, the firm noted that Enron's reported cash flow included customer deposits in California that had to be repaid at a later point. Net of that item, cash flow was negative. This was all solid financial statement analysis, but the problems came to light only in the month before Enron's bankruptcy filing.

Finally, Egan-Jones Ratings Company gained widespread recognition for being swifter to downgrade Enron's bonds to speculative grade than larger competitors such as Moody's and Standard & Poor's. The BB rating to which Egan-Jones lowered the debt, however, connoted only about a 1 percent probability of default within one year. Moreover, the downgrade occurred just 37 days before Enron filed for bankruptcy, although the company's misrepresentations dated back to at least 1997. Egan-Jones deserved credit for its analytical rigor, but like the others, it cannot truly claim that it unearthed a fraud deep enough to destroy the company.

Lessons for Financial Analysts

Enron's success in sustaining its fraud over a long period represents a cautionary tale of the limitations of financial statement analysis. The auditors' failure to curb flagrant abuses of GAAP posed a huge obstacle to analysts. On top of that, the company did its best to make its financial reports unfathomable. "They're not very forthcoming about how they make their money," said John Olson, who headed research at Sanders, Morris & Harris. "I don't know an analyst worth his salt who can seriously analyze Enron."[12]

In a case of this sort, the most diligent investigation of the numbers may not turn up a smoking gun before the company collapses. Accordingly, analysts should be especially wary when a strong likelihood of financial manipulation, as indicated by tools such as the Beneish model, coincides with nontransparent financial reporting. There are many companies to invest in without risking capital on those that fail the smell test.

HEALTHSOUTH'S EXCRUCIATING ORDEAL

After working as a physical therapist and a junior executive of a small Texas hospital chain, 30-year-old Richard Scrushy (pronounced "SCROO-shee") founded HealthSouth in 1984. The business proved highly successful, thanks in large measure to a generous Medicare reimbursement policy for physical rehabilitation of an aging population keen on sports and exercise. Over two decades, Scrushy built the Birmingham, Alabama, company into the largest chain of its kind in the United States, with 1,500 rehabilitation hospitals.

In the process, Scrushy amassed immense wealth, becoming known as the Donald Trump of Birmingham. He acquired seven corporate jets, which he frequently piloted. Several philanthropies that benefited from HealthSouth's generosity named buildings after Scrushy. He also captured attention as the lead singer of his own country music band. Famed athletes John Smoltz and Dan Marino were hired to speak at a children's road show sponsored by HealthSouth.

Scrushy's ascent proceeded without a hitch until 1997, when Congress sharply cut back Medicare reimbursements to hospitals. During the next two years, HealthSouth's operating margins and profits plummeted. Scrushy responded by slashing salaries and divesting unprofitable sidelines. When those measures failed to revive profits, he tightened operations, cutting average patient's stays from 21.5 to 17.5 days. Still, the company struggled to meet Wall Street securities analysts' lofty earnings estimates.

In the end, HealthSouth met the analysts' expectations only by stretching the truth. On March 19, 2003, the Securities and Exchange Commission charged that HealthSouth had overstated earnings by $1.4 billion since 1999. Prosecutors later raised the figure to nearly $2.5 billion. PriceWaterhouseCoopers, the new auditor chosen after the scandal broke, eventually added to this total $500 million in incorrect accounting for goodwill and other acquisition-related items in the period 1994 through 1999, plus $800 million to $1.6 billion in "aggressive accounting" from 1992 to March 2003. In 2005, HealthSouth restated its results for 2001–2002, reducing revenue by about $1.5 billion and changing its originally reported $481 million of earnings for the two years to $555 million of losses.

According to the SEC's complaint, HealthSouth's falsification began shortly after the company went public in 1986. The securities regulator also claimed that Chairman and Chief Executive Officer Scrushy had personally profited from the fraud by selling at least 7.8 million of his own shares and by receiving a $6.5 million bonus based on the false profits. Scrushy, who was placed on leave following the SEC bombshell and fired soon thereafter, had only recently returned to his CEO post after a six-month investigation of insider trading allegations.

Regarding the new charges, his lawyers commented, "Mr. Scrushy was shocked and surprised at the unexpected actions taken by the government over the past two days."[13] Even after all five chief financial officers who worked under Scrushy during the company's history confessed to participating in the fraud, the defense team maintained that Scrushy was unaware of the financial statement manipulation. "I'm not an accountant," the defendant stated in a later civil trial related to the allegations.

Flat denial by Scrushy, regardless of the evidence that emerged, was a consistent theme as the HealthSouth story unfolded. Scrushy disavowed any culpability in an interview on the *60 Minutes* network television program, but when asked to repeat his declaration of innocence in a congressional hearing, he invoked his Fifth Amendment right against self-incrimination. Later, during his trial for fraud, Scrushy said that if acquitted, he would try to regain his position as chief executive officer of HealthSouth, notwithstanding a Securities and Exchange Commission enforcement action pending against him. A woman who worked as a personal shopper for Scrushy's wife said of the couple, "Their life was about as uninhibited by reality as one could imagine."[14]

In a monumental case of unfortunate timing, a book hailing HealthSouth's phenomenal success reached bookstores shortly before the SEC filed its allegations. *The Story of HealthSouth,* by Jeffrey L. Rodengren, was published by Write Stuff Syndicate, a firm specializing in corporate histories. Senators Orrin Hatch of Utah and Tom Harkin of Iowa had contributed an admiring foreword, unaware of the impending storm. (The two senators also participated in Scrushy's 1997 wedding, with Hatch writing a song for the occasion.)

Methods of Misrepresentation

According to HealthSouth whistleblower Weston L. Smith, Scrushy regularly convened so-called family meetings in which he directed company executives to inflate reported earnings to meet securities analysts' estimates. The fake accounting entries were called "dirt."[15] Smith, who pleaded guilty to four federal criminal charges, had been HealthSouth's chief financial officer until August 2002, before switching to head of inpatient operations. The complaint stated that when HealthSouth officials and accountants urged Scrushy to cease inflating profits, he replied, in effect, "Not until I sell my stock."[16]

Among the false filings Smith admitted to was a certification that financial statements sent to the SEC were true. Doing so was a violation of the Sarbanes-Oxley Act, enacted in 2002 following massive financial reporting frauds at Enron and WorldCom. The Sarbox provision requiring CFOs and CEOs to attest to the accuracy of financial statements gave prosecutors a powerful weapon to wield against falsifiers, but HealthSouth's fraud dispelled any notion that the tough new law would end financial misreporting altogether.

HealthSouth exaggerated its earnings by understating the gap between the cost of a treatment and the amount that the patient's insurance would cover. That enabled the company to set aside an unrealistically small allowance for uncollectible accounts. Each time the company overstated its net revenue and earnings in this way, it made a corresponding balance sheet adjustment, raising the value of an asset such as property, plant, and equipment. Another HealthSouth executive who pleaded guilty to participating in accounting fraud said the company overbooked certain reserve accounts referred to internally as "socks," then later "bled them out" into revenue.[17]

To avoid detection, HealthSouth made no large, concentrated adjustments but instead spread them over several different categories, including inventory, intangible assets, and property, plant, and equipment (PP&E). Knowing that the auditors would question an addition to fixed assets only if it was greater than a certain dollar amount, the company officials were careful not to exceed that threshold.

By mid-2002, using this little-by-little approach, the company managed to overstate its PP&E by more than 50 percent. Lehman Brothers accounting analyst Robert Willens later commented, "They were smart enough to realize that, as long as the increases weren't dramatic, the auditors were not going to deviate from the sampling approach they typically take."[18] If the auditors did question an accounting entry, HealthSouth executives reportedly created a phony document to validate the item.

HealthSouth also propped up profits by failing to write off receivables with little chance of being collected. That classic dodge accounted for most of the $500 million of questionable accounting uncovered by an internal investigation, separate from PriceWaterhouseCoopers' study of outright falsification. In addition, the company did not recognize losses when it sold assets that had declined in value. Also, in one instance, the financial statements treated arm and leg braces bearing the HealthSouth logo as inventory, even though the company would generate no revenue from handing them out free at its medical centers.

Securities holders paid a heavy price for HealthSouth's financial hanky-panky. Following the SEC's initial accusation of financial reporting violations on March 19, 2003, HealthSouth lost access to a $1.25 billion line of credit. With a $354 million convertible bond coming due in a little over a week, it appeared doubtful that the company could arrange a new loan to cover the debt maturity without first filing for bankruptcy. (As postbankruptcy lenders, the banks would get first claim on HealthSouth's assets.) According to Premila Peters of KDP Investment Advisors, the company owed $3.5 billion in total, but based on its cash flow, its value was only $2.4 billion.[19]

Shareholders and bondholders were initially trapped in their positions because trading in the company's securities was suspended on March 19. (Bond market participants who misinterpreted the suspension made a few trades on March 20, but the SEC nullified those transactions.) When trading in the company debt resumed on March 21, the convertible **subordinated** bonds closed at 20, down from as high as 98 earlier in the week. Health-South's senior bonds were down from the mid-80s to about 44. Additional bad news for bondholders arrived as bankers blocked the company from making the April 1 principal repayment on the convertible bonds. As for the stock, trading resumed on an over-the-counter basis, and the shares ended March at 8.5 cents, down from $3.91 before the trading halt.

The People versus Scrushy

By October 15, 2003, a total of 15 HealthSouth executives had pleaded guilty to involvement in fraudulent reporting. Several had testified that Scrushy knew about or directed the accounting fraud. "The dominoes are falling, and they are falling fast," said one person involved in the investigation. "It's an investigator's dream."[20] Former SEC attorney Christopher Bebel added, "Scrushy's prospects look bleak."[21]

Compounding Scrushy's legal problems, federal prosecutors disclosed in July 2003 that they had uncovered evidence of tax fraud, obstruction of justice, witness intimidation, money laundering, and public corruption. It also emerged that the Federal Bureau of Investigation was looking into the suicide of William Massey Jr., who managed an umbrella company for Scrushy's personal businesses. Two months before taking his own life, Massey made a hasty business trip to the Bahamas. The FBI suspected Scrushy of setting up offshore bank accounts as a tax dodge.

On November 4, 2003, federal prosecutors charged Richard Scrushy with 85 charges related to a false accounting scheme, including conspiracy, securities fraud, mail and wire fraud, and money laundering. Perjury and obstruction of justice were added the following year, when a revised indictment consolidated the charges into a total of 58. The 2003 indictment made Scrushy the first CEO accused of violating the Sarbanes-Oxley Act because he had signed the financial statements. He pleaded not guilty to all charges, claiming that notwithstanding his reputation as a micromanager, he was oblivious to the massive fraud. Even though several of the 15 Health-South executives who pleaded guilty had implicated him, Scrushy's attorney brushed off the prosecutors' evidence. "They don't have much," he said. "Their primary case is weak."[22]

In his seemingly uphill battle to beat the rap, Scrushy capitalized on the confident prosecutors' decision not to seek a change in venue from Birmingham, where he was admired as a local boy who made good. Scrushy pushed this advantage by hosting a new television series on a Birmingham station. He claimed that the purpose was not to present his own side of the case against him, but he reserved the right to counter "blatantly wrong" statements.[23] The program was taped at Word of Truth Productions, part of the outreach ministry of a predominantly black church that Scrushy joined in 2003.

Both his membership in the congregation and the TV show raised speculation that he hoped to win sympathy from jurors in a city where African Americans constituted 73 percent of the population. Scrushy played the religion card by becoming a nondenominational preacher and delivering guest sermons at several local churches. A former business associate of Scrushy's commented that he had never observed any black executives at HealthSouth and added, "The first time I heard religion and Richard Scrushy mentioned in the same sentence was when I read about him going to Guiding Light Church."[24] According to other accounts, Scrushy was deeply involved in Christianity as a youth but later drifted away. Scrushy remained steadfast in the face of criticism: "I am innocent of the accusations against me," he said, "and have been blessed by the Lord in having the resources to confront my accusers."[25]

During the trial, Scrushy and his lawyers insisted they had nothing to do with another locally telecast program, *The Scrushy Trial with Nikki Preede*. This program aired on a station owned by Scrushy's son-in-law, and its host had done public relations work for Scrushy's law firm. A former Scrushy attorney was a frequent commentator on the show, and the station's general manager had played guitar and fiddle in Scrushy's country-western band. The judge felt obliged to instruct the jury not to watch any television programs dealing with Scrushy and HealthSouth.

Scrushy's defense also employed more conventional tactics, such as attacking one government witness for marital infidelity. His lawyers hammered at the light sentences meted out to HealthSouth executives who confessed and testified against Scrushy. Perhaps effective as well was the lead defense attorney's appearance in a necktie decorated with an image of rats eating cheese, echoing his description of a key prosecution witness's character. In the prosecutors' view, Scrushy benefited as well from the judge's habit of cracking jokes during long stretches of accounting-related testimony, arguing that it may have caused some jurors to take the proceedings less seriously than they ought.

In any event, on June 28, 2005, Richard Scrushy was acquitted of all charges. "It was venue," said former federal prosecutor George B. Newhouse Jr.[26] He echoed a number of legal experts who asserted that the defendant would have been convicted had prosecutors tried him anyplace other than Birmingham.

Scrushy's acquittal did not end his legal troubles, however. Four months later, he was indicted on charges of bribing the former governor of Alabama to appoint him to the state board responsible for approving hospital construction. In addition, he faced a shareholder suit and SEC civil charges arising from the accounting fraud. Scrushy eventually settled the SEC case without admitting guilt, agreeing to give up $77.5 million in stock gains and pay a $3.5 million penalty. The judge in the shareholder suit ordered him to pay $2.8 billion. Finally, Scrushy was convicted of the bribery charge and sentenced to 10 years and six months in prison. The judge rejected his plea that if he were incarcerated, his good work as a minister would suffer.

Audit Failure at HealthSouth

The most dismaying aspect of the performance of HealthSouth's auditor, Ernst & Young, was its failure to challenge a sudden, large increase in cash. The Justice Department claimed that the company's reported $545 million **cash balance** in 2002's second quarter, a jump of more than 50 percent from the preceding quarter, was overstated by more than $300 million. Lehman Brothers accounting analyst Willens noted that auditors were supposed to confirm cash balances by obtaining a sample. "It's one of the easiest things to audit and it does seem amazing," said Willens. "But a sample may have led them to conclude that everything was in order."[27]

Other red flags apparently were ignored. Michael Vines, a bookkeeper who left HealthSouth's accounting department in March 2002, warned Ernst & Young about accounting fraud, but the auditing firm concluded that the company's accounting was legitimate. Additionally, a HealthSouth internal auditor told Ernst & Young that she could not get full access to the company's books. The independent auditor took no action in response to that disturbing statement, according to another partner.

In the view of experts in the field, internal checks and balances also broke down at HealthSouth. The board's audit committee met only once during 2001, three times less than the minimum recommended by the SEC. That should have alerted the company's independent auditor that the company's internal controls were not adequately supervised and might be unreliable. Such infrequent convening of the audit committee meant it was "nonexistent, for all practical purposes," according to Columbia University accounting professor Itzhak Sharav.[28]

Other reasons existed for questioning whether HealthSouth's board was sufficiently independent to fulfill its watchdog responsibilities. "There has been so much sleeping on the job at the HealthSouth board that it could rise to gross negligence," asserted Paul Lapides, head of the Corporate Governance Center.[29] Particularly troubling were directors' transactions with HealthSouth and Scrushy. One director earned $250,000 a year in consulting fees from the company, and another received a $5.6 million contract to install glass at a hospital constructed by HealthSouth. Another director bought a $395,000 resort property in conjunction with Scrushy. Six directors and a seventh's wife were participants (in some instances through related entities) in an online medical supply venture to which HealthSouth directed more than $174 million in business. Moreover, for several years, a single board committee oversaw both corporate audit and compensation. Corporate governance experts could find no parallel at another major company for this arrangement, which was especially problematic considering that the audit failure fattened Scrushy's pay package.

Early Warning Signs

In 1999–2000, when Scrushy instituted an assembly-line-like process to move patients through the system more swiftly, operating earnings skyrocketed by 143 percent. Sales, however, inched up by just 3 percent. Investigators later concluded that this implausibly large gap was a product of fabricated profit numbers. Users of financial statements should be skeptical of such wide disparities between changes in revenue and profit.

Negative surprises can also be a warning sign, as HealthSouth demonstrated. The SEC complaint claimed that when Scrushy told investors on August 27, 2002, that a change in Medicare reimbursements would cost the company $175 million annually, he was overstating the true impact by about $150 million. According to the SEC, other HealthSouth executives were worried that under the newly enacted Sarbanes-Oxley Act, the requirement to certify the company's false financial statements meant they might face prison sentences. The executives claimed that to lower security analysts' expectations and thereby relieve the pressure to falsify, they persuaded Scrushy to abandon the reporting fraud and give securities analysts a bogus profit warning. In response, HealthSouth's stock plunged 44 percent in a single day.

A large stock sale by Scrushy three months before that precipitous drop aroused the SEC's suspicions of insider trading. That trail ultimately led in the unexpected direction of financial reporting fraud. For users of financial statements, the lesson is that a management that appears untrustworthy on other grounds may be tampering with the books as well.

MILK AND OTHER LIQUID ASSETS

Parmalat SpA's rise to the rank of Italy's largest food producer and the world's largest dairy company began in 1961, when Calisto Tanzi inherited a ham and salami business. Two years later, Tanzi created the Parmalat milk brand. He built it into an industry leader by importing technology for packaging milk in distinctive rectangular cartons and preserving it for up to six months without refrigeration. By 1970, the brand was internationally known as the "milk of champions," and the company started sponsoring ski events. Tanzi expanded the product line to desserts, sauces, cookies, and fruit juices and the corporate sponsorship to auto racing and soccer. In the 1990s, Parmalat went public and launched a series of acquisitions in Italy, the United States, Latin America, and Asia. The company's well-known brands included Archway cookies, Pomi pasta sauces, and Sunnydale Farms milk. Along the way, Tanzi became a major contributor to political campaigns and received a knighthood from the Italian state.

On December 19, 2003, Bank of America said documents indicating a $4.7 billion balance in a Parmalat account were not authentic. Standard & Poor's promptly downgraded Parmalat's debt to D, indicating default. Four days later, holding company Parmalat Finanziaria SpA announced plans to file for bankruptcy. As evidence of financial fraud emerged, Tanzi was arrested. He estimated the hole in Parmalat's balance sheet at $10 billion, said he had been falsifying the financial statements for at least a decade, and admitted that he had unlawfully shifted at least $640 million from Parmalat to money-losing travel businesses controlled by his family. Tanzi ultimately received a 10-year prison sentence.

As it turned out, the fraud extended beyond the phantom liquidity on Parmalat's balance sheet. A preliminary report issued in January 2004 revealed that the company had net debt of approximately $18 billion, almost $16 billion of which had not been disclosed previously. Pricewaterhouse-Coopers also found that the company's revenues for the nine months ended September 30, 2003, were only €4 billion, rather than the reported €5.4 billion. Reported as €651 million, EBITDA was actually just €121 million, according to the accounting firm, which was brought in to investigate after the scandal broke. Parmalat's market capitalization prior to the scandal exceeded €2 billion, but according to a report by Enrico Bondi, the special administrator appointed by the Italian government, actual assets totaled less than €1 billion at the end of 2003. In a bizarre touch, company executives attempted to destroy a computer used in the fraud by smashing it with a hammer.

Investors had little official warning of trouble until the month before Parmalat's collapse. As late as October 2003, Deutsche Bank's equity research group rated the company's stock a buy, highlighting its strong reported cash flow, and Citibank put out an optimistic report in November. Furthermore, the company's debt carried an investment grade rating until nine days before the bankruptcy filing. Earlier on, however, there were classic warning signs that may indicate trouble even if a company outwardly appears successful.

A major red flag was Parmalat's voracious appetite for debt, despite claiming to have a huge cash balance. When challenged on this point, Chief Financial Officer Fausto Tonna consistently replied that the company was on the acquisition trail and that its liquid balances were earning good returns. Union officials at the company's main milk plant received a similar answer and were threatened with a lawsuit if they made any public suggestion of financial improprieties. In a similar vein, Calisto Tanzi charged that financial institutions, including Lehman Brothers, were spreading rumors of accounting irregularities to drive down the price of its stock. This sort of response is typical of companies engaged in financial fraud. One investment banker who had declined to deal with Parmalat told *Business Week* that things had "been strange" at the company since the mid-1980s. "It smelled bad," he confided.[30]

Suspiciously high profitability constituted a danger sign to some observers. A Milan banker noted that a very well-managed company in Parmalat's business would achieve an operating margin of 6 to 7 percent, yet Parmalat was reporting 12 percent.[31] Lack of transparency in financial reporting was another warning. "Parmalat was an 'avoid' recommendation," said BarCap high yield bond analyst Robert Jones. "There simply wasn't enough information to form a fundamental credit view."[32] Not everybody steered clear, however. "Everyone who did their research knew this wasn't the cleanest company," commented RBS consumer products analyst Rob Orman, "but many people looked at the spread[33] and thought, how far wrong can you go with a dairy company?"[34]

The 2002 financial statements of Parmalat's Brazilian unit, Parmalat Participacoes do Brasil Ltda., included evidence that Parmalat was prettying up its balance sheet through elaborate financial engineering. Deep in the footnotes of the Brazilian subsidiary's statements was a disclosure that on January 18, 2002, the subsidiary issued a €500 million security convertible into company shares. Unlike the owner of a standard convertible bond, for whom conversion is optional, the buyer of this instrument "made an irrevocable commitment to convert" into shares at the 2008 maturity. Parmalat Participacoes do Brasil Ltda. accounted for the transaction (in U.S. dollars) as $523.8 million of "funds for capital increase," part of an undifferentiated $764 million balance sheet entry encompassing minority interest, funds for capital increase, and shareholders equity.

When this item was consolidated at the parent level, it was simply part of shareholders' equity. Furthermore, analysts suspected that the buyer of the convertible security was another Parmalat unit. On the same day that the convertible was issued, Parmalat Finance Corp. BV issued a €300 million bond. This would mean that by selling debt in one unit and buying it in another, the company increased its shareholders' equity. Management declined to comment when the transaction subsequently came to light, and unfortunately, the Brazilian subsidiary's financial statement was not a public document, so outsiders could not have used it to get wind of Parmalat's hanky-panky. Behind the scenes as well was the information that Parmalat units engaged in currency hedges with related parties. The economic impact of such a transaction does not truly constitute a hedge.

Additional straws in the wind for attentive investors appeared in selected brokerage firm research reports. In December 2002, Merrill Lynch analysts Joanna Speed and Nic Sochovsky downgraded Parmalat to sell, saying that the company's frequent recourse to the bond market, while reporting high cash balances, threw into question its cash-generating ability. The analysts also presciently viewed Parmalat's exceptionally large cash balance as a negative. They appropriately argued that maintaining vast amounts of debt while holding cash that generated a lower interest rate, rather than using the cash to reduce debt, represented "inefficient balance sheet management."[35] The explanation for this uneconomic behavior turned out to be that the cash was fictitious. On January 24, 2003, an analyst at Auerbach Grayson & Co. estimated that Parmalat's net financial debt was $4.5 billion, rather than the $2.3 billion reported by the company.[36] Special administrator Bondi contended that Parmalat's true financial condition was easily determinable by comparing its published debt totals with independently produced data on the amount of bonds it had issued.

Another hazard signal emerged on February 26, 2003, when Parmalat suddenly canceled its plan to sell 30-year bonds. Potential buyers of the issue were voicing uneasiness about the company's need to borrow at the same time that it claimed to have $5.3 billion in cash. The company said it would instead issue bonds with maturities of just seven years, suggesting the market had less confidence in Parmalat's long-run stability than management had thought. This news triggered a fall in the company's stock price to a seven-year low. On February 28, Parmalat called off the seven-year issue.

In the last two months before the bankruptcy filing, the signs of trouble multiplied. On November 6, Consob, the Italian stock market regulator, requested details on how Parmalat had invested €3.5 billion and how it planned to pay back bonds scheduled to mature by the end of 2004. On November 11, auditor Deloitte & Touche disclosed that it was unable to confirm that Parmalat had accounted correctly for a $135 million gain on a currency-related derivatives contract. A classic danger sign, senior management turnover, surfaced on November 14 with the second resignation within a year by a chief financial officer. Next, on November 27, the company announced that it had sold its stake in a hedge fund based in the Cayman Islands for $589.9 million but on December 8 revealed that the proceeds were not recoverable. By that time, it was clear that the company was facing a liquidity squeeze. On December 9, Parmalat failed to pay a €150 million bond maturity. The company made the required principal payment on December 12, but by then, Standard & Poor's had downgraded its debt to speculative grade.

Oddly, the person who achieved the greatest renown for early recognition of the Parmalat's house of cards was not a financial analyst, but a comedian. During a theater presentation in September 2002, more than a year before the bankruptcy filing, the popular Italian entertainer Beppe Grillo recounted to his audience that a Parmalat executive had told him the company had €13 billion in debts and €13 billion in assets. Grillo, an acerbic critic of Italian government and business practices, quipped about Parmalat: "In a normal country, it would collapse, bankrupt."[37] A videotape of Grillo's one-man show was broadcast on Italian television after his joke became reality.

Grillo claimed his anecdote was true but declined to name his informant. Later, though, he was called to testify in the judicial investigation of the Parmalat scandal. Asked to explain how he had managed to foresee the bankruptcy, he stated that anyone could have seen the holes in Parmalat's balance sheet, given that the financial reports were easily accessible. Grillo had a bit of an advantage over the average citizen, however. Prior to becoming a comedian, he earned a degree in accounting.

CONCLUSION

This is a fitting note on which to conclude our discussion of whether fraud is detectable. Beppe Grillo lent a comic twist to the Parmalat case, and Richard Scrushy made a farce of the legal proceedings against him. The downfall of Enron's management contained elements of tragedy that made it adaptable to the stage. Analysts who learn the lessons of events that foreshadowed the revelation of these frauds may become the heroes of future financial reporting dramas.

PART Four

Forecasts and Security Analysis

Forecasting Financial Statements

Analysis of a company's current financial statements, as described in Chapters 2 through 4, is enlightening, but not as enlightening as the analysis of its *future* financial statements. After all, it is future earnings and dividends that determine the value of a company's stock (see Chapter 14) and the relative likelihood of future timely payments of debt service that determines credit quality (see Chapter 13). To be sure, investors rely to some extent on the past as an indication of the future. Because already-reported financials are available to everyone, however, studying them is unlikely to provide any significant advantage over competing investors. To capture fundamental value that is not already reflected in securities prices, the analyst must act on the earnings and credit quality measures that will appear on future statements.

Naturally, the analyst cannot know with certainty what a company's future financial statements will look like. Neither are financial projections mere guesswork, however. The process is an extension of historical patterns and relationships, based on assumptions about future economic conditions, market behavior, and managerial actions.

Financial projections will correspond to actual future results only to the extent that the assumptions prove accurate. Analysts should therefore energetically gather information beyond the statements themselves. They must constantly seek to improve the quality of their assumptions by expanding their contacts among customers, suppliers, and competitors of the companies they analyze.

A TYPICAL ONE-YEAR PROJECTION

The following one-year projection works through the effects of the analyst's assumptions on all three basic financial statements. There is probably no better way than following the numbers in this manner to appreciate the interrelatedness of the income statement, the cash flow statement, and the balance sheet.

Exhibit 12.1 displays the current financial statements of a fictitious company, Colossal Chemical Corporation. The historical statements constitute a starting point for the projection by affirming the reasonableness of assumptions about future financial performance. We will assume throughout the commentary on the Colossal Chemical projection that the analyst has studied the company's results over not only the preceding year but also over the past several years.

Projected Income Statement

The financial projection begins with an earnings forecast (Exhibit 12.2). Two key figures from the projected income statement, net income and depreciation, will later be incorporated into a projected statement of cash flows. The cash flow statement, in turn, will supply data for constructing a projected balance sheet. At each succeeding stage, the analyst will have to make additional assumptions. The logical flow, however, begins with a forecast of earnings, which will significantly shape the appearance of all three statements.

Immediately following is a discussion of the assumptions underlying each line in the income statement, presented in order from top (sales) to bottom (net income).

Sales The projected $2.110 billion for 2011 represents an assumed rise of 6 percent over the actual figure for 2010 shown in Exhibit 12.1. Of this increase, higher shipments will account for 2 percent and higher prices for 4 percent.

To arrive at these figures, the analyst builds a forecast from the ground up, using the historical segment data shown in Exhibit 12.3. Sales projections for the company's business—basic chemicals, plastics, and industrial chemicals—can be developed with the help of such sources as trade publications, trade associations, and firms that sell econometric forecasting models. Certain assumptions about economic growth (increase in gross domestic product) in the coming year underlie all such forecasts. The analyst must be careful to ascertain the forecaster's underlying assumptions and judge whether they seem realistic.

If the analyst is expected to produce an earnings projection that is consistent with an in-house economic forecast, then it will be critical to establish a historical relationship between key indicators and the shipments of the company's various business segments. For example, a particular segment's shipments may have historically grown at 1.5 times the rate of industrial

EXHIBIT 12.1 Financial Statements of Colossal Chemical Corporation Year Ended December 31, 2010 ($000,000 omitted)

Income Statement

Sales	$1,991
Cost of goods sold	1,334
Selling, general, and administrative expense	299
Depreciation	119
Research and development	80
Total costs and expenses	1,832
Operating Income	159
Interest expense	
Interest (income)	(6)
Earnings before income taxes	129
Provision for income taxes	44
Net Income	$ 85
Cash and marketable securities	$ 69
Accounts receivable	439
Inventories	351
Total Current Assets	859
Property, Plant, and Equipment	895
	$1,754

Statement of Cash Flows

Sources:	
Net income	$ 85
Depreciation	119
Deferred income taxes	20
Working capital changes, excluding cash and borrowings	(8)
Funds provided by operations	216
Uses:	
Additions to property, plant, and equipment	125
Dividends	28
Reduction of long-term debt	60
Funds used by operations	213
Net Increase in Funds	$ 3

Balance Sheet

Notes payable	$ 21
Accounts payable	263
Current portion of long-term debt	32
Total Current Liabilities	316
Long-Term Debt	379
Deferred Income Taxes	70
Shareholders' Equity	989
	$1,754

EXHIBIT 12.2 Earnings Forecast

Colossal Chemical Corporation Projected Income Statement
($000,000 omitted)

	2011
Sales	$2,110
Cost of goods sold	1,393
Selling, general, and administrative expense	317
Depreciation and amortization	121
Research and development	84
Total costs and expenses	1,915
Operating Income	195
Interest expense	34
Interest (income)	(5)
Earnings before income taxes	166
Provision for income taxes	56
Net Income	$ 110

production or have fluctuated in essentially direct proportion to housing starts. Similarly, price increases should be linked to the expected inflation level. Depending on the product, this will be represented by either the Consumer Price Index or the Producer Price Index.

Basic industries such as chemicals, paper, and capital goods tend to lend themselves best to the macroeconomic-based approach described here. In technology-driven industries and hits-driven businesses such as motion pictures and toys, the connection between sales and the general economic trend will tend to be looser. Forecasting in such circumstances depends largely on developing contacts within the industry being studied. The objective is to make intelligent guesses about the probable success of a company's new products.

A history of sales by geographic area (Exhibit 12.4) provides another input into the sales projection. An analyst can modify the figures derived from industry segment forecasts to reflect expectations of unusually strong or unusually weak economic performance in a particular region of the globe. Likewise, a company may be experiencing an unusual problem in a certain region, such as a dispute with a foreign government. The geographic sales breakdown can furnish some insight into the magnitude of the expected impact of such occurrences.

Cost of Goods Sold   The $1.393 billion cost-of-goods-sold figure in Exhibit 12.2 represents 66 percent of projected sales. That corresponds to a gross

EXHIBIT 12.3 Sales Forecast

Colossal Chemical Corporation Results by Industry Segment
($000,000 omitted)

	2006	2007	2008	2009	2010
Sales					
Basic chemicals	$ 786	$ 807	$ 878	$ 921	$ 975
Plastics	373	370	399	422	433
Industrial chemicals	461	475	531	546	583
Total	$1,620	$1,652	$1,808	$1,889	$1,991
Operating Income					
Basic chemicals	$ 59	$ 52	$ 65	$ 82	$ 94
Plastics	26	41	25	16	24
Industrial chemicals	28	31	28	35	41
Total	$ 113	$ 124	$ 118	$ 133	$ 159
Depreciation					
Basic chemicals	$ 46	$ 46	$ 50	$ 51	$ 55
Plastics	19	20	22	25	27
Industrial chemicals	31	31	35	36	37
Total	$ 96	$ 97	$ 107	$ 112	$ 119
Identifiable Assets					
Basic chemicals	$ 674	$ 676	$ 741	$ 772	$ 813
Plastics	309	314	352	369	390
Industrial chemicals	456	457	510	530	551
Total	$1,439	$1,447	$1,603	$1,671	$1,754

EXHIBIT 12.4 Colossal Chemical Corporation Results by Geographic Area
($000,000 omitted)

	2006	2007	2008	2009	2010
Sales					
North America	$ 873	$ 896	$ 968	$1,019	$1,077
Europe	526	551	601	622	649
Latin America	103	99	90	87	102
Far East	118	106	149	161	163
Total	$1,620	$1,652	$1,808	$1,889	$1,991
Operating Income					
North America	$ 25	$ 32	$ 29	$ 36	$ 43
Europe	52	47	61	62	77
Latin America	17	24	17	16	26
Far East	19	21	11	19	13
Total	$ 113	$ 124	$ 118	$ 133	$ 159

margin of 34 percent, a slight improvement over the preceding year's 33 percent. The projected gross margin for a company in turn reflects expectations about changes in costs of labor and material. Also influencing the gross margin forecast is the expected intensity of industry competition, which affects a company's ability to pass cost increases on to customers or to retain cost decreases.

In a capital-intensive business such as basic chemicals, the projected capacity utilization percentage (for both the company and the industry) is a key variable. At full capacity, fixed costs are spread out over the largest possible volume, so unit costs are minimized. Furthermore, if demand exceeds capacity so that all producers are running flat out, none will have an incentive to increase volume by cutting prices. When such conditions prevail, cost increases will be fully (or more than fully) passed on, and gross margins will widen. That will be the result, at least, until new industry capacity is built, bringing supply and demand back into balance. Conversely, if demand were expected to fall rather than rise in 2002, leading to a decline in capacity utilization, Exhibit 12.2's projected gross margin would probably be lower than in 2010, rather than higher. (For further discussion of the interaction of fixed and variable costs, see Chapter 3.)

As with sales, the analyst can project cost of goods sold from the bottom up, segment by segment. Since the segment information in Exhibit 12.3 shows only operating income, and not gross margin, the analyst must add segment depreciation to operating income, then make assumptions about the allocation of selling, general, and administrative (SG&A) expense and research and development (R&D) expense by segment. For example, operating income by segment for 2010 works out as shown in Exhibit 12.5, if SG&A and R&D expenses are allocated in proportion to segment sales.

EXHIBIT 12.5 Colossal Chemical Corporation Operating Income by Segment ($000,000 omitted)

	Basic Chemicals	Plastics	Industrial Chemicals	Total
Operating income	$ 94	$ 24	$ 41	$ 159
Plus: Depreciation	55	27	37	119
Plus: SG&A	146	65	88	299
Plus: R&D	39	17	24	80
Equals: Gross Margin	$ 334	$ 133	$ 190	$ 657
Sales	$ 975	$ 433	$ 583	$1,991
Gross Margin Percentage	34.3%	30.7%	32.6%	33.0%
Memo: Segment Sales as Percentage of Total:	49.0%	21.7%	29.3%	100.0%

By compiling the requisite data for a period of several years, the analyst can devise models for forecasting gross margin percentage on a segment-by-segment basis.

Selling, General, and Administrative Expense   The forecast in Exhibit 12.2 assumes continuation of a stable relationship in which SG&A expense has historically approximated 15 percent of sales. The analyst would vary this percentage for forecasting purposes if, for example, recent quarterly income statements or comments by reliable industry sources indicated a trend to a higher or lower level.

Depreciation   Depreciation expense is essentially a function of the amount of a company's fixed assets and the average number of years over which it writes them off. If, on average, all classes of the company's property, plant, and equipment (PP&E) are depreciated over eight years, then on a **straight-line basis**, the company will write off one-eighth (12.5 percent) each year. From year to year, the base of depreciable assets will grow to the extent that additions to PP&E exceed depreciation charges.

Exhibit 12.2 forecasts depreciation expenses equivalent to 13.5 percent of PP&E as of the preceding year-end, based on a stable ratio between the two items over an extended period. Naturally, a projection should incorporate any foreseeable variances from historical patterns. For example, a company may lengthen or shorten its average write-off period, either because it becomes more liberal or more conservative in its accounting practices or because such adjustments are warranted by changes in the rate of obsolescence of equipment. Also, a company's mix of assets may change. The average write-off period should gradually decline as comparatively short-lived assets, such as data-processing equipment, increase as a percentage of capital expenditures and as long-lived assets, such as bricks and mortar, decline.

Research and Development   Along with advertising, R&D is an expense that is typically budgeted on a percentage-of-sales basis. The R&D percentage may change if, for example, the company makes a sizable acquisition in an industry that is either significantly more, or significantly less, research intensive than its existing operations. In addition, changing incentives for research, such as extended or reduced patent protection periods, may alter the percentage of sales a company believes it must spend on research to remain competitive. Barring developments of this sort, however, the analyst can feel fairly confident in expecting that the coming year's R&D expense will represent about the same percentage of sales as it did last year. Such an assumption (at 4 percent of sales) is built into Exhibit 12.2.

Operating Income   The four projected expense lines are summed to derive total costs and expenses. The total ($1,915 million) is subtracted from projected sales to calculate projected operating income of $195 million.

Interest Expense   Exhibit 12.6 displays information found in the notes to financial statements that can be used to estimate the coming year's interest expense. (Not every annual report provides the amount of detail shown here. Greater reliance on assumptions is required when the information is sketchier.)

The key to the forecasting method employed here is to estimate Colossal Chemical's embedded cost of debt, that is, the weighted average interest rate on the company's existing long-term debt. Applying the embedded cost of 5.43 percent to Colossal's 2010 year-end long-term debt *(including*

EXHIBIT 12.6   Details of Long-Term Debt, Short-Term Debt, and Interest Expense

Colossal Chemical Corporation ($000,000 omitted)		
Long Term Debt (Excluding current maturities)	**2001**	**2000**
10.0% notes payable 2003	$ 52	$ 78
8.1% notes payable 2007	77	111
9.5% debentures due 2010	75	75
8.875% debentures due 2014	125	125
6.5% industrial development bonds due 2017	50	50
	$379	$439

Long Term Debt	**2001**
Average interest rate for year	8.50%
Average annual amount outstanding	$29
Annual maturities of long-term debt for the next five years are as follows:	
2002	$27 million
2003	$13 million
2004	$22 million
2005	$18 million
2006	$31 million

Interest Expense	**2001**
Interest incurred	41
Capitalized interest	5
Interest expense	36

current maturities, which are assumed to carry the same average interest rate) produces projected interest charges of $22.32 million. As shown in Exhibit 12.6, the 2011 cash flow projection suggests no substantial reduction in debt outstanding during 2011. Accordingly, the method employed here should not prove far off the mark, even though it is merely an approximation.

To the $22.32 million figure, the forecaster must add interest charges related to the short-term debt (notes payable). These projections are based on an average of the year-end 2010 and projected year-end 2011 outstanding balances, which comes to $30.0 million. The assumed average interest rate is 1.75 percent, based on an expectation of slightly higher rates in 2011.

Bear in mind that the method described here for projecting interest expense involves a certain amount of simplification. Applied retroactively, it will not necessarily produce the precise interest expense shown in the historical financial statements. For one thing, paydowns of long-term debt will not come uniformly at midyear, as implicitly assumed by the estimation procedure for average amounts of long-term debt outstanding. Certainly, analysts should recognize and adjust for major, foreseeable changes in interest costs, such as refinancing of high-coupon bonds with cheaper borrowings. By the same token, forecasters should not go overboard in seeking precision on this particular item. For Colossal Chemical, projected interest for 2011 comes to only 1 percent of sales, so a 10 percent error in estimating the item will have little impact on the net earnings forecast. Analysts should reserve their energy in projecting interest expense for more highly leveraged companies. Their financial viability may depend on the size of the interest expense nut they must cover each quarter.

Interest Income   Exhibit 12.2 incorporates a forecast of an unchanged cash balance for 2011. Based on expectations of an average money market rate of return of 1.5 percent on corporate cash, the average balance of $69 million will generate (in round figures) $1 million of interest income.

Provision for Income Taxes   Following the deduction of interest expense and the addition of interest income, earnings before income taxes stand at $166 million. The forecast reduces this figure by the **statutory tax rate** of 35 percent, based on Colossal's effective rate having historically approximated the statutory rate. For other companies, effective rates could vary widely as a result of tax loss carryforwards and investment tax credits, among other items. Management will ordinarily be able to provide some guidance regarding major changes in the effective rate, and changes in the statutory rate are widely publicized by media coverage of federal tax legislation.

EXHIBIT 12.7 Projected Statement of Cash Flows, 2011

Colossal Chemical Corporation
($000,000 omitted)

Sources:	
Net income	$110
Depreciation	121
Deferred income taxes	25
Working capital changes, excluding cash and borrowings	(43)
Cash provided by operations	213
Uses:	
Additions to property, plant, and equipment	165
Dividends	37
Repayment of current maturities of long-term debt	32
Cash used by operations	234
Net Cash provided (used) by operations	$ (21)
Increase in notes payable	$ 21
Changes in Working Capital	$(25)
Decrease (increase) in accounts receivable	(29)
Decrease (increase) in inventories	11
Increase (decrease) in accounts payable	$(43)

Projected Statement of Cash Flows

The completed income statement projection supplies the first two lines of the projected statement of cash flows (Exhibit 12.7). Net income of $114 million and depreciation of $121 million come directly from Exhibit 12.2 and largely determine the total sources (funds provided by operations) figure. The other two items have only a small impact on the projections.

Deferred Income Taxes   This figure can vary somewhat unpredictably from year to year, based on changes in the gap between tax and book depreciation and miscellaneous factors such as leases, installment receivables, and unremitted earnings of foreign subsidiaries. Input from company management may help in the forecasting of this figure. The $25 million figure shown in Exhibit 12.7 is a trend-line projection.

Working Capital Changes (Excluding Cash and Borrowings)   Details of the derivation of the $43 million projection appear at the bottom of Exhibit 12.7. The forecast assumes that each working capital item remains at the same percentage of sales shown in the historical statements in

Exhibit 12.1. Accounts receivable, for example, at 22 percent of sales, rise from $439 million to $464 million (an increase of $25 million) as sales grow from $1,991 million in 2010 to a projected $2,110 million in 2011. Before assuming a constant-percentage relationship, the analyst must verify that the most recent year's ratios are representative of experience over several years. Potential future deviations from historical norms must likewise be considered. For example, a sharp drop in sales may produce involuntary inventory accumulation or a rise in accounts receivable as the company attempts to stimulate its sales by offering easier credit terms.

Additions to Property, Plant, and Equipment   The first and largest of the uses on this cash flow projection is capital expenditures. A company may provide a specific capital spending projection in its annual report and then, as the year progresses, update its estimate in its quarterly statements or 10-Q reports and in press releases. Even if the company does not publish a specific number, its investor-relations officer will ordinarily respond to questions about the range or at least the direction (up, down, or flat) for the coming year.

Dividends   The $37 million figure shown assumes that Colossal will continue its stated policy of paying out in dividends approximately one-third of its sustainable earnings (excluding extraordinary gains and losses). Typically, this sort of guideline is interpreted as an average payout over time, so that the dividend rate does not fluctuate over a normal business cycle to the same extent that earnings do. A company may even avoid cutting its dividend through a year or more of losses, borrowing to maintain the payout if necessary. This practice often invites criticism and may stir debate within the board of directors, where the authority to declare dividends resides.

Until the board officially announces its decision, an analyst attempting to project future dividends can make only an educated guess. In a difficult earnings environment, moreover, a decision to maintain the dividend in one quarter is no assurance that the board will decide the same way three months later.

Repayment of Current Maturities of Long-Term Debt   The $32 million figure shown comes directly from the current liabilities section of the balance sheet in Exhibit 12.1.

Increase in Notes Payable   Subtracting $234 million of cash used in operations from the $217 million provided by operations produces a net use of $17 million. This projection assumes that any net cash generated will be applied to debt retirement. A net cash use, on the other hand, will be made up through drawing down short-term bank lines. Underlying these assumptions about the company's actions are management's stated objectives and some knowledge of how faithfully management has stuck to its plans in the past. Other assumptions might be more appropriate in other circumstances. For example, a net provision or use of cash might be offset by a reduction or increase in cash and marketable securities. A sizable net cash provision might be presumed to be directed toward share repurchase, reducing shareholders' equity, if management has indicated a desire to buy in stock and is authorized to do so by its board of directors. Instead of making up a large cash shortfall with short-term debt, a company might instead fund the borrowings as quickly as possible (add to its long-term debt). Alternatively, a company may have a practice of financing any large cash need with a combination of long-term debt and equity, using the proportions of each that are required to keep its ratio of debt to equity at some constant level.

Projected Balance Sheet

Constructing the projected balance sheet (Exhibit 12.8) requires no additional assumptions beyond those made in projecting the income statement and statement of cash flows. The analyst simply updates the historical balance sheet in Exhibit 12.1 on the basis of information drawn from the other statements.

Most of the required information appears in the projected statement of cash flows (Exhibit 12.7). Accounts receivable, inventories, and accounts payable, for example, reflect the projected changes in working capital. The cash flow projection would likewise show any increase or decrease in cash and marketable securities, an item that in this case remains flat. Property,

EXHIBIT 12.8 Colossal Chemical Corporation Projected Balance Sheet December 31, 2011 ($000,000 omitted)

Cash and marketable securities	$ 69	Notes payable	$ 42
Accounts Receivable	464	Accounts payable	274
		Current portion of	
Inventories	380	long-term debt	27
Total Current Assets	913	Total Current Liabilities	343
		Long-term debt	352
		Deferred income taxes	95
Property, plant, and equipment	939	Shareholders' equity	1,062
	$1,852		$1,852

plant, and equipment rises from the prior year's level of $895 million by $165 million of additions, less $121 million of depreciation. The projected cash flow statement also furnishes the increases in notes payable and deferred income taxes, as well as the change in shareholders' equity (net income less dividends).

The details of long-term debt in the historical balance sheet (Exhibit 12.6) provide the figures needed to complete the projection of long-term debt. With the 2010 current maturities of long-term debt ($32 million) having been paid off, the 2011 current maturities ($27 million) take their place on the balance sheet. The $27 million figure is also deducted from 2010's (noncurrent) long-term debt of $379 million to produce the new figure of $352 million. (Any further adjustments to long-term debt, of which there are none in these projections, would appear in the projected statement of cash flows.)

SENSITIVITY ANALYSIS WITH PROJECTED FINANCIAL STATEMENTS

Preparing a set of projected financial statements provides a glimpse at a company's future financial condition, given certain assumptions. The analyst can study the projected statements using the same techniques discussed in Chapters 2 through 4 for the historical statements and also use them to calculate the ratios employed in credit analysis (Chapter 13) and equity analysis (Chapter 14). Based on the historical and projected data in Exhibits 12.1 through 12.8, Colossal Chemical's credit quality measures will improve in 2011 (Exhibit 12.9). Total debt will decline, not only in absolute terms but also as a percentage of total capital—from 29.0 percent to 26.5 percent. Similarly, cash provided as a percentage of total debt will rise from 50.8% to 62.2%. (Alternatively, the reciprocals indicate debt as a multiple of cash provided falling from 1.97X to 1.61X.) As explained in Chapter 13, both of these trends indicate reduced financial risk. These projected ratios are only as reliable as the assumptions underlying the projected statements that generated them. Logical though they may seem, the assumptions rest heavily on macroeconomic forecasting, which is far from an exact science, to put it charitably. Typically, the analyst must modify the underlying economic assumptions, and therefore the projections, several times during the year as business activity diverges from forecasted levels.

Knowing that conditions can, and in all likelihood will, change, wise investors and lenders will not base their decisions entirely on a single set of projections, or point forecast. Instead, they will assess the risks and potential rewards in light of a range of possible outcomes.

EXHIBIT 12.9 Trend of Credit Quality Measures—Base Case

Colossal Chemical Corporation
($000,000 omitted)

	2010 (Actual)**	2011 (Projected)*
Total Debt		
Notes payable	$ 21	$ 42
Current portion of long-term debt	32	27
Long-term debt	379	352
	432	421
Deferred income taxes	70	95
Shareholders' equity	989	1,062
Total Capital	$1,491	$1,578
Total debt as a percentage of total capital	29.0%	26.7%
Cash provided by operations (before working captial charges)	224	256
Total Debt	432	421
Cash Provided as a Percentage of Total Debt	51.9%	60.8%

* From Exhibit 12.8
** From Exhibit 12.1

Exhibit 12.10 illustrates how the analyst can modify the underlying assumptions and then observe the extent to which projected ratios will be altered. This process is known as **sensitivity analysis**. In the example, the analyst projects a sales increase over the preceding year of just 3 percent. That is one-half the growth rate assumed in the base case (the most probable scenario) represented by Exhibit 12.2. The less optimistic sales forecast implies a less robust economy than assumed in the base case. For example, the analyst may assume no real growth and a 3 percent inflation rate. In the revised scenario, the analyst assumes that chemical producers will have no opportunity to increase their gross margins over the preceding year. Keeping the other assumptions intact, the revised projections show smaller increases, relative to the base case, in net income, shareholders' equity, and funds provided by operations. Long-term debt declines more slowly under the new assumptions.

Using Exhibit 12.10's revised statements, the analyst can recalculate Exhibit 12.9's credit quality measures as shown in Exhibit 12.11. Under the new, more pessimistic sales growth and gross margin assumptions, projected funds provided by operations represent 56.1 percent of total debt. The implied improvement over 2011 is smaller than indicated by the 62.2 percent

EXHIBIT 12.10 Sensitivity Analysis Projected Financial Statements

Colossal Chemical Corporation Year Ended December 31, 2011 ($000,000 omitted)

Reduce Base Case (Exhibit 12.2) Sales Growth Assumption from 6% to 3%
(No improvement in gross margin over preceding year)

Income Statement

Sales	$2,051
Cost of goods sold	1,374
Selling, general, and administrative expense	308
Depreciation	121
Research and development	82
Total costs and expenses	1,885
Operating Income	166
Interest expense	34
Interest (income)	(5)
Earnings before income taxes	137
Provision for income taxes	47
Net Income	$ 90

Statement of Cash Flow

Sources:	
Net income	$ 90
Depreciation	121
Deferred income taxes	25
Working capital changes, excluding cash and borrowings	(26)
Cash provided by operations	210
Uses:	
Additions to property, plant, and equipment	165
Dividends	30
Repayment of current maturities of long-term debt	32
Cash provided by operations	227
Net cash provided (used) by operations	(17)
Increase in long-term debt	17
Net change in cash	$ 0

Balance Sheet

Cash and marketable securities	$ 69	Notes payable	$ 21
Accounts receivable	451	Accounts payable	267
Inventories	369	Current portion of long-term debt	27
Total Current Assets	889	Total Current Liabilities	315
Property, plant, and equipment	939	Long-term debt	369
		Deferred income taxes	95
		Shareholders' equity	1,049
	$1,828		$1,828

EXHIBIT 12.11   Trend of Credit Quality Comparison

Colossal Chemical Corporation
Year Ended December 31, 2011 (Projected)
($000,000 omitted)

	Pessimistic Case*	Base Case**
Total Debt		
Notes payable	$ 21	$ 42
Current portion of long-term debt	27	27
Long-term debt	369	352
Deferred Income Taxes	417	421
Shareholders' Equity	95	95
Total Capital	1,049	1,062
Total Debt as a Percentage of	$1,541	$1,578
Total Capital	27.1%	26.7%
Funds Provided by Operations		
(Before Working Capital Changes)	236	256
Total Debt	417	421
Cash Provided as a Percentage of		
Total Debt	56.6%	60.8%

* From Exhibit 12.10.
** From Exhibit 12.9.

ratio projected in the base case. Total debt as a percentage of total capital rises modestly under the changed assumptions, to 27.1 percent from 26.5 percent in the base case. Although the addition to retained earnings (and hence growth in shareholders' equity) is smaller in the pessimistic case, so is the need for new working capital to support increased sales. The borrowing need is therefore reduced, partially offsetting the slower growth in equity.

To complete the analysis, an investor or lender will also want to project financial statements on an optimistic, or best-case, scenario. Sample assumptions for a three-scenario sensitivity analysis might be:

	Assumed Sales Growth	Assumed Gross Margin
Optimistic case (best realistic scenario)	8%	36%
Base case (most likely scenario)	6%	34%
Pessimistic case (worst realistic scenario)	3%	33%

Note that the assumptions need not be symmetrical. The optimistic case in this instance assumes sales only two percentage points higher than the base case, whereas the pessimistic case reduces base case sales by three percentage points. The analyst simply believes that the most likely scenario embodies more downside than upside.

Other assumptions can be modified as well, recognizing the interaction among the various accounts. Colossal Chemical may have considerable room to cut its capital spending in the short run if it suffers a decline in funds provided by operations. A projection that ignored this financial flexibility could prove overly pessimistic. Conversely, the assumption that a company will apply any surplus funds generated to debt reduction may produce an unrealistic projected capital structure. Particularly in a multiyear projection for a strong cash generator, the ratio of debt to capital may fall in the later years to a level that the company would consider excessively conservative. In such cases, it may be appropriate to alter the assumption from debt retirement to maintenance of a specified leverage ratio. Surplus cash will thus be applied to stock repurchase to the extent that not doing so would cause the debt component of capital to fall below a specified percentage.

In addition to creating a range of scenarios, sensitivity analysis can also enable the analyst to gauge the relative impact of changing the various assumptions in a projection. Contrast, for example, the impact of a 1 percent change in gross margins with the impact of a 1 percent change in the tax rate on Colossal Chemical's income statement. Exhibit 12.12 shows the effects of these two changes in assumptions on the projected income statement in Exhibit 12.2, holding all other assumptions constant. The sensitivity of net income to a 1 percent change in gross margins is $13 million ($114 million minus $101 million), all other things being equal. A 1 percent change in the tax rate, on the other hand, affects net income by just $1 million, all other things again being equal.

This type of analysis is popular among investors. They may, for example, estimate the impact on a mining company's earnings, and hence on its stock price, of a 10-cent rise in the price of a pound of copper. Another application is to identify which companies will respond most dramatically to some expected economic development, such as a drop in interest rates. A rate decline will have limited impact on a company for which interest costs represent a small percentage of expenses. The impact will be greater on a company with a large interest cost component and with much of its debt at floating rates. (This assumes the return on the company's assets is not similarly rate sensitive.)

Alluring though it may be, sensitivity analysis is a technique that must be used with caution. As suggested, it generally isolates a single assumption and proceeds on the basis that all other things remain equal. In the real

EXHIBIT 12.12   Sensitivity Analysis: Impact of Changes in Selected Assumptions on Projected Income Statement

Colossal Chemical Corporation
Year Ended December 31, 2011
($000,000 omitted)

	Base Case	1% Decline in Gross Margin	1% Rise in Tax Rate
Sales	$2,110	$2,110	$2,110
Cost of goods sold	1,393	1,414	1,393
Selling, general, and administrative expense	317	317	317
Depreciation	121	121	121
Research and development	84	84	84
Total costs and expenses	1,915	1,936	1,915
Operating Income	195	174	195
Interest expense	34	34	34
Interest (income)	(5)	(5)	(5)
Earnings before Income Taxes	166	145	166
Provision for Income Taxes	56	49	58
Net Income	$ 110	$ 96	$ 108

world, this is rarely the case. When sales fall, typically, so do gross margins. The reason is that declining capacity utilization puts downward pressure on prices. Similarly, rising interest rates do not affect only interest expense and interest income. Higher rates depress the level of investment in the economy, which can eventually depress the company's sales.

PROJECTING FINANCIAL FLEXIBILITY

Just as projected statements can reveal a company's probable future financial profile, they can also indicate the likely direction of its financial flexibility, a concept discussed in Chapter 4. For example, the projected statement of cash flows shows by how comfortable a margin the company will be able to cover its dividend with internally generated funds. Likewise, the amount by which debt is projected to rise determines the extent to which nondiscretionary costs (in the form of interest charges) will increase in future income statements.

There is one important aspect of financial flexibility, continuing compliance with loan covenants, for which projections are indispensable. As Exhibit 12.13 illustrates, debt covenants may require the borrower to

EXHIBIT 12.13 Sample Debt Restriction Disclosures

"We have a $9,465 credit agreement with a syndicate of investment and commercial banks, which we have the right to increase up to an additional $2,535, provided no event of default under the credit agreement has occurred. The current agreement will expire in July 2011. We also have the right to terminate, in whole or in part, amounts committed by the lenders under this agreement in excess of any outstanding advances; however, any such terminated commitments may not be reinstated. Advances under this agreement may be used for general corporate purposes, including support of commercial paper borrowings and other short-term borrowings. We must maintain a debt-to-EBITDA (earnings before interest, income taxes, depreciation, and amortization, and other modifications described in the agreement) financial ratio covenant of not more than three-to-one as of the last day of each fiscal quarter for the four quarters then ended. We comply with all covenants under the agreement. At June 30, 2010, we had no borrowings outstanding under this agreement."

—AT&T, Inc. 10-Q, June 30, 2010

"We have a $2.3 billion five-year unsecured revolving credit facility, as amended (the "Credit Facility"), with a syndicate of banks, with no borrowings outstanding at February 27, 2010.

"Our ability to access our facilities is subject to our compliance with the terms and conditions of our facilities, including financial covenants. The financial covenants require us to maintain certain financial ratios. At February 27, 2010, we were in compliance with all such financial covenants. If an event of default were to occur with respect to any of our other debt, it would likely constitute an event of default under our credit facilities as well.

"An interest coverage ratio represents the ratio of pretax earnings before fixed charges (interest expense and the interest portion of rent expense) to fixed charges. Our interest coverage ratio, calculated as reported in Exhibit No. 12.1 of this Annual Report on Form 10-K, was 6.08 and 5.52 in fiscal 2010 and 2009, respectively.

"The Credit Facility is guaranteed by certain of our subsidiaries and contains customary affirmative and negative covenants. Among other things, these covenants restrict or prohibit our ability to incur certain types or amounts of indebtedness, incur liens on certain assets, make material changes to our corporate structure or the nature of our business, dispose of material assets, allow nonmaterial subsidiaries to make guarantees, engage in a change in control transaction, or engage in certain transactions with our affiliates. The Credit Facility also contains covenants that require us to maintain a maximum quarterly cash flow

(Continued)

EXHIBIT 12.13 (*Continued*)

leverage ratio and a minimum quarterly interest coverage ratio. We were in compliance with all such covenants at February 27, 2010.

"The Notes are unsecured and unsubordinated obligations and rank equally with all of our other unsecured and unsubordinated debt. The Notes contain covenants that, among other things, limit our ability and the ability of our North American subsidiaries to incur debt secured by liens, enter into sale and lease-back transactions and, in the case of such subsidiaries, incur unsecured debt."

—Best Buy Co, Inc. 2009 10-K

"Most of our long-term debt obligations contain covenants related to secured debt levels. In addition to a secured debt level covenant, our credit facility also contains a debt leverage covenant. We are, and expect to remain, in compliance with these covenants. Additionally, at July 31, 2010, no notes or debentures contained provisions requiring acceleration of payment upon a debt rating downgrade, except that certain outstanding notes allow the note holders to put the notes to us if within a matter of months of each other we experience both (i) a change in control; and (ii) our long-term debt ratings are either reduced and the resulting rating is noninvestment grade, or our long-term debt ratings are placed on watch for possible reduction and those ratings are subsequently reduced and the resulting rating is noninvestment grade."

—Target Corp. 10-Q, July 31, 2010

"Our credit agreements contain covenants that are typical for large, investment grade companies. These covenants include requirements to pay interest and principal in a timely fashion, to pay taxes, to maintain insurance with responsible and reputable insurance companies, to preserve our corporate existence, to keep appropriate books and records of financial transactions, to maintain our properties, to provide financial and other reports to our lenders, to limit pledging and disposition of assets and mergers and consolidations, and other similar covenants.

"In addition, Verizon Wireless is required to maintain on the last day of any period of four fiscal quarters a leverage ratio of debt to earnings before interest, taxes, depreciation, amortization, and other adjustments, as defined in the related credit agreement, not in excess of 3.25 times based on the preceding twelve months. At December 31, 2009, the leverage ratio was 1.1 times.

"As of December 31, 2009, we and our consolidated subsidiaries were in compliance with all of our debt covenants."

—Verizon Communications Inc. 2009 10-K

"The Company has commercial paper programs that allow for borrowings up to $3.25 billion. All of the Company's short-term borrowings in fiscal 2009 and 2008

EXHIBIT 12.13 (*Continued*)

were under these commercial paper programs. In connection with the commercial paper programs, the Company has a back-up credit facility with a consortium of banks for borrowings up to $3.25 billion. The credit facility expires in December 2010 and contains various restrictive covenants. At January 31, 2010, the Company was in compliance with all of the covenants, and they are not expected to impact the Company's liquidity or capital resources."

—The Home Depot, Inc. 2009 10-K

Source: Company 10-Q and 10-K.

maintain a specified level of financial strength. Compliance may be measured either by absolute dollar amounts of certain items or by ratios.[1] Sanctions against an issuer that commits a technical default (violation of a covenant, as opposed to failure to pay interest or principal on schedule) can be severe. The issuer may be barred from paying further dividends or compelled to repay a huge loan at a time when refinancing may be difficult. Curing the default may necessitate unpleasant actions, such as a dilution of shareholders' interests by the sale of new equity at less than book value. Alternatively, the borrower can request that its lenders waive their right to accelerate payment of the debt. The lenders, however, are likely to demand some quid pro quo along the lines of reducing management's freedom to act without consulting them.

Analysts can anticipate this sort of loss of financial flexibility by applying covenanted tests of net worth, leverage, and fixed charge coverage to projected balance sheets and income statements. General descriptions of the tests can be found in the notes to financial statements. These descriptions may omit some subtleties involving definitions of terms, but since the projections are by their nature also prone to imprecision, the objective is not in any case absolute certainty regarding a possible breach of covenants. Rather, the discovery that a company is likely to be bumping up against covenanted limits a year or two into the future means it is time to ask management how it plans to preserve its financial flexibility. If the answers prove unsatisfactory, the effort of having made the projections and run the tests may be rewarded by a warning, well in advance, of serious trouble ahead.

PRO FORMA FINANCIAL STATEMENTS

Another way that the analyst can look forward with financial statements is to construct pro forma statements that reflect significant developments, prior to reflection of those developments in subsequent published statements. It is unwise to base an investment decision on historical statements that antedate a major financial change such as a stock repurchase, write-off, acquisition, or divestment. By the same token, it can be important to determine quickly whether news that flashes across the screen will have a material effect on a company's financial condition. For example, will a just-announced repurchase of 3.5 million shares materially increase financial leverage? To answer the question, the analyst must adjust the latest balance sheet available, reducing shareholders' equity by the product of 3.5 million and an assumed purchase price per share, then reduce cash or increase debt as the accounting offset.

PRO FORMA STATEMENTS FOR ACQUISITIONS

Pro forma statements are not limited to analysts' rough-and-ready modifications of previously released financial reports, generated in response to corporate announcements. The category also includes detailed income statements and balance sheets that companies provide in connection with major corporate transactions. These unaudited statements contain new disclosures and are filed with the Securities and Exchange Commission on Form 8-K, which is used to notify investors of material, unscheduled events.

Exhibit 12.14 is a pro forma income statement for the proposed acquisition of Dollar Thrifty Automotive Group, Inc. by Hertz Global Holdings, Inc. in 2010. Hertz provided pro forma financials in an 8-K but stated that they were not intended to satisfy any obligation to supply such information upon completion of the merger and were provided for informational purposes only. The question became moot on September 30, 2010, when Dollar Thrifty's shareholders rejected the acquisition offer to which the company's management had agreed. This income statement is a historical artifact of a deal that might have been. Note that Hertz planned to implement the proposed acquisition by merging a specially created subsidiary into Dollar Thrifty, resulting in the 8-K referring to the transaction as a merger.

The key column in Exhibit 12.14 is labeled "Pro Forma Adjustments." To provide insight into the creation of a pro forma statement, the following paragraphs detail the changes summarized in the adjustments column. Observe that some adjustments have genuine economic impact, such as increased interest costs resulting from borrowings to finance the acquisition, while others have none. An example of the latter is the reclassification of items that the acquirer and the acquiree account for differently.

At the level of revenues, consisting primarily of car rentals, the pro forma income statement simply adds the two companies' accounts. The same

EXHIBIT 12.14 Hertz Global Holdings, Inc. Unaudited Pro Forma Condensed Combined Statement of Operations for the Year Ended December 31, 2009

	Hertz	DTG	Pro Forma Adjustments (Note 5)	Pro Forma Combined
		(in thousands of dollars, except per share data)		
Revenues:				
Car rental	$5,872,905	$1,472,918	$ —	$7,345,823
Equipment rental	1,110,243	—	—	1,110,243
Other	118,359	73,331	—	191,690
Total revenues	7,101,507	1,546,249	—	8,647,756
Expenses:				
Direct operating	4,084,176	768,456	—	4,852,632
Depreciation of revenue earning equipment	1,931,358	426,092	—	2,357,450
Selling, general, and administrative	641,148	200,389	(19,932)[a][c][d]	821,605
Interest expense	680,273	102,778	18,987[b]	802,038
Interest and other income, net	(64,439)	(6,218)	—	(70,657)
Impairment charges	—	2,592	—	2,592
Total expenses	7,272,516	1,494,089	(945)	8,765,660

Note: See Appendix for Explanation of Pro Forma Adjustments for Hertz Global Holdings, Inc./DTG.

EXHIBIT 12.14 (Continued)

	Hertz	DTG	Pro Forma Adjustments (Note 5)	Pro Forma Combined
	(in thousands of dollars, except per share data)			
Increase in fair value of derivatives	—	(28,848)	28,848[d]	—
Income (loss) before income taxes	(171,009)	81,008	(27,903)	(117,904)
(Provision) benefit for taxes on income	59,666	(35,986)	10,882[e]	34,562
Net income (loss)	(111,343)	45,022	(17,021)	(83,342)
Less: Net income attributable to noncontrolling interest	(14,679)		—	(14,679)
Net income (loss) attributable to Hertz/DTG common stockholders	$(126,022)	$ 45,022	$(17,021)	$ (98,021)
Weighted average shares outstanding (in thousands)				
Basic	371,456	22,687	(4,428)[f]	389,715
Diluted	371,456	23,967	(5,708)[f]	389,715
Earnings (loss) per share attributable to Hertz/DTG common stockholders:				
Basic	$ (0.34)	$ 1.98		$ (0.25)
Diluted	$ (0.34)	$ 1.88		$ (0.25)

Source: 8-K September 14, 2010.

straightforward treatment handles direct operating expenses, depreciation, interest and other income, and impairment charges. Hertz makes pro forma adjustments to several other items, however.

Selling, general, and administrative expense is adjusted to reflect the amortization of customer relationship intangible assets over 10 years and to eliminate advisory, legal, regulatory, and retention costs directly attributable to the pending merger but not expected to have a continuing impact on the combined entity's results. Additional adjustments to SG&A conform Dollar Thrifty's historical financial statements to Hertz's presentation by reclassifying the increase in fair value of derivatives from a separate line to a component of SG&A.

The adjustments to interest expense involve amortization of the fair value adjustment to debt arising from the acquisition, elimination of interest expense through extinguishment of Dollar Thrifty's nonvehicle debt (letter of credit and revolving credit facility), elimination of amortization of deferred financing costs associated with the extinguished debt, and interest on additional borrowings under Hertz's senior asset-based lending facility used as partial financing for the merger.

Hertz adjusts interest expense for the impact on accrued income taxes in connection with its preclosing retention program and deferred compensation for the write-off of deferred financing costs. The average number of shares outstanding is adjusted to reflect the expected replacement of Dollar Thrifty's outstanding shares by shares to be issued by Hertz in connection with the business combination.

Exhibit 12.15 is a pro forma balance sheet for the aborted Hertz acquisition of Dollar Thrifty. Pro forma adjustments are as follows:

- *Cash and cash equivalents*—Extinguishment of Dollar Thrifty's nonvehicle debt, payment of a special cash dividend to Dollar Thrifty shareholders prior to closing, reflection of the cash portion of the merger consideration, retention payments by Dollar Thrifty prior to closing, estimate of future merger-related transaction costs, additional borrowings under Hertz's senior asset-based lending facility, and reclassification of Dollar Thrifty's cash and cash equivalents, as Dollar Thrifty's required minimum balance would cease to be necessary upon extinguishment of the described debt. (The last item also results in an adjustment to cash and cash equivalents—required minimum balance.)
- *Prepaid expenses and other assets*—Elimination of unamortized deferred financing fees associated with extinguishment of Dollar Thrifty's nonvehicle debt and elimination of prefunding of a trust plan associated with deferred compensation.

EXHIBIT 12.15 Hertz Global Holdings, Inc. Unaudited Pro Forma Condensed Combined Balance Sheet, as of June 30, 2010

	Hertz	DTG	Pro Forma Adjustments (Note 5)	Pro Forma Combined
		(in thousands of dollars)		
Assets				
Cash and cash equivalents	$ 896,848	$ 269,876	$(863,103)(g)	$ 303,621
Cash and cash equivalents—required minimum balance	—	100,000	(100,000)(g)	—
Restricted cash	743,435	113,518	—	856,953
Receivables, less allowance for doubtful accounts	1,400,306	115,279	—	1,515,585
Inventories, at lower of cost or market	88,805	—	—	88,805
Prepaid expenses and other assets	304,296	74,087	(7,196)(h)	371,187
Revenue earning equipment, net				
Cars	8,762,115	1,725,865	—	10,487,980
Other equipment	1,649,095	—	—	1,649,095
Total revenue earning equipment, net	10,411,210	1,725,865	—	12,137,075
Property and equipment, net	1,156,668	93,713	25,445(d)	1,275,826
Other intangible assets, net	2,563,709	25,445	524,555(d)(i)	3,113,709
Goodwill	290,550	—	733,702(i)	1,024,252
Total Assets	$17,855,827	$2,517,783	$ 313,403	$20,687,013

Note: See Appendix for Explanation of Pro Forma Adjustments for Hertz Global Holdings, Inc./DTG.

Liabilities and Equity

Accounts payable	$ 1,467,148	$ 52,104	$ —	$ 1,519,252
Accrued liabilities	915,817	191,200	(6,488)(k)	1,100,529
Accrued taxes	158,114	12,459	(4,316)(e)	166,257
Debt	11,693,823	1,548,934	321,175(l)	13,563,932
Public liability and property damage	261,142	112,857	—	373,999
Deferred taxes on income	1,446,099	132,373	232,240(m)	1,810,712
Total Liabilities	15,942,143	2,049,927	542,611	18,534,681
Common Stock	4,120	350	(167)(n)	4,303
Preferred Stock	—	—	—	—
Additional paid-in capital	3,160,278	937,093	(649,463)(o)	3,447,908
Accumulated deficit	(1,237,844)	(223,630)	174,465(p)	(1,287,009)
Accumulated other comprehensive loss	(30,783)	(18,061)	18,061(q)	(30,783)
Treasury stock	—	(227,896)	227,896(r)	—
Total Hertz/DTG equity	1,895,771	467,856	(229,208)	2,134,419
Noncontrolling interest	17,913			17,913
Total Equity	1,913,684	467,856	(229,208)	2,152,332
Total Liabilities and Equity	$17,855,827	$2,517,783	$ 313,403	$20,687,013

Source: 8-K September 14, 2010.

251

- *Property and equipment, net and other intangible assets, net*—Reclassification of Dollar Thrifty's capitalized software from the other intangible assets category to property and equipment, to conform to Hertz's presentation.
- *Goodwill*—Recording of an estimate of goodwill as of the acquisition date.
- *Accrued liabilities*—Reflection of the settlement of retention and deferred compensation expense in accordance with the merger agreement.
- *Accrued taxes*—Recording of the impact of the preclosing retention program, deferred compensation payments, and the write-off of deferred financing costs.
- *Debt*—Elimination of Dollar Thrifty's nonvehicle debt, adjustment of Dollar Thrifty's remaining debt to an estimate of fair value, and incurrence of additional borrowings under Hertz's senior asset-based lending facility.
- *Deferred taxes on income*—Adjustment on income associated with fair value adjustments on assets acquired and liabilities assumed and reversal of deferred taxes associated with deferred compensation to be paid by Dollar Thrifty prior to closing.
- *Common stock*—Recording of the stock portion of the merger consideration and elimination of Dollar Thrifty's common stock.
- *Additional paid-in capital*—Recording of the stock portion of the merger consideration, at fair value less par, and elimination of Dollar Thrifty's additional paid-in capital.
- *Accumulated deficit*—Elimination of Dollar Thrifty's accumulated deficit and recording of Hertz and Dollar Thrifty's estimated nonrecurring advisory, legal, regulatory, and valuation costs.
- *Accumulated other comprehensive loss*—Elimination of Dollar Thrifty's accumulated other comprehensive loss.
- *Treasury stock*—Elimination of Dollar Thrifty's treasury stock.

For the most part, the company-provided pro forma adjustments take care of accounting niceties. They shed only limited light on probable changes to future cash flow, that is, to the factor that will most influence the company's credit quality and the valuation of its stock. Note that adjusting the acquired company's debt to fair value will not change the ratio of cash flow to actual outstanding debt. Moreover, Hertz makes the following standard disclaimer:

> The pro forma information is not necessarily indicative of what the combined company's financial position or results of operations

actually would have been had the merger been completed as of the dates indicated. In addition, the unaudited pro forma condensed combined financial information does not purport to project the future financial position or operating results of the combined company.[2]

Hertz also states that it has assumed a 39 percent tax rate in estimating the tax impact of the proposed transaction, based on its own statutory rate. The company indicates, however, that the combined company's effective rate could be significantly higher or lower, depending on postmerger activities, cash needs, and the geographical locations of its businesses.

In light of its limitations, a company-provided pro forma statement provides only a starting point for assessing the impact on credit risk and future profitability of a major merger, acquisition, or divestment. Suppose, for instance, a company rated Single-A makes a large, debt-financed acquisition that raises its ratio of total debt to total capital, on a pro forma basis, to a level consistent with a Triple-B rating (see Chapter 13). The bond rating agencies may not downgrade the company despite the increase in financial leverage if management presents a credible plan to bring its leverage back to the Single-A range within a reasonable period. To pay down its acquisition-related borrowings, the company might raise cash from asset sales or increase the portion of cash flow that it devotes to debt repayment. As for future profitability following a merger or acquisition, much will typically depend on the extent to which the business combination produces synergy (see Chapter 3). Management may foresee larger efficiencies from the business combination than indicated by the pro forma statements, which follow the basic accounting principle of conservatism. For these reasons, analysts must make adjustments to the pro forma statements appearing in Form 8-Ks. Still, the company disclosures provide useful information on tax effects and such accounting matters as expected changes in asset valuations and the effects of conforming the two companies' treatment of discretionary items.

MULTIYEAR PROJECTIONS

So far, this chapter has focused on one-year projections and pro forma adjustments to current financial statements. Such exercises, however, represent nothing more than the foundation of a complete projection. A fixed-income investor buying a 30-year bond is certainly interested in the issuer's financial prospects beyond a 12-month horizon. Similarly, a substantial percentage of the present value of future dividends represented by a stock's price lies in years beyond the coming one. Even if particular investors plan to hold the securities for one year or less, they have an interest in estimating longer-term projections. Their ability, 6 or 12 months hence, to sell at attractive prices will depend on other investors' views at the time of the issuer's prospects.

The inherent volatility of economic conditions makes long-term projections a perilous undertaking. In the late 1970s, prognosticators generally expected then-prevailing tightness in energy supplies to persist and worsen, resulting in continued escalation of oil prices. The implications of this scenario included large profits for oil producers and boom conditions for manufacturers of oil exploration supplies, energy-conservation products, and alternative-energy equipment. By the early 1980s, the energy picture had changed from scarcity to glut, and many companies that had expected prosperity instead suffered bankruptcy. In subsequent years, numerous other discontinuities have forced companies to revise their long-range plans. They have included:

- A wave of sovereign debt defaults by less developed countries in Latin America.
- A stock market crash on October 19, 1987.
- A huge wave of leveraged buyout bankruptcies.
- A war in the Persian Gulf.
- A boom and bust in Internet stocks.
- A financial crisis in Asia.
- The September 11, 2001, terrorist attacks on the Pentagon and World Trade Center, followed by new wars in the Persian Gulf and Afghanistan.
- The most severe financial crisis and recession since the 1930s, lasting from 2007 to mid-2009 and leading to reduced expectations for longer-run economic growth.

The frequency of such shocks makes it difficult to have high confidence in projections covering periods even as short as five years.

Notwithstanding their potential for badly missing the mark, multiyear projections are essential to financial analysis in some situations. For example, certain capital-intensive companies such as paper manufacturers have long construction cycles. They add to their capacity not in steady, annual increments but through large, individual plants that take several years to build. While a plant is in construction, the company must pay interest on the huge sums borrowed to finance it. This increased expense depresses earnings until the point, several years out, when the new plant comes onstream and begins to generate revenues. To obtain a true picture of the company's long-range financial condition, the analyst must somehow factor in the income statements for the fourth and fifth years of the construction project. These are far more difficult to forecast than first- or second-year results, which reflect cyclical peak borrowings and interest costs.

Radical financial restructurings also necessitate multiyear projections. Examples include leveraged buyouts, megamergers, and massive stock buybacks. The short-term impact of these transactions is to increase financial risk sharply. Often, leverage rises to a level investors are comfortable with only if they believe the company will be able to reduce debt to more customary levels within a few years. Sources of debt repayment may include both cash flow and proceeds of planned asset sales. Analysts must make projections to determine whether the plan for debt retirement rests on realistic assumptions. A lender cannot prudently enter into a highly leveraged transaction without making some attempt to project results over several years, notwithstanding the uncertainties inherent in such long-range forecasts.

Fortunately for analysts, today's sophisticated financial modeling tools make it feasible to run numerous scenarios for proposed transactions. Analysts can vary the underlying economic assumptions and deal terms as they change from day to day. Once the company's financial structure becomes definitive, the analyst can input the final numbers into the spreadsheet. From that point, the critical task is to monitor the restructured company's quarter-by-quarter progress, comparing actual results with projections.

Financial modeling tools are helpful in analyzing conventionally capitalized companies, as well as highly leveraged transactions. In projecting the financials of companies with already-strong balance sheets, however, analysts should not assume that all excess cash flow will be directed toward debt retirement. Conservatively capitalized companies generally do not seek to reduce their financial leverage below some specified level. Instead, they use surplus funds to repurchase stock or make acquisitions.

Essentially, multiyear projections involve the same sorts of assumptions described in the one-year Colossal Chemical projection (Exhibits 12.1 through 12.12). When looking forward by as much as five years, though, the analyst must be especially cognizant of the impact of the business cycle. Many companies' projected financial statements look fine as long as sales grow like a hockey stick (sloping upward). Their financial strength dissipates quickly, however, when sales turn downward for a year or two.

Notwithstanding the many uncertainties that confront the financial forecaster, carefully constructed projections can prove fairly accurate. The results can be satisfying even when the numbers are strongly influenced by hard-to-predict economic variables. The two detailed projections reproduced as Exhibits 12.16 through 12.22 were generated by independent high-yield bond analyst Stan Manoukian. These exhibits show how the bottom-up approach illustrated in the fictitious Colossal Chemical example can be applied in real life to companies outside the basic industry sphere.

Dex One provides print, online, and mobile search marketing. Its delivery vehicles include the DexKnows.com web site, print yellow pages directories, pay-per-click advertising networks, and voice-based search platforms. Through its Business.com subsidiary, the company also maintains a business search engine and online directory. The company has evolved through a series of mergers-and-acquisitions transactions. The R. H. Donnelley Company (RHD) was spun off from Dun & Bradstreet in 1998. The company made a number of acquisitions, including Dex Media in 2006. Following a bankruptcy filing in 2009, the company emerged in 2009 as Dex One Corporation.

The yellow pages business has been challenged by encroachment of sales of advertising to small businesses by companies such as Google and Microsoft. Dex One maintains a position, however, through its large and effective sales force. On its admittedly shrinking revenue base, the company seeks to capitalize on its marketing strength to reinvent itself.

Exhibit 12.16 shows historical data (2007 through the first half of 2010) and projected data for the second half of 2010. **Fresh start accounting** applies to the 2010 numbers. The historical statements and interspersed financial ratios indicate the base for projected data and the factors for which assumptions are needed, such a year-over-year growth in total revenue and SG&A as a percentage of sales. The ratios shown at the bottom of the exhibit translate the historical and projected financial data into measures of credit quality (see Chapter 13).

A few details of the projections in Exhibit 12.16 shed light on the intricacies of financial forecasting. For instance, the analyst shows separately interest expense ($830.9 million in 2007) and cash interest expense ($721.5 million in that year.) Similarly, the projections differentiate between income taxes ($29.0 million) and cash income taxes ($10.1 million). Most companies provide investors with supplemental information in their quarterly cash flow statements that summarizes cash interest paid and cash taxes paid through the quarter. Usually, these cash numbers are different from those shown in a company's income statements. The difference in interest expense derives from capitalized interest (included in depreciation expense for capital leases, for instance), noncash interest expense on pay-in-kind securities, amortization of debt discount, and several other items. The difference in income taxes arises from deferred income taxes and many other sources. Financial analysts are mostly interested in a company's ability to generate

EXHIBIT 12.16 Dex One Corporation: Historical and Near-Term Projected Data

Column group header spanning the quarterly/annual columns: *Quarterly Revenue/Annual Revenue*

	2007	2008	Q1 2009	Q2 2009	Q3 2009	Q4 2009	2009	Q1 2010	Q2 2010	Q3 2010e	Q4 2010e	2010e
Total Revenue	2,680,299	2,616,811	601,986	565,628	533,990	500,843	2,202,447	468,617	451,791	450,000	445,592	1,816,000
Growth Y/Y	41.1%	(2.4)%	(10.8)%	(14.8)%	(17.6)%	(20.5)%	(15.8)%	(22.2)%	(20.1)%	(15.7)%	(11.0)%	(17.5)%
GOGS, excl.D&A	1,166,587	1,147,921	253,935	253,475	246,129	260,828	1,014,367	210,313	203,978	218,999	239,971	873,261
Total Gross Profit	1,513,712	1,468,890	348,051	312,153	287,861	240,015	1,188,080	258,304	247,813	231,001	205,621	942,739
Gross Margin	56.5%	56.1%	57.8%	55.2%	53.9%	47.9%	53.9%	55.1%	54.9%	51.3%	46.1%	51.9%
SG&A	145,640	120,930	41,562	25,973	24,775	(27,342)	68,968	29,914	40,202	27,656	61,228	159,000
% of Sales	5.4%	4.6%	6.9%	4.6%	5.4%	(5.5)%	3.1%	6.4%	8.9%	6.1%	13.7%	8.8%
Noncash Items	39,017	29,509	2,848	2,848	2,848	2,848	11,392	2,600	4,300	—	—	6,900
EBITDA	1,407,089	1,377,469	309,337	289,028	261,934	270,205	1,130,504	230,990	211,911	203,345	144,393	790,639
EBITDA margin	52.5%	52.6%	51.4%	51.1%	49.1%	54.0%	51.3%	49.3%	46.9%	45.2%	32.4%	43.5%
D&A and Impairment Charges	463,106	4,353,677	142,345	142,322	142,580	7,488,868	7,916,615	7,733,546	829,255	145,678	144,322	8,852,801
Partnership Income	0	0	0	0	0	0	0	0	0	0	0	0
Operating Income	943,983	(2,976,208)	166,492	146,706	119,354	(7,218,663)	(6,786,111)	(7,502,556)	(617,344)	57,667	71	(8,062,162)
Operating Margin	35.2%	(113.7)%	27.7%	25.9%	22.4%	(1,441.3)%	(308.1)%	(1,601.0)%	(136.6)%	12.8%	0.0%	(444.0)%
Nonoperating Income	1,818	265,166	0	(70,781)	(7,107)	77,888	0	0	0	0	0	0
Interest Expense	830,892	835,472	198,835	161,469	63,544	65,694	489,542	68,590	73,423	65,000	60,000	267,013
Income Taxes	29,033	(1,277,696)	366,019	(12,910)	21,925	(1,652,730)	(1,277,696)	516,019	(157,044)	(1,000)	(1,000)	356,975
Net Income	85,876	(2,268,818)	(398,362)	(72,634)	26,778	(5,553,739)	(5,997,957)	(8,087,165)	(533,723)	(6,333)	(58,929)	(8,686,150)
Liquidity												
EBITDA	1,407,089	1,377,469	309,337	289,028	261,934	270,205	1,130,504	230,990	211,911	203,345	144,393	790,639
Capex	(85,000)	(70,542)	(3,937)	(5,909)	(8,347)	(15,192)	(33,385)	(8,152)	(8,806)	(7,000)	(21,042)	(45,000)
Acquisitions, divestitures	(330,000)	4,318	—	—	—	—	—	—	—	—	—	—
Cash Interest Expense	(721,505)	(746,529)	(203,304)	(79,535)	(54,038)	(51,235)	(388,112)	(34,668)	(50,055)	(34,556)	(36,721)	(156,000)
Cash Income Taxes	(10,075)	(1,587)	—	(1,062)	(349)	(6,462)	(7,873)	(2,002)	(146)	(1,345)	(1,507)	(5,000)
Change in Working Capital	(70,170)	(91,307)	(27,387)	(184,926)	89,215	(172,673)	(295,771)	(443,049)	180,548	61,521	(7,423)	(208,403)
Free Cash Flow	190,339	471,722	74,709	17,596	288,415	24,643	405,363	(256,881)	333,452	221,965	77,700	376,236
Cash flow from operations	691,809	548,694	56,135	120,487	231,965	107,235	515,822	177,024	134,777	—	—	—
Cash flow from investments	(409,072)	66,324	(3,937)	(5,909)	(8,347)	(15,192)	(33,385)	(8,152)	(8,806)	—	—	—
Cash flow from financing	(392,910)	(397,247)	349,904	(240,932)	(24,094)	(32,574)	52,304	(687,285)	(151,743)	—	—	—
Total cash flow	(110,173)	217,771	402,102	(126,354)	199,524	59,469	534,741	(518,413)	(25,772)	—	—	—

EXHIBIT 12.16 (Continued)

Balance Sheet	2007	2008	Q1 2009	Q2 2009	Q3 2009	Q4 2009	2009	Q1 2010	Q2 2010	Q3 2010	Q4 2010e	2010e
Cash and Marketable Securities	46,076	131,199	533,301	406,947	606,471	665,940	665,940	147,527	121,755	55,985	55,985	55,985
Accounts Receivable	1,063,468	1,027,027	998,639	951,761	846,057	1,027,027	825,786	753,308	756,472	767,888	780,880	780,880
Days Accounts Receivable	142.8	141.3	151.0	153.1	144.2	186.6	135.0	146.3	152.4	160.6	154.3	154.8
Deferred directory costs	183,687	164,248	163,192	165,662	144,583	164,248	138,061	68,005	133,084	145,788	138,994	138,994
Days deferred costs	56.7	51.5	58.5	59.5	53.5	57.3	49.0	29.4	59.4	60.6	52.7	57.3
Prepaid assets	173,960	193,057	166,746	114,507	82,351	193,057	90,928	75,882	61,479	66,777	79,198	79,198
Days prepaid assets	23.4	26.6	25.2	18.4	14.0	35.1	14.9	14.7	12.4	14.0	15.6	15.7
Accounts Payable	230,693	216,093	180,650	125,716	161,801	216,093	168,488	139,165	119,215	121,333	109,158	109,158
Days Accounts Payable	71.2	67.8	64.7	45.1	59.8	75.4	59.8	60.2	53.2	50.4	41.4	45.0
Accrued Liabilities	1,370,863	1,257,373	1,209,674	983,035	877,226	961,602	961,602	390,296	644,634	733,455	756,827	756,827
Days Accrued Liabilities	423.0	394.3	433.5	352.9	324.3	335.5	341.3	168.9	287.6	304.8	287.0	312.0
Debt												
Total Debt	10,175,649	9,622,256	9,958,616	3,615,434	3,589,256	3,554,776	3,554,776	3,116,916	2,975,004	2,720,170	2,609,569	2,609,569
Net Debt (net of excess cash)	10,129,573	9,491,057	9,425,315	3,208,487	2,982,785	2,888,836	2,888,836	2,969,389	2,853,249	2,664,185	2,553,584	2,553,584
LTM EBITDA	1,407,089	1,377,469	1,342,534	1,276,916	1,227,504	1,130,505	1,130,505	1,052,158	975,041	883,550	790,639	790,639
LTM Interest Expense, cash	721,505	746,529	735,511	650,933	499,012	388,112	388,112	219,476	189,996	170,514	156,000	156,000
LTM Capex	85,000	70,642	64,461	50,184	41,531	33,385	33,385	37,600	40,497	39,150	45,000	45,000
Ratios												
Leverage	7.2x	7.0x	7.4x	2.8x	2.9x	3.1x	3.1x	3.0x	3.1x	3.1x	3.3x	3.3x
Net Leverage (net of excess)	7.2x	6.9x	7.0x	2.5x	2.4x	2.6x	2.6x	2.8x	2.9x	3.0x	3.2x	3.2x
EBITDA/LTM Interest Expense	2.0x	1.8x	1.8x	2.0x	2.5x	2.9x	2.9x	4.3x	5.1x	5.2x	5.1x	5.1x
(LTM EBITDA-LTM Capex)/ LTM Int. exp.	1.8x	1.8x	1.7x	1.9x	2.4x	2.8x	2.8x	4.6x	4.9x	5.0x	4.8x	4.8x

EXHIBIT 12.17 Dex One Corporation: Sales Projection Assumptions

Best and Worst Cases	2010E	2011E	2012E	2013E	2014E
RHDI Best Case	(18.2)%	(10.5)%	(8.9)%	(7.7)%	(6.9)%
RHDI Worst Case	(18.2)%	(17.5)%	(16.0)%	(15.0)%	(14.5)%
Dex East Best Case	(19.4)%	(11.0)%	(9.5)%	(8.8)%	(7.7)%
Dex East Worst Case	(19.4)%	(17.5)%	(16.0)%	(15.0)%	(14.5)%
Dex West Best Case	(20.4)%	(14.0)%	(12.0)%	(10.0)%	(9.5)%
Dex West Worst Case	(20.4)%	(17.5)%	(16.0)%	(15.0)%	(14.5)%

cash flow. Accordingly, when they project operating cash flows (EBITDA – capital expenditures – cash taxes – cash interest), they pay attention mainly to the cash components of interest expense and income taxes. More detailed analysis, however, should take into consideration deferred and capitalized items.

Exhibit 12.17 displays the analyst's assumptions regarding year-by-year sales changes for Dex One subsidiaries, under best-case and worst-case scenarios, from 2010 through 2014. The analyst expects sales to decline over this period, although the rate of decline tapers off. A supporting document for the sales projection (Exhibit 12.18) compares the recent experience of R. H. Donnelley and a competitor. The analysis considers both the number of salespersons and their productivity. Comparing a company with industry peers provides a reality check for estimates of future performance. The comparison also provides insight into the competitive landscape, an essential factor that is dangerous to overlook in making projections.

Exhibit 12.19 shows the assumed EBITDA margins that the analyst applies to the projected sales figures, broken down by subsidiary and divided into best- and worst-case scenarios. These hold steady or improve slightly despite the erosion in revenue. A supporting document (Exhibit 12.20), like Exhibit 12.18, utilizes historical data in an industry peer comparison.

EXHIBIT 12.18 Dex One Corporation: Peer Comparison for Sales Projection

	Idearc	RHD
2007 Sales Force	3,000	1,900
2009 Sales Force	2,300	1,400
2007–2009 change	(12.4)%	(14.2)%
2007 rev./sales person	$1,063,000	$1,410,526
2009 rev./sales person	$1,092,174	$1,573,143
2007–2009 change	1.4%	5.6%

EXHIBIT 12.19　Dex One Corporation: EBITDA Margins Projections

Best and Worst Cases	2010E	2011E	2012E	2013E	2014E
RHDI Best Case	44.1%	45.8%	46.8%	47.9%	48.3%
RHDI Worst Case	44.1%	45.3%	45.7%	46.2%	45.9%
Dex East Best Case	48.6%	48.5%	49.4%	50.0%	50.3%
Dex East Worst Case	48.6%	48.1%	48.4%	48.5%	48.1%
Dex West Best Case	49.6%	49.7%	49.4%	49.5%	49.4%
Dex West Worst Case	49.6%	49.4%	48.7%	48.4%	47.8%

The projection requires assumptions about expenses, as well as revenues. Exhibit 12.21 lays out the analyst's estimates of the costs of materials, production, distribution, selling, and support, as well as bad debt expense, as percentages of sales. These generally remain within narrow bands, but note the projected rise in print, paper, and distribution costs in percentage-of-sales terms.

By varying and modifying the subsidiary revenue assumptions of Exhibit 12.16, the analyst can produce a range of consolidated projections for Dex One. Exhibit 12.22 shows the best-case projection through 2014. The best case is a picture of a company hanging on rather than enjoying robust growth. Sales decline from $2.2 billion in the last historical year to $1.3 billion in the fifth year of the projection. Similarly, EBITDA slides from $1.1 billion to $0.6 billion. The saving grace is that the company is not in a growth mode that requires heavy new investment in its business, Capital expenditures absorb an average of just $53 million a year during the projection period, versus EBITDA averaging $664 million. As a result, the analyst forecasts that Dex One will pay down $2.7 billion of debt as

EXHIBIT 12.20　Dex One Corporation: Peer Comparison for EBITDA Margins

	EBITDA Per Customer	EBITDA Per Customer	Revenue Per Customer	Revenue Per Customer	2007–2009 sales decline	Average customer loss
	2007	2009	2007	2009		
Idearc	$1,429.1	$1,487.1	$3,708.1	$4,617.6	*(11.2)%*	*(20.5)%*
CAGR		2.0%		11.6%		
RHD	$2,280.2	$2,307.4	$4,466.7	$4,541.0	*(9.3)%*	*(10.1)%*
CAGR		0.6%		0.8%		

EXHIBIT 12.21 Dex One Corporation: Operating Assumptions

Production and Distribution Expense	2008	Q1 2009	Q2 2009	2009	Q1 2010	Q2 2010	2010E	2011E	2012E	2013E	2014E
Print, paper, & distribution costs	255.1	59.6	56.6	226.7	49.4	48.1	196.2	176.6	162.7	151.8	143.1
Percentage of sales	9.8%	9.9%	10.0%	10.3%	10.5%	10.6%	10.8%	10.9%	11.0%	11.1%	11.2%
Other production & distribution costs	163.1	42.3	36.2	124	33.7	33.8	135.8	121.5	109.4	99.8	92.0
Percentage of sales	6.2%	7.0%	6.4%	5.6%	7.2%	7.5%	7.5%	7.5%	7.4%	7.3%	7.2%
Selling and support expense											
Bad debt expense		37.9	43.0	154.2	21.6	11.4	81.7	72.9	66.5	61.5	57.5
Percentage of sales		6.3%	7.6%	7.0%	4.6%	2.5%	4.5%	4.5%	4.5%	4.5%	4.5%
Other selling and support expense		114.1	117.8	509.4	105.6	110.8	459.4	421.3	378.6	341.8	316.1
Percentage of sales		18.9%	20.8%	23.1%	22.5%	24.5%	25.3%	26.0%	25.6%	25.0%	24.8%

EXHIBIT 12.22 Dex One Corporation: Best-Case Projection

	2007	2008	Q1 2009	Q2 2009	2009	Q1 2010	Q2 2010	2010E	2011E	2012E	2013E	2014E
Sales	2,680.30	2,616.80	602.00	565.60	2,202.40	468.60	451.80	1,816.00	1,620.40	1,478.70	1,367.30	1,277.40
Change		(2.40)%			(15.80)%	(22.20)%	(20.10)%	(17.50)%	(10.80)%	(8.70)%	(7.50)%	(6.60)%
Production and distribution expense	450.30	418.20	101.90	92.70	350.70	83.10	81.90	332.10	295.70	268.40	246.80	229.30
Percentage of sales	16.80%	15.98%	16.93%	16.40%	15.92%	17.73%	18.13%	18.28%	18.25%	18.15%	18.05%	17.95%
Selling and support expense	716.30	729.70	152.00	160.70	663.60	127.20	122.20	541.20	494.20	445.10	403.40	373.60
Percentage of sales	26.72%	27.89%	25.25%	28.42%	30.13%	27.14%	27.05%	29.80%	30.50%	30.10%	29.50%	29.25%
General and administrative expense	145.60	120.90	41.60	26.00	69.00	29.90	40.20	159.00	120.00	115.00	110.00	105.00
Percentage of sales	5.43%	4.62%	6.91%	4.59%	3.13%	6.38%	8.90%	8.76%	7.41%	7.78%	8.05%	8.22%
EBITDA	1,368.10	1,348.00	306.50	286.20	1,119.10	228.40	207.50	783.70	710.60	650.30	607.20	569.50
Percentage of sales	51.04%	51.51%	50.91%	50.59%	50.81%	48.74%	45.93%	43.16%	43.85%	43.97%	44.41%	44.59%
Debt					3,554.80		2,975.00	2,610.60	2,185.50	1,746.90	1,328.50	914.70
Cash					665.90		121.80	56.00	56.00	56.00	56.00	56.00
Net Debt					2,888.90		2,853.20	2,554.60	2,129.50	1,690.90	1,272.50	858.70
Net Leverage					2.58x			3.26x	3.00x	2.60x	2.10x	1.51x
EBITDA								783.70	710.60	650.30	607.20	569.50
Capex					(33.40)	(8.20)	(8.80)	(45.00)	(54.00)	(54.40)	(54.00)	(56.00)

its revenues shrink, resulting in a reduction of net leverage (defined as debt minus cash divided by EBITDA) from 2.58X to 1.41X. From the standpoint of the fixed-income investors, the picture does not look as bleak as it does to equity investors accustomed to seeing forecasts that show large, steady gains in earnings. Fixed-income investors are in fact the target of the analyst's research, with particular focus on the term loans of Dex One's subsidiaries, RHD, Dex East, and Dex West.

CONCLUSION

Of the various types of analysis of financial statements, projecting future results and ratios requires the greatest skill and produces the most valuable findings. Looking forward is also the riskiest form of analysis, since there are no correct answers until the future statements appear. Totally unforeseeable events may invalidate the assumptions underlying the forecast; economic shocks or unexpected changes in a company's financial strategies may knock all calculations into a cocked hat.

The prominence of the chance element in the forecasting process means that analysts should not be disheartened if their predictions miss the mark, even widely on occasion. They should aim not for absolute prescience but rather for a sound probabilistic model of the future. The model should logically incorporate all significant evidence, both within and external to the historical statements. An analyst can then judge whether a company's prevailing valuations (e.g., stock price, credit rating) are consistent with the possible scenarios and their respective probabilities.

By tracking the after-the-fact accuracy of a number of projections, an analyst can gauge the effectiveness of these methods. Invariably, there will be room for further refinement, particularly in the area of gathering information on industry conditions. No matter how refined the methods are, however, perfection will always elude the modeler since no business cycle precisely recapitulates its predecessor. That is what ultimately makes looking forward with financial statements such a challenging task. The lack of a predictable, recurring pattern is also what makes financial forecasting so valuable. When betting huge sums in the face of massive uncertainty, it is essential that investors understand the odds as fully as they possibly can.

CHAPTER 13

Credit Analysis

Credit analysis is one of the most common uses of financial statements, reflecting the many forms of debt that are essential to the operation of a modern economy. Merchants who exchange goods for promises to pay need to evaluate the reliability of those promises. Commercial banks that lend the merchants the funds to finance their inventories likewise need to calculate the probability of being repaid in full and on time. The banks must in turn demonstrate their creditworthiness to other financial institutions that lend to them by purchasing their certificates of deposit and bonds. In all of these cases, financial statement analysis can significantly influence a decision to extend or not to extend credit.

As important as financial statements are to the evaluation of credit risk, however, the analyst must bear in mind that other procedures also play a role. Financial statements tell much about a borrower's *ability* to repay a loan but disclose little about the equally important *willingness* to repay. Accordingly, a thorough credit analysis may have to include a check of the subject's past record of repayment, which is not part of a standard financial statement. Moreover, to assess the creditworthiness of the merchant in this example, the bank must consider, along with the balance sheet and income statement, the competitive environment and strength of the local economy in which the borrower operates. Lenders to the bank will in turn consider not only the bank's financial position but also public policy. Believing that a sound banking system benefits the economy as a whole, national governments empower central banks to act as lenders of last resort. As a result, fewer bank failures occur than would be the case under pure, unrestrained competition.

An even more basic reason that analyzing a company's financial statements may not be sufficient for determining its credit quality is that the borrower's credit may be supported, formally or informally, by another entity. Many municipalities obtain cost savings on their financings by having their debt payments guaranteed by bond insurers with premier credit ratings. For holders of these municipal bonds, the insurer's creditworthiness, not the municipality's financial condition, is the basis for determining the likelihood of repayment. Corporations, too, sometimes guarantee the debt of weaker credits. Even when the stronger company does not take on a legal obligation to pay if the weaker company fails on its debt, implicit support may affect the latter's credit quality. If a company is dependent on raw materials provided by a subsidiary, there may be a reasonable presumption that it will stand behind the subsidiary's debt, even in the absence of a formal guarantee.

Keeping in mind that the final judgment may be influenced by other information as well, the analyst can begin to extract from the financial statements the data that bear on credit risk. Each of the basic statements—the balance sheet, income statement, and statement of cash flows—yields valuable insights when studied through ratio analysis techniques, as well as when used in the evaluation of fixed-income securities. In each case, the analyst must temper any enthusiasm generated by a review of historical statements with caution based on a consideration of financial ratios derived from projected statements for future years.

BALANCE SHEET RATIOS

The most immediate danger faced by a lender is the risk that the borrower will suffer illiquidity—an inability to raise cash to pay its obligations. This condition can arise for many reasons, one of which is a loss of ability to borrow new funds to pay off existing creditors. Whatever the underlying cause, however, illiquidity manifests itself as an excess of current cash payments due, over cash currently available. The current ratio gauges the risk of this occurring by comparing the claims against the company that will become payable during the current operating cycle (current liabilities) with the assets that are already in the form of cash or that will be converted to cash during the current operating cycle (current assets). Referring to beverage maker Coca-Cola's balance sheet (Exhibit 13.1), the company's current ratio as of December 31, 2009, was 1.28 (dollar figures are in millions):

$$\text{Current ratio} = \frac{\text{Current assets}}{\text{Current liabilities}} = \frac{\$17,551.0}{\$13,721.0} = 1.28$$

Analysts also apply a more stringent test of liquidity by calculating the quick ratio, or acid test, which considers only cash and current assets that can

EXHIBIT 13.1   The Coca-Cola Company Balance Sheet

Company Name: The Coca-Cola Company
Form Type: 10-K
Filed On: 2/26/2010

Balance Sheet

December 31, 2009
(In millions except par value)
ASSETS
CURRENT ASSETS

Cash and cash equivalents	$ 7,021
Short-term investments	2,130
TOTAL CASH, CASH EQUIVALENTS, AND SHORT-TERM INVESTMENTS	9,151
Marketable securities	62
Trade accounts receivable, less allowances of $55 and $51, respectively	3,758
Inventories	2,354
Prepaid expenses and other assets	2,226
TOTAL CURRENT ASSETS	17,551
EQUITY METHOD INVESTMENTS	6,217
OTHER INVESTMENTS, PRINCIPALLY BOTTLING COMPANIES	538
OTHER ASSETS	1,976
PROPERTY, PLANT, AND EQUIPMENT—net	9,561
TRADEMARKS WITH INDEFINITE LIVES	6,183
GOODWILL	4,224
OTHER INTANGIBLE ASSETS	2,421
TOTAL ASSETS	$48,671
LIABILITIES AND EQUITY	
CURRENT LIABILITIES	
Accounts payable and accrued expenses	$ 6,657
Loans and notes payable	6,749
Current maturities of long-term debt	51
Accrued income taxes	264
TOTAL CURRENT LIABILITIES	13,721
LONG-TERM DEBT	5,059
OTHER LIABILITIES	2,965
DEFERRED INCOME TAXES	1,580
THE COCA-COLA COMPANY SHAREOWNERS' EQUITY	
Common stock, $0.25 par value; Authorized—5,600 shares; Issued—3,520 and 3,519 shares, respectively	880
Capital surplus	8,537
Reinvested earnings	41,537
Accumulated other comprehensive income (loss)	($ 757)
Treasury stock, at cost—1,217 and 1,207 shares, respectively	($25,398)
EQUITY ATTRIBUTABLE TO SHAREOWNERS OF THE COCA-COLA COMPANY	24,799
EQUITY ATTRIBUTABLE TO NONCONTROLLING INTERESTS	547
TOTAL EQUITY	25,346
TOTAL LIABILITIES AND EQUITY	$48,671

Source: 10-K.

be most quickly converted to cash (marketable securities and receivables). Coca-Cola's quick ratio on December 31, 2009, was 0.95:

$$\text{Quick ratio} = \frac{\text{Quick assets}}{\text{Current liabilities}} = \frac{\$12{,}971.0}{\$13{,}721.0} = 0.95$$

Besides looking at the ratio between current assets and current liabilities, it is also useful, when assessing a company's ability to meet its near-term obligations, to consider the difference between the two, which is termed *working capital*. Referring once again to Exhibit 13.1, working capital is $3.830 billion.

$$\text{Working capital} = \text{Current assets} - \text{Current liabilities}$$

$$\$3{,}830 = \$17{,}551.0 - \$13{,}721.0$$

Analysis of current assets and current liabilities provides warnings about impending illiquidity, but lenders nevertheless periodically find themselves saddled with loans to borrowers who are unable to continue meeting their obligations and are therefore forced to file for bankruptcy. Recognizing that they may one day find themselves holding defaulted obligations, creditors wish to know how much asset value will be available for liquidation to pay off their claims.[1] The various ratios that address this issue can be grouped as measures of financial leverage.

A direct measure of asset protection is the ratio of total assets to total liabilities, which in the example shown in Exhibit 13.1 comes to:

$$\frac{\text{Total assets}}{\text{Total liabilities}} = \frac{\$48{,}671.0}{\$23{,}872.0} = 2.04$$

(Total liabilities can be derived quickly by subtracting stockholders' equity from total assets.)

Put another way, Coca-Cola's assets of $48,671.0 billion could decline in value by 51 percent before proceeds of a liquidation would be insufficient to satisfy lenders' $23,872.0 billion of claims. The greater the amount by which asset values could deteriorate, the greater the equity cushion (*equity* is, by definition, total assets minus total liabilities), and the greater the creditor's sense of being protected.

Lenders also gauge the amount of equity "beneath" them (junior to them in the event of liquidation) by comparing it with the amount of debt outstanding. For finance companies, where the ratio is typically greater than 1.0, it is convenient to express the relationship as a debt-equity ratio:

$$\frac{\text{Total debt}}{\text{Total equity}}$$

   Conventionally capitalized industrial corporations (as opposed to companies that have undergone *leveraged buyouts*), generally have debt-equity ratios of less than 1.0. The usual practice is to express their financial leverage in terms of a total-debt-to-total-capital ratio:

$$\frac{\text{Total debt}}{\text{Total debt} + \text{Minority interest} + \text{Total equity}}$$

Banks' capital adequacy is commonly measured by the ratio of equity to total assets:

$$\frac{\text{Total equity}}{\text{Total assets}}$$

   Many pages of elaboration could follow on the last few ratios mentioned. Their calculation is rather less simple than it might appear. The reason is that aggressive borrowers frequently try to satisfy the letter of a maximum leverage limit imposed by lenders without fulfilling the conservative spirit behind it. The following discussion of definitions of leverage ratios addresses the major issues without laying down absolute rules about correct calculations. As explained later in the chapter, ratios are most meaningful when compared across time and across borrower. Consequently, the precise method of calculation is less important than the consistency of calculation throughout the sample being compared.

What Constitutes Total Debt?

At one time, it was appropriate to consider only long-term debt in leverage calculations for industrial companies, since short-term debt was generally used for seasonal purposes, such as financing Christmas-related inventory. A company might draw down bank lines or issue commercial paper to meet these funding requirements, then completely pay off the interim borrowings when it sold the inventory. Even today, a firm that zeros out its short-term debt at some point in each operating cycle can legitimately argue that its true leverage is represented by the permanent (long-term) debt on its balance sheet. Many borrowers have long since subverted this principle, however, by relying heavily on short-term debt that they neither repay on an interim basis nor fund (replace with long-term debt) when it grows to sufficient size to make a bond offering cost-effective. Such short-term debt must be viewed as permanent and included in the leverage calculation. (Current maturities of long-term debt should also enter into the calculation of total debt, based on a conservative assumption that the company will replace maturing debt with new long-term borrowings.)

As an aside, the just-described reliance on short-term debt is not necessarily as dangerous a practice as in years past, although it should still raise a caution flag for the credit analyst. Two risks are inherent in depending on debt with maturities of less than one year. The first is potential illiquidity. If substantial debt comes due at a time when lenders are either unable to renew their loans (because credit is tight) or unwilling to renew (because they perceive the borrower as less creditworthy than formerly), the borrower may be unable to meet its near-term obligations. This risk may be mitigated, however, if the borrower has a revolving credit agreement, which is a longer-term commitment by the lender to lend (subject to certain conditions, such as maintaining prescribed financial ratios and refraining from significant changes in the business). The second risk of relying on short-term borrowings is exposure to interest-rate fluctuations. If a substantial amount of debt is about to come due, and interest rates have risen sharply since the debt was incurred, the borrower's cost of staying in business may skyrocket overnight.

Note that exposure to interest rate fluctuations can also arise from long-term **floating-rate debt.** Companies can limit this risk by using **financial derivatives.** One approach is to cap the borrower's interest rate, that is, set a maximum rate that will prevail, no matter how high the market rate against which it is pegged may rise. Alternatively, the borrower can convert the floating-rate debt to **fixed-rate debt** through a derivative known as an interest-rate swap. (The forces of supply and demand may make it more economical for the company to issue floating-rate debt and incur the cost of the swap than to take the more direct route to the same net effect, that is, to issue fixed-rate debt.) Public financial statements typically provide only general information about the extent to which the issuer has limited its exposure to interest rate fluctuations through derivatives.

Borrowers sometimes argue that the total debt calculation should exclude debt that is convertible, at the lender's option, into common equity. Hard-liners on the credit analysis side respond: "It's equity when the holders convert it to equity. Until then, it's debt." Realistically, though, if the conversion value of the bond rises sufficiently, most holders will in fact convert their securities to common stock. This is particularly true if the issuer has the option of calling the bonds for early retirement, which results in a loss for holders who fail to convert. Analysts should remember that the ultimate objective is not to calculate ratios but to assess credit risk. Therefore, the best practice is to count convertible debt in total debt but to consider the possibility of conversion when comparing the borrower's leverage with that of its peer group.

Preferred stock[2] is a security that further complicates the leverage calculation. From a legal standpoint, preferred stock is clearly equity; in liquidation, it ranks junior to debt. Preferred stock pays a dividend rather than interest, and failure to pay the dividend does not constitute a default. On the other hand, preferred dividends, unlike common dividends, are contractually fixed in amount. An issuer can omit its preferred dividend but not without also omitting its common dividend. Furthermore, a preferred dividend is typically **cumulative**, meaning that the issuer must repay all preferred dividend arrearages before resuming common stock dividends. Furthermore, not all preferred issues have the permanent character of common stock. A preferred stock may have a sinking fund provision, much like the provision typically found in bonds, that requires redemption of a substantial portion of the outstanding par amount prior to final maturity. Such a provision implies less financial flexibility than is the case for a perpetual preferred stock, which requires no principal repayment at any time. Another preferred security, exchangeable preferred stock, can be transformed into debt at the issuer's option. Treating it purely as equity for credit analysis purposes would understate financial risk. In general, the credit analyst must recognize the heightened level of risk implied by the presence of preferred stock in the capital structure. A formal way to take this risk into account is to calculate the ratio of total fixed obligations to total capital:[3]

$$\frac{\text{Total debt} + \text{Preferred stock} + \text{Preference stock}}{\text{Total debt} + \text{Minority interest} + \text{Preferred stock} + \text{Preference stock} + \text{Common equity}}$$

Off-balance-sheet lease obligations, like preferred stock, enable companies to obtain many of the benefits of debt financing without violating covenanted limitations on debt incurrence. Accounting standards have partially brought these debtlike obligations out of hiding by requiring capital leases to appear on the balance sheet, either separately or as part of long-term debt. Credit analysts should complete the job. In addition to including capital leases in the total debt calculation, they should also take into account the off-balance-sheet liabilities represented by contractual payments on operating leases, which are reported (as "rental expense") in the notes to financial statements. The rationale is that although the accounting rules distinguish between capital and operating leases, the two financing vehicles frequently differ little in economic terms. Indeed, borrowers have used considerable ingenuity in structuring capital leases to qualify as operating leases under generally accepted accounting principles (GAAP), the benefit being that they will consequently be excluded from the balance sheet and, it is hoped, from credit analysts' scrutiny. Analysts should not fall for this ruse but should instead capitalize the current year rental payments shown in the notes to financial statements. The most common method is to multiply the payments by seven or eight, a calculation that has been found to be reasonably accurate when actual figures on capitalized value of leases have been available for comparison.

Other Off-Balance-Sheet Liabilities

In their quest for methods of obtaining the benefits of debt without suffering the associated penalties imposed by credit analysts, corporations have by no means limited themselves to the use of leases. Like leases, the other popular devices may provide genuine business benefits, as well as the cosmetic benefit of disguising debt. In all cases, the focus of credit-quality determination must be economic impact, which may or may not be reflected in the accounting treatment.

A corporation can employ leverage yet avoid showing debt on its consolidated balance sheet by entering joint ventures or forming partially owned subsidiaries. At a minimum, the analyst should attribute to the corporation its proportionate liability for the debt of such ventures, thereby matching the cash flow benefits derived from the affiliates. (Note that cash flow is generally reduced by unremitted earnings—the portion not received in dividends—of affiliates that are not fully consolidated.) In some cases, the affiliate's operations are critical to the parent's operations, as in the case of a jointly owned pulp plant that supplies a paper plant wholly owned by the parent. There is a strong incentive, in such instances, for the parent to keep the jointly owned operation running by picking up the debt service commitments of a partner that becomes financially incapacitated, even though it may have no legal obligation to do so. (In legal parlance, this arrangement is known as a *several* obligation, in contrast to a *joint* obligation in which each partner is compelled to back up the other's commitment.) Depending on the particular circumstances, it may be appropriate to attribute to the parent more than its proportionate share—up to 100 percent—of the debt of the joint venture or unconsolidated subsidiary.

Surely one of the most ingenious devices for obtaining the benefits of debt without incurring balance sheet recognition was described by *The Independent* in 1992. According to the British newspaper, the Faisal Islamic Bank of Cairo had provided $250 million of funding to a troubled real estate developer, Olympia & York. As an institution committed to Islamic religious principles, however, the bank was not allowed to charge interest. Instead, claimed *The Independent,* Faisal Islamic Bank in effect had acquired a building from Olympia & York, along with an option to sell it back. The option was reportedly exercisable at $250 million plus an amount equivalent to the market rate of interest for the option period. Because the excess was not officially classified as interest, said *The Independent,* the $250 million of funding did not show up as a loan on Olympia & York's balance sheet.

The Independent noted a denial by an Olympia & York spokesperson that "any such *loan* existed" (emphasis added). If, however, the account was substantially correct, then the religious-prohibition-of-interest gambit succeeded spectacularly in diverting attention from a transaction that had all the trappings of a loan. Barclays Bank, one of Olympia & York's most important lenders, commented that it had never heard of the Faisal Islamic Bank transaction.[4]

Of a somewhat different character within the broad category of off-balance-sheet liabilities are employee benefit obligations. Under Statement of Financial Accounting Standards (SFAS) 87, balance sheet recognition is now given to pension liabilities related to employees' service to date. Similarly, SFAS 106 requires recognition of postretirement health care benefits as an on-balance-sheet liability. Additional requirements are set out in SFAS 158. Projected future wage increases are still not recognized, although they affect the calculation of pension expense for income statement purposes. Unlike some other kinds of hidden liabilities, these items arise exclusively in furtherance of a business objective (attracting and retaining capable employees), rather than as a surreptitious means of leveraging shareholders' equity.

Generally speaking, pension obligations that have been fully funded (provided for with investment assets set aside for the purpose) present few credit worries for a going concern. Likewise, a modest underfunding that is in the process of being remediated by an essentially sound company is no more than a small qualitative factor on the negative side. On the other hand, a large or growing underfunded liability can be a significantly negative consideration—albeit one that is hard to quantify explicitly—in assessing a deteriorating credit. In bankruptcy, it becomes essential to monitor details of the Pension Benefit Guaranty Corporation's efforts to assert its claim to the company's assets, which, if successful, reduce the settlement amounts available to other creditors.

Are Deferred Taxes Part of Capital?

Near the equity account on many companies' balance sheets appears an account labeled "Deferred Income Taxes." This item represents the cumulative difference between taxes calculated at the statutory rate and taxes actually paid. The difference reflects the tax consequences, for future years, of the differences between the tax bases of assets and liabilities and their carrying amounts for financial reporting purposes.

Many analysts argue that net worth is understated by the amount of the deferred tax liability, since it will in all likelihood never come due and is therefore not really a liability at all. (As long as the company continues to pay taxes at less than the statutory rate, the deferred tax account will continue to grow.) Proponents of this view adjust for the alleged understatement of net worth by adding deferred taxes to the denominator in the total-debt-to-total-capital calculation, thus:

$$\frac{\text{Total debt}}{\text{Total debt} + \text{Deferred taxes} + \text{Minority interest} + \text{Total equity}}$$

In general, this practice is sound. Analysts must, however, keep in mind that the precise formula for calculating a ratio is less important than the assurance that it is calculated consistently for all companies being evaluated. The caveat is that many factors can contribute to deferred taxes, and not all of them imply a permanent deferral. A defense contractor, for example, can defer payment of taxes related to a specific contract until the contract is completed. The analyst would not want to add to equity the taxes deferred on a contract that is about to be completed, although in such situations specific figures may be hard to obtain.

The Importance of Management's Attitude toward Debt

As the preceding discussion has established, companies use numerous gambits in their quest to enjoy the benefits of aggressive financial leverage without suffering the consequences of low credit ratings and high borrowing costs. Analysts should note that corporations' bag of tricks is not confined to accounting gimmicks. Some management teams also rely on a bait-and-switch technique.

The ploy consists of announcing that management has learned the hard way that conservative financial policies serve shareholders best in the long run. Never again, vows the chief executive officer, will the company undergo the financial strain that it recently endured as a result of excessive borrowing a few years earlier. To demonstrate that they truly have gotten religion, the managers institute new policies aimed at improving cash flow and pay down a slug of short-term borrowings. On the strength of the favorable impression that these actions create among credit analysts who rely heavily on trends in financial ratios, the company floats new long-term bonds at an attractive rate. Once the cash is in the coffers, management loses its motivation to present a conservative face to lenders and reverts to the aggressive financial policies that so recently got the company into trouble.

Not everybody is taken in by this ruse. Moody's and Standard & Poor's place heavy emphasis on management's attitude toward debt when assigning bond ratings (see "Relating Ratios to Credit Risk" later in this chapter). They strive to avoid upgrading companies in response to balance sheet improvements that are unlikely to last much beyond the completion of the next public offering. In reward for such vigilance, the agencies are routinely accused of being backward-looking. The corporations complain that the bond raters are dwelling unduly on past, weaker financial ratios. In reality, the agencies are thinking ahead. Based on their experience with management, they are inferring that the recent reduction in financial leverage reflects expediency, rather than a long-term shift in debt policy. In general, credit analysts should assume that the achievement of higher bond ratings is a secondary goal of corporate management. If a company's stock has been languishing for a while, management will not ordinarily feel any urgency about eliminating debt from the capital structure, an action that reduces return on shareholders' equity (see Chapter 14). Similarly, the typical chief executive officer, being only human, finds it difficult to resist a chance to run a substantially bigger company. Therefore, if a mammoth acquisition opportunity comes along, the CEO is likely to pursue it, even if it means borrowing huge amounts of money and precipitating a rating downgrade, rather than the hoped-for upgrade.

Like other types of financial statement analysis, finding meaning in a company's balance sheet requires the analyst to look ahead. When management's probable future actions are taken into account, the company's prospects for repaying its debts on schedule may be better or worse than the ratios imply. The credit analyst cannot afford to take management's representations at face value, however. When a chief executive officer claims that obtaining a higher bond rating is the corporation's overriding objective, it is essential to ask for specifics: What are the elements of the company's action plan for achieving that goal? Which of the steps have been achieved so far?

Above all, the credit analyst must listen closely for an escape clause, typically uttered while the company is engaged in a debt offering. It can be heard when a prospective buyer asks whether management will stay on course for a rating upgrade come hell or high water. The CEO casually replies, "Of course, if a once-in-a-lifetime major acquisition opportunity were to come along, and it required us to borrow, we would have to delay our plans for debt reduction temporarily." The credit analyst can generally assume that shortly after the bond deal closes, the once-in-a-lifetime opportunity will materialize.

INCOME STATEMENT RATIOS

Although an older approach to credit analysis places primary emphasis on liquidity and asset protection, both of which are measured by balance sheet ratios, the more contemporary view is that profits are ultimately what sustain liquidity and asset values. High profits keep plenty of cash flowing through the system and confirm the value of productive assets such as plant and equipment. In line with this latter view, the income statement is no longer of interest mainly to the equity analyst but is essential to credit analysis as well.

A key income statement focus for credit analysis is the borrower's profit margin (profit as a percentage of sales). The narrower the margin, the greater is the danger that a modest decline in selling prices or a modest increase in costs will produce losses, which will in turn begin to erode such balance sheet measures as total debt to total capital by reducing equity.

Profit can be measured at several levels of the income statement, either before or after deducting various expenses to get to the bottom line, net income. The most commonly used profit margins are the following:

$$\text{Gross margin} = \frac{\text{Sales} - \text{Cost of goods sold}}{\text{Sales}}$$

$$\text{Operating margin} = \frac{\text{Operating income}}{\text{Sales}}$$

$$\text{Operating Margin} = \frac{\begin{array}{c}\text{Net Income} + \text{Income Taxes} + \text{Interest Expense} \\ - \text{Interest Income} - \text{Other Income}\end{array}}{\text{Sales}}$$

$$\text{Pretax margin} = \frac{\text{Net income} + \text{Income taxes}}{\text{Sales}}$$

$$\text{Net margin} = \frac{\text{Net income}}{\text{Sales}}$$

Applying these definitions to Coca-Cola's income statement (Exhibit 13.2), the company's profit margins in 2009 were:

$$\text{Gross margin} = \frac{\$30,990.0 - 11,088.0}{\$30,990.0} = 64.2\%$$

$$\text{Operating margin} = \frac{\begin{array}{c}\$6,824.0 + \$2,040.0 + \$355.0 - \$267.0 \\ - (\$781.0 + \$80.0 - \$115.0)\end{array}}{\$30,990.0} = 26.5\%$$

$$\text{Pretax margin} = \frac{\$6,824.0 + 2,040}{\$30,990.0} = 28.6\%$$

$$\text{Net margin} = \frac{\$6,824.0}{\$30,990.3} = 22.0\%$$

EXHIBIT 13.2   The Coca-Cola Company Income Statement

Company Name: The Coca-Cola Company
Form Type: 10-K
Filed On: 2/26/2010

Income Statement

Year Ended December 31, 2009
(In millions except percentages and per share data)

NET OPERATING REVENUES	$30,990
Cost of goods sold	11,088
GROSS PROFIT	19,902
GROSS PROFIT MARGIN	64.20%
Selling, general and administrative expenses	11,358
Other operating charges	313
OPERATING INCOME	8,231
OPERATING MARGIN	26.60%
Interest income	249
Interest expense	355
Equity income (loss)—net	781
Other income (loss)—net	40
INCOME BEFORE INCOME TAXES	8,946
Income taxes	2,040
Effective tax rate	22.80%
CONSOLIDATED NET INCOME	6,906
Less: Net income attributable to noncontrolling interests	82
NET INCOME ATTRIBUTABLE TO SHAREOWNERS OF THE COCA-COLA COMPANY	$ 6,824
NET INCOME PER SHARE	
Basic net income per share	$ 2.95
Diluted net income per share	$ 2.93

Source: 10-K.

Coca-Cola's comparatively high profit margins give creditors confidence that the beverage maker is a successful business that can continue attracting new capital from investors. A company's ability to maintain its funding capability is an essential component of a strong credit profile. In qualitative terms, Coca-Cola strives to ensure its future profitability through heavy advertising aimed at reinforcing its almost universally recognized brand name.

Observe that in the operating margin calculation, the deduction of other income called for by the formula includes an addback of one negative figure (Other Nonoperating Expense). Note as well that the formula does not call for adding back the $273.0 million restructuring charge, which does not qualify for after-tax treatment as an *extraordinary item* (see Chapter 3). Analysts should nevertheless be cognizant of such nonrecurring charges when forming an impression of a company's bona fide profitability.

In some instances, an after-tax nonoperating item can produce a disparity between the numerators in the pretax and operating margins, as calculated from the bottom up in accordance with the formula, and the corresponding figure derived by working from the top down. For example, the cumulative effect of a change in accounting procedures will appear below the line, or after income taxes have already been deducted. The sum of net income and provision for income taxes will then differ from the pretax income figure that appears in the income statement. To ensure comparability across companies, analysts should take care to follow identical procedures in calculating each company's margins, rather than adopting shortcuts that may introduce distortion.

The various margin measures reflect different aspects of management's effectiveness. Gross margin, which is particularly important in analyzing retailers, measures management's skill in buying and selling at advantageous prices. Operating margin shows how well management has run the business—buying and selling wisely and controlling selling and administrative expenses—before taking into account financial policies (which largely determine interest expense) and the tax rate (which is outside management's control).[5] These last two factors are sequentially added to the picture by calculating pretax margin and net margin, with the latter ratio reflecting all factors, whether under management's control or not, that influence profitability.

In calculating profit margins, analysts should eliminate the effect of extraordinary gains and losses to determine the level of profitability that is likely to be sustainable in the future.

Fixed-charge coverage is the other income statement ratio of major interest to credit analysts. It measures the ability of a company's earnings to meet the interest payments on its debt, the lender's most direct concern. In its simplest form, the fixed-charge coverage ratio indicates the multiple by which operating earnings suffice to pay interest charges:

$$\text{Fixed-charge coverage} = \frac{\text{Net income} + \text{Income taxes} + \text{Interest expense}}{\text{Interest expense}}$$

This basic formula requires several refinements, however. As with profit margins, extraordinary items should be eliminated from the calculation to arrive at a sustainable level of coverage. The other main adjustments involve capitalized interest and payments on operating leases.

Capitalized Interest

Under SFAS 34, companies may be required to capitalize, rather than expense, a portion of their interest costs. The underlying notion is that like the actual bricks and mortar purchased to construct a plant, the cost of the money borrowed to finance the purchase provides benefits in future periods and therefore should not be entirely written off in the first year. Whether it is expensed or capitalized, however, all interest accrued must be covered by earnings and should therefore appear in the denominator of the fixed-charge coverage calculation. Accordingly, the basic formula can be rewritten to include not only the interest expense shown on the income statement but also capitalized interest, which may appear either on the income statement or in the notes to financial statements. (If the amount is immaterial, capitalized interest will not be shown at all, and the analyst can skip this adjustment.) The numerator should not include capitalized interest, however, for the amount is a reduction to total expenses and consequently reflected in net income. Including capitalized interest in the numerator would therefore constitute double counting:

$$\text{Fixed-charge coverage (adjusted for capitalized interest)} = \frac{\text{Net income} + \text{Income taxes} + \text{Income expenses}}{\text{Interest expense} + \text{Capitalized interest}}$$

Lease Expense

As mentioned, off-balance-sheet operating leases have virtually the same economic impact as on-balance-sheet debt. Just as credit analysts should take into account the liabilities represented by these leases, they should also factor into coverage calculations the annual fixed charges associated with them. One approach simply adds the total current-year rental expense from notes to financial statements to both the numerator and denominator of the fixed-charge coverage calculation. An alternate method includes one-third of rentals (as shown in the following calculation) on the theory that one-third of a lease payment typically represents interest that would be paid if the assets had been purchased with borrowed money, and two-thirds is equivalent to principal repayment:

$$\text{Fixed-charge coverage (adjusted for capitalized interest and operating leases)} = \frac{\text{Net income} + \text{Income taxes} + \text{Income expense} + 1/3 \text{ Rentals}}{\text{Interest expense} + \text{Capitalized interest} + 1/3 \text{ Rentals}}$$

Two complications arise in connection with incorporating operating lease payment into the fixed-charge coverage calculation. First, the SEC does not require companies to report rental expense in quarterly statements. The analyst can therefore only estimate where a company's fully adjusted coverage stands, on an interim basis, in relation to its most recent full-year level. (Capitalized interest, by the way, presents the same problem, although a few companies voluntarily report capitalized interest on an interim basis.) Second, retailers in particular often negotiate leases with rents that are semi-fixed, tied in part to revenues of the leased stores. Some argue that the variable portion—contingent rentals—should be excluded from the fixed-charge coverage calculation. That approach, however, results in a numerator that includes income derived from revenues in excess of the threshold level, while omitting from the denominator charges that were automatically incurred when the threshold was reached. A better way to recognize the possible avoidance of contingent lease payments is by capitalizing only the mandatory portion when calculating the balance sheet ratio of total debt to total capital.

Interest Income

A final issue related to fixed-charge coverage involves interest income. Companies sometimes argue that the denominator should include only net interest expense: the difference between interest expense and income derived from interest-bearing assets, generally consisting of marketable securities. They portray the two items as offsetting, with operating earnings having to cover only the portion of interest expense not automatically paid for by interest income. Such treatment can be deceptive, however, when a company holds a large but temporary portfolio of marketable securities. In this situation, fixed-charge coverage based on net interest expense in the current year can greatly overstate the level of protection that may be expected in the succeeding year, after the company has invested its funds in operating assets. If, however, a company's strategy is to invest a substantial portion of its assets indefinitely in marketable securities (as some pharmaceutical manufacturers do, to capture certain tax benefits), analysts should consider the associated liquidity as a positive factor in their analysis.

STATEMENT OF CASH FLOWS RATIOS

Ratios related to sources and uses of funds measure credit quality at the most elemental level—a company's ability to generate sufficient cash to pay its bills. These ratios also disclose a great deal about financial flexibility; a company that does not have to rely on external financing can take greater operating risks than one that would be forced to retrench if new capital suddenly became scarce or prohibitively expensive. In addition, trends in sources-and-uses ratios can anticipate changes in balance sheet ratios. Given corporations' general reluctance to sell new equity, which may dilute existing shareholders' interest, a recurrent cash shortfall is likely to be made up with debt financing, leading to a rise in the total-debt-to-total-capital ratio.

For capital-intensive manufacturers and utilities, a key ratio is cash flow to capital expenditures:

$$\frac{\text{Cash flow from operations}}{\text{Capital expenditures}}$$

The higher this ratio, the greater the financial flexibility implied. It is important, though, to examine the reasons underlying a change in the relationship between internal funds and capital outlays. It is normal for a capital-intensive industry to go through a capital-spending cycle, adding capacity by constructing large-scale plants that require several years to complete. Once the new capacity is in place, capital expenditures ease for a few years until demand growth catches up and another round of spending begins. Over the cycle, the industry's ratio of cash falls. By definition, the down leg of this cycle does not imply long-term deterioration in credit quality. In contrast, a company that suffers a prolonged downtrend in its ratio of cash flow to capital expenditures is likely to get more deeply into debt and therefore become financially riskier with each succeeding year. Likewise, a rising ratio may require interpretation. A company that sharply reduces its capital budget will appear to increase its financial flexibility, based on the cash-flow-to-capital-expenditures ratio. Cutting back on outlays, however, may impair the company's long-run competitiveness by sacrificing market share or by causing the company to fall behind in technological terms.

Although the most recent period's ratio of cash flow to capital expenditures is a useful measure, the credit analyst is always more interested in the future than in the past. One good way of assessing a company's ability to sustain its existing level of cash adequacy is to calculate depreciation as a percentage of cash flow:

$$\frac{\text{Depreciation}}{\text{Cash flow from operations}}$$

Unlike earnings, depreciation is essentially a programmed item, a cash flow assured by the accounting rules. The higher the percentage of cash flow derived from depreciation, the more predictable a company's cash flow and the less dependent its financial flexibility on the vagaries of the marketplace.

Also important among the ratios derived from the statement of cash flows is the ratio of capital expenditures to depreciation:

$$\frac{\text{Capital expenditures}}{\text{Depreciation}}$$

A ratio of less than 1.0 over a period of several years raises a red flag, since it suggests that the company is failing to replace its plant and equipment. Underspending on capital replacement amounts to gradual liquidation of the firm. By the same token, though, the analyst cannot necessarily assume that all is well simply because capital expenditures consistently exceed depreciation. For one thing, persistent inflation means that a **nominal dollar** spent on plant and equipment today will not buy as much capacity as it did when the depreciating asset was acquired. (Technological advances in production processes may mitigate this problem because the cost in real terms of producing one unit may have declined since the company purchased the equipment now being replaced.) A second reason to avoid complacency over a seemingly strong ratio of capital expenditures to depreciation is that the depreciation may be understated with respect either to wear and tear or to obsolescence. If so, the adequacy of capital spending will be overstated by the ratio of capital spending to depreciation. Finally, capital outlays may be too low even if they match in every sense the depreciation of existing plant and equipment. In a growth industry, a company that fails to expand its capacity at roughly the same rate as its competitors may lose essential economies of scale and fall victim to a **shakeout**.

Credit analysts carry further the concept underlying the ratio of capital expenditures to depreciation by bringing other cash flow items and dividends into the picture and calculating free cash flow as follows:

$$\text{Free Cash Flow} = \text{Cash Flow from Operating Activities}$$
$$- \text{Capital Expenditures} - \text{Dividends}$$

Some credit analysts who focus on debt of highly leveraged companies put primary emphasis on a company's ability to generate positive free cash flow. They reason that as long as a company has sufficient cash flow to replace its fixed assets and satisfy shareholders' demands for payout of a portion of profits, it will not be dependent on outside financing. Management will have the option of retiring debt and thereby reducing financial risk. The key question, naturally, is whether the profitability underlying the cash flow from operating activities is sustainable.

COMBINATION RATIOS

Each of the financial ratios discussed so far in this chapter is derived from numbers collected from just one of the three basic financial statements. In financial analysis, these rudimentary tools are analogous to the simple machines—the wedge, the lever, the wheel, and the screw—that greatly increased the productivity of their prehistoric inventors. How much more remarkable an advance it was, however, when an anonymous Chinese combined two simple machines, a lever and a wheel, to create a wheelbarrow! In similar fashion, combining numbers from different financial statements unleashes vast new analytical power.

Rate-of-Return Measures

One of the most valuable types of combination ratios combines earnings with balance sheet figures. Such ratios measure the profit that an enterprise is generating relative to the assets employed or the capital invested in it. This kind of measure provides a link between credit analysis and the economic concept of productivity of capital.

To illustrate, consider Companies A, B, and C, all of which are debt-free. If we look only at net margin, a ratio derived solely from the income statement, Company A is superior to both its direct competitor, Company B, and Company C, which is in a different business. Looking at the combination ratio of return on equity, however, we find that Company C ranks highest, notwithstanding that sales margins tend to be narrower in its industry:

	Company A	Company B	Company C
Sales	$1,000,000	$1,000,000	$2,000,000
Net income	50,000	40,000	60,000
Equity	500,000	500,000	500,000
Net margin	5.0%	4.0%	3.0%
$\left(\dfrac{\text{Net Income}}{\text{Net Sales}}\right)$			
Return on equity	10.0%	8.0%	12.0%
$\left(\dfrac{\text{Net Income}}{\text{Equity}}\right)$			

To an economist, this result suggests that investors earning 8 percent to 10 percent in Company A and Company B's industry will seek to shift their capital to Company C's industry, where 12 percent returns are available. The credit implication of this migration of capital is that Companies A and B will have greater difficulty raising funds and therefore less financial flexibility. The credit impact on Company C, conversely, is favorable.

There are several variants of the rate-of-return combination ratio, each with a specific analytical application. Return on equity, which has already been alluded to, measures a firm's productivity of equity and therefore provides an indication of its ability to attract a form of capital that provides an important cushion for the debtholders:

$$\text{Return on equity} = \frac{\text{Net income}}{\text{Common equity} + \text{Preferred equity}}$$

In calculating this ratio, analysts most commonly use as the denominator equity as of the final day of the year in which the company earned the income shown in the numerator. This method may sometimes produce distortions. A company might raise a substantial amount of new equity near the end of the year. The denominator in the return-on-equity calculation would consequently be increased, but the numerator would not reflect the benefit of a full year's earnings on the new equity because it was employed in the business for only a few days. Under these circumstances, return on equity will compare unfavorably (and unfairly) with that of a company that did not abruptly expand its equity base.

The potential for distortion in the return-on-equity calculation can be reduced somewhat by substituting for end-of-year equity so-called average equity:

$$\text{Return on average equity} = \frac{\text{Net income}}{\dfrac{(\text{Equity at beginning of year} + \text{Equity at end of year})}{2}}$$

(Some analysts prefer this method to the year-end-based calculation, even when sudden changes in the equity account are not an issue.)

Another limitation of combination ratios that incorporate balance sheet figures is that they have little meaning if calculated for portions of years. Suppose that in 2010 a company earns $6 million on year-end equity of $80 million, for a return on equity of 7.5 percent. During the first half of 2011, its net income is $4 million, of which it pays out $2 million in dividends, leaving it $82 million in equity at June 30, 2011. With the company having earned in half a year two-thirds as much as it did during all of 2010, it is illogical to conclude that its return on equity has fallen from 7.5 percent to 4.9 percent ($4 million ÷ $82 million).

To derive a proper return on equity, it is necessary to annualize the earnings figure. Merely doubling the first half results can introduce some distortion, though, since the company's earnings may be seasonal. Even if not, there is no assurance that the first-half rate of profitability will be sustained in the second half. Accordingly, the best way to annualize earnings is to calculate a trailing 12-months' figure:

$$\frac{\text{Net income for second half of 2010} + \text{Net income for first half of 2011}}{\text{Equity at June 30, 2011}}$$

If the analyst is working with the company's 2010 annual report and 2011 second-quarter statement, 2010 second-half earnings will not be available without backing out some numbers. For ease of calculation, the numerator in the preceding ratio can be derived as follows:

Net income for full year 2010.

Less: Net income for first half of 2010.

Plus: Net income for first half of 2011.

For the credit analyst, return on equity alone may be an insufficient or even misleading measure. The reason is that a company can raise its return on equity by increasing the proportion of debt in its capital structure, a change that reduces credit quality. In Exhibit 13.3, Company Y produces a higher return on equity than the more conservatively capitalized Company X, even though both have equivalent operating margins.

Note that Company Y enjoys its edge despite having to pay a higher interest rate on account of its riskier financial structure.

Income statement ratios such as net margin and fixed-charge coverage, which point to higher credit quality at Company X, serve as a check against return on equity, which ranks Company Y higher. A later section of this chapter explores systematic approaches to reconciling financial ratios that give contradictory indications about the relative credit quality of two or more companies. The more immediately relevant point, however, is that other combination ratios can also be used as checks against an artificially heightened return on equity. Using the same figures for Companies X and Y, the analyst can calculate return on total capital, which equalizes for differences in capital structure. On this basis, Company Y enjoys only a

EXHIBIT 13.3   Effect of Debt on Return on Equity ($000,000 omitted)

	Company X				Company Y			
	12/31/10		12/31/11		12/31/10		12/31/11	
Total debt	$ 25.0	25.0%	$ 25.0	23.5%	$ 50.0	50.0%	$ 50.0	47.5%
Total equity	75.0	75.0%	81.4	76.5%	50.0	50.0%	55.3	52.5%
Total capital	$100.0	100.0%	$106.4	100.0%	$100.0	100.0%	$105.3	100.0%

2011 Results

	Company X	Company Y
Sales	$125.0	$125.0
Operating expenses	108.5	108.5
Operating income	16.5	16.5
Interest expense	2.0*	4.5
Pretax income	14.5	12.0†
Income taxes	4.9	4.1
Net income	9.6	7.9
Dividends	3.2	2.6
Additions to retained earnings	6.4	5.3
Operating margin	16.5/125.0 = 13.2%	16.5/125.0 = 13.2%
Net margin	9.6/125.0 = 7.7%	7.9/125.0 = 6.3%
Return on equity	9.6/81.4 = 11.8%	7.9/55.3 = 14.3%
Fixed-charge coverage	(9.6 + 4.9 + 2.0)/2.0 = 8.25 X	(7.9 + 4.1 + 4.5)/4.5 = 3.7 X

*At 8%.
†At 9%.

negligible advantage related to its slower growth in retained earnings (and hence in capital):

$$\text{Return on total capital} = \frac{\text{Net income} + \text{Income taxes} + \text{Interest expense}}{\text{Total debt} + \text{Total equity}}$$

Company X

Company Y

$$\frac{9.6 + 4.9 + 2.0}{25.0 + 81.4} = \frac{16.5}{106.4} = 15.5\% \qquad \frac{7.9 + 4.1 + 4.5}{50.0 + 55.3} = \frac{16.5}{105.3} = 15.7\%$$

Total debt in this calculation includes short-term debt, current maturities of long-term debt, and long-term debt, for reasons described earlier under "What Constitutes Total Debt?" Similarly, total equity includes both preferred and preference stock. If there is a minority interest, the associated income statement item should appear in the numerator and the balance sheet amount in the denominator.

Turnover Measures

In addition to measuring return on investment, a particular type of combination ratio known as a turnover ratio can provide valuable information about asset quality. The underlying notion of a turnover ratio is that a company requires a certain level of receivables and inventory to support a given volume of sales. For example, if a manufacturer sells its goods on terms that require payment within 30 days, and all customers pay exactly on time, accounts receivable on any given day (barring seasonality in sales) will be $30 \div 365$, or 8.2 percent of annual sales. Coming at the question from the opposite direction, the analyst can calculate the average length of time that a receivable remains outstanding before it is paid (the calculation uses the average amount of receivables outstanding during the year):

$$\text{Average days of receivables} = \frac{\dfrac{(\text{A}/\text{R beginning of year} + \text{A}/\text{R end of year})}{2}}{\times 365 \text{ Annual sales}}$$

This ratio enables the analyst to learn the company's true average collection period, which may differ significantly from its stated collection period.

By inverting the first portion of the average days of receivables calculation, one can determine how many times per year the company turns over its receivables:

$$\text{Receivables turnover} = \frac{\text{Annual sales}}{\dfrac{(\text{ARBY} + \text{AREY})}{2}}$$

where　ARBY = Accounts receivable at beginning of year
　　　　AREY = Accounts receivable at the end of year

As long as a company continues to sell on the same terms, its required receivables level will rise as its sales rise, but the ratio between the two should not change. A decline in the ratio may signal that the company's customers are paying more slowly because they are encountering financial difficulties. Alternatively, the company may be trying to increase its sales by liberalizing its credit standards, allowing its salespeople to do more business with less financially capable customers. Either way, the ultimate collectibility of the accounts receivable shown on the balance sheet has become less certain. Unless the company has reflected this fact by increasing its allowance for doubtful receivables, it may have to write off a portion of receivables against income at some point in the future. The analyst should therefore adjust the company's total-debt-to-total-capital ratio for the implicit overstatement of equity.

Another asset quality problem that can be detected with a combination ratio involves unsalable inventory. A fashion retailer's leftover garments from the preceding season or an electronics manufacturer's obsolete finished goods can be worth far less than their balance sheet values (historical cost). If the company is postponing an inevitable write-off, it may become apparent through a rise in inventory without a commensurate rise in sales, resulting in a decline in inventory turnover:

$$\text{Inventory turnover} = \frac{\text{Annual sales}}{\dfrac{(\text{IBY} + \text{IEY})}{2}}$$

where　IBY = Inventory at beginning of year
　　　　IEY = Inventory at end of year

A drop in sales is another possible explanation of declining inventory turnover. In this case, the inventory may not have suffered a severe reduction in value, but there are nevertheless unfavorable implications for credit quality. Until the inventory glut can be worked off by cutting back production to match the lower sales volume, the company may have to borrow to finance its unusually high working capital, thereby increasing its financial leverage. Profitability may also suffer as the company cuts its selling prices, accepting a lower margin to eliminate excess inventory.

One objection to the preceding inventory-turnover calculation involves the variability of selling prices. Suppose that the price of a commodity chemical suddenly shoots up as the result of a temporary shortage. A chemical producer's annual sales—and hence its inventory turnover—may rise, yet the company may not be physically moving its inventory any faster than before. Conversely, a retailer may respond to a drop in consumer demand and cut its prices to avoid a buildup of inventory. The shelves and back room have no more product than previously, yet the ratio based on annual sales indicates that turnover has declined.

To prevent such distortions, the analyst can use the following variant ratio:

$$\text{Inventory turnover} = \frac{\text{Annual cost of goods sold}}{\dfrac{(\text{IBY} + \text{IEY})}{2}}$$

This version should more closely capture the reality of a company's physical turnover. Cost of goods sold and inventory are both based on historical cost, whereas selling prices fluctuate with market conditions, causing a mismatch between the numerator and denominator of the turnover calculation.

Total-Debt-to-Cash-Flow Ratio

A final combination ratio that is invaluable in credit analysis is the ratio of total debt to cash flow:

$$\text{Total debt to cash flow} = \frac{\begin{array}{c}\text{Short-term debt} + \text{Current maturities}\\ + \text{Long-term debt}\end{array}}{\text{Cash flow from operations}}$$

This ratio expresses a company's financial flexibility in a most interesting way. If, for the sake of illustration, a company has total debt of $60 million and cash flow from operations of $20 million, it has the ability to liquidate all its debt in three years by dedicating 100 percent of its cash flow to that purpose. This company clearly has greater financial flexibility than a company with $80 million of debt and a $10 million annual cash flow, for an eight-year debt-payback period. In the latter case, flexibility would be particularly limited if the company's debt had an average maturity of significantly less than eight years, implying the possibility of significant refinancing pressure under tight credit conditions.

All very interesting, one might say, but in reality, how many companies dedicate 100 percent of their cash flow to debt retirement? The answer is very few, but total debt to cash flow is still a good ratio to monitor for credit quality. It enjoys distinct advantages over some of the more frequently invoked credit-quality measures, which are derived from the balance sheet or income statement alone. The total-debt-to-total-capital ratio has the inherent flaw that equity may be understated or overstated relative to its economic value. After all, the accounting rules do not permit a write-up of assets unless they are sold, nor do the rules require a write-down until someone makes the often subjective determination that the assets have fallen in value. In comparison, total debt is an objective number, a dollar amount that must contractually be repaid. Fixed-charge coverage, too, has a weakness, for it is based on earnings, which are subject to considerable manipulation. Cash flow eliminates one major opportunity for manipulation: underdepreciation. If a company inflates its reported earnings by writing down its fixed assets more slowly than economic reality dictates, it is merely taking money out of one cash flow pocket and putting it into the other. Cash flow, then, puts companies on equal footing, whatever their depreciation policies.

Built from two comparatively hard numbers, the ratio of total debt to cash flow provides one of the best single measures of credit quality. Analysts should not worry about whether its literal interpretation—the period required for a total liquidation of debt—is realistic but instead focus on its analytical value.

RELATING RATIOS TO CREDIT RISK

The discussion of financial ratios up to this point has sidestepped an obvious and critical question: How does an analyst who has calculated a ratio know whether it represents good, bad, or indifferent credit quality? Somehow, the analyst must relate the ratio to the likelihood that the borrower will satisfy all scheduled interest and principal payments in full and on time. In practice, this is accomplished by testing financial ratios as predictors of the borrower's propensity not to pay (to default). For example, a company with high financial leverage is statistically more likely to default than one with low leverage, all other things being equal. Similarly, high fixed-charge coverage implies less default risk than low coverage. After identifying the factors that create high default risk, the analyst can use ratios to rank all borrowers on a relative scale of propensity to default.

Many credit analysts conduct their ratio analyses within ranking frameworks established by their employers. Individuals engaged in processing loan applications may use criteria derived from the lending institution's experience over many years in recognizing the financial characteristics that lead to timely payment or to default. In the securities field, bond ratings provide a structure for analysis. Exhibits 13.4 and 13.5 show the rating definitions of two leading bond-rating agencies, Moody's Investors Service and Standard & Poor's. (The following discussion uses the rating notations and their

---

EXHIBIT 13.4 Moody's Bond Ratings (Definitions)

Long-Term Obligation Ratings
Moody's long-term ratings are opinions of the relative credit risk of financial obligations with an original maturity of one year or more. They address the possibility that a financial obligation will not be honored as promised. Such ratings use Moody's Global Scale and reflect both the likelihood of default and any financial loss suffered in the event of default.

Aaa   Obligations rated Aaa are judged to be of the highest quality, with minimal credit risk.

Aa   Obligations rated Aa are judged to be of high quality and are subject to very low credit risk.

A   Obligations rated A are considered upper-medium grade and are subject to low credit risk.

Baa   Obligations rated Baa are subject to moderate credit risk. They are considered medium grade and as such may possess certain speculative characteristics.

Ba   Obligations rated Ba are judged to have speculative elements and are subject to credit risk.

B   Obligations rated B are considered speculative and are subject to high credit risk.

Caa   Obligations rated Caa are judged to be of poor standing and are subject to very high credit risk.

Ca   Obligations rated Ca are highly speculative and are likely in, or very near, default, with some prospect of recovery of principal or interest.

C   Obligations rated C are the lowest rated class and are typically in default, with little prospect for recovery of principal or interest.

Note: Moody's appends numerical modifiers 1, 2, and 3 to each generic rating classification from Aa through Caa. The modifier 1 indicates that the obligation ranks in the higher end of its generic rating category; the modifier 2 indicates a mid-range ranking; and the modifier 3 indicates a ranking in the lower end of that generic rating category.

Source: Moody's Investors Service.

EXHIBIT 13.5 Standard & Poor's Bond Ratings (Definitions)

Issue-Specific Credit Ratings
Our issue credit rating is a current opinion of the credit risk pertaining to a specific financial obligation, a specific class of financial obligations, or a specific financial program.

Long-Term Ratings Definitions
AAA: An obligation rated AAA has the highest rating we assign. The obligor's capacity to meet its financial commitments on the obligation is extremely strong.

AA: An obligation rated AA differs from the highest-rated obligations only to a small degree. The obligor's capacity to meet its financial commitment on the obligation is very strong.

A: An obligation rated A is somewhat more susceptible to the adverse effects of changes in circumstances and economic conditions than obligations in higher rated categories. However, the obligor's capacity to meet its financial commitment on the obligation is still strong.

BBB: An obligation rated BBB exhibits adequate protection parameters. However, adverse economic conditions or changing circumstances are more likely to lead to a weakened capacity of the obligor to meet its financial commitment on the obligation.

Obligations rated BB, B, CCC, CC, and C are regarded as having significant speculative characteristics. BB indicates the least degree of speculation, and C the highest. While such obligations likely will have some quality and protective characteristics, these may be outweighed by large uncertainties or major exposure to adverse conditions.

BB: An obligation rated BB is less vulnerable to nonpayment than other speculative issues. However, it faces major ongoing uncertainties or exposure to adverse business, financial, or economic conditions that could lead to the obligor's inadequate capacity to meet its financial commitment on the obligation.

B: An obligation rated B is more vulnerable to nonpayment than obligations rated BB, but the obligor currently has the capacity to meet its financial commitment on the obligation. Adverse business, financial, or economic conditions likely will impair the obligor's capacity or willingness to meet its financial commitment on the obligation.

CCC: An obligation rated CCC is vulnerable to nonpayment within one year, and depends on favorable business, financial, and economic conditions for the obligor to meet its financial commitment on the obligation. In the event of adverse business, financial, or economic conditions, the obligor is unlikely to have the capacity to meet its financial commitment on the obligation.

CC: An obligation rated CC currently is highly vulnerable to nonpayment.

C: The C rating is also used when a bankruptcy petition has been filed or similar action has been taken but payments on this obligation are being continued. C is also used for a preferred stock that is in arrears (as well as for junior debt of issuers rated CCC– and CC).

D: Default; SD: Selective default. The D and SD ratings, unlike other ratings, are not prospective; rather, they are used only when a default actually has occurred—not when default is only expected.

Plus (+) or minus (−): The ratings from AA to CCC may be modified by the addition of a plus or minus sign to show relative standing within the major rating categories.

Source: Standard & Poor's.

corresponding spoken equivalents interchangeably—AAA and Triple-A, AA and Double-A, and so on.)

Because much credit work is done in the context of established standards, the next order of business is to explain how companies can be ranked by ratios on a relative scale of credit quality. Bond ratings are the standard on which the discussion focuses, but the principles are applicable to in-house credit-ranking schemes that analysts may encounter. Following a demonstration of the use of credit rating standards, this chapter concludes with an examination of the methods underlying the construction of standards to show readers how financial ratios are linked to default risk.

The analysis in this section focuses primarily on determining the probability that a borrower will pay interest and principal in full and on time. It does not address the percentage of principal that the lender is likely to recover in the event of default. Certainly, expected recoveries have an important bearing on the decision to extend or deny credit, as well as on the valuation of debt securities. Bankruptcy analysis, however, is a huge topic in its own right. Its proper practice depends on a detailed knowledge of the relevant legislation and a thorough understanding of the dynamics of the negotiations between creditors and the management of a company in Chapter 11 **reorganization** proceedings. Such matters are beyond the scope of the present work. For the securities of highly rated companies, moreover, the potential percentage recovery of principal tends to be a comparatively minor valuation factor. Over the short to intermediate term, the probability of a bankruptcy filing by such a company is small.

Although the reader will not find a complete guide to bankruptcy analysis in these pages, Chapter 14 is relevant from the standpoint of determining the failed firm's equity value, a key step in the reorganization or liquidation of the company. In addition, the bibliography includes books that discuss bankruptcy in extensive detail.

Comparative Ratio Analysis

The basic technique in assigning a relative credit ranking is to compare a company's ratio with those of a peer group. Size and line of business are the key criteria for identifying a company's peers.

On the matter of size, a manufacturer with $5 billion in annual sales will ordinarily be a better credit risk than one with similar financial ratios but only $5 million in sales. As a generalization, bigger companies enjoy economies of scale and have greater leverage with suppliers by virtue of their larger purchasing power. A big company can spread the risks of obsolescence and competitive challenges over a wide range of products and customers, whereas a smaller competitor's sales are likely to be concentrated on a few products and customers. Particularly vulnerable is a company with just a single manufacturing facility. An unexpected loss of production could prove fatal to such an enterprise. Lack of depth in management is another problem commonly associated with smaller companies.

Unquestionably, some very large companies have failed in the past. There is ample evidence, as well, of inefficiency in many large, bureaucratic organizations. The point, however, is not to debate whether big corporations are invincible or nimble, but to determine whether they meet their obligations with greater regularity, on average, than their pint-size peers. Statistical models of default risk confirm that they do. Therefore, the bond-rating agencies are following sound methodology when they create size-based peer groups.

Line of business is another basis for defining a peer group. Because different industries have different financial characteristics, ratio comparisons across industry lines may not be valid. A machinery manufacturer's sales may fluctuate substantially over the capital goods cycle. In contrast, a personal care products manufacturer derives its revenues from essential products that are in demand year in and year out. The personal care products company therefore has greater predictability of earnings and cash flow. It can tolerate a higher level of fixed charges, implying a larger proportion of debt in its capital structure, than the machinery manufacturer. The rating agencies may assign Single-A ratings to a manufacturer of personal care products with a ratio of total debt to total capital that would earn a machinery maker with similar ratio ratings no higher than Triple-B.

For this reason, a ratio comparison between companies in different industries can be misleading. One company can look superior based on a particular ratio, yet still be excessively leveraged in view of the operating risks in its industry. Comparability problems become even more pronounced when ratio analysis crosses boundaries of broadly defined sectors of the economy (e.g., industrial, financial, utility, and transportation).

Carrying this principle to its logical conclusion, however, requires a peer group of companies with virtually identical product lines. Operating risk varies to some extent even among closely allied businesses. Strictly speaking, a producer of coated white paper is not comparable to a producer of kraft linerboard, nor a producer of facial tissue to a producer of fine writing paper.

Too zealous an effort to create homogeneous peer groups, though, narrows the field to such an extent that ratio comparisons begin to suffer from having too few data points. At the extreme, a comparison with only one other peer company is not terribly informative. The company being evaluated may rank above its lone peer, but the analyst does not know whether the peer is strong or weak.

Suppose, on the other hand, that with respect to a particular financial ratio, a company ranks fourth among a peer group of 10 companies, with eight in the group tightly distributed around the median and with one outlier each at the high and low ends. It is valid to say that the company has average risk within its peer group, at least in terms of one particular ratio.

There are two techniques for resolving the trade-off between strict comparability and adequate sample size. Both consist of peer group comparisons. By employing both approaches, the analyst can achieve a satisfactory assessment of relative credit risk.

The first technique is to compare the company against a reasonably homogeneous industry peer group, such as the food producers shown in Exhibit 13.6. Credit analysts can use this type of analysis to slot a company within its industry. The ratios in the 21-company sample comparison are averages, computed over three years. Averaging minimizes the impact of unrepresentative results that any company may report in a single year.

Standard & Poor's conducts far more analysis in assigning the ratings indicated in the table, yet it is notable how well these basic financial ratios sort the companies by rating. In the case of pretax interest coverage and funds flow as a percentage of total debt, for both of which a higher ratio connotes better credit quality, the A ratings are all in the top third of the rankings and the B ratings are all in the bottom third. In ranking the 21 companies by the median of these two ratios, the top third have an average rating of BBB+, the middle third have an average rating of BBB−, and the bottom third have an average rating of BB−.

Strikingly, total debt as a percentage of capital, also known as the debt ratio, is the least effective of the three ratios as a ranking device. For example, the companies with the highest rating within the peer group (A) are scattered across the top, middle, and bottom thirds of the rankings. It is little wonder that specialists in credit analysis, particularly those who focus on the lower end of the ratings spectrum, pay little if any attention to the classic debt ratio.

A key reason for the debt ratio's limited ability to discriminate according to credit risk is that it is calculated on the basis of book value. There are great disparities between book value and market value of equity, with food processing a prime example. The companies' earnings power and by extension their share prices largely reflect the value embedded in the brand names they own, rather than their physical assets.

Notwithstanding the analytical limitations of the debt ratio, the concept underlying it has considerable merit. Suppose a company defaults on its debt payments and files for bankruptcy as a consequence of taking on excessive debt. Creditors then become the company's owners and may be able to recover a substantial portion of their principal through a sale of the company.

EXHIBIT 13.6 Comparative Ratio Analysis of Packaged Foods and Meats Annual Average 2007–2009

Pretax Interest Coverage			Funds Flow as a Percentage of Total Debt			Total Debt as a Percentage of Capital		
Company Name	Times	Rating	Company Name	Percentage	Rating	Company Name	Percentage	Rating
Flowers Foods, Inc. (NYSE:FLO)	29.7	BBB–	Flowers Foods, Inc. (NYSE:FLO)	213.1	BBB–	Hormel Foods Corp. (NYSE:HRL)	15.6	A
Hormel Foods Corp. (NYSE:HRL)	18.8	A	Hormel Foods Corp. (NYSE:HRL)	109.4	A	Flowers Foods, Inc. (NYSE:FLO)	21.2	BBB–
Campbell Soup Co. (NYSE:CPB)	9.6	A	Hershey Co. (NYSE:HSY)	43.8	A	Tyson Foods Inc. (NYSE:TSN)	39.1	BB+
Hershey Co. (NYSE:HSY)	8.1	A	Wimm-Bill-Dann Foods OJSC (NYSE:WBD)	41.3	BB–	Treehouse Foods Inc. (NYSE:THS)	42.6	BB–
McCormick & Co. Inc. (NYSE:MKC)	7.7	A–	Campbell Soup Co. (NYSE:CPB)	34.0	A	ConAgra Foods, Inc. (NYSE:CAG)	42.7	BBB
Kellogg Company (NYSE:K)	6.7	BBB+	McCormick & Co. Inc. (NYSE:MKC)	32.8	A–	Kraft Foods Inc. (NYSE:KFT)	44.4	BBB
Wimm-Bill-Dann Foods OJSC (NYSE:WBD)	5.9	BB–	Kellogg Company (NYSE:K)	28.6	BBB+	Ralcorp Holdings Inc. (NYSE:RAH)	44.9	BBB–
Sara Lee Corp. (NYSE:SLE)	5.8	BBB	Sara Lee Corp. (NYSE:SLE)	27.3	BBB	McCormick & Co. Inc. (NYSE:MKC)	45.5	A–
General Mills Inc. (NYSE:GIS)	5.6	BBB+	General Mills Inc. (NYSE:GIS)	26.2	BBB+	Wimm-Bill-Dann Foods OJSC (NYSE:WBD)	46.3	BB–
Kraft Foods Inc. (NYSE:KFT)	5.0	BBB	Treehouse Foods Inc. (NYSE:THS)	26.2	BB–	Chiquita Brands International Inc. (NYSE:CQB)	51.4	B
Treehouse Foods Inc. (NYSE:THS)	4.7	BB–	HJ Heinz Co. (NYSE:HNZ)	25.4	BBB	Del Monte Foods Co. (NYSE:DLM)	51.4	BB
HJ Heinz Co. (NYSE:HNZ)	4.6	BBB	Tyson Foods Inc. (NYSE:TSN)	23.3	BB+	Sara Lee Corp. (NYSE:SLE)	52.5	BBB

Company	Value	Rating	Company	Value	Rating	Company	Value	Rating
ConAgra Foods, Inc. (NYSE:CAG)	4.2	BBB	Kraft Foods Inc. (NYSE:KFT)	21.4	BBB	General Mills Inc. (NYSE:GIS)	55.6	BBB+
Ralcorp Holdings Inc. (NYSE:RAH)	3.9	BBB−	Del Monte Foods Co. (NYSE:DLM)	20.1	BB	Campbell Soup Co. (NYSE:CPB)	69.4	A
Del Monte Foods Co. (NYSE:DLM)	3.3	BB	Ralcorp Holdings Inc. (NYSE:RAH)	19.7	BBB−	Kellogg Company (NYSE:K)	71.5	BBB+
Dean Foods Co. (NYSE:DF)	2.2	BB−	ConAgra Foods, Inc. (NYSE:CAG)	16.9	BBB	B&G Foods Inc. (NYSE:BGS)	73.7	B+
Tyson Foods Inc. (NYSE:TSN)	1.9	BB+	Reddy Ice Holdings, Inc. (NYSE:FRZ)	12.7	B−	HJ Heinz Co. (NYSE:HNZ)	75.5	BBB
B&G Foods Inc. (NYSE:BGS)	1.6	B+	Dean Foods Co. (NYSE:DF)	12.3	BB−	Hershey Co. (NYSE:HSY)	76.5	A
Reddy Ice Holdings, Inc. (NYSE:FRZ)	1.4	B−	Chiquita Brands International Inc. (NYSE:CQB)	10.7	B	Dole Food Company Inc. (NYSE:DOLE)	78.6	B
Chiquita Brands International Inc. (NYSE:CQB)	1.4	B	B&G Foods Inc. (NYSE:BGS)	9.2	B+	Dean Foods Co. (NYSE:DF)	88.2	BB−
Dole Food Company Inc. (NYSE:DOLE)	1.2	B	Dole Food Company Inc. (NYSE:DOLE)	7.1	B+	Reddy Ice Holdings, Inc. (NYSE:FRZ)	90.2	B−

Standard & Poor's Ratings

Source: Capital IQ, Bloomberg, and author calculations.

If the company's value is high relative to its debt, creditors should recover a high percentage of what they are owed. Capital as measured by debt plus the book value of equity is not an especially good gauge of company value, but credit analysts can gain a fair idea of their prospects for recovery by substituting a measure based on the company's cash-generating capability. The most common such measure is a multiple of EBITDA (see Chapter 8).

The second technique of comparative ratio analysis that is useful in evaluating credit quality is ranking a company within a rating peer group. As noted, it is not appropriate to compare companies in disparate sectors of the economy, such as industrials and utilities. A rating peer group can, however, legitimately include a variety of industries within a broadly defined economic sector. The expanded sample available under this approach enables the analyst to fine-tune the slotting achieved via the industry peer group comparisons.

Instead of displaying ratios for all industrial companies rated Single-A by Standard & Poor's, Exhibit 13.7 lists the medians for the Single-A group. As a further aid in slotting companies, the table includes the cutoff points for the upper and lower quartiles in the rankings of Single-A companies.

The table shows that companies within a rating category vary substantially by key quantitative criteria. The lesson is that although comparative ratio analysis plays a large role in the bond-rating process, Moody's and Standard & Poor's also consider factors outside the financial statements. Therefore, analysts working outside the rating agencies must be cautious about concluding that a company is rated incorrectly. If they make such an inference without exploring the possibility of extenuating circumstances, they may recommend buying or selling a bond in expectation of an upgrade or downgrade that has little chance of materializing.

With that proviso, analysts can derive considerable value from comparative ratio analysis. It is helpful to determine that a company not rated by Moody's or Standard & Poor's most closely resembles the companies in

EXHIBIT 13.7 Average Ratios for Standard & Poor's Single-A Industrials 2007–2009

	Pretax Interest Coverage	Funds Flow as a Percentage of Total Debt	Total Debt as a Percentage of Capital
Best quartile	18.8	51.5	26.6
Median	10.1	31.0	37.1
Worst quartile	6.5	17.3	49.4

Source: Standard & Poor's.

EXHIBIT 13.8 Median Ratios by Bond-Rating Category (Industrials, 2007–2009)

	AAA	AA	A	BBB	BB	B
Oper. income (bef. D&A)/ revenues (%)	28.2	25.3	19.5	17.0	17.2	15.8
Return on capital (%)	34.2	25.4	21.1	14.1	12.2	8.3
EBIT interest coverage (×)	30.5	18.3	11.0	5.8	3.5	1.4
EBITDA interest coverage (×)	33.5	20.5	14.3	7.6	5.2	2.3
FFO/debt (%)	200.7	73.4	53.0	34.0	25.3	12.0
Free oper. cash flow/debt (%)	157.8	49.8	34.0	17.0	11.9	3.2
Disc. cash flow/debt (%)	96.8	29.4	22.7	11.0	9.1	2.3
Debt/EBITDA (×)	0.4	1.1	1.5	2.3	3.0	5.3
Debt/debt plus equity (%)	15.1	34.7	35.7	44.7	50.4	73.1
No. of companies	4.0	16.0	92.0	213.0	245.0	325.0

Source: Standard & Poor's.

a particular rating category. In assigning a nonrated company to a rating category based on ratio comparisons, analysts should keep in mind the size criterion, previously discussed, for creation of peer groups.

Comparative ratio analysis is also useful in assessing the credit impact of a major transaction, such as a debt-financed acquisition or a major stock repurchase. The analyst can calculate ratios based on pro forma financial statements (see Chapter 12) and slot the company in a grid of median ratios by rating category (see Exhibit 13.8). In view of changes in the peer group ratios that arise from fluctuations in business conditions, it is important to use data that is as up-to-date as possible for the exercise.

Analysts should also bear in mind that a company can potentially avert a downgrade implied by the pro forma ratios, provided management's credibility with the rating agencies is high. The key is to present a plausible plan for restoring financial leverage to its pretransaction level within a few years. Note, however, that the company will merely delay the downgrade if it does not begin fairly quickly to make palpable progress toward the long-range target. The rating agencies tend to be skeptical about a company's ability to implement a three-year plan entirely in the third year.

Ratio Trend Analysis

Comparative ratio analysis is an effective technique for assessing relative credit risk, yet it leaves the analyst exposed to a major source of error. Suppose two companies in the same industry posted an identical fixed-charge coverage of 3.5 times last year. On a ratio comparison, the two appear to be equally risky. Suppose, however, that one company had coverage of 5.0 times five years ago and has steadily declined to 3.5 times. Imagine, as well, that the other company's coverage has improved over the same period from 2.0 times to 3.5 times. If the two companies' trends appear likely to continue, based on analysis, then the happenstance that both covered their interest by 3.5 times last year should have little bearing on the credit assessment. The company that will have stronger coverage in the future is the better risk.

A further complication is that improving or deteriorating financial ratios can have different implications for different companies. In some cases, a declining trend over several years signals that a company has genuinely fallen to a new, lower level of credit quality. For other companies, negative year-over-year comparisons merely represent the down legs of their normal operating cycles.

Certain industries enjoy fairly stable demand, year in and year out. Small-ticket nondurables such as food, beverages, and beauty aids are not items that consumers cease to buy during recessions. At worst, people trade down to cheaper products within the same categories. In contrast, consumers tend to postpone purchases of big-ticket durable goods when credit is tight or when they have misgivings about economic conditions. Producers of automobiles, houses, and major appliances are among the businesses that experience wide swings in demand between peaks and troughs in the economy. Profits typically fluctuate even more dramatically in these industries, due to the high fixed costs entailed in capital-intensive production methods.

In evaluating the long-range creditworthiness of cyclical companies, the bond-rating agencies historically focused on cycle-to-cycle, rather than year-to-year, trends. Their notion was that a cycle-to-cycle pattern of similar highs and similar lows (Exhibit 13.9) did not imply a true impairment of financial strength. Deterioration was indicated only when a company displayed a trend of successively lower highs and lower lows (Exhibit 13.10).

EXHIBIT 13.9 Cycle-to-Cycle Stability (Similar Highs and Lows)
*Examples: Operating margin, fixed charge coverage, ratio of cash flow to total debt.

EXHIBIT 13.10 Cycle-to-Cycle Deterioration (Successively Lower Highs and Lower Lows)

Moody's and Standard & Poor's label this traditional approach "rating through the cycle." Although it still influences the agencies' analysis, they have deemphasized the concept somewhat in recent years. They are more likely than formerly to assume that an extended upturn or downtrend in a company's ratios represents a longer-lived shift.

Even in years past, when the agencies adhered more closely to the doctrine of rating through the cycle, it was often difficult to distinguish a normal, cyclical decline from more permanent deterioration, without the benefit of hindsight. There was always a danger that a company's management was portraying a permanent reduction in profitability as a routine cyclical slump. Then, as now, an analyst had to look beyond the financial statements to make an informed judgment about the likely persistence of an improvement or deterioration in financial measures.

Default Risk Models

As noted, comparative ratio analysis and ratio trend analysis are techniques for placing companies on a relative scale of credit quality. Many analysts have no need to look more deeply into the matter, but it is impossible to cover the topic of credit analysis satisfactorily without discussing two more fundamental issues. First, there is the question of how to set up a ranking scheme such as bond ratings in the first place. Second, there is the problem of conflicting indicators. How, for example, should an analyst evaluate a company that ranks well on fixed-charge coverage but poorly on financial leverage? A rigorous approach demands something more scientific than an individual analyst's subjective opinion that coverage should be weighted twice as heavily as leverage, or vice versa.

The solution to both of these problems lies in establishing a statistical relationship between financial ratios and default. This requires, first of all, collecting data on the default experience in a given population. Next, statistical methods are employed to determine which financial ratios have historically predicted defaults most reliably. Using a model derived from the best predictors, the analyst can then rank companies on the basis of how closely their financial profiles resemble the profiles of companies that defaulted.

One example of the various models that have been devised to predict defaults is Edward I. Altman's Z-Score model, which takes the following form:

$$Z = 1.2x_1 + 1.4x_2 + 3.3x_3 + 0.6x_4 + 1.0x_5$$

where $x_1 = $ Working capital/Total assets (%, e.g., 0.20, or 20%)
$x_2 = $ Retained earnings/Total assets (%)
$x_3 = $ Earnings before interest and taxes/Total assets (%)
$x_4 = $ Market value of equity/Total liabilities (%)
$x_5 = $ Sales/Total assets (number of times, e.g., 2.0 times)

In this model, scores below 1.81 signify serious credit problems, whereas a score above 3.0 indicates a healthy firm.

A refinement of the Z-Score model, the Zeta model developed by Altman and his colleagues,[6] achieved greater predictive accuracy by using the following variables:

$x_1 = $ Earnings before interest and taxes (EBIT)/Total assets

$x_2 = $ **Standard error of estimate** of EBIT/Total assets (normalized) for 10 years

$x_3 = $ EBIT/Interest charges

$x_4 = $ Retained earnings/Total assets

$x_5 = $ Current assets/Current liabilities

$x_6 = $ Five-year average market value of equity/Total capitalization

$x_7 = $ Total tangible assets, normalized

Quantitative models such as Zeta, as well as others that have been devised using various mathematical techniques, have several distinct benefits. First, they are developed by objectively correlating financial variables with defaults. They consequently avoid guesswork in assigning relative weights to the variables. Second, the record of quantitative models is excellent from the standpoint of classifying as troubled credits most companies that subsequently defaulted. In addition, the scores assigned to nondefaulted companies by these models correlate fairly well with bond ratings. This suggests that although Moody's and Standard & Poor's originally developed their rating methods along more subjective lines, their conclusions are at least partially vindicated by statistical measures of default risk. Therefore, the credit analyst can feel comfortable about using methods such as ratio trend analysis to slot companies within the ratings framework. Although one can quarrel with the rating agencies' assessments of particular companies or particular industries, there is strong statistical support for the notion that in the aggregate, ratings provide a valid, if rough, assessment of default risk. The lower a company's present rating, the higher its probability of defaulting over the next year, next two years, and so on up to 20 years.[7]

Useful as they are, though, quantitative default models cannot entirely replace human judgment in credit analysis.

For one thing, quantitative models tend to classify as troubled credits not only most of the companies that eventually default but also many that do not default.[8] Often, firms that fall into financial peril bring in new management and are revitalized without ever failing in their debt service. If faced with a huge capital loss on the bonds of a financially distressed company, an institutional investor might wish to assess the probability of a turnaround—an inherently difficult-to-quantify prospect—instead of selling purely on the basis of a default model.

The credit analyst must also bear in mind that companies can default for reasons that a model based solely on reported financial data cannot pick up. For example, U.S. Brass entered Chapter 11 proceedings in 1994 in an effort to resolve litigation involving defective plastic plumbing systems that it had manufactured. Dow Corning's 1995 bankruptcy filing offered a possible means of resolving massive litigation arising from silicone gel breast implants sold by the company, which were alleged to cause autoimmune disease and other maladies. In 1999, Gulf States Steel, Inc. of Alabama filed for bankruptcy to address, among other matters, pending litigation with the Environmental Protection Agency and other potential environmentally related claims.[9] Typically, in such cases, neither the company's balance sheet nor its income statement signals an impending collapse. Eljer Industries, U.S. Brass's parent company, specifically indicated that the bankruptcy filing did not result from a cash flow shortfall. The problems were apparent in the company's notes to financial statements, but default models based entirely on financial statement data do not deal with contingent liabilities.

In the case of the Zeta model, the default hazard posed by a company's environmental or product liability litigation may be picked up, at least in part, by the ratio of market value of equity to total capitalization. Stock market investors consider such risks in determining share prices.

Some default risk models dispense with statement data altogether in favor of complete reliance on the equity market's wisdom. The best known are marketed by Moody's KMV and Helix Investment Partners, L.P. BondScore, a product of CreditSights, combines quantitative analysis based on equity pricing with traditional credit analysis. Underlying these models is the observation that a company's debt and equity both derive their value from the same assets. Equity holders have only a residual claim after bond-holders have been paid. Therefore, if the market value of a company's assets falls below the value of its liabilities, the stock becomes worthless. At the same time, the company becomes bankrupt; its liabilities exceed its assets. Extending the logic, a declining stock price indicates that the company is getting closer to bankruptcy. In theory, then, credit analysts can skip the financial statement work and monitor companies' default risk simply by watching their stock prices.

Like the quantitative models consisting of financial ratios, the default risk models based on stock prices provide useful, but not infallible, signals. For example, when a company dramatically increases its total-debt-to-total-capital ratio by borrowing money to repurchase stock, its default risk clearly rises. At the same time, its stock price may also rise, reflecting the positive impact on earnings per share of increased financial leverage and a reduction in the number of shares outstanding. According to the theory underlying the stock-based default risk models, however, a rising share price indicates declining default risk. This is one of several caveats typically accompanying credit opinions derived from stock-based models.

Even if share prices were perfect indicators of credit risk, credit ana-lysts would not escape the rigors of tearing apart financial statements. To begin with, not every company's shares trade in the public market. The pro-ducers of stock-based models attempt to get around this problem by using share prices of industry peers to create surrogates for private companies' unobservable equity values. This method, however, cannot capture the sort of company-specific risks that led to the bankruptcies of U.S. Brass, Dow Corning, and Gulf States Steel, Inc. of Alabama. Neither can stock-based default risk models relieve the analyst of such tasks as creating pro forma financial statements to gauge the impact of a potential merger or major asset sale. At most, incorporating stock prices into credit analysis is a useful com-plement to plumbing the financial statements for meaning with time-tested ratio calculations.

CONCLUSION

Default risk models can provide a solid foundation for credit analysis but must be complemented by the analyst's judgment on matters too complex to be modeled. Much the same applies to all of the quantitative techniques discussed in this chapter. A lender should not provide credit before first running the numbers. By the same token, it is a mistake to rely solely on the numbers to sidestep a difficult decision. This can take the form either of rejecting a reasonable risk by inflexibly applying quantitative criteria or of approving a credit against one's better judgment while counting on financial ratios that are technically satisfactory as a defense against criticism if the loan goes bad.

As other chapters in this book demonstrate, financial statements are vulnerable to manipulation, much of which is perfectly legal. Often, the specific aim of the manipulators is to outfox credit analysts who mechanically calculate ratios without pausing to consider whether accounting ruses have defeated the purpose. Another danger in relying too heavily on quantitative analysis is that a company may unexpectedly and radically alter its capital structure to finance an acquisition or defend itself against a hostile takeover. Such action can render ratio analysis on even the most recent financial statements largely irrelevant. In the end, credit analysts must equip themselves with all the tools described in this chapter yet not be made complacent by them.

CHAPTER 14

Equity Analysis

Countless books have been written on the subject of picking stocks. The approaches represented in their pages cover a vast range. Some focus on technical analysis, which seeks to establish the value of a common equity by studying its past price behavior. Others take as their starting point the efficient market hypothesis, which in its purest form implies that no sort of analysis can identify values not already recognized and properly discounted by the market.

This chapter does not attempt to summarize or criticize all the methods employed by the legions who play the market. Rather, the discussion focuses primarily on the use of financial statements in **fundamental analysis.** This term refers to the attempt to determine whether a company's stock is fairly valued, based on its financial characteristics.

Certain elements of fundamental analysis do *not* use information found in the financial statements. For example, a company may seem like a good candidate for a bust-up, or hostile takeover, premised on selling portions of the company to realize value not reflected in its stock price. As discussed later in this chapter, the analyst can estimate the firm's ostensible breakup value by studying its annual report. The feasibility of a hostile raid, however, may hinge on the pattern of share ownership, the availability of financing for a takeover, or laws applicable to tender offers. All these factors lie outside the realm of financial statement analysis but may have a major bearing on the valuation process.

A final point regarding the following material is that it should be read in conjunction with Chapter 12, "Forecasting Financial Statements." A company's equity value lies wholly in its future performance, with historical financial statements aiding the analysis only to the extent that they provide a basis for projecting future results. Into the formulas detailed in this chapter, the analyst must plug earnings and cash flow forecasts derived by the techniques described in Chapter 12.

THE DIVIDEND DISCOUNT MODEL

Several methods of fundamental common stock analysis have been devised over the years, but few match the intuitive appeal of regarding the stock price as the discounted value of expected future dividends. This approach is analogous to the yield-to-maturity calculation for a bond and therefore facilitates the comparison of different securities of a single issuer. Additionally, the method permits the analyst to address the uncertainty inherent in forecasting a noncontractual flow[1] by varying the applicable discount rate.

To understand the relationship between future dividends and present stock price, consider the following fictitious example: Tarheel Tobacco's annual common dividend rate is currently $2.10 a share. Because the company's share of a nonexpanding market is neither increasing nor decreasing, it will probably generate flat sales and earnings for the indefinite future and continue the dividend at its current level. Tarheel's long-term debt currently offers a yield of 6 percent, reflecting the company's credit rating and the prevailing level of interest rates. Based on the greater uncertainty of the dividend stream relative to the contractual payments on Tarheel's debt, investors demand a risk premium of four percentage points—a return of 6 percent + 4 percent = 10 percent—to own the company's common stock rather than its bonds.

The stock price that should logically be observed in the market, given these facts, is the price at which Tarheel's annual $2.10 payout equates to a 10 percent yield, or algebraically:

$$P = \frac{D}{K}$$

$$P = \frac{\$2.10}{.10}$$

$$P = \$21.00$$

where P = Current stock price
  D = Current dividend rate
  K = Required rate of return

If the analyst agrees that 10 percent is an appropriate discount rate, based on a financial comparison between Tarheel and other companies with similar implicit discount rates, then any price less than $21 a share indicates that the stock is undervalued. Alternatively, suppose the analyst concludes that Tarheel's future dividend stream is less secure than the dividend streams of other companies to which a 10 percent discount rate is being applied. The analyst might then discount Tarheel's stream at a higher rate, say 12 percent, and recalculate the appropriate share price as follows:

$$P \times K = \frac{\$2.10}{.12}$$
$$P/K = \$17.50$$

A market price of \$17.50 a share would then indicate an overvaluation of Tarheel Tobacco.

Dividends and Future Appreciation

When initially introduced to the dividend-discount model, many individuals respond by saying, "Dividends are not the only potential source of gain to the stockholder. The share price may rise as well. Shouldn't any evaluation reflect the potential for appreciation?" It is in responding to this objection that the dividend-discount model displays its elegance most fully. The answer is that there is no reason for the stock price to rise in the future unless the dividend rises. In a no-growth situation such as Tarheel Tobacco, the valuation will look the same five years hence (assuming no change in interest rates and risk premiums) as today. There is consequently no fundamental reason for a buyer to pay more for the stock at that point. If, on the other hand, the dividend payout rises over time (the case that immediately follows), the stock *will* be worth more in the future than it is today. The analyst can, however, incorporate the expected dividend increases directly into the present-value calculation to derive the current stock price, without bothering to determine and discount back the associated future price appreciation. By thinking through the logic of the discounting method, the analyst will find that value always comes back to dividends.

Valuing a Growing Company

No-growth companies are simple to analyze, but in practice most public corporations strive for growth in earnings per share, which, as the ensuing discussion demonstrates, will lead to gains for shareholders. In analyzing growing companies, a somewhat more complex formula must be used to equate future dividends to the present stock price:

$$P = \frac{D(1+g)^1}{(1+K)^1} + \frac{D(1+g)^2}{(1+K)^2} + \cdots \frac{D(1+g)^n}{(1+K)^n}$$

where P = Current stock price
          D = Current dividend rate
          K = Required rate of return
          g = Growth rate

A number of dollars equivalent to P, if invested at an interest rate equivalent to K, will be equal, after n periods, to the cumulative value of dividends paid over the same interval, assuming the payout is initially an amount equivalent to D and increases in each period at a rate equivalent to g.

Fortunately, from the standpoint of ease of calculation, if n, the number of periods considered, is infinite, the preceding formula reduces to the simpler form:

$$P = \frac{D}{K - g}$$

In practice, this is the form ordinarily used in analysis, since companies are presumed to continue to operate as going concerns, rather than to liquidate at some arbitrary future date.

Figures projected from the financial statements of the fictitious Wolfe Food Company (Exhibit 14.1) illustrate the application of the dividend-discount model. Observe that the company is expected to pay out $33\frac{1}{3}$ percent of its earnings to shareholders in the current year:

$$\text{Dividend payout ratio} = \frac{\text{Dividends to common shareholders}}{\text{Net income available to common shareholders}}$$

$$= \frac{\$15,000,000}{\$45,000,000}$$

$$= 33\frac{1}{3}\%$$

If Wolfe maintains a constant dividend **payout ratio**, it follows that the growth rate of dividends will equal the growth rate of earnings, which is

EXHIBIT 14.1   Selected Financial Data for Wolfe Food Company

Net income available to common shareholders	$45,000,000
Dividends to common shareholders	$15,000,000
Common shares outstanding	10,000,000
Expected annual growth in earnings	6%
Investors' required rate of return, given predictability of Wolfe's earnings	9%

expected to be 10 percent annually. On a per share basis, the initial dividend comes to $1.50:

$$\text{Dividend rate} = \frac{\text{Dividends to common shareholders}}{\text{Common shares outstanding}}$$

$$= \frac{15,000,000}{10,000,000}$$

$$= \$1.50 \text{ per share}$$

With these numbers, the analyst can now use the valuation formula to derive a share price of $50 for Wolfe:

$$P = \frac{D}{K - g}$$

$$P = \frac{\$1.50}{.09 - .06}$$

$$P = \frac{\$1.50}{.03}$$

$$P = \$50$$

The execution of this model rests heavily on the assumptions underlying the company's projected financial statements. To estimate the future growth rate of earnings, the analyst must make informed judgments both about the growth of the company's markets and about the company's ability to maintain or increase its share of those markets. Furthermore, the company's earnings growth rate may diverge from its sales growth due to changes in its operating margins that may or may not reflect industrywide trends.

Because of the uncertainties affecting such projections, the analyst should apply to equity valuation the same sort of sensitivity analysis discussed in connection with financial forecasting (see Chapter 12). For instance, if Wolfe Foods ultimately falls short of the 6 percent growth rate previously projected by one percentage point, then the $50 valuation will prove in retrospect to have been $12.50 too high:

$$P = \frac{D}{K - g}$$

$$P = \frac{\$1.50}{.09 - .05}$$

$$P = \$37.50$$

Therefore, an analyst whose forecast of earnings growth has a margin of error of one percentage point should not put a strong buy recommendation on Wolfe when it is trading at $45 a share. By the same token, a price of $25, which implies a 3 percent growth rate, can safely be regarded as an undervaluation, provided the other assumptions are valid.

Earnings or Cash Flow?

Intuitively appealing though it may be, relating share price to future dividends through projected earnings growth does not jibe perfectly with reality. In particular, highly cyclical companies do not produce steady earnings increases year in and year out, yet the formula $P = D/K - g$ demands a constant rate of growth. If, as assumed previously, the company's dividend payout ratio remains constant, the pattern of its dividends will plainly fail to fit neatly into the formula.

What saves the dividend discount method from irrelevance is that companies generally do not strive for a constant dividend payout ratio at all costs. More typically, they attempt to avoid cutting the amount of the payout, notwithstanding declines in earnings. For example, a company that aims to pay out 25 percent of its earnings over a complete business cycle might record a payout ratio of 15 percent in a peak year and 90 percent or 100 percent in a trough year. Indeed, a company that records net losses may maintain its dividend at the established level, at least for a few years, resulting in a meaningless payout ratio calculation. (If losses persist, financial prudence will usually dictate cutting or eliminating the dividend to conserve cash.) As a rule, a cyclical company will not increase its dividend on a regular, annual basis. Nevertheless, the board will ordinarily endeavor to raise the payout over the longer term. In all of these cases, the $P = D/K - g$ formula will work reasonably well as a valuation tool, with the irregular pattern of dividend increases recognized through adjustments to the discount rate (K).

Although the dividend discount model can accommodate earnings' cyclicality, the analyst must pay close attention to the method by which a company finances the continuation of its dividend at the established rate. A chronically money-losing company that borrows to pay dividends is simply undergoing slow liquidation. (It is replacing its equity, ultimately 100 percent of it, with liabilities.) In such circumstances, the key assumption that dividends will continue for an infinite number of periods becomes unsustainable.

On the other hand, a cyclical company may sustain losses at the bottom of a business cycle but never reach the point at which its funds from operations, net of capital expenditures required to maintain long-term competitiveness, fail to cover the dividend. Maintaining the dividend under these circumstances poses no financial threat. Accordingly, many analysts argue that cash flow, rather than earnings, is the true determinant of dividend-paying capability. By extension, they contend that projected cash flow, rather than earnings-per-share forecasts, should be the main focus of equity analysis.

Certainly, analysts need to be acutely conscious of changes in a company's cash-generating capability that are not paralleled by changes in earnings. For example, a company may for a time maintain a given level of profitability even though its business is becoming more capital intensive. Rising plant and equipment requirements might transform the company from a self-financing entity into one that is dependent on external financing. Return on equity (ROE) will not reflect the change until, after several years, either the resulting escalation in borrowing costs or the increase in the equity base required to support a given level of operating earnings becomes material. Furthermore, as detailed in Chapters 6 and 7, reported earnings are subject to considerable manipulation. In fact, that is the flaw that helped to popularize the use of cash flow analysis in the first place. Cash generated from operations, which is generally more difficult for companies to manipulate than earnings, can legitimately be viewed as the preferred measure of future dividend-paying capability.

Notwithstanding these arguments, earnings per share forecasts remain the main focus of equity research on Wall Street and elsewhere. EBITDA, which first became popular in the analysis of speculative-grade debt and leveraged buyouts, has gained some traction in conventional equity analysis. For many companies, however, the components of EBITDA other than net income, especially depreciation, are highly predictable over the near term. By accurately forecasting the more variable component, earnings, an investor can get a fairly good handle on EBITDA as well. To some extent, too, the unflagging focus on earnings probably reflects institutional inertia. Portfolio managers measure the accuracy of brokerage houses' equity analysis in terms of earnings per share (EPS) forecasts, and investment strategists rely on aggregate earnings per share forecasts to gauge the attractiveness of the stock market as a whole. Analysts who lack an EPS forecast simply have a hard time getting into the discussion. Despite the entrenched position of earnings forecasts, however, a mechanism is available for adjusting a stock evaluation when the quality of the forecasted earnings is questionable. Investors can reduce the earnings multiple, as explained in the following section.

THE PRICE-EARNINGS RATIO

Although the dividend discount model is an intuitively satisfying approach to valuing a common stock, it is not the most convenient method of comparing one stock's value with another's. Better suited to that task is the price-earnings ratio, alternately known as the P/E ratio or earnings multiple:

$$\text{Price} - \text{earnings ratio} = \frac{\text{Stock price}}{\text{Earnings per share}}$$

Based on this formula, Wolfe Food Company (see preceding section) has a price-earnings ratio of:

$$\text{Stock price} = \$50$$

$$\text{Net income available to common shareholders} = \$45,000,000$$

$$\text{Common shares} = 10,000,000$$

$$\text{Earnings per share} = \frac{\$45,000,000}{10,000,000}$$

$$= \$4.50$$

$$\text{Price} - \text{earnings ratio} = \frac{\$50}{\$4.50}$$

$$= 11.1X$$

To understand how the price-earnings ratio may be used to compare companies with one another, consider a competitor of Wolfe Food Company, Grubb & Chao (Exhibit 14.2). Grubb & Chao has the same expected earnings growth rate as Wolfe (6 percent) and is assigned the same required rate of return (9 percent). Its price-earnings ratio, however, is higher than Wolfe's (13.5X vs. 11.1X):

$$\text{Price} - \text{earnings ratio} = \frac{\text{Stock price}}{\text{Earnings per share}}$$

$$= \frac{\$48.75}{\left(\dfrac{\$54,000,000}{15,000,000}\right)}$$

$$= \frac{\$48.75}{\$3.60}$$

$$= 13.5X$$

EXHIBIT 14.2 Selected Financial Data for Grubb & Chao

Net income available to common shareholders	$54,000,000
Dividends to common shareholders	$18,000,000
Common shares outstanding	15,000,000
Expected annual growth in earnings	9%
Investors' required rate of return, given predictability of company's earnings	6%
Current stock price	$ 48.75

Based on the information provided, an investor would regard Wolfe as a better value than Grubb & Chao. This conclusion proceeds from applying the dividend discount model to the latter's numbers:

$$P = \frac{D}{K - g}$$

$$P = \frac{\left(\dfrac{\$18,000,000}{15,000,000}\right)}{.09 - .06}$$

$$P = \frac{\$1.20}{.03}$$

$$P = \$40$$

The price thus derived is lower than the actual price of $48.75, implying an overvaluation by the market. Observe as well that the correct price for Grubb & Chao produces the same price-earnings ratio as calculated for Wolfe Food Company:

$$\text{Price} - \text{earnings ratio} = \frac{\$40}{\$3.60}$$

$$= 11.1X$$

The P/E-based value comparisons can go well beyond this sort of company-to-company matchup. The analyst can rank all the companies within an industry (Exhibit 14.3), then judge whether the variations in price-earnings ratios appear justified, or whether certain companies seem out of line. Note that the table ranks companies on the basis of actual earnings over the preceding four quarters, rather than estimated earnings for the coming year, another typical format employed in P/E ratio comparisons. Earnings exclude extraordinary items (see Chapter 3). Earnings per share are

EXHIBIT 14.3 Companies within an Industry
Ranked by Price-Earnings Ratio: Cosmetics and
Personal Care Industry—November 2010

Company	Share Price Divided by Trailing Earnings per Share
Estee Lauder	23.43
Alberto-Culver	23.04
Inter Parfums	21.76
Elizabeth Arden	21.11
Procter & Gamble	17.52
Colgate-Palmolive	16.33
Avon Products	15.67
Revlon	9.63

Source: Bloomberg.

customarily calculated on a diluted basis by taking into account the possibility that new shares will be created through conversion of outstanding **convertible** securities.

WHY P/E MULTIPLES VARY

Justifications for differences in earnings multiples derive from the variables of the preceding valuation formulas. Consider the following two equations:

$$P = \frac{D}{K - g} \text{ and } P/E = \frac{P}{EPS}$$

where
P = Current stock price
D = Current dividend rate
K = Required rate of return
g = Growth rate
P/E = Price-earnings ratio
EPS = Current earnings per share (annual)

Substituting $D/K - g$, which equals P, for the P in the other equation, produces the following expanded form:

$$P/E = \frac{\left(\dfrac{D}{(K - g)}\right)}{EPS}$$

Using this expanded equation permits the analyst to see quickly that an increase in the expected growth rate of earnings produces a premium multiple. For example, both Wolfe Food Company and Grubb & Chao have 0.06 percent growth factors, and both stocks currently trade at 11.1 times earnings. Suppose another competitor, Eatmore & Co., can be expected to enjoy 7 percent growth, by virtue of concentration in faster-growing segments of the food business. A substantially higher multiple results from this modest edge in earnings growth:

$$P/E = \frac{\left(\dfrac{D}{(K-g)}\right)}{EPS}$$

$$P/E = \frac{\left(\dfrac{\$1.60}{(.09-.07)}\right)}{\$4.80}$$

$$P/E = 16.7X$$

Eatmore & Co.'s earnings will not, however, command as big a premium (16.7X vs. 1.1X for its competitors) if the basis for its higher projected growth is subject to unusually high risks. For example, Eatmore's strategy may emphasize expansion in developing countries, where the rate of growth in personal income is higher than in the more mature economy of the United States. If so, Eatmore may be considerably more exposed than Wolfe or Grubb & Chao to the risks of nationalization, new restrictions on repatriation of earnings, protectionist trade policies, and adverse fluctuations in exchange rates. If so, the market will raise its discount rate (K) on Eatmore's earnings. An increase of just half a percentage point (from 9.0 percent to 9.5 percent) wipes out more than half the premium in Eatmore's multiple, dropping it from 16.7X to 13.3X:

$$P/E = \frac{\left(\dfrac{D}{(K-g)}\right)}{EPS}$$

$$P/E = \frac{\left(\dfrac{\$1.60}{(.095-.07)}\right)}{\$4.80}$$

$$P/E = 13.33X$$

In effect, the ability to vary the discount rate, and therefore assign a lower or higher multiple to a company's earnings, is the equity analyst's defense against the sort of earnings manipulation by management described in Chapter 3. A company may use liberal accounting practices and skimp on long-term investment spending, yet expect the resulting artificially inflated earnings per share to be valued at the same multiple as its competitor's more legitimately derived profits. Indeed, the heart of many management presentations to analysts is a table showing that the presenting company's multiple is low by comparison with its peers. Typically, the chief executive officer cites this table as proof that the company is undervalued. The natural corollary is that in time investors will become aware of the discrepancy and raise the multiple and therefore the price of shares owned by those who are astute enough to buy in at today's dirt-cheap level.

These stories are sometimes persuasive, yet one must wonder whether such discrepancies in earnings multiples are truly the result of inattention by analysts. In the case of a large-capitalization company, hundreds of Wall Street and institutional analysts probably are making the comparison on their own. If so, they are fully aware of the below-average multiple but consider it justified for one or more reasons, including the following:

- The company's earnings are more cyclical than those of its peer group.
- The company's earnings depend on a special tax break or other legislative or regulatory preference that could be rescinded as the political winds shift.
- The company has historically been prone to earnings surprises, which raise suspicions that the reported results reflect an exceptionally large amount of earnings management.
- Management has a reputation for erratic behavior (e.g., abrupt changes in strategy, ill-conceived acquisitions) that makes future results difficult to forecast.

Analysts may be mistaken in these perceptions and may genuinely be undervaluing the stock. The low multiple is a conscious judgment, however, not a function of neglect. Even a small-capitalization company, which can more credibly claim that its stock is underfollowed by Wall Street, may have the multiple it deserves, notwithstanding that its competitors sport higher P/E ratios. It is appropriate to assign an above-average discount factor to the earnings of a company that competes against larger, better-capitalized firms. A small company may also suffer the disadvantages of lack of depth in management and concentration of its production in one or two plants.

Recognizing that qualitative factors may depress their multiples, companies often respond in kind, arguing that their low valuations are based on misperceptions. For example, a company in a notoriously cyclical industry may argue that it is an exception to the general pattern of its peer group.

Thus, a manufacturer of automotive components may claim that its earnings are protected from fluctuations in new car sales by a heavy emphasis on selling replacement parts. Regardless of whether consumers are buying new cars, the reasoning goes, they must keep their existing vehicles in good repair. In fact, sales of replacement parts should rise if the existing fleet ages because fewer individuals buy new autos. Similarly, a building-materials manufacturer may claim to be cushioned against fluctuations in housing starts because of a strong emphasis in its product line on the remodeling and repair markets.

These arguments may contain a kernel of truth, but investors should not accept them on faith. Instead of latching on to the concept as a justification for immediately pronouncing the company's multiple too low, an analyst should independently establish whether an allegedly countercyclical business has in fact fit that description in past cycles. It is also important to determine whether the supposed source of earnings stability is truly large enough to offset a downturn of the magnitude that can realistically be expected in the other areas of the company's operations.

A good rule to remember is that a company can more easily create a new image than it can recast its operations. Analysts should be especially wary of companies that have tended to jump on the bandwagon of concepts associated with the hot stocks of the moment. During the late 1970s, skyrocketing oil prices led directly to higher expected earnings growth (g) and hence higher P/E multiples and stock prices for oil producers. Suddenly, chemical companies, capital-goods producers, and others began presenting themselves as energy plays. Some did so by acquiring oil properties, but others simply began publicizing their existing, albeit tangential, links to the oil business in markets that might conceivably have benefited from rising petroleum prices. A few years later, when oil prices collapsed, these same companies deleted from their annual reports the glowing references and photographs playing up their energy-relatedness. Around the same time, as the economic boom ended in Houston and other cities that had benefited from surging oil prices, national retailing chains became less vocal about their concentration in the Sunbelt, which had for several years been synonymous with high growth and therefore high P/E ratios.

Normalizing Earnings

Companies have strong incentives to obtain incremental increases in their earnings multiples, even at the cost of stretching the facts to the breaking point (or beyond). Accordingly, it is prudent to maintain a conservative bias in calculating appropriate multiples. In addition to upping the discount rate (K) when any question arises about the quality of earnings, the analyst should normalize the earnings per share trend when its sustainability is doubtful.

EXHIBIT 14.4 PPE Manufacturing
Corporation Earnings History Table

Year	Earnings per Share
2006	$1.52
2007	1.63
2008	1.86
2009	2.04
2010	2.67 (Estimated)

Suppose, for example, that the fictitious PPE Manufacturing Corporation's earnings per share over the past five years are as shown in Exhibit 14.4. Customarily, PPE has commanded a multiple in line with the overall market, which is at present trading at 12 times estimated current-year earnings. By this logic, a price of 12 times $2.67, or approximately 32, seems warranted for PPE stock.

Exhibit 14.5 shows, however, that the current-year earnings estimate is well above PPE's historical trend line, making the sustainability of the

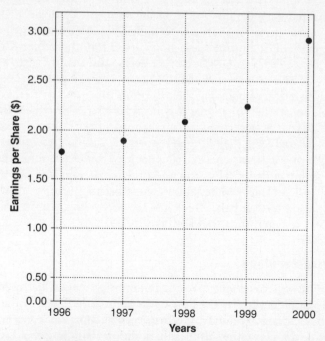

EXHIBIT 14.5 PPE Manufacturing Corporation Earnings History Graph

current level somewhat suspect. As it turns out, the $2.67 estimate is bloated by special conditions that will probably not recur in the near future. Specifically, the customers for PPE's major product are stepping up their purchases in anticipation of an industrywide strike later in the year. A temporary shortage has resulted, causing buyers to raise their bids. With its plants running flat out (reducing unit costs to the minimum) and its price realizations climbing, PPE is enjoying profit margins that it has never achieved before—and probably never will again.

It hardly seems appropriate to boost PPE's valuation from $24\frac{1}{2}$ (12 times last year's earnings per share) to 32, a 31 percent increase, solely on the basis of an EPS hiccup that reflects no change in PPE's long-term earnings power. Accordingly, the analyst should normalize PPE's earnings by projecting the trend line established in preceding years. Exhibit 14.6 shows such a projection, using the least-squares method. The formula for this method is as follows

$$y = a + m(x - \bar{x})$$

$$a = \bar{y}$$

$$m = \frac{\Sigma xy - n\overline{xy}}{\Sigma x^2 - n\bar{x}^2}$$

$$\bar{x} = \frac{0 + 1 + 2 + 3}{4} = 1.5$$

$$\bar{y} = \frac{1.52 + 1.63 + 1.86 + 2.04}{4} = 1.7625$$

$$\Sigma xy = (0 \times 1.52) + (1 \times 1.63) + (2 \times 1.86) + (3 \times 2.04) = 11.47$$

$$n\overline{xy} = 4 \times 1.5 \times 1.7625 = 10.575$$

$$\Sigma x^2 = 0^2 + 1^2 + 2^2 + 3^2 = 14$$

$$n\bar{x}^2 = (4) \times (1.5)^2 = 9$$

$$m = \frac{11.47 - 10.575}{14 - 9} = 0.179$$

$$y = 1.7625 + 0.79(x - 1.5)$$

Solving for $x = 4$, we derive a current-year trend-line value of $2.21. Applying the market multiple of 12 produces an indicated stock price of $26\frac{1}{2}$. Some modest upward revision from this point may be warranted, for if nothing else, the company can reinvest its windfall profit in its business and generate a small, incremental earnings stream. By no means, though,

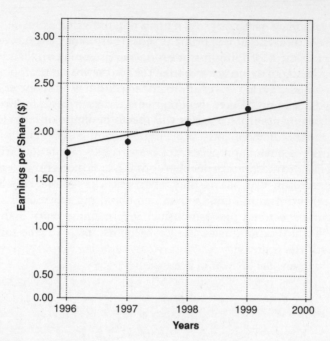

EXHIBIT 14.6   PPE Manufacturing Corporation Earnings Trend—Least-Squares
Method

should the company be evaluated on the basis of an earnings level that is
not sustainable.

Sustainable Growth Rate

Sustainability is an issue not only in connection with unusual surges in earnings but also when it comes to determining whether a company's historical
rate of growth in earnings per share is likely to continue. The answer is
probably no if the growth has been fueled by anything other than additions
to retained earnings per share.

Consider the following derivation of earnings per share:

$$\frac{\text{Asset}}{\text{turnover}} \times \frac{\text{Return on}}{\text{sales}} \times \text{Leverage} \times \frac{\text{Book value}}{\text{per share}} = \text{Earnings per share}$$

Or:

$$\frac{\text{Sales}}{\text{Assets}} \times \frac{\text{Net income}}{\text{Sales}} \times \frac{\text{Assets}}{\text{Net worth}} \times \frac{\text{Net worth}}{\text{Shares outstanding}} = \frac{\text{Net income}}{\text{Shares outstanding}}$$

Earnings per share will not grow merely because sales increase. Any such increase will be canceled out in the preceding formula, since sales appears in the denominator of return on sales as well as in the numerator of asset turnover. Only by an increase in one of the four terms on the left side of the equation, or by a reduction in the number of shares outstanding, will the product (earnings per share) rise. Aggressive management may boost asset turnover, but eventually the assets will reach the limits of their productive capacity. Return on sales, likewise, cannot expand indefinitely because too-fat margins will invite competition. Leverage also reaches a limit because lenders will not continue advancing funds beyond a certain point as financial risk increases. This leaves only book value per share, which can rise unceasingly through additions to retained earnings, as a source of sustainable growth in earnings per share. As long as the amount of equity capital invested per share continues to rise, more income can be earned on that equity, and (as the reader can demonstrate by working through the preceding formula) earnings per share can increase.

A company's book value per share will not rise at all, however, if it distributes 100 percent of its earnings in dividends to shareholders. (This, by the way, is why an immediate increase in the dividend-payout ratio will not ordinarily cause a direct, proportionate rise in the stock price, as might appear to be the implication of the equation $P = D/K - g$.) Assuming the company can earn its customary return on equity on whatever profits it reinvests internally, raising its dividend-payout ratio reduces its growth in earnings per share (g). Such a move proves to be self-defeating, as both the numerator and the denominator (D and $K - g$, respectively) rise and P remains unchanged.

To achieve sustainable growth in earnings per share, then, a company must retain a portion of its earnings. The higher the portion retained, the more book value is accumulated per share and the higher can be the EPS growth rate. By this reasoning, the following formula is derived:

Sustainable growth rate = (Return on equity) × (Income reinvestment rate)

where Income reinvestment rate = 1 − Dividend payout ratio

As mentioned, the one remaining way to increase earnings per share, after exhausting the possibilities already discussed, is to reduce the number of shares outstanding. During the 1990s, a number of companies used stock buybacks to maintain EPS growth in the face of constrained opportunities for revenue growth. Between 1995 and 1999, International Business Machines spent $34.1 billion to repurchase shares, more than its cumulative net income for the period of $31.3 billion. By reducing its shareholders' equity through stock purchases, IBM increased its **leverage** and, therefore, its financial risk. Moreover, the company intensified this effect by adding to its debt. Financial commentator James Grant quipped that if IBM continued to buy in shares, it would undergo a slow-motion leveraged buyout.[2] Such EPS-boosting plans tend to be self-limiting, for as already noted, lenders refuse at some point to countenance increased indebtedness.

Analysts should note one subtlety in calculating the impact of stock repurchases on earnings per share. To the extent that the company funds the buybacks with idle cash, the increase in EPS is offset by a reduction arising from forgone income on investments. If a company has far more cash on its balance sheet than it can employ profitably in its operations, it is unfair to accuse management of deceitfully inflating its per share income by buying in stock.

THE DU PONT FORMULA

The preceding discussion of sustainable growth introduced a formula that provided insight into earnings per share by disaggregating it into several simple financial ratios. Disaggregation can be applied in other beneficial ways in equity analysis, most notably in a technique known as the Du Pont Formula. (The idea is generally credited to Donaldson Brown, who developed the formula while at E. I. du Pont de Nemours, then applied it during the 1920s as vice president of finance at General Motors.) With the aid of the Du Pont Formula, the analyst can more readily perceive the sources of a firm's return on assets:

$$\text{Asset turnover} \times \text{Return on sales} = \text{Return on assets}$$

$$\frac{\text{Sales}}{\text{Assets}} \times \frac{\text{Income}}{\text{Sales}} = \frac{\text{Income}}{\text{Assets}}$$

This analysis can be expanded to ascertain the contribution of financial leverage to return on equity:

$$\text{Asset turnover} \times \text{Return on sales} \times \text{Financial Leverage} = \text{Return on Equity}$$

$$\frac{\text{Sales}}{\text{Assets}} \times \frac{\text{Income}}{\text{Sales}} \times \frac{\text{Assets}}{\text{Equity}} = \frac{\text{Income}}{\text{Equity}}$$

Note that "financial leverage" is not directly defined as a ratio of debt to assets or equity, as in most other contexts. Rather, it is the ratio of assets to equity. By definition, the excess of assets over equity consists of liabilities, not limited to debt. Conceptually, this version of financial leverage indicates how large an asset base is supported by the company's equity.

Like most ratio analysis, the Du Pont Formula is valuable not only for the questions it answers but also for the new ones it raises. If a company increases its return on assets by finding ways to reduce working capital without impairing competitiveness (thereby improving asset turnover), then it is likely to be able to perform at the higher level. On the other hand, cutting back on necessary capital expenditures will also have a positive effect—in the short run—on return on assets. Not only will the denominator decline in the asset turnover factor as a result of depreciation but also return on sales will rise as future depreciation charges are reduced by lower capital outlays in the current year. Underspending will eventually hurt competitiveness, and therefore the company's long-run return on assets, so analysts must probe to determine the true nature of shifts in these ratios.

A Du Pont analysis of the food processing industry (Exhibit 14.7) confirms the value of examining the components of return on equity. Based on ROE alone, for example, Dean Foods (17.77 percent) and Hormel Foods (16.86 percent) appear similar. They achieved those numbers by very different methods, however. Dean Foods turned over its assets less frequently (1.42 times versus 1.76 times) and earned a lower margin on sales (2.15 percent versus 5.67 percent), resulting in a return on assets less than one-third as high (3.06 percent versus 9.99 percent). The higher return on equity for Dean Foods is purely a consequence of using more than three times as much leverage (5.80 times versus 1.69 times). Investors in Dean Foods stock should expect to experience volatility as a function of the company's comparatively high financial risk. Its bond ratings at the point of this analysis are in the low Double-B category versus the medium Single-A category for Hormel Foods.

Also noteworthy in Exhibit 14.7 is the negative financial leverage of Mead Johnson Nutrition Company. The manufacturer of infant formulas has net worth of −$674.9 million. This does not indicate that the company is bankrupt. In fact, Mead Johnson boasts the group's highest return on sales and has investment grade ratings (medium to high Triple-B). For this company, the DuPont analysis is meaningful only up to the point of return on assets, as Mead Johnson's positive net income divided by its negative equity produces a negative figure, implying that the profitable company has a negative return on equity.

The Mead Johnson Nutrition case is just an extreme case of a phenomenon observed with several companies in Exhibit 14.7. They have low, although not negative, equity balances, resulting in spectacularly higher returns on equity, for example, Campbell Soup (78.79 percent) and Hershey (60.51 percent). In part, those results reflect the two companies' employment

EXHIBIT 14.7 Du Pont Analysis of Food Processing Industry's 2009 Results*

Company Name	Asset Turnover (X)	x	Return on Sales (%)	=	Return on Assets (%)	x	Financial Leverage (X)	=	Return on Equity
Campbell Soup Co. (NYSE:CPB)	1.23		10.65%		13.10%		6.01		78.79%
ConAgra Foods, Inc. (NYSE:CAG)	1.05		6.35%		6.69%		2.32		15.52%
Dean Foods Co. (NYSE:DF)	1.42		2.15%		3.06%		5.80		17.77%
General Mills Inc. (NYSE:GIS)	0.79		11.08%		8.80%		3.05		26.83%
Hershey Co. (NYSE:HSY)	1.44		8.23%		11.86%		5.10		60.51%
HJ Heinz Co. (NYSE:HNZ)	1.02		8.26%		8.42%		5.52		46.48%
Hormel Foods Corp. (NYSE:HRL)	1.76		5.67%		9.99%		1.69		16.86%
Kellogg Company (NYSE:K)	1.12		9.64%		10.82%		4.93		53.35%
Kraft Foods Inc. (NYSE:KFT)	0.61		7.48%		4.53%		2.58		11.67%
McCormick & Co. Inc. (NYSE:MKC)	0.94		9.39%		8.85%		2.54		22.46%
Mead Johnson Nutrition Company (NYSE:MJN)	1.37		14.14%		19.30%		(3.07)		NM
Sara Lee Corp. (NYSE:SLE)	1.28		6.36%		8.12%		3.61		29.28%
The J. M. Smucker Company (NYSE:SJM)	0.58		10.16%		5.92%		1.51		8.93%
Tyson Foods Inc. (NYSE:TSN)	2.47		(1.03)%		(2.53)%		2.39		(6.05)%

*Calculations are subject to rounding error
NM = Not meaningful
Source: Capital IQ and author calculations.

of the comparatively high financial leverage within the industry. In addition, though, the outlandishly high ROEs result from the companies' very low levels of book value. Producers of branded food products typically derive their equity value primarily from consumer acceptance of their well-known brands, rather than the physical plants in which they produce their goods. Under generally accepted accounting principles (GAAP), the costs of these companies' product development and advertising, which create enduring value just as a factory or an oil well does, is expensed rather than capitalized. Unlike the accounting system, the financial markets recognize the economic value of brand names. Exhibit 14.8 shows that Campbell Soup's book value is a mere one-twelfth of its market value. The median company's market value is 3.44 times book value, underscoring how little attention investors pay to accounting-based net worth.

Branded food and consumer goods producers are not the only ones with value based largely on intellectual capital. Like those companies'

EXHIBIT 14.8 Market Value to Book Value Ratios of Packaged Foods and Meats Industry

Company Name	Market Value*	Book Value**	Ratio
Campbell Soup Co.	11,118.7	926.0	12.01
ConAgra Foods, Inc.	9,478.7	4,923.9	1.93
Dean Foods Co.	3,028.7	1,351.9	2.24
General Mills Inc.	21,675.3	5,402.9	4.01
Hershey Co.	8,546.0	720.5	11.86
HJ Heinz Co.	12,922.7	1,891.3	6.83
Hormel Foods Corp.	5,039.6	2,123.5	2.37
Kellogg Company	19,805.9	2,272.0	8.72
Kraft Foods Inc.	39,522.9	25,876.0	1.53
McCormick & Co. Inc.	4,587.0	1,334.6	3.44
Mead Johnson Nutrition Company	8,998.0	(674.9)	NM
Sara Lee Corp.	8,151.5	1,487.0	5.48
The J. M. Smucker Company	6,266.2	5,326.3	1.18
Tyson Foods Inc.	4,851.2	4,352.0	1.11
Average			4.48

*Latest one-year
**Latest annual
All data extracted November 2010
NM = Not meaningful
Source: Capital IQ and author calculations.

expenditures aimed at building the economic value of their brands, the research and development outlays of technology and pharmaceutical companies are written off as incurred and consequently are assigned no asset value under GAAP. For these exemplars of the postindustrial economy, return on equity looks less stratospheric when equity is viewed in terms of market capitalization rather than historical cost (see "Pros and Cons of a Market-Based Equity Figure" in Chapter 2).

VALUATION THROUGH RESTRUCTURING POTENTIAL

A subtler benefit of the Du Pont analysis is the insight it can provide into companies' potential for enhancing value through corporate restructuring. Whether initiated internally or imposed from outside, major revisions in operating and financial strategies can dramatically increase the price of a corporation's common shares. The analysis illustrated in Exhibit 14.7 helps to identify the type of restructuring that can unlock hidden value in a particular instance. Some companies have the potential to raise their share prices by utilizing their assets more efficiently, whereas others can increase their value by increasing their financial leverage.[3]

By way of background, corporate managers frequently find themselves at odds with stock market investors and speculators over issues of corporate policy. In general, managers prefer to maintain a certain amount of slack in their organizations, that is, a reserve capacity to deal with crises and opportunities. They tend to be less troubled than investors if their companies generate excess cash that remains on the balance sheet earning the modest returns available on low-risk, short-dated financial instruments. That cash may come in handy, they argue, if earnings and cash flow unexpectedly turn down or if an outstanding acquisition opportunity suddenly presents itself. Investors and speculators, in contrast, prefer to see the cash used to repurchase stock or returned to shareholders. Managers also tend to be more inclined than shareholders to believe that underperforming units can be rehabilitated. Their judgment is sometimes influenced by reluctance to admit that acquisitions in which they had a hand have worked out poorly.

Over the years, management-shareholder disputes over such operating- and financial-policy issues have featured a variety of tactics. As far back as 1927 and 1928, pioneer securities analyst Benjamin Graham waged a successful campaign to persuade the management of Northern Pipeline to liquidate certain assets that were not essential to the company's crude oil transportation business and distribute the proceeds to shareholders. Graham enlisted pivotal support for his effort from a major institutional holder, the

Rockefeller Foundation. The outcome was unusual, as institutional investors generally sided with management, both at the time and for many years afterward. At most, institutions sold their shares if they became thoroughly dissatisfied with the way a company was being run. Trying to bring about change was not a widespread institutional practice, even in the 1980s. Therefore, management's main adversaries in battles over corporate governance were aggressive financial operators. During the 1950s, these swashbucklers attracted considerable attention by pushing for strategic redirection through proxy battles. Their modus operandi consisted of striving to obtain majority control of the board through the election of directors at the annual meeting of shareholders.

The 1970s brought the tactical shift to hostile takeovers, a type of transaction previously regarded as unsavory by the investment banks that acted as intermediaries in mergers and acquisitions. Hostile takeovers became especially prominent in the 1980s, fueled in part by the greatly increased availability of high-yield debt (informally referred to as *junk bond*) financing. High-yield bonds also financed scores of leveraged buyouts (LBOs), whose sponsors defended these controversial transactions in part by arguing that corporations could improve their long-run performance if they were taken private and thereby shielded from the public market's insatiable demand for short-run profit increases.

In the 1990s, institutional investors finally began to understand the influence they could wield in corporate boardrooms by virtue of their vast share holdings. Large institutional shareholders began to prod corporations to increase their share prices by such measures as streamlining operations, divesting unprofitable units, and using excess cash to repurchase shares. In some instances, where merely making their collective voice heard had no discernible effect, the institutions precipitated the ouster of senior management.

The shareholder activism of the 1990s flourished in an environment of comparatively high price-earnings ratios. Additionally, the period was characterized by a backlash against the previous decade's trend toward increased financial leverage. Conditions were not conducive to the sort of borrow-and-acquire transactions that drove much of the corporate restructurings of the 1980s.

Leveraged buyouts did not disappear, however. After the early-1990s wave of LBO bankruptcies, the buyout firms resumed their deal making. Under the banner of private equity, the LBO shops gained new prominence in the 2000s. It seemed clear that this category of alternative investments (those outside the traditional categories of public equities, bonds, and cash) had become a standard feature of the financial markets. A recurring boom-and-bust cycle in LBOs also appeared to have gotten ingrained into the investment landscape.

The prototypical leveraged buyout consists of gaining control of a company by buying its stock at a depressed price, then adding a large amount of debt to the capital structure. In the initial stage of the cycle, opportunities of this sort are abundant, because institutional investors are recovering from the previous bust. Absent the pressure of too many dollars chasing too few deals, it is feasible to extract value without creating undue bankruptcy risk, simply by increasing the ratio of debt to equity. The private equity firms emphasize the second factor in the modified Du Pont Formula—financial leverage.

In assessing a company's potential as a leveraged buyout candidate, private equity firms do not focus on traditional equity valuation techniques. Consider the fictitious Sitting Duck Corporation (Exhibit 14.9). Under conventional assumptions, and given a prevailing earnings multiple of 15 on similar companies, Sitting Duck's equity will be valued at $975 million, about 2.4 times its book value of $413 million.

Leveraged buyout sponsors, however, would approach the valuation much differently. Their focus would not be on earnings, but on cash flow.

EXHIBIT 14.9   Sitting Duck Corporation

Year Ended December 31, 2010
($000,000 omitted)

Balance Sheet		Statement of Cash Flows	
Current assets	$ 594	Net income	$ 65
Property, plant, and		Depreciation	38
equipment	406	Cash generated by operations	103
Total assets	$1,000	Dividends	22
Current liabilities	$ 350	Capital expenditures	41
Long-term debt	237	Increase in working capital	10
Shareholders' equity	413	Cash used in operations	73
Total liabilities and equity	$1,000	Net cash available	30
		Reduction of long-term debt	25
Income Statement		Increase in cash and equivalents	$ 5
Sales	$1,253		
Cost of goods sold	972		
Selling, general, and			
administrative expense	95		
Operating income	186		
Interest expense	19		
Pretax income	167		
Income taxes	102		
Net income	$ 65		

After paying out approximately one-third of its earnings in dividends and more than offsetting depreciation through new expenditures for plant and equipment, Sitting Duck generated $30 million of cash in 2010. The incumbent management group used this cash to reduce an already conservative (36 percent) total-debt-to-total-capital ratio and to add to the company's existing portfolio of marketable securities. To a buyout specialist, a more appropriate use would be to finance a premium bid for the company.

The arithmetic goes as follows: Assume lenders and bond buyers are currently willing to finance sound leveraged buyout projects that can demonstrate EBITDA coverage of 2.5 times. (The debt providers do not care about the company's book profits, but rather about its ability to repay debt. Cash generation is a key determinant of that ability.) Sitting Duck's operating income of $186 million, with $38 million of depreciation added back, produces EBITDA of $224 million. The amount of interest that $224 million can cover by 2.5 times is $90 million, an increase of $71 million over Sitting Duck's present interest expense. Assuming a blended borrowing cost of 10 percent on the LBO financing, a raider can add $710 million of debt to the existing $237 million, for a total of $947 million. If prevailing lending standards require equity of at least 25 percent in the transaction, the raider must put up an additional $320 million, for a total capitalization of $1.267 billion. By this arithmetic, the takeover artist can pay a premium of 30 percent ($1.267 billion ÷ $975 million = 1.30) over Sitting Duck's present market capitalization. The purchase price equates to a multiple of 19.5 times earnings, rather than the 15X figure currently assigned by the market. The LBO sponsor got to this number, however, through a measure of cash flow, rather than earnings. The EBITDA multiple of the bid is 5.7 times, not an astronomical level by the standards of LBO specialists. (As explained in Chapter 8, EBITDA is by no means the *best* measure of cash flow, but it can be fairly described as the standard in leveraged finance circles.)

Stepping back from these calculations, one is bound to wonder whether the LBO sponsor can truly expect to earn a high return on investment after paying 30 percent above the prevailing price for Sitting Duck's shares. Many such transactions do prove highly profitable, with the new owners eventually exiting through sale of the company or an **initial public offering**, that is, returning the company to the public market. In some cases, the buyout sponsor takes out substantial dividends before exiting, adding to its profits. Although private equity firms downplay the role of timing in their success, buying companies when equity market valuations are low and selling when they are high is a winning formula. The only problem is that peaks in LBO activity—and EBITDA multiples—tend to be followed by recessions and bear markets in stocks. Late-cycle deals consequently become plagued by depressed earnings, making it difficult to cover the company's vastly increased interest charges at a time when exiting through an IPO is not feasible.

Rather than rely entirely on their ability to catch the highs and lows in the equity market, private equity firms try to enhance their probability of success by the following means:

1. *Profit Margin Improvement.* A leveraged buyout can bring about improved profitability for either of two reasons. First, a change in ownership results in a fresh look at the company's operations. The newcomers typically have less sentimental attachment to product lines that are long on tradition but are no longer profitable. In addition, they can more easily take the emotionally difficult but necessary steps to re-store competitiveness, such as reducing the work force and outsourcing production. Second, management may obtain a significantly enlarged stake in the firm's success as the result of a buyout. In lieu of stock op-tions that could leave them comfortably provided for in their retirement, senior and even middle-level executives may receive equity interests that can potentially make them immensely wealthy within a few years. The change in incentives can reduce managers' zeal for maintaining slack in their operations and cause them instead to squeeze every possible dollar of profit out of their company's assets. With an enhanced opportunity to participate in the benefits, managers may crack down on unnecessary costs that they formerly tolerated and pursue potential new markets more aggressively than in the past. Regardless of how it comes about, however, improvement in profit margins means higher EBITDA. That, in turn, leads to a higher valuation and generates a profit for the LBO's equity investors.

   As a caveat, analysts must watch out for improvements in reported profit margins that represent nothing more than reductions in invest-ment spending. Following an LBO, a company can report an immediate improvement in earnings by cutting back expenditures on advertising and research and development. Even though the accounting rules do not permit these items to be capitalized, the outlays provide benefits in future periods. Sharply reducing such outlays, or delaying capital expen-ditures to conserve cash, can impair a company's future competitiveness, making the increase in current-period earnings illusory. Today's profit improvement can be a precursor of tomorrow's bankruptcy by a com-pany that has economized its way to an uncompetitive state.

   Regrettably, the income statement may provide too little detail to determine whether specific kinds of investment spending have been curtailed. Analysts must therefore query industry sources for evidence regarding the adequacy of the company's investment spending. If the company's customers report a drop in the quality of service following a leveraged buyout, it may indicate that important sales support functions have been eviscerated. Earnings may rise in the short run but suffer soon as customers switch to other providers.

2. *Asset Sales.* As a function of the stock market's primary focus on earnings, a company's market capitalization may be far less than the aggregate value of its assets. For example, a subsidiary that contributes little to net income but generates substantial cash flow from depreciation has a potentially large value in the private market. In that realm, the unit would be priced on a multiple of EBITDA. Alternatively, a subsidiary might be unprofitable only because its scale is insufficient. A competitor might be willing to buy the unit and consolidate it with its own operations. The result would be higher combined earnings than the two operations were able to generate independently. An LBO sponsor who spies this sort of opportunity within a company may invest a small amount of equity and borrow the greater part of the purchase price, then liquidate the low-net-income operations to repay the borrowings. If carried out as planned, the asset sales will leave the acquirer debt-free and in possession of the remainder of the company, that is, the operations that previously contributed almost all of the net income. In the P/E-multiple-oriented stock market, that portion of the company will be worth as much as the entire company was previously. The LBO sponsor may then cash out by taking it public again. After all the dust has settled, the sponsor should have cleared more than enough to cover the premium paid to original shareholders who sold into the buyout.

Unrealized earnings potential and EBITDA multiples are by no means the only valuation factors that come into play in corporate governance controversies. Proponents of policy changes in pursuit of enhanced shareholder value sometimes focus on the values of specific assets identified in the financial statements. For example, oil companies disclose the size of their reserves in their annual reports. Because energy companies frequently buy and sell reserves, and because the prices of larger transactions are widely reported, current market valuations are always readily at hand. If recent sales of reserves in the ground have occurred at prices that equate to $18 a barrel, then a company with 50 million barrels of reserves could theoretically liquidate those assets for $900 million.[4] It may be that the sum of $900 million and a P/E-multiple-based price for the company's refining, marketing, and transportation assets substantially exceeds the company's current market capitalization. If so, the so-called unrecognized value of the oil reserves can be the basis of an alternative method of evaluating the company's stock.

Would-be corporate restructurers also seek unrecognized value in other types of minerals, real estate, and long-term investments unrelated to a company's core business. Methods of realizing the value of such an asset include:

- Selling the asset for cash.
- Placing it in a separate subsidiary, then taking a portion of the subsidiary public to establish a market value for the company's residual interest.
- Placing the asset in a master limited partnership, interests in which are distributed to shareholders.

The key message to take away from this overview of valuation via restructuring potential is that a focus on price-earnings multiples, the best-known form of fundamental analysis, is not the investor's sole alternative to relying on technicians' stock charts. There are in fact several approaches to fundamental analysis. A solid understanding of financial statements is essential to all of them, even though factors outside the financial statements also play a role in fundamental valuation.

CONCLUSION

As noted at the outset of this chapter, valuations derived from financial statements represent only a portion of the analyses being conducted by millions of stock buyers and sellers during each trading session. Indeed, the split-second decision making of traders on the exchange floors can scarcely be described as analysis of any kind. Rather, it amounts to a highly intuitive response to momentary shifts in the balance of supply and demand.

For the investor who takes a longer view, however, financial statement analysis provides an invaluable reference point for valuation. A stock may temporarily soar or plummet in frenzied reaction to a development of little ultimate consequence. Eventually, however, rationality usually reasserts itself. The share price then returns to a level that is justifiable on the basis of the company's long-range capacity to generate earnings and cash. Focusing on breakup values, as well as P/E and EBITDA multiples, is consistent with this thesis. Ultimately, the value of previously unrecognized assets likewise rests on their potential to generate cash, which must be measured in the context of previous performance. By studying the company's historical financial statements to forecast its future results, the analyst can derive an intrinsic value for a stock that is unaffected by the market's transitory mood.

Explanation of Pro Forma Adjustments for Hertz Global Holdings, Inc./DTG

Adjustments included in the column under the heading "Pro Forma Adjustments" represent the following:

a. To adjust amortization expense for the estimated amortization expense of customer relationship intangible assets acquired, with an estimated fair value of $105 million and an estimated useful life of ten years.

b. To adjust interest expense as follows:

	Year Ended December 31, 2009	Six Months Ended June 30, 2010
	(In thousands)	
Amortization of the fair value adjustment to debt	$ 24,840	$ 7,320
Elimination of interest expense due to the extinguishment of DTG's existing non-vehicle debt[i]	(9,405)	(4,111)
Elimination of amortization of deferred financing costs associated with extinguished debt	(3,392)	(726)
Interest expense on additional borrowings under Hertz's Senior ABL facility used to partially finance the merger[ii]	6,944	3,472
Total	$ 18,987	$ 5,955

[i] Includes the elimination of letter of credit and commitment fees relating to DTG's revolving credit facility.

[ii] Represents interest expense at an assumed current rate of 1.85% (June 30, 2010 LIBOR plus 150 basis points) net of assumed savings of 50 basis points on the drawn amount, as historical information includes a facility fee equal to 50 basis points on any available and undrawn amount. A change of one-eighth of 1% (12.5 basis points) in the interest rate associated with this variable rate borrowing would result in additional annual interest expense (if the interest rate increases) or a reduction to annual interest expense (if the interest rate decreases) of approximately $0.7 million.

c. To eliminate advisory, legal, regulatory and retention costs that are directly attributable to the pending merger but that are not expected to have a continuing impact on the combined entity's results, as follows:

	Year Ended December 31, 2009	Six Months Ended June 30, 2010
	(In thousands)	
Eliminate Hertz's advisory, legal and regulatory costs assumed to be non-recurring	$ 1,584	$ 10,774
Eliminate DTG's acquisition-related transaction and retention costs assumed to be non-recurring	—	8,521
Total	$ 1,584	$ 19,295

d. Certain adjustments have been made to the historical financial statements of DTG to conform to Hertz's presentation. For the pro forma condensed combined statements of operations, the increase in the fair value of derivatives, which DTG presents as a separate line item, has been reclassified to the "Selling, general and administrative" line item. For the pro forma condensed combined balance sheet, "Other intangible assets, net," presented by DTG represents capitalized software, and in order 10 conform to Hertz's presentation, $525,445,000 has been reclassified from "Other intangible assets, net" to "Property and equipment, net."

e. To record the impact on accrued income taxes in relation to pre-closing retention program and deferred compensation payments and the write-off of deferred financing costs.

Hertz has generally assumed a 39% tax rate when estimating the tax impacts of the merger, representing the statutory tax rate for Hertz. The effective tax rate of the combined company could be significantly different (either higher or lower) depending on post-merger activities, cash needs and the geographical location of businesses.

f. The unaudited pro forma condensed combined basic and diluted income (loss) per share calculations are based on the combined basic and diluted weighted average shares outstanding. The historical basic and diluted weighted average shares of DTG outstanding are assumed to be replaced by the shares expected to the issued by Hertz in connection with the merger. No dilution from common stock equivalents is reflected in these unaudited pro forma condensed combined financial statements, as such impact would be antidilutive.

g. To adjust cash and cash equivalents, as follows:

	(In thousands)
Extinguishment of DTG's non-vehicle debt prior to closing	$ (153,125)
Special Cash Dividend paid to DTG shareholders prior to closing (see Note 4(a))	(200,000)
Cash portion of merger consideration (see Note 3)	(1,071,933)
Retention payments paid by DTG prior to closing[i] (see Note 4(a))	(3,880)
Estimate of future merger-related transaction costs	(49,165)
Additional borrowings under Hertz's Senior ABL facility	515,000
Reclassification of DTG's cash and cash equivalents—required minimum balance[ii]	100,000
Total	$ (863,103)

[i]DTG has established a retention program with a pool of approximately $7,760,000 for DTG employees who are not executive officers, as to which DTG and Hertz have agreed that 50% of the approximately $7,760,000 charge is payable upon completion of the merger and 50% is payable upon completion of a six-month requisite service period following the merger. As such, Hertz will incur charges following the merger of approximately $3,880,000 in retation to the retention program.

[ii]DTG's cash and cash equivalents required minimum balance designation is no longer necessary upon extinguishment of DTG's non-vehicle debt prior to closing.

h. To adjust prepaid expenses and other assets, as follows:

	(In thousands)
Eliminate unamortized deferred financing fees associated with DTG's extinguished non-vehicle debt	$ (4,100)
Eliminate Rabbi trust plan (prefunding) associated with deferred compensation	(3,096)
Total	$ (7,196)

i. To record intangible assets acquired at an estimate of fair value of $550,000,000 (see Note 4(c)), and to reclassify DTG software of $25,445,000 into "Property and equipment" in order to conform with Hertz's presentation.

j. To record an estimate of acquisition date goodwill (see Note 4(g)).

k. To reflect the settlement of retention and deferred compensation expense in accordance with the amended merger agreement.

l. To eliminate DTG's non-vehicle debt, adjust DTG's remaining debt to an estimate of fair value, and incur additional borrowings under Hertz's Senior ABL facility as follows:

	(In thousands)
Eliminate DTG non-vehicle debt	$ (153,125)
Estimated fair value decrease to remaining debt assumed	(40,700)
Additional borrowings under Hertz's Senior ABL facility	515,000
Total	$ 321,175

m. To adjust deferred taxes on income associated with the estimated fair value adjustments of assets to be acquired and liabilities to be assumed, at 39% (see Note 4(f)), and to reverse deferred taxes of $1,867,000 associated with deferred compensation to be paid by DTG prior to closing.

n. To record the stock portion of the merger consideration, at par, and to eliminate DTG's common stock, at par, as follows:

	(In thousands)
Eliminate DTG common stock	$ (350)
Issuance of Hertz common stock[i]	183
Total	$ (167)

[i]Represents the issuance of approximately 18.3 million shares associated with exchange of DTG shares for Hertz shares at an exchange ratio of 0.6366 (see Note 3).

o. To record the stock portion of the merger consideration, at fair value less par, and to eliminate DTG's additional paid-in-capital, as follows:

	(In thousands)
Eliminate DTG's additional paid-in capital	$ (937,093)
Issuance of Hertz common stock and options	287,630
Total	$ (649,463)

p. To eliminate DTG's accumulated deficit, and to record estimated non-recurring costs of Hertz and DTG for advisory, legal, regulatory and valuation costs, as follows:

	(In thousands)
Eliminate DTG's accumulated deficit	$ 223,630
Estimated remaining merger related transaction costs assumed to be non-recurring	(49,165)
Total	$ 174,465

q. To eliminate DTG's accumulated other comprehensive loss.
r. To eliminate DTG's treasury stock.

The unaudited pro forma condensed combined financial statements do not reflect Hertz's expected realization of annual cost savings of $180 million by 2013. These savings are expected indirect operating, depreciation of revenue earning equipment and selling, general and administrative functions. Although Hertz management expects that cost savings will result from the merger, there can be no assurance that these cost savings will be achieved. The unaudited pro forma condensed combined financial statements do not reflect estimated restructuring and integration charges associated with the expected cost savings, which are estimated to be approximately $70 million, of which approximately $23 million (associated with the purchase of information technology hardware and software) will be capitalized and the remainder will be expensed as incurred. Additionally, severance charges for DTG senior management of approximately $23 million are not reflected in these pro forma financial statements, and will be expensed as incurred.

Notes

CHAPTER 1   The Adversarial Nature of Financial Reporting

1. Howard M. Schilit, *Financial Shenanigans: How to Detect Accounting Gimmicks and Fraud in Financial Reports* (New York: McGraw Hill, 1993), 153.
2. Although this book focuses on for-profit companies, nonprofit companies and governmental entities also produce financial statements. Readers should not presume that those entities invariably eschew reporting trickery. Like their for-profit counterparts, nonprofit organizations seek to raise capital. They have incentives to portray their financial positions in as favorable a light as possible, when trying to borrow or to demonstrate their financial viability to providers of grants. On the other hand, nonprofits sometimes strive to make themselves appear less flush than they really are, to impress on donors the urgency of their appeal for funds. Governmental units sometimes resort to disingenuous reporting to avoid political fallout from the consequences of unsound fiscal policies. Anticapitalist ideologues cannot truthfully contend that the profit motive alone leads to devious financial reporting.
3. Stuart Elliott, "Advertising," *New York Times,* November 11, 2002, C10.
4. Vanessa O'Connell and Suzanne Vranica, "Interpublic Says SEC Seeks Data Related to Its Bookkeeping Errors," *Wall Street Journal,* November 20, 2002, A3.
5. Nick Wingfield and Paul Beckett, "MicroStrategy, Results Restated, Is MacroLoser," *Wall Street Journal,* March 21, 2000, B1, B4.
6. Floyd Norris, "A Hard Fall as Highflier Revises Figures," *New York Times,* March 21, 2000, C1, C16.
7. Floyd Norris, "Failed Audit: The Humiliation of PricewaterhouseCoopers," *New York Times,* March 24, 2000, C1.
8. Alan Abelson, "Up & Down Wall Street: Way to Go," *Barron's,* July 19, 1999, 5. The $59 million purchase price that Lernout & Hauspie paid for Brussels Translation Group was neither a revenue nor an expense, but an exchange of one asset (cash) for another (BTG's stock).
9. John Carreyrou and Mark Maremont, "Lernout Files for Bankruptcy Protection," *Wall Street Journal,* November 30, 2000, A3, A6.
10. Randall Smith, Steven Lipin, and Amal Kumar Naj, "Managing Profits: How General Electric Damps Fluctuations in Its Annual Earnings," *Wall Street Journal,* November 3, 1994, A1, A6.
11. In financial statements prepared for tax purposes, the corporation minimizes its taxable income by writing off fixed assets over the shortest allowable period.

This is both a lawful and a customary practice. Companies are permitted to prepare separate sets of accounts for tax and financial reporting purposes. In the latter, they can make choices on discretionary accounting items that result in lower profits than shown in the former.

12. Senior executives typically own stock in their corporations, so to some extent they penalize their wealth by undercutting quality of earnings. Unless their stock holdings are very large, however, the direct benefits of increased bonuses more than fully offset the impact of reduced valuations on their shares.

13. Richard Zeckhauser, Jayendu Patel, Francois Degeorge, and John Pratt, "Reported and Predicted Earnings: An Empirical Investigation Using Prospect Theory." Project for David Dreman Foundation (1994).

14. Ibid.

15. As December 31, 1999, approached, economic pundits warned of massive dislocations arising from a programming quirk whereby many computer systems would interpret the following date to be January 1, 1900. Many corporations attributed sluggish sales during the latter part of 1999 to customers' unwillingness to make major commitments in advance of impending chaos, fears of which proved to be greatly overstated.

16. See, for example, Michael C. Jensen and William H. Meckling, "Theory of the Firm: Managerial Behavior, Agency Costs and Ownership Structure," *Journal of Financial Economics* 3 (1976), 305–360.

CHAPTER 2   The Balance Sheet

1. For the record, the accounting profession defines *assets* as "probable future economic benefits obtained or controlled by a particular entity as a result of past transactions or events" (Statement of Financial Accounting Concepts No. 6, Financial Accounting Standards Board, Stamford, Connecticut, December 1985, p. 10).

2. Barry Libert and Barbara Sayre Casey, "Accounting for Value" (letter to editor), *Barron's,* December 11, 2000, 65.

3. Jonathan R. Laing, "The New Math: Why an Accounting Guru Wants to Shake Up Some Basic Tenets of His Profession," *Barron's,* November 20, 2000, 31–36.

4. Henny Sender and Aline van Duyn, "Lack of Consistency in Lehman's Asset Valuations," *Financial Times,* March 15, 2010, 17.

5. Barnaby J. Feder, "JDS Uniphase Will Write Down $44.8 Billion in Assets," *New York Times,* July 27, 2001, C1–C2.

6. Richard H. Thaler, ed., *Advances in Behavioral Finance* (New York: Russell Sage Foundation, 1993).

CHAPTER 3   The Income Statement

1. There are a few exceptions to this generalization. Tax collectors, for example, examine a company's income statement to determine its tax liability. For them,

next year is irrelevant because they can assess a tax only on what has already been earned.
2. Financial Accounting Standards: Original Pronouncements, as of June 1, 1980, Financial Accounting Standards Board, Stamford, Connecticut, 371–373. The APB opinion covering the issue became effective on October 1, 1973.
3. Floyd Norris, "No Special Accounting Breaks for Recent Corporate Setbacks," *New York Times,* October 2, 2001, C9.
4. Emily Nelson, "P&G's One-Time Charges Make Critics Look Twice at Earnings," *Wall Street Journal,* April 4, 2001, C1–C2.

CHAPTER 4   The Statement of Cash Flows

1. Exhibit 4.2 and the accompanying narrative simplify the concept of cash flow to introduce it to the reader. Only the two major sources of cash, net income and depreciation, appear here, leaving to subsequent exhibits refinements such as deferred taxes, which arise from timing differences between the recognition and payment of taxes. Similarly, the uses of cash exclude a working capital factor, which is discussed in connection with Exhibit 4.9.
2. For a detailed rationale for the use of the EBITDA multiple to evaluate a firm, see "Valuation through Restructuring Potential" in Chapter 14. See also Chapter 8, "The Applications and Limitations of EBITDA."
3. Michael C. Jensen, "The Free Cash Flow Theory of Takeovers: A Financial Perspective on Mergers and Acquisitions and the Economy," in *The Merger Boom: Proceedings of a Conference*, ed. Lynn E. Browne and Eric S. Rosengren (Boston: Federal Reserve Bank of Boston, 1987), 102–137. This article provides the basis for the synopsis of the free cash flow argument described here, as well as the definition quoted.
4. Ibid.

CHAPTER 5   What Is Profit?

1. John Francis Fowler Jr., *Introduction to Wall Street: A Practical Guide Book for the Investor or Speculator* (New York: Harper & Brothers, 1930), 76.
2. This was probably even truer in 1930 than today, for it was only with the passage of the Securities Act of 1933 that it became a requirement for most U.S. public companies to have their financial statements audited by independent public accountants. Even then, financial reporting rules remained fairly loose while the federal government and accounting profession wrestled with the question of how best to establish standards.

CHAPTER 6   Revenue Recognition

1. Gardiner Harris, "Bristol-Myers Says Accounting Was 'Inappropriate,' Inflated Sales," *Wall Street Journal,* March 11, 2003, A2, A8.

NOTES

2. Gardiner Harris, "At Bristol-Myers, Ex-Executives Tell of Numbers Games," *Wall Street Journal,* December 12, 2002, A1, A13.

3. Stephanie Saul, "Fraud Case Filed against Ex-Officers of Bristol," *New York Times,* June 16, 2005, C1, C17.

4. Steven C. Tighe, *Bristol-Myers: Analysis Reveals Excess Inventory in the Trade,* Merrill Lynch & Co., March 25, 2002.

5. In this analysis, it is essential to carry out the full growth-rate calculations, rather than simply add the percentage increases for price and units, then subtract the reported revenue gain. To illustrate, suppose a manufacturer sells 100 units at $5.00 each for revenue of $500 in Year 1. In Year 2, unit sales grow by 12 percent, and the price increases by 8 percent. Revenue increases to 112 units @ $5.40 = $604.80. That represents a revenue increase of $604.8 ÷ $500 = 20.96 percent. In round terms, the revenue increase is 21 percent, rather than the sum of the percentage volume and price increases, that is, 12 percent + 8 percent = 20 percent.

6. Warren St. John, "With Games of Havoc, Men Will Be Boys," *New York Times,* May 12, 2002, Section 9, pp. 1, 4.

7. Gene Marcial, "Take-Two Gets a Second Chance," *BusinessWeek Online,* December 19, 2001.

8. Ibid.

9. Greg Chang, "Take-Two Drops on U.S. SEC's Accounting Investigation," *Bloomberg News,* February 15, 2002.

10. Ibid.

11. U.S. Securities and Exchange Commission Release No. 19260, June 9, 2005.

12. The account of Kendall Square's revenue recognition controversies draws on the following articles: John R. Dorfman and William M. Bulkeley, "Supercomputer Maker Kendall Square's Effort to Crack Business Market Has Some Skeptics," *Wall Street Journal,* October 11, 1993, C2; Liz Roman Gallese, "Kendall Square Fires Founder Burkhardt, Two Demoted Executives," *Bloomberg News,* October 26, 1993; "Kendall Square Closes Down 32%," *Bloomberg Business News,* October 29, 1993; David Zielenziger, "Kendall Square Drops 21% after Auditors Withdraw Backing," *Bloomberg News,* November 29, 1993.

13. Chip Cummins, "Wal-Mart's Net Income Increases 28%, but Accounting Change Worries Investors," *Wall Street Journal,* August 10, 2000, A6.

14. Heather Landy, "Wal-Mart 2nd-Quarter Net to Miss Forecasts," *Bloomberg,* August 9, 2000.

15. Linda Sandler, "Bally Total Fitness's Accounting Procedures Are Getting Some Skeptical Investors Exercised," *Wall Street Journal,* August 26, 1998, C2.

16. Eric Matejevich, "Bally Total Fitness: Flexing Its Muscles; Buy Reiterated," *Merrill Lynch HYLights,* September 2, 1999, 18–24.

17. Sandler, "Bally," C2.

18. "BJ's Wholesale Club, Inc. Says Membership Income Accounting Complies with All Applicable Standards," *Business Wire,* September 3, 1998.

19. Elizabeth MacDonald, Laura Johannes, and Emily Nelson, "Discount-Club Retailers Shift Accounting," *Wall Street Journal,* October 28, 1998, B4.

20. "MemberWorks Reports Record Fiscal 2000 Fourth Quarter Financial Results," *Business Wire,* July 28, 2000.
21. Elizabeth MacDonald, "Are Those Revenues for Real?" *Forbes,* May 29, 2000, 108–110. The author credits Bear Stearns & Co. with identifying 120 companies that announced they had changed or would change their revenue recognition policies in recent months.
22. "Sequoia, Ex-Officials Settle SEC Charges of Inflating Results," *Wall Street Journal,* February 17, 1996, B6.
23. *SEC v. Scott A. Livengood, John W. Tate, and Randy S. Casstevens*, SEC Complaint against Scott A. Livengood, John W. Tate, and Randy S. Casstevens, May 4, 2009.
24. Mark Maremont and Rick Brooks, "Krispy Kreme Franchise Buybacks May Spur New Concerns," *Wall Street Journal,* May 25, 2004, C4–C5.
25. Gretchen Morgenson, "Did Someone Say Doughnuts? Yes. The S.E.C." *New York Times,* July 30, 2004, C1, C6.
26. Mark Maremont and Rick Brooks, "Krispy Kreme Operating Chief to Join Restoration Hardware," *Wall Street Journal,* August 17, 2004, B3.
27. Lauren R. Rublin, "Full of Holes," *Barron's,* September 13, 2004, 16.
28. Melanie Warner, "Report Details Some Failures That Hurt Krispy Kreme," *New York Times,* August 11, 2005, C7.
29. Alex Berenson and Lowell Bergman, "Under Cheney, Halliburton Altered Policy on Accounting," *New York Times,* May 22, 2002, C1–C2.
30. Ibid., C2.
31. *SEC Charges Halliburton and Two Former Officers for Failure to Disclose a 1998 Change in Accounting Practice,* Securities and Exchange Commission Press Release, August 3, 2004.
32. Melody Peterson, "S.E.C. Charges Grace and 6 Former Executives with Fraud," *New York Times,* December 23, 1998, C1, C6.
33. Ann Davis, "SEC Claims Profit 'Management' by Grace," *Wall Street Journal,* April 7, 1999, C1, C20.
34. Ibid., C20.
35. Ibid.
36. Peter Ramjug, "W. R. Grace Settles SEC Income Manipulation Case," *Reuters,* June 30, 1999.
37. Michael C. Jensen, "Why Pay People to Lie?" *Wall Street Journal,* January 8, 2001, A32.
38. Elizabeth MacDonald and Daniel Kruger, "Aiding and Abetting," *Forbes,* April 2, 2001, 82–84.
39. Ibid., 84.
40. Davis, "SEC Claims," C1.
41. "Cincinnati Milacron Overstated Earnings by $300,000 for Half," *Wall Street Journal,* August 4, 1993, C9.
42. "Net of First Financial Management Corp. Restated for 3 Periods," *Wall Street Journal,* December 30, 1991, B7.

43. Shawn Young and Dennis K. Berman, "SEC Staff Recommends Penalty against Lucent of $25 Million," *Wall Street Journal,* March 18, 2004, B5.

CHAPTER 7 Expense Recognition

1. *Bloomberg News*, "Nortel to Restate Results of Past Years," October 23, 2003.
2. Ian Austen, "Nortel Faces Credibility Questions in New Audit," *New York Times,* March 22, 2004, C1–C6.
3. Ibid., C6.
4. Ibid.
5. Ibid.
6. Mark Heinzl, "Nortel's Books Face SEC Investigation," *Wall Street Journal,* April 6, 2004, A3, A6.
7. *Financial Times*, "Wrong Number, Approximately," August 30, 2004, 10.
8. Mark Heinzl, "Nortel Again Delays Financial Report," *Wall Street Journal,* November 12, 2004, A3, A8.
9. Ken Brown and Mark Heinzl, "Nortel Board Finds Accounting Tricks behind '03 Profits," *Wall Street Journal,* July 2, 2004, A1, A8.
10. This account draws on Floyd Norris, "Now G.M. Has Woes on Audits," *New York Times,* March 18, 2006, C1, C4.
11. Joseph B. White and Lee Hawkins Jr., "GM Will Restate Results for 2001 in Latest Stumble," *Wall Street Journal,* November 10, 2005, A1, A13.
12. Ibid., A13.
13. Floyd Norris, "The World Is Volatile, So Why Should Earnings Show Smooth Gains?" *New York Times,* November 28, 2003, C1.
14. Alex Berenson, "Report Says Freddie Mac Misled Investors," *New York Times,* July 24, 2003, C1–C2.

CHAPTER 8 The Applications and Limitations of EBITDA

1. Failures by leveraged buyouts largely accounted for the escalation in the default rate on speculative grade bond issuers, as reported by Moody's Investors Service, from 3.5 percent in 1988 to a peak of 10.5 percent in 1991.
2. William H. Beaver, "Financial Ratios as Predictors of Failure," *Journal of Accounting Research* (Supplement 1966), 71–111.
3. The development of this tradition is more fully explored in Martin S. Fridson, "EBITDA Is Not King," *Journal of Financial Statement Analysis* (Spring 1998), 59–62.
4. Edward I. Altman, "Financial Ratios, Discriminant Analysis, and the Prediction of Corporate Bankruptcy," *Journal of Finance* (September 1968), 589–609.
5. Richard Bernstein, "An Analysis of Low EV/EBITDA," Merrill Lynch & Co., September 4, 2001.
6. Defined as Equity Market Capitalization + Long-Term Debt + Short-Term Debt + Preferred Stock + Minority Interest – (Cash + Cash Equivalents).

CHAPTER 9   The Reliability of Disclosure and Audits

1. James Bandler, "Computer Associates Says Error Boosted Annual Earnings," *Wall Street Journal,* May 7, 2001, B9.
2. Jacqueline Doherty, "Fuzzy Numbers from Mr. Trump," *Barron's,* November 1, 1999, MW16.
3. "Trump Hotels & Casino Resorts Third Quarter Results," *Business Wire,* October 25, 1999.
4. Christina Binkley, "Trump Hotels Failed to Disclose Gain, so Firm Appeared to Beat Estimates," *Wall Street Journal,* November 8, 1999, p. B12.
5. Ibid.
6. Doherty, "Fuzzy Numbers."
7. Steve Lohr, "Trump Hotels Settles Case Accusing It of Misleading Investors," *New York Times,* January 17, 2002, C4.
8. Adam Steinhauer, "Park Place CEO Goldberg Is out of Hospital," *Bloomberg News,* July 7, 2001.
9. Jeannine DeFoe, "Park Place Taps Hilton Exec to Succeed Goldberg," *Bloomberg News,* October 23, 2000.
10. Shawn Tully, "The New King of Casinos," *Fortune,* September 18, 2000, 156.
11. Judy DeHaven, "What Now for Park Place?" *Star-Ledger,* October 20, 2000, 53.
12. Cassell Bryan-Low, "Accounting Firms Earn More from Consulting," *Wall Street Journal,* April 16, 2003, C9.
13. Ibid.
14. This discussion draws extensively on Jonathan Weil, "Behind Wave of Corporate Fraud: A Change in How Auditors Work," *Wall Street Journal,* March 25, 2004, A1, A14.
15. Ibid., A14.
16. This discussion draws extensively on Mark Maremont and Deborah Solomon, "Behind SEC's Failings: Caution, Tight Budget, '90s Exuberance," *Wall Street Journal,* December 24, 2003, A1, A5.
17. Ibid., A5.
18. Jeanne Patterson and Nell Minow, "Blame Directors for Accounting Practices, Managing Earnings," *Pensions & Investments,* May 28, 2001, 12.

CHAPTER 10   Mergers-and-Acquisitions Accounting

1. Floyd Norris, "At Tyco, Accounting 'Baths' Begin before the Deals Close," *New York Times,* October 29, 1999, C1.
2. Mark Maremont, "Tyco Sleuth Has History of Uncovering Bad Numbers," *Wall Street Journal,* October 15, 1999, C1, C8.
3. Ibid., C8.
4. Ibid.
5. Floyd Norris, "Tyco Shares Plunge after Company Discloses SEC Inquiry," *New York Times,* December 10, 1999, C2.

6. Jonathan R. Laing, "Tyco's Tumble," *Barron's,* December 13, 1999, 15.

7. Mark Maremont, "Tyco's Shares Rise 13% after Concern Restates Results following SEC Review," *Barron's,* June 27, 2000, C8.

8. Ibid.

9. Herb Greenberg with Lisa Muñoz, "Does Tyco Play Accounting Games?" *Fortune,* April 1, 2002, 83–86.

10. Ibid., 86.

11. Andrew Ross Sorkin, and Alex Berenson, "Tyco Admits Using Accounting Tricks to Inflate Earnings," *New York Times,* December 31, 2002, A1, C2.

12. Andrew Ross Sorkin, "Tyco, after the Glitter and the Agile Math," *New York Times,* January 1, 2003, C1–C2.

13. Maremont, "Tyco Sleuth," C8.

14. Thatcher Thompson, "Navigant: Downgrading NCI Shares," Merrill Lynch & Co. Research Comment, November 5, 1999.

15. Barry Henderson, "Number Theory: Navigant's Growth Rate May Not Be What It Seems," *Barron's,* October 25, 1999, 24.

16. Barry Henderson, "Follow the Money," *Barron's,* November 29, 1999, 15–17.

17. James P. Miller, "Navigant CEO Resigns, Two Officials Are Fired over Stock-Purchase Deals," *Wall Street Journal,* November 23, 1999, A4.

18. A month later, when Navigant announced that it was not for sale, the stock receded to $41.44.

CHAPTER 11   Is Fraud Detectable?

1. Messod D. Beneish, "The Detection of Earnings Manipulation," *Financial Analysts Journal,* September–October 1999, 24–36.

2. David F. Larcker and Anastasia A. Zakolyukina. *Detecting Deceptive Discussions in Conference Calls,* Working Paper Series No. 63 (Stanford, CA: Rock Center for Corporate Governance, 2010).

3. Nicholas Stein, "The World's Most Admired Companies," *Fortune,* October 2000.

4. Jeremy Gerard, "Did Goldman Sachs on TV Kill 'Enron' on Broadway?" *Bloomberg News,* May 11, 2010.

5. John R. Emshwiller, and Rebecca Smith, "Behind Enron's Fall, a Culture of Operating outside Public's View," *Wall Street Journal,* December 5, 2001, A1, A10.

6. Richard A. Oppel Jr. and Andrew Ross Sorkin, "Enron Admits to Overstating Profits by About $600 Million," *New York Times,* November 9, 2001, C1, C5.

7. Dan Ackman, "Enron the Incredible," *Forbes.com,* January 15, 2002.

8. "Jeff Skilling's Spectacular Career," www.chron.com/disp/story.mpl/jenny/2404018.html.

9. Jonathan Weil, "Energy Traders Cite Gains, but Some Math Is Missing," *Wall Street Journal,* September 20, 2000, Texas Journal section, 1.

10. Ibid.

11. Joe Nocera, "Tipping over a Defense of Enron," *New York Times,* January 6, 2007, C1, C8.
12. Anne Kates Smith, "Enron's Biggest Assets Are on Paper," *U.S. News & World Report,* June 18, 2001, 30.
13. Milt Freudenheim, "Hospital Chain Is Accused of Accounting Fraud," *New York Times,* March 20, 2003, C1, C4.
14. Simon Romero, "The Rise and Fall of Richard Scrushy, Entrepreneur," *New York Times,* March 21, 2003, C4.
15. Judy Mathewson, Keith Snider, William McQuillen, and James Rowley, "HealthSouth, Scrushy Accused of $1.4 Billion Fraud," *Bloomberg News,* March 19, 2003.
16. Freudenheim, "Hospital Chain," C4.
17. Ann Carrns, Carrick Mollenkamp, Deborah Solomon, and John R. Wilke, "HealthSouth Case Unveils a Shock Strategy," *Wall Street Journal,* April 4, 2003, C1, C9.
18. Jonathan Weill, "Accounting Scheme Was Straightforward but Hard to Detect," *Wall Street Journal,* March 20, 2003, C1, C13.
19. Reed Abelson, "HealthSouth Fires Chief Executive and Audit Firm," *New York Times,* April 1, 2003, C1, C13.
20. Kurt Eichenwald, "Key Executive at HealthSouth Admits to Fraud," *New York Times,* March 27, 2003, C1–C2.
21. David Voreacos, with reporting by Bob Van Voris, "HealthSouth Officers Plead Guilty to $2.5 Billion Fraud," *Bloomberg News,* April 3, 2003.
22. Greg Farrell, "Scrushy Sticks to His Defense: They're All Lying," *USA Today,* November 5, 2003, 1B–2B.
23. Carrick Mollenkamp and Ann Carrns, "As Trial Looms, HealthSouth's Ex-CEO Starts a TV Show," *Wall Street Journal,* March 3 2004, B1, B5.
24. Simon Romero, "Will the Real Richard Scrushy Please Step Forward," *New York Times,* February 17, 2005, C1, C6.
25. Brian Grow, "All Scrushy, All the Time," *BusinessWeek,* April 12, 2004, 86–87.
26. Reed Abelson and Jonathan Glater, "A Style That Connected with Hometown Jurors," *New York Times,* June 29, 2005, C1, C4.
27. Adrian Michaels and Lisa Fingeret Roth, "HealthSouth Auditors Facing Federal Probe," *Financial Times,* March 28, 2003, 17.
28. Jonathan Weil and Cassell Bryan-Low, "Audit Committee Met Only Once during 2001," *Wall Street Journal,* March 21, 2003, A2, A10.
29. Joann S. Lublin and Ann Carrns, "Directors Had Lucrative Links at Health-South," *Wall Street Journal,* April 11, 2003, B1, B3.
30. Gail Edmondson, with David Fairlamb and Nanette Byrnes, "The Milk Just Keeps on Spilling," *BusinessWeek,* June 24, 2004, 54–58.
31. Ibid., 55–58.
32. Oliver Holtaway, "Tragedy or Farce?" *US Credit* (February 2004), 22–26.
33. The *spread* is the risk premium on the issue, measured in the yield differential between Parmalat debt and default-risk-free government debt. Parmalat's bonds yielded around 8 percent, a high rate compared with bonds of other companies with the same (Triple-B) credit rating.

34. Holtaway, "Tragedy," 26.
35. Joanna Speed and Nic Sochovsky, *Parmalat: The Straws That Break the Camel's Back*, Merrill Lynch & Co., December 5, 2002.
36. Edmondson, "The Milk," 55.
37. Daniel J. Wakin, "There Were Earlier Signs of Trouble at Parmalat," *New York Times,* January 14, 2004, C1, C6.

CHAPTER 12   Forecasting Financial Statements

1. A less restrictive type of covenant merely prohibits incurrence of new debt or payment of dividends that would cause financial measures to deteriorate below a targeted level. No violation occurs if, for example, net worth declines as a result of operating losses.
2. Hertz Global Holdings, Inc. 8-K Current Report Filing filed on September 14, 2010, p. 1.

CHAPTER 13   Credit Analysis

1. In practice, the U.S. Bankruptcy Code encourages companies to reorganize, rather than simply liquidate, if they become insolvent. Typically, a reorganization results in settlement of creditors' claims via distribution of securities of a firm that has been rehabilitated through forgiveness of a portion of its debt. Determination of the value of securities awarded to each class of creditor is related to asset protection, however, so the analysis that follows applies equally to reorganization and liquidation.
2. The comments on preferred stock in this paragraph also apply generally to preference stock, which is similar to preferred stock in form but junior to it in the capital structure.
3. In this and subsequent definitions of total capital, minority interest is included. This item should be viewed as equity in leverage calculations because it involves no contractual payment and ranks junior to debt.
4. Nick Fielding, Richard Thomson, and Larry Black, "Undisclosed Debt Worries Hang over O&Y," *The Independent,* May 10, 1992, Business on Sunday Section, 1.
5. Technically speaking, the effective tax rate is somewhat manageable, even though the statutory rate is not. It is nevertheless useful to calculate the operating margin separately from the pretax margin, to measure management's operating prowess separately from its financial acumen.
6. See Edward I. Altman, Robert G. Haldeman, and Paul Narayanan, "Zeta Analysis: A New Model to Identify Bankruptcy Risk of Corporations," *Journal of Banking and Finance,* June 1977, 29–54.
7. See, for example, Kenneth Emery, Sharon Ou, and Jennifer Tennant, *Corporate Default and Recovery Rates of Corporate Bond Issuers, 1920–2009,* Moody's Investors Service, February 2010. The analysts report average one-year default

rates that increase with each step down the rating scale, from 0.00% for issuers rated Aaa to 22.15% for issuers rated Ca or C.

8. Altman, Haldeman, and Narayanan set the Zeta model's cutoff score (the level at which a loan request is rejected on grounds of excessive default risk) with an explicit goal of achieving the optimal trade-off between the costs of making loans that default and rejecting loans that do not default.

9. Christopher M. McHugh, ed., *The 2000 Bankruptcy Yearbook & Almanac* (Boston: New Generation Research, 2000), 187–190.

CHAPTER 14   Equity Analysis

1. Dividends, unlike interest payments on debt, are payable at the discretion of the board of directors, rather than in fulfillment of a contractual obligation. They are consequently subject to greater variability—through reduction, increase, or suspension—than bond coupons or scheduled principal repayments.

2. Bethany McLean, "Hocus-Pocus: How IBM Grew 27% a Year," *Fortune,* June 26, 2000, 165.

3. The notion that a company can increase its market capitalization by boosting its financial leverage appears to fly in the face of a fundamental tenet of modern finance. Nobel economics laureates Franco Modigliani and Merton Miller demonstrated that under certain critical assumptions, a company's stock market value was insensitive to the proportions of debt and equity in its capital structure. Modigliani and Miller followed up on this pioneering work, however, by exploring what happened when the assumptions were relaxed to reflect real-world conditions. In particular, they and subsequent researchers found that the company's stock market value could in fact rise as a result of boosting financial leverage to take fuller advantage of the tax shield provided by debt. Interest on borrowings is a tax-deductible expense, whereas dividends on stock are not.

4. Note, however, the uncertainties associated with reserve valuations, discussed in Chapter 2 under the heading "The Value Problem."

accelerate To demand immediate repayment of debt in default, exercising thereby a right specified in the loan contract.

Accounting Principles Board (APB) Formerly, a rule-making body of the American Institute of Certified Public Accountants. Predecessor of the Financial Accounting Standards Board (see).

accrual accounting An accounting system in which revenue is recognized during the period in which it is earned and expenses are recognized during the period in which they are incurred, whether or not cash is received or disbursed.

APB Accounting Principles Board (see).

bona fide profit A reported profit that represents a genuine increase in wealth as opposed to one that exploits a flaw in the accounting system and reflects no economic gain.

book value The amount at which an asset is carried on the balance sheet. Book value consists of the asset's construction or acquisition cost, less depreciation (see) and subsequent impairment of value, if applicable. An asset's book value does not rise as a function of an increase in its market value or inflation. (See also *historical cost accounting*.)

breakeven rate The production volume at which contribution (see) is equivalent to fixed costs (see), resulting in a pretax profit of zero.

Example:

$$
\begin{aligned}
\text{Price per unit} &= \$2.50 \\
\text{Variable cost per unit} &= \$1.00 \\
\text{Fixed costs} &= \$600 \\
\text{To calculate breakeven: } [(\$2.50 - \$1.00) \times B] - \$600 &= 0 \\
(\$1.50 \times B) &= \$600 \\
B &= 400 \text{ units}
\end{aligned}
$$

broadcast cash flow A measure of financial performance used by operators of radio and television stations, defined as Operating Income + Depreciation and Amortization + Corporate Overhead − Cash Outlays for Acquisition of New Programming + Amortization of Cost of Previously Acquired Programming.

business cycle Periodic fluctuations in economic growth, employment, and price levels. Phases of the classic cycle, in sequence, are peak, recession, trough, and recovery.

capital-intensive Characterized by a comparatively large proportion of plant and equipment in asset base. The heavy depreciation charges that arise from capital intensity create a high level of fixed costs and volatile earnings.

capitalization (of an expenditure) The recording of an expenditure as an asset, to be written off over future periods, on the grounds that the outlay produces benefits beyond the current accounting cycle.

carrying cost Charges associated with warehousing of goods, such as financing, insurance, storage, security, and spoilage.

cash-on-cash profit In real estate, the cash flow from a property divided by the cash equity invested. Unlike conventional rate-of-return measures calculated in accordance with accrual accounting (see), cash-on-cash profit is not reduced by noncash charges such as depreciation (see). This reflects a presumption that land and buildings tend to increase in value over time, rather than lose value through wear and tear, as in the case of plant and equipment.

Chapter 11 Under the Bankruptcy Code, a method of resolving bankruptcy that provides for reorganization of the failed firm as an alternative to liquidating it.

class-action suit A type of lawsuit filed under Federal Rule of Civil Procedure 23, which allows one member of a large group of plaintiffs with similar claims to sue on behalf of the entire class, provided certain conditions are met. Damages awarded in certain class-action suits have been large enough to compromise the solvency of corporate defendants.

comparability In accounting, the objective of facilitating financial comparisons of a group of companies, achieved by requiring them to use similar reporting practices.
Example:

Year	Value of Asset ($)
0	377
1	421
2	414
3	487
4	541
5	596

The year-to-year increase in the asset's value has been uneven, ranging from −1.7 percent in Year 2 to 17.6 percent in Year 4. If the increase had been 9.6 percent in each year, however, the value would have grown from the beginning figure of $377 to the terminal figure of $596. Computation of the compound annual growth rate is a standard function on sophisticated hand-held calculators. CAGRs can also be derived from compound interest tables.

consolidation (of an industry) A reduction in the number of competitors in an industry through business combinations.

contribution Revenue per unit minus variable costs (see) per unit.

convertible   With reference to bonds or preferred stock, redeemable at the holder's option for common stock of the issuer, based on a specified ratio of bonds or preferred shares to common shares. (See also *exchangeable*.)

cost of capital   The rate of return that investors require for providing capital to a company. A company's cost of capital consists of the cost of capital for a risk-free borrower, a premium for business risk (the risk of becoming unable to continue to cover operating costs), and a premium for financial risk (the risk of becoming unable to continue covering financial costs, such as interest). The risk-free cost of capital is commonly equated with the prevailing interest rate on U.S. Treasury obligations.

cumulative   A characteristic of the dividends of most preferred stocks whereby any dividends in arrears must be paid before dividends may be paid to common shareholders.

default   The failure of a debt obligor to make a scheduled interest or principal payment on time. A defaulting issuer becomes subject to claims against its assets, possibly including a demand by creditors for full and immediate repayment of principal.

depreciation   A noncash expense meant to represent the amount of capital equipment consumed through wear and tear during the period.

derivative   (see *financial derivative*).

dilution   A reduction in present shareholders' proportional claim on earnings. Dilution can occur through the issuance of new shares in an acquisition if the earnings generated by the acquired assets are insufficient to maintain the level of earnings per share previously recorded by the acquiring company. Existing shareholders' interest is likewise diluted if the company issues new stock at a price below book value. In this circumstance, a dollar invested by a new shareholder purchases a larger percentage of the company than is represented by a dollar of net worth held by an old shareholder.

discount rate   The interest rate used to equate future value (see) with present value (see). Also referred to as cost of capital (see).

discounted cash flow   A technique for equating future cash flows to a present sum of money, based on an assumed interest rate. For example, $100 compounded annually at 8 percent over three years will cumulate to a sum of $125.97, ignoring the effect of taxes. This figure can be calculated via the equation

$$P \times (1+r)^n = F$$

where P = Principal value at beginning of period (Present value)
r = Interest rate
n = Number of periods
F = Principal value at end of period (Future value)

In this case, $100 \times (1.08)^3 = \$125.97$. (Note that this formula implicitly assumes reinvestment of cash interest received at the original rate of interest throughout the period.)

If $125.97 three years hence is equivalent to $100 today—given the assumed discount rate (see) of 8 percent per annum—then the ratio $100.00/$125.97, or 0.794, can be used to determine the present value (see) of any other amount discounted back from the same date and at the same rate.

By using the same general formula, it is possible to assign a value to an asset, based on a series of cash flows it is expected to generate. By way of illustration, suppose the right to distribute a particular product is expected to generate cash flow of $5,000 a year for four years, then expire, leaving no terminal value. At a discount rate of 15 percent, the distribution rights would be valued at $14,820, derived as follows:

Year	Expected Cash Flow	Discount Factor	Present Value
1	$5,000	.870	$ 4,350
2	5,000	.756	3,780
3	5,000	.658	3,290
4	5,000	.572	2,860
		Total:	$14,280

discretionary cash flow   Cash flow that remains available to a company after it has funded its basic operating requirements. There is no universally accepted, precise definition of discretionary cash flow, but conceptually it includes funds from operations less required new investment in working capital and nondiscretionary capital expenditures. The latter figure is difficult to quantify with precision, but it exceeds the required maintenance level required to keep existing plant and equipment in good working order. Ordinarily, some additional expenditures, which may be designated semidiscretionary, are necessary to keep a company competitive with respect to capacity, costs, and technology. Only a portion of the total capital budget, including expansion-oriented outlays that can be deferred in the event of slower-than-expected growth in demand, can truly be considered discretionary. In a similar vein, mandatory principal repayments of debt, by definition, cannot be regarded as discretionary. Still, a company with strong cash flow and the assurance, as a practical matter, of being able to refinance its maturing debt, has considerable freedom in the disposition even of amounts that would appear to be earmarked for debt retirement.

diversification   In portfolio management, the technique of reducing risk by dividing one's assets among a number of different securities or types of investments. Applied to corporate strategy, the term refers to participation in several unrelated businesses. The underlying premise is often countercyclicality, or the stabilization of earnings over time through the tendency of profits in certain business segments to be rising at times when they are falling in others.

double-entry bookkeeping   A system of keeping accounts in which each entry requires an offsetting entry. For example, a payment to a trade creditor causes both cash and accounts payable to decline.

Dow Jones Industrial Average A widely followed index of the U.S. stock market composed of the common stocks of 30 major industrial corporations.

EBIT Earnings before deduction of interest expense and income taxes.

EBITDA Earnings before deduction of interest expense, income taxes, depreciation, and amortization.

economies of scale Reductions in per unit cost that arise from large-volume production. The reductions result in large measure from the spreading of fixed costs (i.e., those that do not vary directly with production volume) over a larger number of units than is possible for a smaller producer.

economies of scope Reductions in per unit cost that arise from applying knowledge or technology to related products.

external growth Revenue growth achieved by a company through acquisition of other companies.

factor A financial institution that provides financing to companies by buying accounts receivable at a discount.

Fair Value Accounting An accounting system in which certain assets and liabilities are recorded at their market values. Also known as *mark-to-market accounting.*

FASB Financial Accounting Standards Board (see).

Financial Accounting Standards Board (FASB) A rule-making body for the accounting profession. Its members are appointed by a foundation, the members of which are selected by the directors of the American Institute of Certified Public Accountants.

financial derivative A financial instrument with a return linked to the performance of an underlying asset, such as a bond or a currency.

financial flexibility The ability, achieved through such means as a strong capital structure and a high degree of liquidity, to continue to invest in maintaining growth and competitiveness despite business downturns and other financial strains.

financial leverage (See *leverage (financial)*.)

fixed costs Costs that do not vary with the volume of production. Examples include rent, interest expense, senior management salaries, and, unless calculated by the units-of-production method, depreciation (see).

fixed-rate debt A debt obligation on which the interest rate remains at a stated level until the loan has been liquidated. (Compare *floating-rate debt*.)

floating-rate debt A debt obligation on which the interest rate fluctuates with changes in market rates of interest, according to a specified formula. (Compare *fixed-rate debt*.)

free cash flow Operating cash flow minus capital expenditures and dividends.

fresh start accounting Accounting for a company that emerges from bankruptcy, in which assets and liabilities are recorded at fair value, with the result that the new reporting entity's financial statements generally are not comparable to the prebankruptcy historical statements.

fundamental analysis A form of security analysis aimed at determining a stock or bond's intrinsic value, based on such factors as the issuer's expected earnings and financial risk. In contrast, technical analysis aims to predict a security's future value based on its past price changes.

future value The amount to which a known sum of money will accumulate by a specified future date, given a stated rate of interest. For example, $100 compounded annually at 8 percent over three years will cumulate to a sum of $125.97, ignoring the effect of taxes. This figure can be calculated via the formula

$$P \times (1 + r)^n$$

where $P =$ Principal at beginning of period
$r =$ Interest rate
$n =$ Number of periods

In this case, $100 \times (1.08)^3 = $125.97. (This formula implicitly assumes that cash interest received will be reinvested at the original rate of interest throughout the period.) (See also *discounted cash flow, net present value,* and *present value.*)

GAAP Generally accepted accounting principles (see).

GDP Gross domestic product (see).

generally accepted accounting principles Rules that govern the preparation of financial statements, based on pronouncements of authoritative accounting organizations such as the Financial Accounting Standards Board, industry practice, and the accounting literature (including books and articles).

goodwill A balance sheet item arising from accounting for a business combination, representing the excess of the purchase price over the acquired company's tangible asset value.

Gross domestic product The value of all goods and services that residents and nonresidents produce in a country.

guidance An earnings per share projection provided to investors to convey management's expectations.

historical cost accounting An accounting system in which assets are recorded at their original value (less any applicable depreciation or other impairment of value), notwithstanding that the nominal dollar value of the assets may rise through some cause such as inflation or increased scarcity. (See also *book value.*)

hostile takeover An acquisition of a corporation by another corporation or by a group of investors, typically through a tender for outstanding shares, in the face of initial opposition by the acquired corporation's board of directors.

initial public offering (IPO) A first-time sale of stock to the public by a previously privately owned company. The IPO process is called going public.

internal growth Revenue growth achieved by a company through capital investment in its existing business.

internally generated funds Cash obtained through operations, including net income, depreciation, deferred taxes, and reductions in working capital.

investor-relations officer An individual designated by a corporation to handle communications with securities analysts.

involuntary inventory accumulation An unintended increase in a company's inventory levels, resulting from a slowdown in sales that is not offset by a reduced rate of production.

LBO Leveraged buyout (see).

leverage (financial) The use of debt financing in hopes of increasing the rate of return on equity. In the following example, the unleveraged company, with no debt in its capital structure, generates operating income of $30.0 million, pays taxes of $10.2 million, and nets $19.8 million for a return on equity (net income divided by shareholders' equity) of 13.2 percent. The leveraged company, with an equivalent amount of operating income, relies on long-term debt (at an interest rate of 12 percent) for one-third of its capital. Interest expense causes its net income before taxes to be lower ($24 million) than the unleveraged company's ($30 million). After taxes, the leveraged company earns less ($15.8 million) than the unleveraged company ($19.8 million), but on a smaller equity base ($100 million versus $150 million) provides shareholders a higher rate of return (15.8 percent versus 13.2 percent).

Note, however, that leverage works in reverse as well. In the following scenario, operating income declines by two-thirds (to $10 million) at both companies. With no interest expense, the unleveraged company manages to net $6.6 million for a 4.4 percent return on equity. The leveraged company, obliged to pay out 60 percent of its operating income in interest expense, suffers a sharper decline in return on equity (to 2.6 percent). Incurring financial leverage increases the risk to equity holders, whose returns become more subject to fluctuations. The greater the percentage of the capital structure that consists of debt, the greater the potential for such fluctuations.

	($ Million)	
	Unleveraged Company	Leveraged Company
Operating income	$ 30.0	$ 30.0
Interest expense	0.0	6.0
Net income before taxes	30.0	24.0
Taxes	10.2	8.2
Net income	$ 19.8	$ 15.8
Long-term debt	$ 0.0	$ 50.0
Shareholders' equity	150.0	100.0
Total capital	$150.0	$150.0
$\dfrac{\text{Net Income}}{\text{Shareholders' Equity}}$	13.2%	15.8%

leverage (operating) The substitution of fixed costs (see) for variable costs (see) in hopes of increasing return on equity. In the following example, Company A's cost structure is dominated by variable expenses, of which labor represents a substantial portion. A 5 percent increase in sales volume (from 500,000 to 525,000 units) raises the rate of return on shareholders' equity from

	($ Million)	
	Unleveraged Company	Leveraged Company
Operating income	$ 10.0	$ 10.0
Interest expense	0.0	6.0
Net income before taxes	10.0	4.0
Taxes	3.4	1.4
Net income	$ 6.6	$ 2.6
Long-term debt	$ 0.0	$ 50.0
Shareholders' equity	150.0	100.0
Total capital	$150.0	$150.0
Net Income / Shareholders' Equity	4.4%	2.6%

11.0 percent to 13.7 percent. Company B, on the other hand, has installed labor-saving equipment that sharply reduces man-hours per unit of production. Its variable costs are lower than Company A's ($50.00 versus $30.00 per unit), but as a function of its greater depreciation (see) charges, its fixed costs are higher ($30 million versus $25 million per annum). The benefit of Company B's higher operating leverage is that a 5 percent increase in its unit sales raises its return on shareholders' equity from 11.0 percent to 14.7 percent, a larger boost than Company A receives from a comparable rise in volume. By the same token, Company B's return on shareholders' equity will fall more sharply than Company A's if unit volume at both companies subsequently recedes from 525,000 to 500,000 units.

	Company A		Company B	
Sales (units)	500,000	525,000	500,000	525,000
Price per unit	$ 100.0	$ 100.0	$ 100.0	$ 100.0
Fixed costs ($ million)	$ 25.0	$ 25.0	$ 30.0	$ 30.0
Variable cost per unit	$ 50.0	$ 50.0	$ 30.0	$ 30.0
	($ Million)			
Sales	$ 50.0	$ 52.5	$ 50.0	$ 52.5
Fixed costs	25.0	25.0	30.0	30.0
Variable costs	25.0	26.3	15.0	15.8
Income before taxes	5.0	6.2	5.0	6.7
Taxes	1.7	2.1	1.7	2.3
Net income	$ 3.3	$ 4.1	$ 3.3	$ 4.4
Shareholders' equity	$ 30.0	$ 30.0	$ 30.0	$ 30.0
Net income / Shareholders' equity	11.0%	13.7%	11.0%	14.7%

leveraged buyout (LBO) An acquisition of a company or a division, financed primarily with borrowed funds. Equity investors typically hope to profit by repaying debt through cash generated by operations (and possibly from proceeds of asset sales), thereby increasing the net value of their stake.

leveraged recapitalization A corporate strategy involving the payment of a large, debt-financed cash dividend. The strategy is often employed as a defense against an attempted hostile takeover, for two reasons. First, by increasing the company's financial leverage (see), the transaction reduces the potential for a raider to use borrowed funds, lest the posttakeover company become excessively debt-laden. Second, the recapitalization increases the concentration of ownership in the hands of those attempting to retain control.

liquidity The ability of a company to meet its near-term obligations when due.

macroeconomic Pertaining to the economy as a whole or its major subdivisions, such as the manufacturing sector, the agricultural sector, the government. (See also *microeconomic.*)

market capitalization The aggregate market value of all of a company's outstanding equity and debt securities. Also used loosely to represent the product of a company's share price and number of shares outstanding. (See also *total enterprise value.*)

mark-to-market accounting The practice of valuing a holding of a financial instrument according to its fair market price on the date of the financial statement. If the instrument does not trade on a regular basis, a current market value may be inferred from the prices of comparable instruments that do.

mature With respect to a product, firm, or industry, at a stage of development at which the rate of sales growth remains positive but no longer exceeds the general growth rate of the economy.

microeconomic Pertaining to a small segment of the economy, such as an individual industry or a particular firm. (See also *macroeconomic.*)

multiple With respect to a common stock, the ratio of the share price to earnings per share. Similarly, the price paid in an acquisition can be viewed as a multiple of the acquired company's earnings, cash flow, or EBITDA (see).

multivariate In the field of quantitative modeling, having the characteristic of employing more than one explanatory factor.

net present value The present value (see) of a stream of future cash inflows, less the present value of an associated stream of current or future cash outflows. This calculation is useful for comparing the attractiveness of alternative investments, as shown in the example on the following page. Both proposed capital projects require an expenditure of $60 million during the first year. Project A generates a higher cash flow, without trailing off in the latter years as Project B is projected to do. Residual value in year 10 is likewise superior in Project A. Even so, Project B is the more profitable investment, based on a higher net present value ($17.7 million versus $14.3 million for Project A).

nominal dollar A monetary sum expressed in terms of its currency face amount, unadjusted for changes in purchasing power from a designated base period. (See also *real dollar.*)

Net Present Value Illustration (Presumed Discount Rate = 20%) ($000,000 omitted)

					Year							Net Present Value
	0	1	2	3	4	5	6	7	8	9	10	
Project A												
Cash flow*	(40)	(20)	16	18	21	24	24	26	26	26	20	
Discount factor	1.000	.833	.694	.579	.482	.402	.335	.279	.233	.194	.162	
Present value	(40.00) +	(16.66) +	11.10 +	10.42 +	10.12 +	9.65 +	8.04 +	7.25 +	6.06 +	5.04 +	3.24 =	14.26
Project B												
Cash flow*	(10)	(50)	17	20	22	23	23	23	22	21	17	
Discount factor	1.000	.833	.694	.579	.482	.402	.335	.279	.233	.194	.162	
Present value	(10.00) +	(41.65) +	11.80 +	11.58 +	10.60 +	9.25 +	7.71 +	6.42 +	5.13 +	4.07 +	2.75 =	17.66

*Figures in parentheses represent projected outflows, i.e., construction costs. Figures for years 2–9 represent projected inflows, i.e., net income plus noncash expenses. Year 10 figure represents expected residual value of equipment.

operating leverage   (See *leverage (operating)*.)

organic growth   Increases in revenues and earnings arising from internal operations as opposed to mergers and acquisitions.

payout ratio   Dividends per share divided by earnings per share. In financial theory, a low payout ratio (other than as a result of a dividend reduction forced on the company by financial distress) is generally viewed as a sign that the company has many opportunities to reinvest in its business at attractive returns. A high payout ratio, in contrast, is appropriate for a company with limited internal reinvestment opportunities. By distributing a large percentage of earnings to shareholders, the company enables them to seek more attractive returns by investing elsewhere.

portfolio   A group of securities. Barring the unlikely circumstance that all securities contained in a portfolio produce identical returns in all periods, it generally produces a steadier return than a single security. The comparative stability arises from the tendency of declines in the prices of certain securities to be offset by rises in the prices of others during the same period. (See *diversification*.)

present value   The sum that, if compounded at a specified rate of interest, or discount rate (see), will accumulate to a particular value at a stated future date. For example: To calculate the present value of $500, five years hence at a discount rate of 7 percent, solve the equation:

$$\frac{F}{(1+r)^n}$$

where F = Future value
r = Interest rate
n = Number of periods
p = Present value

In this case $500/(1.07)^5 = $356.49.

(See also *discounted cash flow, future value,* and *net present value*.)

pro forma   Describes a financial statement constructed on the basis of specified assumptions. For example, if a company made an acquisition halfway through its fiscal year, it might present an income statement intended to show what the combined companies' full-year sales, costs, and net income would have been, assuming that the acquisition had been in effect when the year began.

rationalization   In reference to a business or an industry, the process of eliminating excess capacity and other inefficiencies in production.

real dollar   A monetary sum expressed in terms of its purchasing-power equivalent, relative to a designated base period. For example, at the end of the third quarter of 2001, $500 (face amount) had only 56.1 percent of the purchasing power that $500 had in the base period 1982–1984. The erosion reflected price inflation during the intervening years. The real value of $500 in September 2001 was therefore $280.50 in 1982–1984 dollars. This calculation employs a series of the purchasing power of the consumer dollar, published by the United States

Bureau of Labor Statistics. See the Bureau's web site, www.bls.gov. (See also *nominal dollar.*)

reorganization proceedings A procedure under Chapter 11 of the Bankruptcy Code that permits a bankrupt company to continue in operation, instead of liquidating, while restructuring its liabilities with an aim toward ensuring its future financial viability.

reported earnings A company's profit or loss for a specified period, as stated in its income statement. The figure may differ from the company's true economic gain or loss for the period for such reasons as delayed recognition of items affecting income, changes in accounting practices, and discrepancies between accruals and actual changes in asset values.

Disparities between reported and economic earnings can also arise from certain nuances of inventory accounting. For example, under the last-in, first-out (LIFO) method, a company's inventory account may include the historical acquisition costs of goods purchased several years earlier and unaffected (for book purposes) by inflation in the interim period. To the extent that a surge in sales causes a company to recognize the liquidation of older inventories during the current period, revenues will reflect postinflation (i.e., higher) values, but expenses will not. The mismatch will produce unusually wide reported profit margins in the current period, even though the nominal dollar (see) gains arising from inflation are in reality benefits that accumulated over several preceding periods.

sale-leaseback A transaction in which a company sells an asset and immediately leases it back. The lessee thereby obtains cash while retaining use of the asset. An additional motivation for the transaction may be a difference in the marginal tax rates of the lessee and lessor. The tax shelter provided by depreciation charges on the asset are more valuable to the party paying the higher tax rate.

same-store sales A measure of revenue growth for retailing chains, consisting of the increase in revenue in a quarter or year over the preceding comparable period, for stores that were open during both periods. This measure excludes sales growth that reflects opening of additional stores.

scale economies (See *economies of scale.*)

SEC Securities and Exchange Commission (see).

Securities and Exchange Commission (SEC) An arm of the federal government that regulates the issuance and trading of securities, the activities of investment companies and investment advisers, and standards for financial reporting by securities issuers.

sensitivity analysis The testing of what-if scenarios in financial statement analysis. Typically, sensitivity analysis measures the potential impact (on earnings, cash flow, etc.) of a change of a stated amount in another variable (sales, profit margins, etc.). In connection with financial forecasting, sensitivity analysis may be used to gauge the variation in projected figures that will occur if a particular assumption proves either too optimistic or too pessimistic by a given amount.

SFAS Statement of Financial Accounting Standards. Designation for a numbered series of statements of accounting rules promulgated by the Financial Accounting Standards Board (see).

shakeout A reduction in the number of competitors (through failures or through mergers) that typically occurs as a rapidly growing industry begins to mature. Factors that may contribute to a firm's survival during a shakeout include advantages in raising new capital, economies of scale (see), and superior management.

short interest ratio The ratio between the number of a company's shares that are sold short and remain uncovered and the stock's average daily trading volume. A high ratio indicates a widespread expectation that the stock's price will decline.

slack Unutilized productive capability within a company. Although the term ordinarily connotes inefficiency, management may have a conscious strategy of maintaining a certain amount of slack. For example, a company may benefit from keeping skilled employees on the payroll during recessions, when demand can be met with a reduced workforce. The cost savings entailed in laying off the workers may be offset by the costs of replacing them with equally skilled employees during the next boom. Another example is a backup trading floor maintained by a company engaged in trading securities or commodities. The associated cost may be justified by the potentially devastating loss of business that could result in a shutdown of the primary trading floor because of a natural disaster or civil disturbance.

standard error of estimate A measure of the scatter of the observations in a regression analysis. In statistical terms, the standard error of the estimate is equivalent to the standard deviation of the vertical deviations from the least-squares line.

statutory tax rate The percentage of pretax income that would be recorded as income tax if all of a company's reported income were subject to the corporate tax rate specified by federal law. Disparities between the statutory rate and the effective rate (that which is actually recorded) arise from such reasons as tax credits and differences between U.S. and foreign tax rates.

straight-line method A depreciation method that charges off an equivalent portion of the asset in each period. During inflationary periods, straight-line depreciation may understate the true economic impact of capital consumption. That is, as the replacement cost of the asset rises in nominal terms, the dollar amount required to offset wear and tear during a period grows to exceed a pro rata write-off based on the original acquisition cost. In these circumstances, accelerated methods of depreciation, which result in larger amounts being written off in earlier than in later years, represent more conservative reporting of expenses.

subordinated debt Borrowings that have a lesser preference in liquidation vis-à-vis senior debt. In the event of a bankruptcy, subordinated lenders' claims cannot be provided for until senior claims have been satisfied.

synergy An increase in profitability arising from a merger or acquisition, relative to the stand-alone profitability of the companies involved. Synergy may result from economies of scale (see) or economies of scope (see).

technical default A default on debt that does not involve failure to make a scheduled payment of principal or interest but instead results from the violation of a covenant requirement, such as maintaining a minimum ratio of earnings to interest expense.

total enterprise value   The value that a business would fetch if put up for sale, commonly estimated as a multiple of its sales, earnings, or EBITDA (see). (See also *market capitalization*.)

variable costs   Costs that increase as the volume of production rises. Examples include materials, fuel, power, and wages.

working capital   Current assets minus current liabilities. Working capital is commonly employed as an indicator of liquidity, but care must be taken in interpreting the number. The balance sheets of some corporations that are strong credits by all other methods ordinarily have little (or even negative) working capital. These companies manage inventories closely and extract generous terms from creditors, including long payment periods, which result in chronically high trade payable balances. In such cases, no threat of illiquidity is implied by the fact that more liabilities than assets will be liquidated during the current operating cycle.

Bibliography

BOOKS

Browne, Lynn E., and Eric S. Rosengren (Eds.). *The Merger Boom: Proceedings of a Conference Held in October 1987*. Boston: Federal Reserve Bank of Boston, 1988.

Fabozzi, Frank J., and T. Dessa Fabozzi (Eds.). *The Handbook of Fixed Income Securities*, 4th ed. Burr Ridge, IL: Irwin, 1995.

Fridson, Martin S. *High Yield Bonds: Identifying Value and Assessing Risk of Speculative-Grade Securities*. Chicago: Probus, 1989.

Gitman, Lawrence J. *Principles of Managerial Finance*, 7th ed. New York: Harper-Collins, 1994.

Hale, Roger H. *Credit Analysis: A Complete Guide*. New York: John Wiley & Sons, 1983.

Levine, Sumner N. (Ed.). *Handbook of Turnaround & Bankruptcy Investing*. New York: Harper & Row, 1991.

Maginn, John L., and Donald L. Tuttle (Eds.). *Managing Investment Portfolios: A Dynamic Process*, 2nd ed. Boston: Warren, Gorham & Lamont, 1989.

Malonis, Jane A. (Ed.). *Encyclopedia of Business*, 2nd ed. Detroit: Gale, 1999.

McConnell, Campbell R. *Economics: Principles, Problems and Policies*, 10th ed. New York: McGraw-Hill, 1987.

Mosteller, Frederick, Robert K. E. Rourke, and George B. Thomas Jr. *Probability with Statistical Applications*, 2nd ed. Reading, MA: Addison-Wesley, 1970.

Moyer, Stephen. *Distressed Debt Analysis: Strategies for Speculative Investors*. Ft. Lauderdale, FL: J. Ross Publishing, 2004.

Pass, Christopher, Bryan Lowes, Leslie Davis, and Sidney J. Kronish (Eds.). *The HarperCollins Dictionary of Economics*. New York: HarperCollins, 1991.

Prochnow, Herbert V. (Ed.). *Bank Credit*. New York: Harper & Row, 1981.

Reilly, Frank K. *Investment Analysis and Portfolio Management*, 3rd ed. Orlando, FL: Dryden, 1989.

Roe, Mark J. *Bankruptcy and Corporate Reorganization: Legal and Financial Materials*, 2nd ed. New York: The Foundation Press.

Siegel, Joel G., and Jae K. Shim. *Dictionary of Accounting Terms*. New York: Barron's, 1987.

Standard & Poor's Municipal Finance Criteria. New York: Standard & Poor's, 1989.

White, Gerald I., and Ashwinpaul C. Sondhi (Eds.). *CFA Readings in Financial Statement Analysis*. Charlottesville, VA: Institute of Chartered Financial Analysts, 1985.

Martin Fridson is Global Credit Strategist at BNP Paribas Investment Partners. Over a 25-year span with brokerage firms including Salomon Brothers, Morgan Stanley, and Merrill Lynch, he became known for his innovative work in credit analysis and investment strategy. For the last nine years of that span, participants in the Institutional Investor All-America research survey ranked Fridson number one in high yield bond strategy. Fridson has served as president of the Fixed Income Analysts Society, governor of the Association for Investment Management and Research (now CFA Institute), and director of the New York Society of Security Analysts. Since 1989 he has been book review editor of the *Financial Analysts Journal*.

The *New York Times* described Fridson as "one of Wall Street's most thoughtful and perceptive analysts." *Investment Dealers Digest* called him "perhaps the most well-known figure in the high yield world." In 2000, Fridson became the youngest person inducted into the Fixed Income Analysts Hall of Fame. The Financial Management Association named him Financial Executive of the Year in 2002.

Fridson is the author of six books on investments and political economy. The *Boston Globe* said *Unwarranted Intrusions: The Case Against Government Intervention in the Marketplace* (2006), should be short-listed for best business book of the decade. A study based on 16 core journals ranked Fridson among the ten most widely published authors in finance in the period 1990–2001. His writings have appeared in *Barron's,* the *Financial Times*, and *WSJ.com*. He is a regular contributor to Forbes.com's *Intelligent Investing* and *Credit Magazine*, as well as a frequent guest on CNBC, Bloomberg, and Consuelo Mack WealthTrack on PBS. Fridson received a Bachelor of Arts cum laude from Harvard College and a Masters of Business Administration from Harvard Business School.

Fernando Alvarez (PhD New York University) is currently Adjunct Associate Professor of Finance and Economics at the Columbia University Graduate Business School, where he teaches Entrepreneurship Finance. From 2003 until 2008, he was Associate Professor in the Finance and Economics Department and Director of Entrepreneurship Programs at Rutgers Business

School, Newark and New Brunswick. He has taught at New York University's Stern School of Business, where he was Clinical Associate Professor on Innovation and Entrepreneurship from 1998 to 2003, and Babson College in Wellesley, MA, where he was Assistant Professor of Finance from 1992 to 1996. He was visiting Associate Professor of Finance at Rutgers from 1996 to 1998.

He has taught Financial Management, Long-Term Finance with an emphasis in Shareholder Value/Economic Value Added, Short-Term Finance and Cash Flow Management, Fixed Income Analysis, Investments, Financial Statement Analysis, and Portfolio Analysis and Management. He was affiliated with the Shulman Chartered Financial Analyst Review Program in Boston. He has also taught a seminar in financial engineering at ITESM Graduate School of Management in Mexico City. Prof. Alvarez has a B.S. in Civil Engineering from the University of Nebraska at Lincoln.

Professor Alvarez's primary research areas include the growth of entrepreneurial firms, financing for start-up and growth, and the interaction of strategy, financial statement analysis, and valuation models in business decisions. His writings include the management of cash flows resulting from changes in working capital requirements, the structure of cash flows after the IPO, and the uses and sources of capital for the entrepreneurial firm. His research has been funded by the MacArthur Foundation, the Kaufman Foundation, U.S. Trust Bank of Boston, and Wells Fargo Bank.

He is co-author, with Martin Fridson, of the fourth edition of *Financial Statement Analysis: A Practitioner's Guide* (John Wiley & Sons, 2011). He contributed a chapter on business planning for the *Next Generation Business Handbook* (John Wiley & Sons, 2004), where he was recognized as one of the 50 thought leaders of tomorrow. From 1999 to 2003, he was on the Advisory Board of McGraw-Hill's Annual Editions in Entrepreneurship. Professor Alvarez has written or supervised over 50 cases and technical notes developed for the purposes of class discussion in entrepreneurship courses and cash flow analysis.

Index